China

Reform and the Role of the Plan in the 1990s

The World Bank
Washington, D.C.

Copyright © 1992
The International Bank for Reconstruction
and Development/THE WORLD BANK
1818 H Street, N.W.
Washington, D.C. 20433, U.S.A.

All rights reserved
Manufactured in the United States of America
First printing September 1992

World Bank Country Studies are among the many reports originally prepared for internal use as part of the continuing analysis by the Bank of the economic and related conditions of its developing member countries and of its dialogues with the governments. Some of the reports are published in this series with the least possible delay for the use of governments and the academic, business and financial, and development communities. The typescript of this paper therefore has not been prepared in accordance with the procedures appropriate to formal printed texts, and the World Bank accepts no responsibility for errors.

The World Bank does not guarantee the accuracy of the data included in this publication and accepts no responsibility whatsoever for any consequence of their use. Any maps that accompany the text have been prepared solely for the convenience of readers; the designations and presentation of material in them do not imply the expression of any opinion whatsoever on the part of the World Bank, its affiliates, or its Board or member countries concerning the legal status of any country, territory, city, or area or of the authorities thereof or concerning the delimitation of its boundaries or its national affiliation.

The material in this publication is copyrighted. Requests for permission to reproduce portions of it should be sent to the Office of the Publisher at the address shown in the copyright notice above. The World Bank encourages dissemination of its work and will normally give permission promptly and, when the reproduction is for noncommercial purposes, without asking a fee. Permission to copy portions for classroom use is granted through the Copyright Clearance Center, 27 Congress Street, Salem, Massachusetts 01970, U.S.A.

The complete backlist of publications from the World Bank is shown in the annual *Index of Publications,* which contains an alphabetical title list (with full ordering information) and indexes of subjects, authors, and countries and regions. The latest edition is available free of charge from the Distribution Unit, Office of the Publisher, Department F, The World Bank, 1818 H Street, N.W., Washington, D.C. 20433, U.S.A., or from Publications, The World Bank, 66, avenue d'Iéna, 75116 Paris, France.

ISSN: 0253-2123

Library of Congress Cataloging-in-Publication Data

China : reform and the role of the plan in the 1990s.
    p.   cm. — (A World Bank country study)
  ISBN 0-8213-2230-3
    1. China—Economic policy—1976–   2. Central planning—China.
  3. Economic forecasting—China.   I. World Bank. II. Series.
  HC427.92.C46454   1992
  338.951—dc20
                                      92-30849
                                       CIP

338.951
C44W

Abstract

The focus of this report is on the government's reform and development policies for the decade of the nineties. The assessment is based on a review of the successes and failures of China's reform experience over the past decade. Particular attention is paid to the key reform areas that appear to deserve increased attention. Development policies are examined on the basis of the Eight Five-Year Plan, with a particular focus on transport policies. The report also reviews economic developments during the 1990-91 period, when China was emerging from recession. Finally, after examining reform and development options, the report develops a set of alternative scenarios for the economy for the rest of the decade, depending upon the set of policy options selected.

188312

CURRENCY EQUIVALENTS

Up to December 15, 1989	Up to November 29, 1990	At March 31, 1992:
$1.00 = Y 3.72	$1.00 = Y 4.72	$1.00 = Y 5.46
Y 1.00 = $0.27	Y 1.00 = 0.21	Y 1.00 = $0.18

FISCAL YEAR

January 1 - December 31

ABBREVIATIONS AND ACRONYMS

7thFYP	-	Seventh Five-Year Plan, 1986-90
8thFYP	-	Eighth Five-Year Plan, 1991-95
CAAC	-	Civil Aviation Authority of China
CIECC	-	China International Engineering Consulting Corporation
CTRI	-	Comprehensive Transport Research Institute
DRC	-	Development Research Center of the State Council
GNFS	-	Goods and Nonfactor Services
IMF	-	International Monetary Fund
IOT	-	Investment Orientation Tax
MME	-	Ministry of Materials and Equipment
MOC	-	Ministry of Communications
MOF	-	Ministry of Finance
MOR	-	Ministry of Railways
NDA	-	Net Domestic Assets
NFA	-	Net Foreign Assets
PBC	-	People's Bank of China
SAEC	-	State Administration of Exchange Control
SOE	-	State-Owned Enterprise
SPC	-	State Planning Commission
SRC	-	State Commission for Restructuring the Economic System
TVE	-	Township and Village Enterprise
SCIC	-	State Communications Investment Corporation

- v -

Preface

This report is based on a mission which visited China in May/June 1991. Mission members were Peter Harrold (Principal Economist, Mission Leader, Reform Issues), Fernando Montes-Negret (Senior Economist, Macroeconomics), Michael Bell (Deputy Division Chief, IMF, Macroeconomics), Anand Rajaram (Economist, Development Plan), Thomas Chan (Consultant, Reform Plan), Hernan Levy (Principal Transport Economist, Transport Plan) and Tejaswi Raparla (Research Analyst, Statistics and Projections). The mission received great support from the World Bank Resident Mission in China, and especially Chen Xingdong (Economic Officer) and Dai Dongchang (Transport Operations Officer), as well as from Zhang Shaojie (Local Consultant).

The mission was hosted by and received great support from the Ministry of Finance. In particular, MOF put together a very capable counterpart team to work with the mission: Liu He, Ning Jizhe, Wu Qing, Zhu Zhixin, Li Tiejun, Yang Weimin, all of the State Planning Commission; Wang Hong, Ministry of Finance; Wang Huijiong, Li Poxi, Development Research Center; Fan Hengshan, Systems Reform Commission; and Huang Dehai, Comprehensive Transport Research Institute. The team was led by Zhang Shengman (World Bank Department, Ministry of Finance), and support was ably coordinated by Wu Jingkang. The team produced nine background papers in preparation for the mission.

The mission visited Henan Province, where it was hosted by the local Bureau of Finance. This was a most useful and enlightening visit, the results of which are illustrated at various points in the report.

The support of all the Chinese counterparts is duly acknowledged, for without it, this report would not have been possible.

Table of Contents

Page No.

EXECUTIVE SUMMARY   xi

I.   RECENT ECONOMIC DEVELOPMENTS   1

     A. Introduction   1
     B. Monetary and Credit Policies   1
     C. The Real Sector   8
     D. Price Developments   15
     E. The State Sector   18
     F. The External Sector   25
     G. Conclusions   31

II. CHINESE REFORM EXPERIENCE TO DATE   34

     A. Introduction   34
     B. The Initial Conditions   34
     C. China's Reform Style   37
     D. China's Major Reform Steps   42
     E. The Impact of Reforms   49
     F. Reform Priorities   60
     G. Some Tentative Conclusions   66

III. CHINA'S DEVELOPMENT PLAN, 1991-95   70

     A. Introduction   70
     B. The Evolution of Planning   70
     C. Role of the Plan in the 1990s   73
     D. The Macroeconomic Framework and Development Policy . . .   75
     E. Planning to Correct Market Failures   85
     F. Planning for the State Sector   94
     G. Conclusions and Issues for Future Plans   97

IV. THE REFORM PLAN   100

     A. Introduction   100
     B. Reform in 1989/91   100
     C. The Reform Plan   103
     D. The Implied Shape of the Reformed Chinese Economy . . .   116
     E. Timing, Sequencing and Reform Style   117
     F. Links with the Development Plan   120
     G. Specific Reform Areas   122
     H. Conclusions   127

		Page No.
V.	THE PLAN FOR THE TRANSPORT SECTOR	131
A.	Background	131
B.	The Eighth Five-Year Plan, 1991-95	133
C.	Financing of the Plan	141
D.	Sectoral and Institutional Reforms	146
E.	Conclusions	151
VI.	SCENARIOS FOR THE CHINESE ECONOMY	154
A.	Introduction	154
B.	The Base Case	155
C.	Scenario 2: Slow Policy Change/Macroeconomic Instability	158
D.	Scenario 3: Accelerated Reform	160
E.	Conclusions	162
	END NOTES	163

BOXES IN TEXT

1.1	Fiscal Policy in Henan Province	23
3.1	The 7th FYP and its Outcome	72
3.2	Development Plans in an Interior and a Coastal Province	88
3.3	Eleven Measures to Revitalize SOEs	96
4.1	The Future Chinese Policy Framework	118
5.1	Organizational Reforms in Air Transport and Ports	132
5.2	Transport Development and Market Integration	136
5.3	Growing Role for Local Railways	139
5.4	The Bank for Public Works, Mexico	145

TABLES IN TEXT

1.1	Relative Composition of Reserve Money	4
1.2	Specialized and Comprehensive Banks: Total Deposits	7
1.3	China: Sources of Growth of GDP (1988-90)	9
1.4	China: Comparative Supply and Demand-Side Contributions to Growth	10
1.5	China: Price Adjustments During 1990/91	18
1.6	China--State Budgetary Operations, 1986-91	20
1.7	China: Selected Indicators for the SOEs, 1984-91	25
1.8	Sources of Foreign Exchange, 1988-90	28
1.9	China: Balance of Payments, 1986-91	29
1.10	China: Effective Exchange Rate, 1986-91	30
2.1	Output Gains in the Reform Era	50
2.2	Consumption Indicators, 1978 and 1988	51
2.3	Economic Gains during the Reform Era	52
2.4	Changing Role of the State	54
2.5	Shares of Industrial Output of Nonstate Industry	55
2.6	Structure of Government Expenditures, 1978-90	57
2.7	Trade in the Chinese Economy, 1978-90	59

Page No.

3.1   8th FYP Objectives and Targets   78
3.2   Provincial Allocation of State Investment, 1981-90   86
3.3   Labor and Employment Under Eighth Plan   90
3.4   Employment Elasticity of GNP by Sectors, 1980-89   91
3.5   Possible Employment Growth, 1991-95   91
3.6   Share of Services in Current GDP in Selected Countries,
       1965-90   93
3.7   Sectoral Composition of China's GNP, 1979-90   93
3.8   Performance of Industrial SOEs in Central Budget   95
5.1   Financing of 8th FYP Highway Program, Henan Province   143
6.1   The Base Case, 1989-2000   155
6.2   The Slow Reform Scenario, 1989-2000   159
6.3   The Accelerated Reform Scenario, 1989-2000   161

GRAPHS IN TEXT

1.1   Monetary Aggregates   6
1.2   Real Gross Value of Industrial Output and Retail Sales . . .   11
1.3   Commercial Inventory Changes   14
1.4   Retail Price Inflation   16

CHARTS IN TEXT

2.1   Ownership Shares in Industrial Output   56
2.2   Regional Development and Nonstate Industry   58
5.1   International Comparison of Transport Networks   134
5.2   Passenger and Freight Volumes in China   138

MATRIX IN TEXT

4.1   Reform Priorities and the Reform Plan 128-29

ENDNOTES

ANNEX

  A RMSM-X Model for China

STATISTICAL APPENDIX

Executive Summary

Introduction

i.   China entered the decade of the 1990s at a crucial stage both in its own development path and in the world economy. China emerged in 1990 from a painful period of economic stabilization and from the domestic and international repercussions of the May-June 1989 events. It did so with an apparent determination to avoid the sharp economic cycles of the 1980s, or at least to dampen the amplitude of such cycles. Moreover, after a period in which it seemed the government was tending to look towards administrative measures to solve economic problems, there has been a clear revival of attention to reform issues, and a renewed recognition that only further economic reform can solve the fundamental issues facing the economy. Moreover, this recognition comes at a time when the state sector itself faces increasingly severe problems, to which solutions have yet to be clearly identified. Finally, all these domestic issues are occurring at a time of rapid changes in the world economy, not only in terms of unclear global economic prospects, but more particularly, the collapse of the former USSR, and a less benign international environment for China.

ii.   This report focuses on China's recent economic developments and future prospects in the light of the reform and development strategy set out in the "Outline of the Ten-Year Program and of the Eighth Five-Year Plan for National Economic and Social Development", which was prepared in 1991. In particular, it proposes a range of economic policies and reforms that may be necessary to achieve a strong, sustainable growth path over the rest of this decade. These proposals are based on an analysis of the reform experience of the past decade, and the lessons to be drawn both from this experience and from China's macroeconomic performance over this decade, especially the 1988-91 period.

iii.   The report concludes that China's economic prospects are extremely bright if the government continues to pursue a strong program of economic reform and appropriate development policies. Many of the economic problems that China has encountered in recent years are considered to be the consequence of incomplete reforms, and the judgement of the report is that these problems can be avoided or minimized in the future if the program of reform is widened and deepened across a broad policy spectrum, which is spelled out in the report. Moreover, it appears that the likelihood that such reforms will continue has increased in recent months.

Current Economic Situation

iv.   By early 1990, the serious inflationary pressures of 1988 had been eliminated and the economy was showing signs of severe strain from the austerity policies. In particular, the state sector, with much less flexibility in adjusting to the recessionary environment, was facing cash flow difficulties in the face of sluggish demand. From the second quarter of 1990, the authorities began to relax monetary policy, and in particular to expand working capital for state owned enterprises, as well as relaxing investment controls. Thus, in deciding to reflate the economy, the government chose the same two instruments that had been employed in 1989 to dampen inflation. Once it got underway the recovery in output was very rapid indeed, and the key issue raised by the speed and manner of the recovery is its sustainability and whether it will lead the economy straight back into a strong upswing, bringing a return to inflation and overheating.

v.   Money and credit policies have been the key area of economic policy once more. From an original planned credit growth of 14 percent, the level of loans outstanding grew by over 22 percent for the year in 1990, and particularly large increases went to finance SOEs' inventories and the purchase of the record grain harvest. This was repeated in 1991, when loans grew by 19 percent, again well above the 14 percent target. This source of money supply growth was further boosted by the very large balance of payments surplus, and broad money rose by 28 percent in 1990 and by a similar level in 1991. Similar trends in credit growth appear to be continuing in 1992, with growth rates well over 20 percent in the first six months, which is significantly above the credit target. Fortunately, both households and enterprises proved to be very willing to increase their savings, and total bank deposits grew by a remarkable 30 percent in both 1990 and 1991, with particularly fast growth of enterprise deposits, as enterprises rebuilt deposits which had been run down in 1989 in the face of the austerity program. This rapid growth of savings meant that the build-up of inventories and of foreign exchange reserves was achieved without increasing inflationary pressures, and inflation has remained at very low levels, falling to only 2.9 percent in 1991. However, it has also meant that banks' profitability and the ratio of their equity to assets have fallen significantly.

vi.   The real impact of the austerity program in China was felt from mid-1989 to mid-1990, a period which saw no real growth. As noted, once recovery began, it took off very rapidly. In the 18 months after October 1990, industrial output grew by over 15 percent, close to 1988 levels. Overall GDP grew by 5.6 percent in 1990, and 7 percent in 1991. The first six months of 1992 saw their growth accelerate to 10.6 percent. While agriculture and trade were key sources of growth in 1990, this shifted to industry and investment in 1991. However, while output was recovering rapidly, final demand was not, and the "sluggish market" became a major issue as retail sales grew by only 1.9 percent for 1990 as a whole, having declined substantially in the first half. As a consequence, inventories grew very rapidly. Although data is very poor in this regard, inventories probably reached a peak of about 20 percent of GDP in early 1991 and were particularly large in those sectors where production is dominated by SOEs, such as textiles and large consumer durables. A concerted effort was made in late 1991 to reduce these inventories, with some initial success. The level of consumer demand recovered in 1991, growing at 13 percent, and is continuing to grow in 1992, but inventories still remained high, given the high growth of industrial output, although inventory accumulation appears to have stopped.

vii.   It should be no surprise that the economic downturn strongly affected China's state-owned enterprises, especially in terms of profitability. However, while profits fell, and about one third of SOEs were losing money, this had no noticeable impact on tax receipts. Overall, the open fiscal deficit was only 2 percent of GDP in 1990, and 2.6 percent in 1991, higher than projected (primarily because of higher administrative expenditures) but still manageable. However, MOF was, for the second year, unable to service maturing bonds held outside the household sector. The greater impact has been on the public sector's borrowing requirement more broadly defined, which appears to have risen from 8 percent of GDP in 1987 to 11 percent in 1990, and a similar level in 1991.

viii.   The strongest area of performance in China in the last year has been the external sector, with record external surpluses in 1990 and 1991. Exports have continued to perform very well, in response both to declining domestic demand, and to improved incentives, notably successive real devaluations. As a result of the austerity program and intensified restrictions, imports fell 10 percent in 1990, but as the economy recovered, imports registered growth of almost 20 percent in 1991, a trend which is continuing in 1992. The trade surplus was accompanied by a recovery of tourism and by greater willingness to lend to China, and therefore the current account surplus of $12 billion in each of the two years resulted in a cumulative $26 billion improvement in reserves during 1990/91 to the equivalent of about ten months of imports.

ix.   China has therefore had in many ways an enviable emergence from recession, with rapid output growth accompanied by low inflation and a strong external position. However, while fully recognizing this success, three issues arise: (a) the strong growth of credit could, if permitted to continue, lead China back to an inflationary situation, especially given highly liquid savings. For this reason, a more moderate credit stance, consistent with non-inflationary growth, is now called for, and restoration of the provisions for index-linked interest rates would be desirable in case of a change in inflationary expectations; (b) the severe difficulties of the SOEs during the last three years merit a focus on restructuring and reform issues for these enterprises; and (c) the growing open and quasi-fiscal deficit, now of the order of 9 percent of GNP (through forced lending by banks to loss-making SOEs) merits attention not only to the SOEs, but also more generally to fiscal and financial sector reforms.

Development Policies

x.   The new five-year plan can be seen as part of an evolving pattern for the role of planning. Over time, the plans have gradually developed from being an exercise in numerical targeting and in calling for mobilization of effort, to an attempt at a realistic macroeconomic assessment and statement of government intent. The previous plan (the 7th FYP, 1986-90) had suffered from a macroeconomic framework that was very divergent from actual government policy, and from an attempt to provide targets and goals for sectors beyond the government's direct influence. While the present plan has more of a focus on the macroeconomic framework and development policy, and on the reforms necessary to achieve those goals, it continues to suffer from some of the same difficulties as past plans, and as such, it runs the risk of rapidly becoming irrelevant.

xi.   In this report, we assess the plan in the light of the three key roles for planning: the provision of a macroeconomic framework and set of accompanying policies that can act as a guide for the actions of others; planning to correct market failures, which can be expected to be quite serious under China's partially-reformed economy; and planning for the state sector and specifically for the avoidance of bottlenecks. With respect to this

latter role for planning, particular focus is paid to what is probably the
single most important sector in this regard: the provision of transport.

xii.   The macroeconomic framework and its associated development strategy
and policies calls for a much more moderate pace of growth (6 percent per
annum) than in the recent past, and while the framework appears in general to
be easily achievable, there are three particular issues:

   (a) It suffers from a rather incomplete coverage--for example, by the
absence of trade and external accounts projections--and from a lack
of exposition of macroeconomic policies.

   (b) More serious, it suffers from the same problem as the 7th FYP, in
that actual economic policy in the first year of the Plan differed
radically (by promoting rapid growth) from the Plan, not least
because the Plan's target was below the growth level that was both
desirable and achievable.

   (c) While the development strategy seems sensible, there is very little
exposition of policies and programs to support the achievement of
the strategy, such as pricing policies for the key 'basic' industries.

xiii.   Where the exposition is fairly explicit is with respect to industrial policies. These show a continued move away from mechanical targeting
policies and associated credit allocations towards greater use of indirect
instruments, such are the new Investment Orientation Tax. While this trend is
welcomed it will need to accelerate and to place less emphasis on the use of
countervailing distortions, such as this tax.

xiv.   With respect to policies to correct market failure, we have focussed
our analysis on two such issues: balancing the pace of regional development;
and creation of sufficient employment generation via the tertiary sector.
This plan does not have regional policy as a key instrument of the overall
development strategy, as was the case of the 7th FYP with its emphasis on the
coastal development strategy. Rather, it focusses on ways to maximize growth
in each region, and to re-distribute income as appropriate. However, the Plan
pays no attention to the major policy issues that appear to have generated the
present pattern of income distribution, notably pricing policies, provincial
economic policy-making discretion, and the location of SOEs. If the authorities are concerned about emerging patterns of regional income distribution,
these seem to be the issues to be addressed. While general economic reform
and progress will, therefore, be the key to continued poverty reduction in
China, recent analysis has shown there to be pockets of absolute poverty in
certain resource-poor areas, where more direct action is warranted.

xv.   The Plan recognizes the heavy burden of employment creation facing
the economy, and has only modest aims in this regard. For example, it anticipates that open unemployment will rise from 2.5 percent to 3.5 percent and
that no significant progress will be made on reducing underemployment. However, it recognizes the potential key role of the services sector in creating
employment opportunities, by targeting for a 9 percent growth in the tertiary
sector. However, while the target seems appropriate and potentially achiev-

able, no supporting policies are outlined. Among the more important that seem to merit attention are those that would create an enabling framework for the sector, including efficient licensing systems, access to credit and contracting out of various government services.

xvi.   Increasingly, the more traditional aspects of the plan, in terms of investment programming and output targeting, will have to be limited to those parts of the economy where government provision of services or production of goods will remain dominant, as in the transport sector (paras. xxviii.-xxxii.). Similarly, there will be the need for continued government attention to issues concerned with improving the environment. One key issue for the future will be industrial restructuring for the SOEs, especially given the increasing burden they are placing on the budget. However, while the policy framework includes some appropriate concerns--such as the granting of trade rights and the reduction of mandatory plans--too much of the solution is being sought through technical improvements and through disguised subsidies, especially on credit and via tax exemptions. In short, as restructuring policies are refined, they should concentrate more on the removal of disadvantages imposed on the SOEs and less on the provision of countervailing advantages.

China's Reform experience since 1979

xvii.   In identifying reform priorities for the coming period, it is appropriate to start from an assessment of the successes and failures of past reform experience. Such an assessment can now be done on an objective basis because of the passage of time and the availability of recent research results. However, in drawing broader lessons from this experience, it is important to understand clearly the initial conditions under which the reform was launched. Three factors are key in China in this regard: the absence of severe macroeconomic crisis at the start of the program, so that harsh stabilization measures could be avoided; the state of agriculture, with its good infrastructure but poor incentives; and the presence of Hong Kong, as a source of inspiration, expertise and investment.

xviii.   As the reform program has developed in China, four distinctive features in terms of reform style have emerged:

   (a) Gradualism and Experimentation. China has tended to spread changes over several years, and usually after considerable experimentation and adaptation. Its large size and provincial structure foster such experiments and make such an approach appropriate, if not inevitable.

   (b) Partial Reforms. One of the distinctive features of China's reform has been the apparent success of partial reforms within sectors, notably the two-tier price system, which has created a situation in which marginal decisions are based on market prices, and market skills can be learned without economic dislocation.

   (c) Decentralization. Decentralization of decision-making power to enterprises, individuals and local governments has been a key theme of reforms, enhancing microeconomic incentives and creating a strong interest group in favor of continued reform deepening.

(d) <u>Self-Reinforcing Reforms</u>. Reforms in one area created pressures for matching reforms in other areas, and policymakers have in general seen their interests served best by meeting such pressures with new reforms rather than by administrative protectionism, albeit sometimes with a considerable lag.

xix. China's approach to reform has been demonstrably effective, particularly in terms of its impact in four distinct areas:

(a) <u>Output and Welfare</u>. GNP has grown about 50 percent faster during the reform period, especially in light industry and services. This has resulted in enormous improvements in consumption levels (more than doubled over the decade) and in the lifting of 160 million from poverty since 1979.

(b) <u>Productivity</u>. The key to this has been that growth has come via productivity gains, which were close to zero in the 1949-79 period, but accounted for 3-4 percent per annum of growth during reforms.

(c) <u>The Role of the State</u>. The state used to dominate savings and investment, but now, most savings are generated by individuals and enterprises, and investment is financed by retained profits and banks. Even more dramatic is the changing role of state-owned enterprises, which accounted for almost all output in the prereform period, but now nonstate industry employs almost 100 million people and produces 45 percent of industrial output.

(d) <u>Trade</u>. The share of trade in GNP has risen from just under 10 percent in 1978 to over 30 percent in 1990, and there are over 20,000 sino-foreign joint ventures in operation.

xx. Despite the great progress achieved to date, the gradual approach means that much remains to be done, and reform priorities can be identified in six key areas: (a) <u>enterprise reform</u>, especially the question of ownership reform for the state-owned enterprises; (b) <u>financial sector issues</u>, especially the reduction of forced policy lending by commercial banks; (c) <u>fiscal reforms</u>, to replace the present <u>revenue</u> generation system with a diversified <u>tax</u> system; (d) <u>external reforms</u>, and especially reduced import protection; (e) further <u>price reform</u>, particularly for such distorted prices of raw materials and agriculture; and (f) <u>social sector reforms</u>, primarily those which improve labor mobility by converting nonwage benefits such as housing and pension rights, to wages. In addition, the government will need to be increasingly concerned in this decade with issues that affect the environment and with poverty alleviation, although these topics are not addressed directly in this report. The adequacy of the reform plan's proposals in each of these areas is discussed in the next section.

xxi. The final issues addressed in considering China's reform experience to date are concerned with conclusions of more general applicability that can be reached, and the sustainability of the approach. Five key features of China's experience seem to have wider applicability: agriculture as an entry point for reform; the success of "marketization" of the enterprise sector, instead of privatization; the key role of changing the interest of the bureaucracy; the impact of developing exports at an early stage; and the role of the state in maintaining stability by looking after the most affected.

xxii.   Given the lack of historical precedents for the Chinese approach, the question of its sustainability overtime must be addressed. On balance, it is judged that the approach is sustainable, because: (a) the Chinese reform has generated intensive development, and the consequent generation of true welfare changes; and (b) China has generally responded to the problems arising out of reform by deepening reforms, which suggests that deep crisis can be avoided via a process of continued incremental change. Nevertheless, the key will be in how well China responds to the reform challenges still to be addressed (para. xx).

Reform Prospects

xxiii.   During three years of stabilization during 1988-91, when reforms were given less prominence, a surprising degree of progress was achieved, not least because of the imperatives of the fiscal situation. Most important, several key prices were adjusted substantially, notably the prices of grain, oilseeds, coal, and transportation, in some cases for the first time in 20 years. In addition, a new round of trade reform and extension of the coverage of the foreign exchange adjustment centers lent further impetus to the export drive. Finally, reform experiments were extended and widened in various areas, notably in housing and in the separation of profits and taxes.

xxiv.   The prospects for a deepening of economic reform have improved sharply of late, since the visit of Deng Xiaoping to Southern China in the spring, and various reform initiatives have either been launched or are being actively prepared at the local level since that time. However, this report takes as its point of basic reference the reform plan contained in the 8th FYP issued in 1991, and some of the observations made about the shortcomings of this plan are already being addressed by the Chinese authorities at various levels. Nevertheless, these shortcomings merit continued attention as the government reviews its overall reform strategy and its specific reform proposals in preparation for the 14th Party Congress later in 1992.

xxv.   This reform plan is a rather comprehensive statement of intention in all the major areas of reform, some of which are new and of considerable interest and importance. Notable among these are: a program to expand the number of enterprise groups to 100 from the present 57, with groups which would cross ministerial, bureau or even provincial boundaries, and be the locus of many other reforms initiatives, such as the formation of joint stock companies; a renewed emphasis on price reform and a clear commitment to eliminate major distortions, even if not necessarily via markets; a new focus on reform of the distribution system, and on the formation of an integrated national market; a major initiative on social sector reforms, especially housing, social security and unemployment and medical insurance; and further reforms of the investment system.

xxvi.   In reviewing this reform plan, it can be seen to be relatively comprehensive, and to propose appropriate reforms in many areas. One general issue is that, in most areas, it suggests only preparatory actions during the 8th FYP, leaving implementation to the 9th FYP, although recent announcements suggest this position may already have been overtaken. Such caution seems neither desirable, nor necessary, given the state of the economy, and the state of preparation. This would seem to be the case in particular for price reforms, and for fiscal reforms. In addition, four key areas of reform seem to merit particular care or greater attention.

(a) <u>Ownership Reform Issues</u>. Enterprise reform remains the central challenge in China, particularly those reforms which will enable SOEs to become efficient and competitive. The government has very little to say at present as to how it will represent its ownership function in the future. Experience suggests that the preparation time in this regard can be extensive, so this would call for a much more aggressive program of reform experiments, especially in such areas as joint-stock companies, and the separation of profits from taxes, as well as the improvement of the legal framework and accounting systems. Nevertheless, while there are clear incremental gains to be made in China's SOEs, it must be noted that international experience casts doubt on the ability of the SOEs to attain the same level of efficiency as private enterprises, so long as the SOEs remain dominant.

(b) <u>Enterprise Groups</u>. The great interest in this idea is that such groups would cut across the present interest structure that currently impacts on the performance of the SOEs. As such, it is a development to be very much welcomed, but with one major caveat. Great care will need to be taken with respect to competition policy, as such groups could rapidly create monopolistic positions. In particular the role of the TVEs should be invoked in this regard, both as a direct source of competition, and potentially as leading enterprises of such groups. A key to the achievement of greater efficiency gains could be the future taking over of loss-making SOEs by efficient, aggressive nonstate-owned enterprises.

(c) <u>Financial Sector Issues</u>. The government hopes to create banks that are fully responsible for credit risk, but at the same time, it continues to impose tight control on banks to ensure that its key enterprises and key projects receive funding, which is clearly contradictory with the first aim. The solution seems to be to find alternative methods to fund these priorities, and the suggested route is to convert the State Investment Corporations into true investment banks issuing bonds to generate financing for such investments.

(d) <u>Role of the External Sector</u>. While much progress has been made on the export policy framework, and the performance of China's external sector has been remarkable, it continues to have relatively little impact on the domestic economy, except in provinces such as Guangdong and Fujian. In particular, the external sector--with respect to both imports and foreign investment--is seen only as a source of foreign capital and technology, and not as a source of competitive pressure for innovation for domestic enterprises. This crucial link between an outward orientation and enterprise reform deserves to be revisited as the reform plan is refined.

xxvii.   It seems clear that there is once again a major impetus for reform
in China, and a recognition that only via reform can further efficiency gains
be achieved. Moreover, it is also beginning to be seen that, far from the
economic cycles of the latter 1980s having been caused by reform, rather they
reflected inadequate reform in the area of the development of instruments of
indirect economic management. Indeed, only with further, deeper reforms can
there be economic gains while avoiding the strong cyclical pattern of the
1980s. However, the reform program seems to be weakest in the very areas that
would do most to strengthen macroeconomic management capability, and it is
therefore in these same areas that incremental attention should be addressed.

The Transport Plan

xxviii.   The transport sector has long been one of the main bottlenecks in
the economy, serving not only as a constraint to the achievable rate of non-
inflationary growth, but also as an impediment to efficiency gains through
greater integration of the national market. As such, the plan for the transport sector should be seen very much in the light of its links to the rest of
the economy, and to the achievement of the development and reform plans.

xxix.   The reason that this sector has for so long been a constraint on the
rest of the economy is clear: there have been decades of underinvestment in
the sector, not least because of the importance attached to regional self-
sufficiency during the pre-reform era. It must also be recognized that any
economy would have had difficulties keeping up in terms of the provision of
transport infrastructure with the rapid overall rate of economic growth in the
1980s. When compared to other countries, China has a very small transport
network in terms of population and area covered. China's investment in transport in the last ten years has been 1.4 percent of GDP, compared with 2-3
percent for countries such as Korea, India and Brazil.

xxx.   The plan for the transport sector gives an appropriate emphasis to
transport investments that would help to integrate the national market. In
particular, there is a focus on two key areas: expansion of highways and
efficiency improvements on the railways. For the latter, the main priority
continues to be to relieve coal transport bottlenecks, but the focus is on
double-tracking, electrification and related improvements rather than new
lines. The railways will dominate overall investments in the sector, at an
estimated Y 116 billion in today's prices, about 0.8 percent of GNP. The
highways plan is based on traffic growth projections of 14-15 percent per
annum, with a particular focus on interprovincial highways and expressways,
reflecting the key importance being attached to the role of the trucking
industry. Given good progress in the 1980s, less attention is given to ports,
but civil aviation is expected to expand rapidly, at about 12 percent per
annum, with major focus not on network expansion but on airport improvement
and increased numbers of aircraft.

xxxi.   There are three key issues that emerge within the transport plan;
financing, pricing and competition, and the role of the trucking industry.

    (a) Financing. While there may be some increased budget allocation for
         transport investments, the main source of incremental revenue is
         seen as higher use charges, both at the national and local levels.

While there is much scope for this, and it is an appropriate direc-
tion--especially with respect to tariff adjustment--care will need
to be taken to select fitting instruments. This is especially so in
highways, where there is an absence of sufficient use charges on
fuels, but the presence of many toll roads. A greater reliance on
the former could lead to efficiency gains, especially in terms of
road selection by users, and average speeds. Similarly, use of
bonds could be expanded as a source of financing for some high utilization, high quality facilities. However, with full financing by
no means assured, government will need to monitor this carefully and
take appropriate actions if necessary.

(b)   Pricing and Competition. Major progress has been made during the
7th FYP period in eliminating some of the most serious pricing distortions. Nevertheless, further progress is needed if the sector is
to generate the necessary investment resources. In contrast, trucking tariffs are unusually high, and five to ten times unit rates on
the railways. The key to stimulating road-rail competition is
bringing these rates closer together, and while some further adjustment of rail tariffs can be expected, much will have to come from
lowering trucking rates through encouraging competition. In particular, this should come through stimulating the role of TVEs in the
provision of trucking services.

(c)   The Trucking Industry. This is the most backward sector in relative
terms in China's transport sector and will have a critical role to
play in transport diversification, and new initiatives are needed to
increase efficiency and lower costs. The key issue is the common
practice of trucking via own account trucks, with very few common
carriers, and these mainly publicly owned. One consequence of this
is very low load factors, as many trucks return empty. Similarly,
the low load-bearing capacity of most roads reduces the average
truck size. In addition, as noted, this is a sector where small
enterprises could play a key role given the opportunity.

xxxii.   In short, the 8th FYP for transport appears to give the sector the
priority it requires and attempts to remedy longstanding neglect. However,
the pricing and institutional reforms that have been identified are critical
to the achievement of the aims of the transport plan, and thus to the wider
aims of the development plan itself.

Macroeconomic Prospects

xxxiii.   China's macroeconomic prospects have been considered under three
scenarios, which differ in terms of the policy framework to be adopted and the
associated efficiency gains. The base case assumes a moderate, steady pace of
reform over the decade. The accelerated reform case assumes that the pace of
reform quickens in the next year or so, particularly in price, financial, trade
and fiscal reforms, with consequent gains in efficiency. The slow case, in
contrast, assumes a repetition of some of the economic cycles of the 1980s, with
their associated reform cycles. In each case, however, we see a strong growth
performance, and continued creditworthiness. The key distinctions between the

cases are in the degree of efficiency improvement, and consequently in the level of welfare.

xxxiv.   The base case assumes that China makes good progress with a wide range of reforms, on an accelerated schedule compared with the reform plan. It thus assumes that growth will be on average rather higher than the government target at about 7.5 percent per annum. The impact of reform is reflected in a gradually falling investment requirement over the period, from 37 percent of GDP in 1990, to 33 percent by the end of the decade, indicating efficiency improvements. Inflation control is assumed to remain a priority for the government--hence the lower rate of growth than in the 1980s--and inflation is expected to be in the 5-6 percent range over the period. Any sign of a return to double-digit inflation is expected to generate the sort of firm policy response that was witnessed in 1988-89. The growth pattern under this scenario is projected to be in line with the 8th FYP's targets, with industry showing more moderate growth, at about 6-8 percent in GDP terms, while the services sector, and especially transport, finance and information services, is projected to be the leading source of growth, at around 9 percent per annum.

xxxv.   The external sector is also projected to continue to expand its role in the economy, with both exports and imports growing faster than GDP. The export (volume) growth rate is projected to be in the 7.5-9 percent range, while we expect a very rapid growth of imports for a year or two, to eliminate the present trade surplus, and thereafter growth at about 8 percent. The strong emphasis on technical modernization in the development strategy is thus expected to be reflected in particular in higher capital goods imports, which we expect to grow at about 10 percent a year. Nevertheless, the current account deficit is not expected to exceed 1.3 percent of GDP, keeping debt within manageable levels, and in fact declining as a share of GDP. With relatively small additions to the level of reserves, the net external financing requirement barely exceeds the current account deficit. In the base, about $4 billion is projected on average to come from foreign direct investment, and thus the net external borrowing requirement is about $6 billion per annum on average over the course of the decade. The distribution of such borrowing between official and private sources is expected to be a bit more favorable to China than in the last decade, as more and larger sources of official financing are now available.

xxxvi.   The slow reform scenario assumes that with less progress in reform in particular with respect to the development of macroeconomic management capability, and the state-owned enterprises, there would be a consequent repetition of the stop-go cycles of the 1980s. It is not expected that this would have a severe impact on the average growth rate--even in 1989, at the height of the austerity program, GDP grew by 4.6 percent--but rather it would be reflected in three things: a higher investment requirement and thus significantly lower rate of consumption growth; a higher average inflation rate, nearer to 10 percent per annum on average, because of the high rates during the "booms"; and a lower rate of foreign direct investment, because of the economic instability.

xxxvii.   The accelerated reform case assumes a much more aggressive attack on these issues, commencing in the next year or so. This would have three primary effects: GDP would rise by an average of about 8.5 percent a year in response to efficiency gains, as experience has shown in China that reforms launched in periods of macroeconomic stability have a strong growth effect as people respond to the new incentives; similarly, more products would become export-competitive, raising average trade levels; and in response to these reforms, foreign direct investment would rise rapidly. In the higher scenario, FDI would rise to about $5 billion per annum, while in the slow case it would be about $3 billion, the lowest it has been in the recent past. In the slow case, therefore, debt ratios are somewhat worse than the base case, while in the accelerated case they are better. It is to be noted that in this scenario we do not project any increase in the rate of inflation above the base case of 5-6 percent rate, associated with the higher growth rate. This is because it is assumed that the accelerated reform would strongly impinge upon fiscal and financial areas, which would reinforce the effectiveness of macroeconomic management under conditions of rapid growth. <u>Nevertheless, we would urge caution in permitting sustained growth above this rate, and specifically sustained growth rates of 10 percent per annum or more, as these would cause overheating and inflation, which would interfere with the orderly implementation of reforms.</u>

xxxviii. Under all three of our scenarios China would continue to enjoy a strong creditworthiness position, with all indicators remaining very good. Total debt outstanding stood at only 15.4 percent of GDP in 1991, and under our base scenario, this would <u>fall</u> to 11.4 percent in the year 2000, and stay between these two levels throughout the decade. Even in the low case, debt would not rise above 16 percent of GDP, and would be only 9.4 percent in the high case. The associated debt service levels also remain manageable, at a peak of 11.5 percent of export earnings in 1992, falling to only 7.7 percent in the year 2000. However, even with these modest indicators, it should be emphasized that in a different sense they cannot be regarded as conservative, in that the absolute level of debt would double over the decade to $113 billion in the year 2000, placing China among the ranks of the most highly indebted developing countries in absolute terms, which would mean that China would account for a very substantial proportion of total new net debt to developing countries over the decade.

xxxix. In summary, these scenarios demonstrate two things: first, the policy decisions that will be taken will have a clear and measurable impact on economic variables, and we have attempted to indicate the orders of magnitude of such impact under different policy frameworks; second, our assessment has shown that within the range of what could be considered likely outcomes, China is likely to continue to enjoy healthy growth, and to continue to enjoy a strong creditworthiness position.

xl. This report has reviewed China's past experience with reform and its prospects for the future. It finds great opportunities for China to move forward and enjoy a continued strong economic performance if these opportunities are grasped. But this will require strong reform efforts by the Chinese government, for without changes to the present policy framework, it is unlikely that the current problems facing the economy could be solved. The indications are that these opportunities will indeed be grasped, and that the decade will see economic gains at least as great as those of the 1980s.

I. RECENT ECONOMIC DEVELOPMENTS

A. Introduction

1.1   By early 1990, the serious inflation and overheating of the economy that had been seen in 1987/88 had been overcome, and the more pressing issue had become the need to restart the economy, which was suffering heavily from the downturn in economic activity.[1] Therefore, this chapter is concerned primarily with the manner of China's emergence from recession since 1990. In many respects, this recovery has been remarkable, in that growth in 1991 has returned to the 7 percent region, with industrial output growth well into double figures, but without the reemergence of inflation or with any negative impact on the external accounts. This growth has returned partly as a natural upswing in activity at the end of the cycle, and even more as a result of explicit government policies to stimulate economic activity.

1.2   There are two main questions that this chapter attempts to address. First, there is the question of the sustainability of the recovery in view of the way in which it has been initiated. Just as there was a heavy reliance on a tightening of money and credit policies in 1989 to overcome inflation, so has there also been a heavy reliance on such policies to stimulate the recovery, which raises the obvious question of whether this approach is likely to generate inflationary pressures. The second issue is therefore whether the recovery can be sustained without a repetition of the earlier economic cycles that have characterized the Chinese economy in the 1980s, or at least with a dampening of their amplitude.

1.3   To a large extent, these past cycles have occurred because of the inadequacy of the macroeconomic policy instruments and, in particular, the lack of indirect economic levers available to the government.[2] More recently, however, such tools have been used with greater frequency and effect, which permits more emphasis to be placed on an assessment of the efficacy with which such tools have been used. The links between these assessments and the rest of the report should be clear: continued success of the reform process and attainment of the goals of the Eighth Five-Year Plan (8th FYP) depend on achieving sustainable growth with macroeconomic stability, primarily through indirect management of the economy.[3]

B. Monetary and Credit Policies

Background

1.4   In 1988, Chinese policymakers confronted an economy which was seriously overheated, as described in detail in the World Bank's last two CEMs on China. This prompted the authorities to act quickly, shelving plans for further price adjustments and adopting a stabilization program, consisting both of direct administrative interventions, including reduction of state investment outlays by 20 percent, freezing prices of basic goods and tight credit controls and also more intensive and successful use of indirect policy levers. Nominal interest rates on deposits were increased by more than four percentage points, and the People's Bank of China (PBC) introduced long-term indexed savings accounts to reverse the depletion of deposits and to encourage longer-term savings. These decisive actions proved to be highly effective in reducing inflation and, by restoring confidence, curbing inflationary expectations. By mid-1989, the annualized monthly rate of inflation, seasonally adjusted, had already declined to single-digit levels. However, measures to establish stricter controls over aggregate demand led to a sharp contraction of output growth and sales, especially in late 1989. The authorities were therefore faced in 1990 with a very different set of economic problems to address.

Money and Credit in 1990 and 1991

1.5   It is clear that, by early 1990, it was appropriate to begin to reflate the economy, as inflation was no longer a short-term threat, and the economy presented Chinese policymakers with a somber picture characterized by rising (open and disguised) unemployment; rising losses or declining profits in most large and medium state-owned enterprises (SOEs);1/ stagnant industrial production and retail sales; rising tax and credit delinquency and major fiscal difficulties; and high and rising inventories of unsold (industrial, agricultural and finished) goods. Moreover, 1989 had witnessed considerable disintermediation in the banking system, with rapidly growing interenterprise arrears (the so-called "debt-triangle"), and all these circumstances called for some relaxation by PBC of monetary policy in 1990.2/

1.6   The 1990 Credit Plan. PBC's initial credit plan was Y 170 billion for the year--about the same as the actual credit growth for 1989--but this was raised on three occasions, for a total credit expansion of Y 276 billion in 1990, yielding total credit growth of 22.3 percent for the year. Several factors explain this outcome. First, it was decided to guarantee credit to key state enterprises and projects. The result was, on the one hand, that as much as 80 percent of working capital loans, above the initial credit target, went to finance the rapid accumulation of inventories, and to finance operational expenditures of SOEs such as overdue taxes and salaries. In addition, as much as Y 30 billion went to help clear interenterprise arrears, which reached a peak of Y 158 billion during the year. At the same time, as part of the reflation strategy, the level of fixed asset investment financed by the specialized banks rose significantly, which facilitated a growth in investment by state-owned units of 11.5 percent, and it was these units that explained

---

1/   "Poor economic performance in enterprises constitutes the main obstacle to China's economic development and the major cause of its financial difficulties. In the past few years, the enterprises' economic performance has been fairly poor, and the profit from their operation, both the total and the part turned over to the financial authorities, has been steadily decreasing, while their losses have been increasing," Report on the Implementation of the State Budget for 1990 and on the Draft State Budget for 1991, Speech delivered at the 4th Session of the 7th NPC Congress on March 26, 1991 by Finance Minister Wang Bingqian.

2/   Three alternative strategies were discussed in China for the reflation of the economy: to relax credit, especially to SOEs; to expand public investment rapidly in economic infrastructure; or to increase incentives for consumption through reduced interest rates. While all three were used to some extent, it was the first that received greatest attention.

the <u>entire</u> growth in fixed investment in 1990.<u>3</u>/ It should be noted that restraints on lending to Township and Village Enterprises (TVEs), introduced in the last quarter of 1988, were also relaxed, and Rural Credit Cooperatives (RCCs) increased their lending to TVEs by 35 percent in 1990.

1.7   Second, it was necessary for the authorities to guarantee credit to procure 1990's bumper grain harvest, and PBC allocated above Y 20 billion in new credits for this purpose. In practice, credits to procure agricultural crops are excluded from the credit ceiling, as illustrated by the credit plan of Henan, a largely wheat-producing province.<u>4</u>/ Third, PBC executed the 1990 credit plan with more flexibility than in previous years, letting its provincial branches exceed their credit quotas by up to 5 percent, allocating any excess among the banks under their jurisdiction. It also appears to be the case, however, that this flexibility was exercised primarily in the interior provinces and the Northeast, and that credit limits continued to be applied quite strictly in the major cities and coastal areas.

1.8   Most of the additional requests for credit financing during 1990 could not be foreseen by the monetary authorities at the beginning of the year, such as unplanned losses of SOEs and to finance crop purchases, given the record grain harvest. In other countries, these are usually the responsibility of the budget authorities. This delayed progress in achieving a more complete separation of fiscal and monetary functions. As a result of the expansionary pressures from the domestic front, Net Domestic Assets (NDA) grew at an annual rate of 24 percent by the end of 1990.

1.9   The <u>credit plan for 1991</u> postulated a <u>reduction</u> of credit expansion from the Y 276 billion level of 1990 to Y 210 billion in 1991, with Y 145 billion for working capital, Y 10 billion for agriculture and Y 50 billion for

---

<u>3</u>/   In spite of the rapid growth of these longer-term loans in 1990, their relative importance in the stock of total outstanding bank loans remained under 10 percent.

<u>4</u>/   <u>Henan's Credit Plan</u>. Henan's 1990 credit plan amounted to Y 12.4 billion (4.5 percent of the national plan), well in excess of the allocation at the beginning of the year. This outcome reflected the rapid growth in lending to procure agricultural products, as well as the increase in working capital loans to finance the accumulation of unsold inventories in the province., A feature giving an expansionary bias to the provincial credit plan results from the flexibility and practical automaticity in exceeding the planned allocation of funds when bank loans are granted to procure agricultural goods. The initial credit plan for 1991 foresaw an expansion of Y 6.3 billion, which was seen as clearly insufficient by the provincial authorities, given the demand for working capital to finance inventories and the rapid growth in bank deposits in Henan which has resulted in a rapid rise in excess reserves. Demand pressures generally become particularly intense during the second semester of the year, when--given the marked seasonal pattern of the demand for agricultural loans--about 70 percent of total annual bank credit is granted, while banks are extremely liquid and anxious to expand their assets in order to improve their financial results.

fixed capital investment. Most of the proposed cuts would have fallen on working capital, based on the notion that the recovery of retail sales would reduce the need for bank credit for this purpose. As it turned out, the credit plan target was exceeded by Y 80 billion in 1991, driven in part by a credit infusion of an additional Y 35 billion to reduce the problem of inter-enterprise debt as well as credit to finance recovery from flood damage.5/ Seasonally adjusted domestic credit increased by more than 20 percent in each of the first three quarters (23.8, 20.5 and 22.9 percent, respectively) before slowing to 14.4 percent growth in the final quarter of 1991. The 1992 credit plan had not been finalized at the time of preparation of this report, and the PBC intends to monitor the performance of the economy and inflation in the first two quarters before setting a target for the year. The Governor of the PBC indicated, however, that credit expansion in 1992 would not exceed the nominal increase in 1991, i.e., Y 345 billion.

1.10   Net Foreign Assets, Reserve Money and Broad Money. The balance of payments strengthened sharply in response to the stabilization program (see Section E below). Therefore, the financing of the large accumulation of for-eign reserves in 1990 and 1991 ($11.6 and $14.1 billion respectively) provided an additional impetus to the overall level of domestic liquidity, while also changing the relative composition of the monetary base significantly. As shown in Table 1.1, Net Foreign Assets (NFA) trebled from 5 percent of PBC's reserve money in 1988 to over 16 percent at the end of 1991. In addition, due to the rapid growth of international reserves, broad money (M2) grew faster than Net Domestic Assets in 1990 and again in 1991, albeit by a smaller amount, fueling a rapid growth of reserve money (see Graph 1.1).6/

Table 1.1: RELATIVE COMPOSITION OF RESERVE MONEY
(Percentages)

| | December | | | | |
	1987	1988	1989	1990	1991
Net foreign assets	4.6	5.1	6.6	10.4	16.0
Claims on financial institutions	86.1	83.6	83.8	78.3	72.6
Other domestic assets	9.3	11.3	9.6	11.3	11.4
Reserve Money	100.0	100.0	100.0	100.0	100.0

5/ Total domestic credit expanded by Y 345 billion in 1991. However, using the credit plan definition, credit expansion was Y 289.5 billion.

6/ Since evidence in China indicates that broad money is a good leading indicator of inflation, targeting broad money may be an efficient way to achieve macroeconomic stability and reduce the frequency and amplitude of the business cycles.

1.11   One result of this growth has been the reversal of the decline in the ratio of excess reserves to deposits. With unchanged legal reserve requirements, the spectacular increase in bank deposits caused the ratio to double from 5.9 percent in 1988 to 13.5 percent at the end of 1991. The increase in bank deposits also allowed the rapid growth of credit to have minimal short-term impact on the price level, but this rate of credit expansion is clearly inconsistent with low and stable inflation in the medium term.

Savings Deposits and Interest Rates

1.12   In 1989 total bank deposits grew by 19.3 percent, with household deposits rising by about 33 percent. In contrast, enterprise deposits rose only 5 percent, a steep decline in real terms, as enterprises were forced to draw down their deposits in the face of the shortage of credit, and to finance the rising level of interenterprise arrears.7/ In 1990, total bank deposits grew by 31 percent, a remarkably fast increase in real terms. Household total and time deposits continued to grow at annual rates of 30 and 41 percent, respectively, but it was the growth of enterprise sight and time deposits, by about 26 and 55 percent respectively, that caused this acceleration in total savings.8/ By the end of 1990, total deposits in the specialized and universal banks had reached the level of Y 1,046 billion, equivalent to 60 percent of GDP (Table 1.2). This trend continued in 1991; by the end of the year, household deposits were 29 percent larger and enterprise deposits were 27 percent greater than in 1990, while total deposits had grown to Y 1,330 billion, or 67.9 percent of GNP.

1.13   The increase in household savings in 1990 and 1991, which was particularly rapid in urban areas which accounted for 90 percent of growth, can be attributed to a mixture of policy and structural factors:

(a) low inflationary expectations as a result of the impact of the austerity program, strengthened by an ample supply of agricultural goods and the reassuring presence of the indexation mechanism for longer-term deposits;

7/ Interestingly, however, enterprise term deposits, which accounted for only about 17 percent of total enterprise deposits at the beginning of the year, grew by almost 32 percent in that year. This was probably in response to two things: the postponement of investment projects during the "retrenchment program," resulting in a temporary increase in demand for financial assets; and the abolition of punitively low interest rates on such deposits. Although enterprises were not eligible for indexed deposits, they received the same interest rates as individuals with effect from September 1988.

8/ By the end of 1990, enterprise deposits were 36.2 percent higher than at the end of 1988, while nominal GDP was up 24.5 percent, and if the comparison is made on the basis of 1987, such deposits are still below "normal." Therefore, a good proportion of the growth in such deposits in 1990 can be attributed to enterprises restoring balances to a normal level.

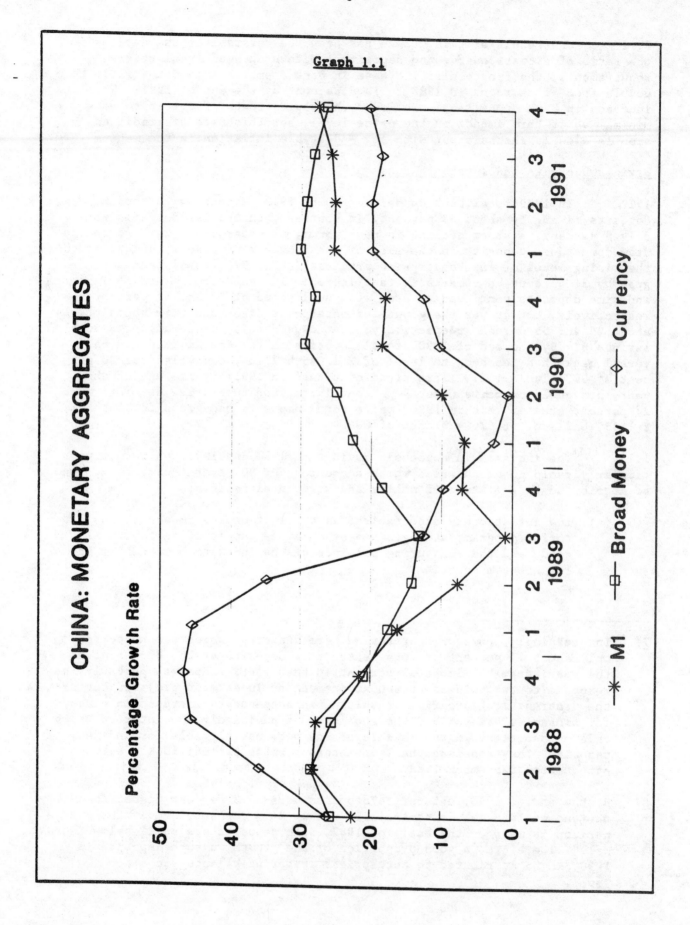

Graph 1.1

CHINA: MONETARY AGGREGATES

Percentage Growth Rate

—✳— M1   —▱— Broad Money   —◇— Currency

Table 1.2: SPECIALIZED AND COMPREHENSIVE BANKS: TOTAL DEPOSITS

	Year-End (Y billion)				Growth Rate (%)	
	1988	1989	1990	1991	1990	1991
Enterprise Deposits	293	308	399	505	29.6	26.6
Sight	262	267	336	455	25.7	35.4
Term	31	41	64	50	55.0	-14.1
Household Deposits	259	363	501	647	38.0	29.1
Sight	60	61	76	102	24.4	34.2
Term	199	302	424	545	40.7	28.5
TVEs	6	6	7	9	18.3	28.6
Agricultural Collectives	2	2	2	2	11.8	5.3
RCCs	59	64	76	92	18.8	21.1
Other Deposits	50	56	61	74	9.5	21.3
Total Deposits	669	798	1,046	1,330	31.0	27.2
Memorandum Items:						
Total Deposits/Total Liabilities	58.0	58.0	60.1	62.8	3.6	4.5
Household Deposits/Total Deposits	38.7	45.5	47.9	48.7	5.3	1.7
Liabilities to PBC/Total Liabilities	29.2	30.5	29.2	27.9	-4.3	-4.5
Total Deposits/GDP	47.7	50.3	59.0	67.9	19.1	15.1
Total Liabilities/GDP	82.3	86.8	98.1	108.1	14.9	10.3

Source: Annex Table 6.7.

(b) record high real interest rates on bank deposits;

(c) a rapid increase in urban real wages and incomes, of a reported 9.7 percent in urban areas in 1990 and a further 13.2 percent in 1991;9/

(d) an apparent increasing concentration of savings among nonstate and private workers, with a high propensity to save in view of both the relatively high level of their incomes as well as uncertainty over their future incomes; and

(e) factors which might explain a more permanent shift in the savings function,[4] including the aging of China's population, the increased uncertainty associated with a reduction of pension and health bene-

9/ Report on the Implementation of the 1990 Plan for National Economic and Social Development and the Draft 1991 Plan: speech delivered at the 4th Session of the NPC on March 26, 1991, by Zou Jiahua, Minister in charge of the State Planning Commission.

fits,[5] opportunities for financial bequests, and the expectation of
an attractive housing reform, which might facilitate the purchase of
new or existing properties.

While the structural factors seem to explain an upward shift of the savings
function over time, they seem less adequate to explain the recent acceleration. This suggests that the shorter term factors, and especially high interest rates and low price expectations, have been more important, casting some
doubt on the longer-term stability of the incremental deposits in 1990, which
exceeded incremental GDP by 55 percent in 1990, and 49 percent in 1991, with
household deposits alone growing by the equivalent of 80 percent of incremental GNP.

1.14   In the short term, however, the growth in savings had two important
effects. First, from a macroeconomic point of view, the very fast increase in
household savings and enterprise deposits in the last two years made it possible to finance the large accumulation of foreign assets and inventories of
domestically-produced goods without exacerbating inflationary pressures.
Second, the rapid increase of household savings deposits had two important
sectoral effects. First, the relative share of the different sources of bank
funds has changed significantly, in favor of the more expensive deposits,
increasing the cost of funding bank operations. The share of household deposits in total bank deposits rose by more than 9 percentage points over the
period 1988-91, while term deposits rose from 34.5 percent of total deposits
in 1988, to 45 percent at the end of 1991, putting additional pressure on the
banks' financial margins. Second, the rapid increase of bank total assets and
liabilities during 1990/91 resulted in a significant fall of the ratio of
equity to assets, weakening the banks' capital adequacy.

1.15   Interest rate policy played a positive role in the stabilization
program, with rates becoming highly positive in 1990 as a result of the rapid
decline in the rate of inflation. In 1990, in an effort to stimulate the
economy, PBC reduced rates across the board on two occasions (March and
August) by a total of about 2.7 percentage points, followed by a further
reduction of 1.08 points in April 1991. Nominal interest rates on one-year
bank deposits have thus fallen from a peak of 11.34 percent in February 1989
to 7.56 percent in the second quarter of 1992, although this still leaves real
rates higher than at the time of the first rate cut. The consensus forecast
for the expected rate of inflation for 1992 is about 6 percent. If inflation
were to rise beyond that range, real interest rates could become negative, and
the government will need to be ready to use interest rate policy again to
reduce inflationary expectations if this proves necessary, which would imply,
inter alia, restoring the provisions for the indexation of interest rates on
medium-term deposits.

C. The Real Sector

Overview

1.16   China's real GDP growth averaged a remarkable 9.6 percent per year
between 1979, when major economic reforms were initiated, and 1988. Over the
last two years of the decade, real growth slowed down substantially, falling
from 11.2 percent in 1988, to 4.6 percent and 5.6 percent in 1989 and 1990,

respectively, as the government sought to cool down the economy in order to eliminate inflation. Economic activity was sluggish in the first half of 1990, but it accelerated in the second half, 10/ aided by the rapid increase in credit, a moderate rise in public investment and a fast expansion of exports, and these trends continued throughout 1991, with GDP growing by 7 percent.

<u>Table 1.3</u>: CHINA: SOURCES OF GROWTH OF GDP (1988-90)
(Percentage Growth Rate in Constant 1980 Prices)

| | Annual Percentage Change | | | |
	1988	1989	1990	1991
GDP	11.2	4.6	5.6	7.0
Agriculture	2.5	3.1	7.5	3.2
Industry	15.3	5.1	5.7	11.4
Services and Other	12.3	4.8	3.9	2.8
<u>Memorandum Items</u>:				
Imports of GNFS /a	25.0	12.1	-13.0	13.5
Exports of GNFS	15.4	5.4	10.7	16.1
GNP Deflator	11.4	8.9	5.1	4.1
Consumption	11.7	7.3	5.7	7.8
Gross Domestic Investment	10.8	-15.5	2.3	13.9

/a GNFS = Goods and Nonfactor Services.

Source: Annex Tables 1.7 and 1.8.

Sources of Growth Analysis

1.17   Industrial GNP growth slowed to 5.7 percent in 1990, and its share in total GNP growth fell to 43 percent. The services and construction sector grew steadily over these two years, but it was the agricultural sector, which grew by 7.5 percent, that enabled overall GDP growth to accelerate to 5.6 percent in 1990 while accounting for a remarkable 35 percent of aggregate GNP growth, its highest since 1982.

1.18   Similar shifts are also evident in the relative roles of demand-side factors in explaining aggregate growth since 1989. Whereas consumer spending has been the predominant influence in the past, slack domestic demand in 1990 had the result that only 24 percent of growth was generated by this source. The weak domestic market compelled many enterprises to look to foreign markets and a successful export drive increased the contribution of exports to 35 percent, while the cutback in imports contributed another 37 percent of the

---

10/ The quarterly rates of growth of GVIO were 0 percent, 4.1 percent, 5 percent and 14.2 percent.

growth in 1990. This is the biggest contribution of the foreign trade sector to China's growth since 1949.

Table 1.4: CHINA: COMPARATIVE SUPPLY AND DEMAND-SIDE CONTRIBUTIONS TO GROWTH
(In Percentage Points)

	1988 Rate	1988 Share	1989 Rate	1989 Share	1990 Rate	1990 Share	1991 Rate	1991 Share
GDP Growth Rate	11.2	100	4.6	100	5.6	100	7.0	100
Supply Side								
Agriculture	0.7	6.3	0.8	17.8	2.0	34.7	0.9	12.0
Industry	6.2	55.4	2.2	47.1	2.4	43.3	4.8	69.2
Services and Other	4.3	38.3	1.6	35.1	1.2	22.0	1.3	18.8
Demand Side								
Total Consumption	7.7	69.1	4.0	87.1	1.4	24.8	4.5	65.1
Gross Domestic Investment	4.7	41.6	0.6	14.5	0.2	3.4	1.6	22.9
Exports of GNFS	2.1	18.9	1.2	25.7	1.9	34.5	2.3	32.6
Imports of GNFS	-3.3	-29.6	-1.2	-27.3	2.1	37.3	-1.4	-20.6

Source: Annex Table 1.9(b).

1.19   Preliminary statistics for 1991 indicate that the economy returned to a much more "normal" pattern, with industry contributing two thirds of growth on the supply side, and consumption leading on the demand side, with trade more neutral. This is a further indication that after the extraordinary economic events of 1988-90, the last year has seen a return to the growth path of the mid-1980s.

Industrial Output

1.20   The recovery of GVIO in 1990 followed very closely the expansion of credit and the subsequent improvement of consumer demand and retail sales (see Graph 1.2). One remarkable aspect of the industrial output picture in 1990 was that output of the SOEs grew by only 2.9 percent,[6] compared with 11.1 percent for industrial TVEs, in spite of the strong preferential treatment received by SOEs in terms of access to credit, raw materials, imports and transport. Light industry grew 60 percent faster than heavy industry, thus maintaining the longer-term trend of a shrinking share of both SOEs and heavy industry in total GVIO (see Annex Table 9.2). As recently as 1985 SOEs had a 65 percent share of total GVIO, while in 1990 such share had fallen below 55 percent.[7] The recovery of GVIO had also an important regional dimension, with coastal provinces like Guangdong, Fujian and Hainan growing in double figures (Guangdong by 17 percent), while the older industrial cities (e.g., Shanghai) and the Northeast showed very little growth. These trends continued in 1991, with the share of SOEs in GVIO falling to 52.8 percent, despite a

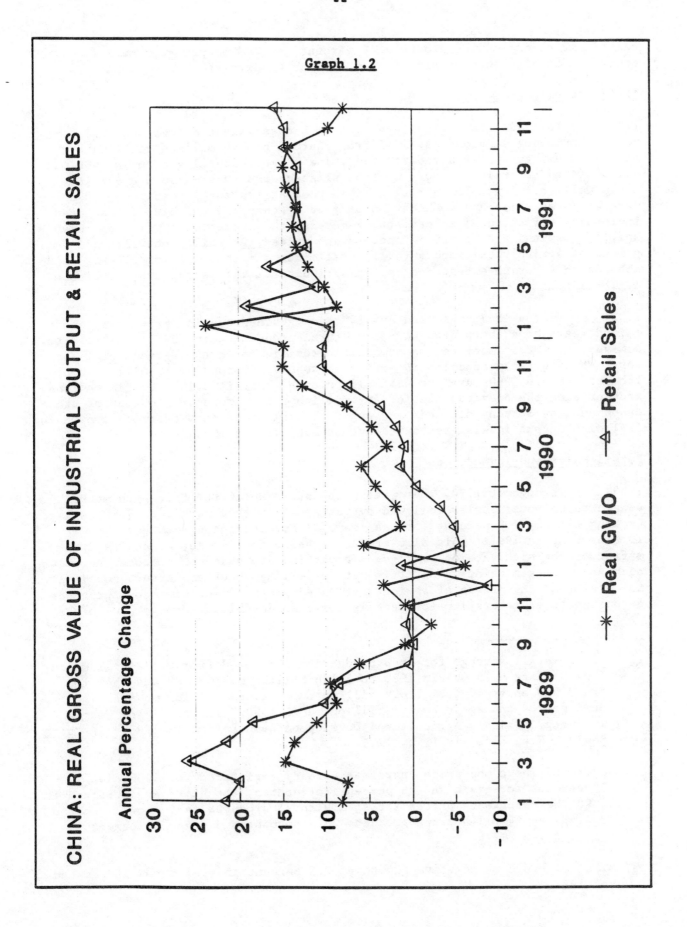

Graph 1.2

CHINA: REAL GROSS VALUE OF INDUSTRIAL OUTPUT & RETAIL SALES

Annual Percentage Change

—*— Real GVIO   —△— Retail Sales

relatively strong output growth of 8 percent, as TVE output grew over 14 percent, and foreign enterprises' output by over 45 percent.

Agricultural Output

1.21   In 1990, the agricultural sector had excellent summer and fall harvests, achieving a record level of grain output of 446 million tons, with annual output growth of 6.7 percent. China's agricultural growth in 1990 was not confined to grains alone. Cotton, oilseeds and sugar also did particularly well (see Annex Table 8.1). These good agricultural results in 1990 were achieved through a combination of good weather and policies directed at increasing agricultural investment, reversing the reduction in farming acreage,11/ continuing to increase procurement prices,12/ while controlling prices of agricultural inputs (e.g., pesticides and chemical fertilizers) and mobilizing labor to extend and repair agricultural infrastructure, particularly irrigation.

1.22   Floods in Jiangsu and Anhui, major grain-producing provinces, had raised fears of a sharp drop in agricultural production in 1991. The results, however, bear testimony to the remarkable resilience of the agricultural sector. While grain production is estimated to have dropped by 11 million tons from the record 1990 level to 435 million tons, this is still 28 million tons greater than the previous high of 407 million tons. Moreover, output of other crops such as cotton, oilseeds and sugar-bearing crops showed strong growth in 1991 with output levels greater than that achieved in 1990.

Retail Sales and Inventories

1.23   Throughout 1990, there was much debate about the "sluggish market," as growth in retail sales followed output growth with a very considerable lag, growing by only 1.9 percent for the year,13/ but recording growth of 13.2 percent in 1991. This slow growth of sales in 1990 is, of course, the mirror of the high rate of savings. In particular, sales of consumer durables such as washing machines and refrigerators fell by about a quarter, confirming the view that the growth of savings reflected postponement of major purchases, or perhaps even saturation for certain consumer durables. However, with the

---

11/   "The overall acreage for crop production increased from 2.173 billion mu (one hectare = 15 mu) in 1988 to 2.198 billion mu in 1989 and that for grain was enlarged from 1.652 billion mu to 1.683 billion mu over the same period and again to 1.7 billion mu in 1990," in You Ji and Wang Yuesheng, "China's Agricultural Development and Reform in 1990," in China Review, Hong-Kong, 1991, p. 12.6.

12/   Over and above the price increases already registered for 1989, i.e., 27 percent for grain and 23 percent for cotton, the state again raised in 1990 the purchasing prices for agricultural products as follows: cotton 27.1 percent, oil-bearing products 28.3 percent and sugar 10 percent. Op. cit., p. 12.6.

13/   The low had been negative growth of 8.5 percent in real terms at the end of 1989.

relaxed credit stance financing output growth, the sluggish market rapidly generated large accumulations of inventories.

1.24   The mismatch between industrial production and retail sales during 1989-91 created a disequilibrium growth of inventory both at enterprise level and, to a lesser extent, with commercial departments. Graph 1.3 indicates the behavior of inventory held by commercial units as a reflection of their procurement and sales between January 1989 and September 1991. The period between September and December 1990 saw a buildup of inventory with commercial departments, driven largely by the procurement of the bumper harvest of grain and edible oil.14/ For the year as a whole, the inventory of grain and edible oil grew by 31 and 27 percent, respectively. Commercial units also saw a sharp increase in their inventories of specific consumer durables such as television sets (which increased by 22 and 37 percent, respectively, in 1989 and 1990) and electric fans (which rose by 37 and 22 percent, respectively, in 1990 and 1991), and faced difficulties in unloading previously built-up stocks of other items such as refrigerators and washing machines. However, the period 1990 and 1991 also saw commercial units cutting back on purchases of consumer durables, backing the problem of excess production to the enterprise. Commercial inventories of several consumer goods had declined substantially by the end of 1991 and stocks of producer goods with commercial units had also been reduced after peaking in 1989. The inventory problem in 1991 was thus largely concentrated in the enterprise sector. The value of inventories with enterprises and industrial departments increased from Y 90 billion in 1989 to Y 116 billion by 1990 and reached a peak of Y 136 billion in June 1991.15/ In September, the authorities initiated measures to curb production of items in excess supply--enterprises producing unsalable products were asked to curb production and banks were instructed to extend credit only to enterprises that succeeded in reducing their inventory. Whereas the first half of 1991 saw industrial production rise by 9.9 percent and inventories grow by 20 percent, the growth rate of industrial output fell by 5.5 percent in the second half of 1991, while inventories fell by 13.4 percent, from Y 136 billion in June 1991 to Y 113.1 billion by year-end. Correspondingly, enterprise profitability improved from -17.5 percent to +2.8 percent.

1.25   What Annex Tables 13.6-13.9 indicate clearly is that enterprises reacted slower than consumers to the austerity program of 1989, in that sales fell faster than output, but were faster than consumers to respond to the subsequent relaxed credit stance, as output grew more rapidly than sales. This is the expected response of enterprises not fully subject to hard budget constraints, and reflects strategic behavior directed at putting pressure on policymakers to reverse contractionary policies,[8] given the authorities' desires to maintain employment. In other words, enterprises doubt the cred-

---

14/   The purchases of grain in November and December 1990 were 19 and 40 percent greater than the corresponding months in 1989.

15/   These inventory figures refer to stockpiles held by budgeted state-owned industrial enterprises which are additional to the figure for inventory held by commercial units. The latter are cited by the China Statistics Monthly and are three times as large. Most of the recent growth in inventory has been in the stocks held by enterprises.

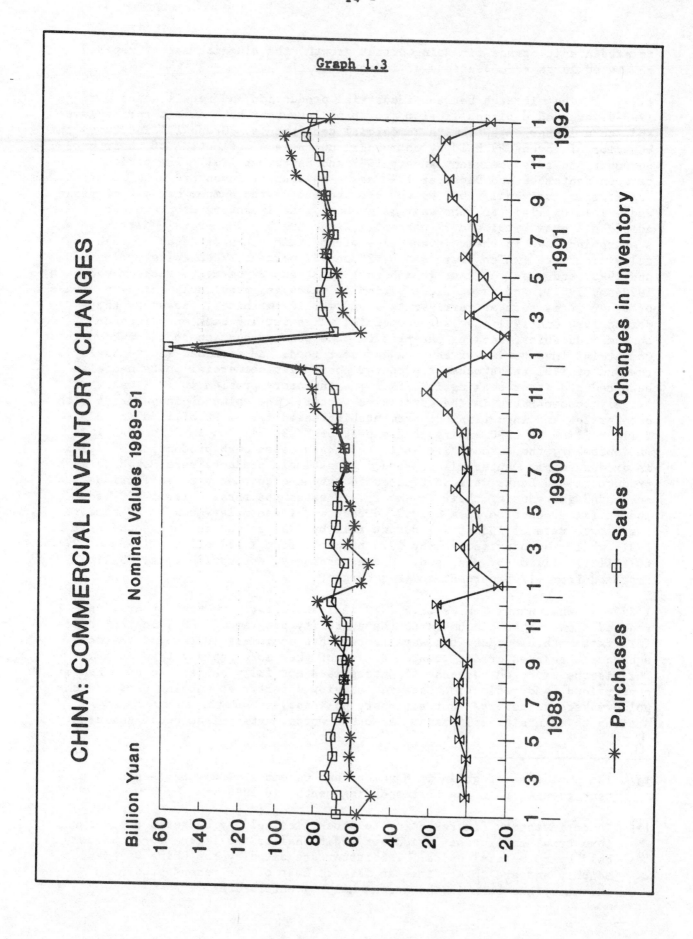

Graph 1.3

CHINA: COMMERCIAL INVENTORY CHANGES

Billion Yuan   Nominal Values 1989-91

—✳— Purchases   —□— Sales   —▷— Changes in Inventory

ibility of contractionary policies, and try to position themselves well for the economic conditions that will exist if contractionary policies are abandoned.[9] It had appeared that the determination of the authorities in 1989 to implement the austerity program was going to moderate this kind of behavior by enterprises, but the manner of the relaxation of the policy in 1990 has served to reinforce the appearance that such behavior actually pays.

D. Price Developments

1.26   The most significant and obvious achievement of the rectification program in China has been the remarkable speed with which the rate of inflation has declined. The retail price index, and the index of free market prices were both growing at close to 30 percent at the end of 1988, and within one year this was down to single digits. The average increase in the retail price index for 1990 was only 2.1 percent and 2.9 percent for 1991, with market price indices falling in both years. The question to be addressed, however, is whether there is imminent risk that inflation will reemerge some time in the near future.

1.27   In 1990 price pressures continued to fall. The most significant factors to explain this were sluggish domestic demand, large inventories, and the second bumper grain harvest in succession. In these circumstances, China witnessed the unexpected phenomenon of appreciable reductions in the free market price index, which fell by 9 percent in 1990, while retail prices rose by 2.1 percent in 1990 and the broader based cost of living index (which includes the effect of service price movements) increased by 1.3 percent. In 1991, despite a decline in market prices, the retail price index grew by 2.9 percent and the cost of living index increased by 5.1 percent as the government seized the opportunity to adjust administered prices. The upward adjustment of food ration prices and increases in the administered price of urban services had the effect of increasing the cost of living index for 35 large and medium cities by approximately 8 percent in 1991.[16] Graph 1.4 illustrates the sharp upward spike in the retail price index in May 1991 as a reflection of the ration price adjustment in that month.

1.28   Evidence of inflationary pressure is best gauged by movements of market prices and while these largely showed a tendency to decline, the period since May 1991 has seen market prices firming up and even inching up slightly. The market price index, which had been negative from November 1989 to May 1991, was 1.7 percent higher in October 1991 than in October 1990, indicating the emergence of demand pressure. Moreover, nominal per capita urban incomes rose by 9.7 percent in 1990 and 13.2 percent in 1991, translating into sizable real income increases in both years as basic wages in SOEs increased by 13 percent in 1990 while bonuses expanded by 30.5 percent. At present most of this increased income has been saved, minimizing demand pressure, but the

---

16/   By October 1991, the prices of several urban services in the 35 large and medium cities had been raised--commuter bus fares were raised by 18.8 percent, running water by 16.6 percent, public bath charges by 20.4 percent, hospital registration fees by 12 percent, household electricity by 5.3 percent, and house rents by 4.2 percent.

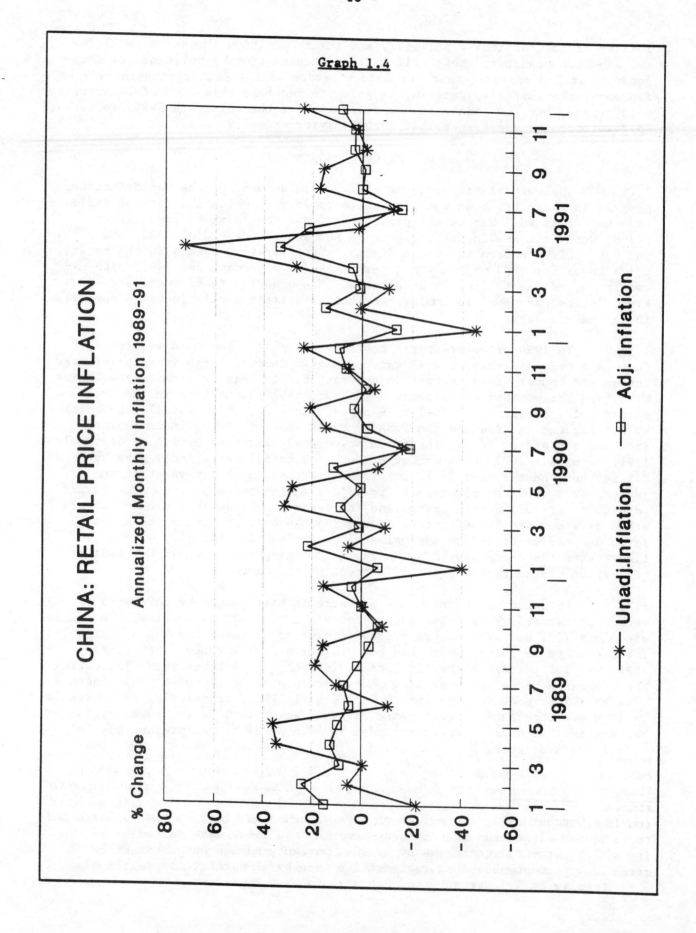

Graph 1.4

CHINA: RETAIL PRICE INFLATION

Annualized Monthly Inflation 1989-91

% Change

—*— Unadj.Inflation   —□— Adj. Inflation

possibility remains of the tiger emerging from the cage should consumers' expectations about price stability change.

1.29   The overall price reform program in China has two essential compo- nents: the introduction of greater use of markets in determining prices; and the adjustment of state fixed prices closer to market levels. While the move towards the greater use of markets has been gradual, there was significant relaxation in price control. This came in the form of a substantial reduction in the number of commodities where price adjustments remain subject to State Council approval, by relaxation of some of the additional administrative con- trols that had been imposed in 1989.[10] By the end of 1989, some 50 items had been returned to central control, but by the second quarter of 1991 the list had been reduced to only six. Nevertheless, a substantial degree of indirect control remains through the continued operation of a system under which pro- vincial authorities are given targets for price increases in commodities which are part of the monitored basket for the retail price indices. The provincial price controllers are expected to keep annual price increases in these commod- ities to within a margin of 0.5 to 1.0 percentage point of these targets, which are designed to yield the Plan target for inflation for the year in question (e.g., 6 percent in 1991).

1.30   The Chinese government has taken advantage of the sluggish market to make a relatively large number of adjustments to administered prices during 1990 and 1991, a selective list of which appears at Table 1.5.[11]   These adjustments are across the board in a wide range of commodities, but include some in which the government had for many years been unwilling to take any action at all. Indeed, it is these price adjustments that have probably accounted for much of the price increase so far registered (para. 1.26). Most notable of these were the increases of about 60 percent in urban grain prices and of over 150 percent in edible oil prices. However, the list of adjust- ments is very long, and in fact represents the highest level of activity in this area since the reform program began.[12] This experience has demonstrated a major lesson: if carried out in a period of tight macroeconomic management and excess supply, price reform has little impact on the overall price level in the short term. Rather, it has been reflected in declining rates of profit--and higher rates of loss--in the enterprise sector, as enterprises have not been able to pass on higher costs at this stage in the economic cycle. This is a second factor to consider in assessing the potential for a return of inflation.

1.31   While the maintenance of administrative controls has helped to restrain the rate of increase of the price indices, the question remains as to why more general inflation has not reemerged in the Chinese economy, given the size of the monetary expansion described in Section A above. There are two overriding reasons for this, in our judgment. First, short-term inflationary expectations remained low, as demonstrated by the fact that even the signifi- cant administered price adjustments in 1990/91 did not provoke panic buying. Thus, as discussed earlier (paras. 1.12-1.13), the savings propensity remained extremely high. Second, inventories were still high, and for some commodities continued to grow despite price-cutting by state-owned outlets. What remains to be seen is how long such inventories will be able to exercise this cushion- ing effect, since the quality and composition of such stocks may well not match demand patterns as retail sales continue to build. Inflation, there-

Table 1.5: CHINA: PRICE ADJUSTMENTS DURING 1990/91

	Date change	Unit	Old price	New price	Range /a	Percentage
1990						
Agricultural commodities /b						
Food oil	Apr 1	50 kg			47	...
Soybean	Apr	50 kg	165	215	50	30.3
Sugarcane		tons	125	140	15	12.0
Sugar beet		tons	140	155		10.7
Tobacco		50 kg	109.42	120.6		10.2
Cotton		50 kg	236.42	300.00		26.9
Timber	Nov	meters	144.97	214.83		48.2
Industrial commodities /c						
Crude oil	Mar	tons	137	167		21.9
Residual oil	Mar	tons			60	...
Railway freight	Mar	ton-km	0.02	0.25		25.0
Water freight	Mar	ton-km	0.01051	0.01353		28.7
Mineral ore (42%)	Jul	tons	188	242		28.7
Iron ore (68%)	Jul	tons	93.5	115		23.0
Mail post	Jul	a letter	0.08	0.2		150.0
Corrugated aluminum	Aug	tons	800	1,000		66.7
Coal	Aug	tons			10	...
Copper ore (25%)	Sep	tons	5,700	7,560		32.6
Electrolytic copper (99.95%)	Sep	tons	7,500	9,700		29.3
Tin ore (60%)	Sep	tons	2,700	3,550		31.5
Living commodities						
Detergent	Jul	500 g			0.4	...
White cloth	Oct	meters		2.79		...
Sugar	Nov	500 g		1.90		...
1991						
Industrial commodities /d						
Steel	Q I					15
Transport fares	Q I					23
Consumer goods						
Grain (state-rationed)	May /e					67
Edible oil	May /f					159

/a Difference of old and new price.
/b Mainly procurement prices.
/c Mainly ex-factory prices.
/d Retail prices.
/e Price change from Y 0.06 to Y 0.10 per 0.5 kg.
/f Price change from Y 52 to Y 1.55 per 0.5 kg.

Source: Data provided by the Chinese authorities.

fore, is one of the most hotly debated topics in Chinese economic circles, and is one of the main issues to emerge from this review of recent developments as needing the continued close attention of the authorities.

E. The State Sector

1.32   Throughout the 1980s, the overall fiscal deficit (including both local and central government) fluctuated in the relatively narrow range of 1.5 percent to 3 percent of GNP. Although not exceptional by international standards, even this level proved difficult to finance at times. But it is necessary to look beyond this relatively narrow concept of deficit to the much larger financial requirements of the state enterprises to realize the full financial consequences of government policy. In particular, there is a high level of policy-related bank lending to the SOEs because of the constraints placed on the state budget. This section analyzes both the government budget situation and the difficult-to-quantify broader issue of the public sector deficit as a whole.

The Government

1.33   Revenue and Expenditure Trends. There were two major reforms of the fiscal system in the 1980s, each of which reduced the ratio of revenue to GDP: the switch from profit surrender to income taxes for enterprises in the first half of the decade, and the move to the fiscal contract responsibility system in the latter half. In effect, the primary impact of these reforms was to transfer responsibility for investment financing from the central government to enterprises. With rising enterprise losses in sectors subject to price controls, the overall result was that the net contribution of the SOEs and collectives to the budget (that is income tax and related taxes, levies, and profits, net of subsidies to loss-making enterprises) declined from 6 percent of GNP in 1984 to 2 percent of GNP in 1989 (see section "Enterprises" below). The overall level of revenue was maintained by the broadening of the tax base through indirect taxes (Table 1.6). The expenditure/GNP ratio was compressed by holding capital expenditure constant in nominal terms, and by a gradual reduction in consumer subsidies. The effects of these measures were counteracted by the marked increase in subsidies to loss-making enterprises. Recurrent expenditure other than subsidies has stabilized relative to GNP since 1987, suggesting that there may be little prospect for major reduction in the future.

1.34   Performance in 1990. The overall deficit in 1990, only marginally higher than the preceding year, was 2 percent of GNP, about 0.5 percent of GNP larger than budgeted. This overrun was entirely financed by net credit from the PBC. However, while the overall outcome was close to target, not all components were so close to their estimated levels. First, tax revenue fell 6 percent short of target because of the decision not to implement the budgeted increase (from 3 percent to 5 percent) in the business tax rate, owing to fears as to the impact on retail prices, and because of below-budget receipts from value added taxes and customs duties, reflecting weak domestic demand and import compression during much of the year. This latter factor accounted for about two-thirds of the shortfall. Although enterprise finances remained weak, it is noteworthy, and somewhat surprising, that in 1990 for the first time net flows from the enterprises rose in nominal terms for the first time in the reform era.

1.35   Total expenditure was marginally below the budget target, despite overruns in several areas of current expenditure and an increase in capital expenditures authorized during the year. This out-turn was largely attributable to lower subsidies, because the procurement prices of some foodstuffs (notably pork) were lower than expected, and because transfers to loss-making enterprises were less than budgeted. As described in the section on "Center-Local Fiscal Relations" below, overruns in current expenditure came from local government outlays, primarily on administration, reflecting higher wages.

Table 1.6: CHINA--STATE BUDGETARY OPERATIONS, 1986-91

	1986	1987	1988	1989	1990 Budget	1990 Actual	1991 Budget	1991 Prelim
			(in billions of yuan)					
Total Revenue	244.6	257.6	280.4	326.4	356.1	351.8	364.8	363.4
Tax	224.8	232.1	257.6	301.7	333.9	313.9	336.8	330.2
Nontax	19.8	25.5	22.8	24.7	22.2	37.9	28.0	33.2
Total Expenditure and net lending	263.2	282.4	313.7	364.3	382.0	388.5	395.8	413.5
Current	188.0	206.8	237.6	288.7	307.5	306.9	317.9	330.4
of which: subsidies	58.2	67.0	76.3	97.3	106.4	96.0	89.0	87.7
Capital	75.2	75.6	76.1	75.6	74.5	81.6	77.9	83.1
Overall deficit	-18.6	-24.8	-33.3	-37.9	-25.9	-36.7	-31.0	-50.1
Financing	18.1	24.6	33.5	37.4	25.9	36.8	31.0	50.1
Domestic	12.8	17.8	22.0	26.1	14.0	23.7	20.3	38.2
Peoples Bank of China, net	12.7	8.4	11.5	-7.5	8.8	17.4	12.3	21.1
Other domestic	0.1	9.4	10.5	33.6	5.2	6.3	8.0	17.1
Foreign	5.3	6.8	11.5	11.3	11.9	13.1	10.7	11.9
Gross foreign borrowing	7.6	10.6	13.9	14.4	16.4	17.8	16.2	17.4
Amortization	-2.3	-3.8	-2.4	-3.1	-4.5	-4.7	-5.5	-5.5
			(as a percent of GNP)					
Revenue	25.2	22.8	20.1	20.7	20.1	20.2	18.6	18.6
Expenditure	27.1	25.0	22.4	23.1	21.6	22.3	20.2	21.1
Current expenditure	19.4	18.3	17.0	18.3	17.4	17.6	16.2	16.9
Subsidies	6.0	5.9	5.5	6.2	6.0	5.5	4.5	4.5
Capital expenditure	7.8	6.7	5.4	4.8	4.2	4.7	4.0	4.2
Overall balance	-1.9	-2.2	-2.4	-2.4	-1.5	-2.1	-1.6	-2.6

Sources: Ministry of Finance; State Statistical Bureau; and staff estimates.

1.36   The 1991 Budget. The budget for 1991 was intended to reduce the overall deficit from the 2.1 percent of 1990 to 1.6 percent of GDP in 1991. The budget had anticipated a 1.3 percentage point decline in the revenue/GNP ratio, as a consequence of weak state enterprise performance and in spite of a proposed increase in the business tax rate. However, the deficit was to be reduced by a sharper cutback in expenditure--by reducing outlays on subsidies and limiting the nominal growth of nonsubsidy current and capital expenditure. The Budget presentation for 1992 revealed that the targeted reduction in the deficit was not achieved and it in fact increased to 2.6 percent of GNP. While the business tax increase was not implemented, the revenue/GNP ratio declined by 1.6 percentage points. Wage pressure, indicated by a 13 percent growth of wages in 1991, continues to weaken the budget position. However, the government was successful in reducing expenditure on subsidies which has been cut by 1 percent of GNP to 4.5 percent of GNP.

1.37   Financing. In addition to a modest level of net foreign financing, and the residually determined level of net borrowing from the PBC, the Government has financed about one third of the deficit, on average, through the issue of domestic bonds. The management of these bonds has created a number of problems. There was strong growth during the 1980s in the holdings--mainly by individuals and enterprises--of government securities. For the most part these were sold through involuntary placement, and, for enterprises and financial institutions, at interest rates that were far below market (typically half the rate offered to households). What is more, the Government's financing needs were compounded by the progressive reduction in the average maturity of treasury bonds, which resulted in a bunching of debt service, exacerbated by the Chinese practice of paying interest only at maturity.

1.38   In 1990, the total value of maturing bonds rose to Y 30 billion from Y 5 billion in the previous year. Only a small part of the resulting gross financing needs could be met by the issue of new bonds to households and enterprises, so the government resorted to the forced rollover of bonds held by enterprises. In 1991, similar demands arose, and so, in addition to the planned issue of new bonds, the Government once again postponed redemption of enterprise-held bonds, resorting for a second time to the device of conversion bonds.17/ To balance this, however, a new method of placement was used for new bonds held by individuals, relying on voluntary placement via financial institutions instead of the usual compulsory placement via work units.

1.39   This practice of non-redemption is not conducive to the development of a market for the voluntary placement of government securities, a key element of financial sector reform. There is an urgent need for the authorities to develop more rational public debt management techniques, in parallel with the gradual relaxation of the direct methods of monetary control in favor of indirect instruments that would foster government securities markets.

Center-Local Fiscal Relations[13]

1.40   Since 1988, center-local fiscal relations have been regulated by contracts, usually of 3-4 years' duration, struck between the central Government and provincial and municipal governments. The importance of these contracts cannot be overstated since local governments account for the majority (about 60 percent in 1990) of both revenue collection and expenditure. There are several different forms of contract, but a common one is demonstrated by the case of Henan province (see Box 1.1). One feature of these contracts is that, after the provinces have satisfied their contractual tax obligations to the center, they are permitted to retain, and spend, about 75 percent (on average) of the incremental revenue. One consequence of this arrangement is that the central government has lost a degree of fiscal control, because it cannot anticipate the magnitude of total government spending, and at the same time the buoyancy of fiscal revenues has been severely limited. In particular, it is the central government that has had to cope with shortfalls in revenues, while the local governments get the benefits of any above-budget revenues.[14]

1.41   The largest deviation from budget in 1990 was in expenditure by the local governments which overshot by about 5 percent, even though revenue collection was close to target. As noted earlier, the overrun was mainly the result of natural disasters and expenditure on priority projects. Expansion of administrative expenses has also contributed as wages caught up with their

---

17/ These were bonds issued to enterprises in replacement for the maturing bonds. Interest was not paid on the latter, merely a promise to pay on maturity of the conversion bonds.

<u>Box 1.1</u>: FISCAL POLICY IN HENAN PROVINCE

Henan is the second most populous province in China, and a leading producer of many basic commodities and raw materials processed in other provinces. Its economic conditions are in many senses typical of the inland provinces, which have not benefited from reform to the same extent as the coastal provinces. The following are selected basic statistics for 1990 for Henan province:

Population as a proportion of total	7.7 percent
GNP as a proportion of total	5.1 percent
Fixed investment/GNP	23.1 percent
Government revenue/GNP	9.5 percent
Government expenditure/GNP	10.1 percent

Comparisons between national statistics and those for Henan are complicated, by the following considerations: (i) a larger than average proportion of Henan's output comes from commodities produced under the Plan, distortions in the prices of which are reflected in both GNP estimates, and the level of revenue and expenditure; and (ii) the fiscal data exclude revenue and expenditure relating to centrally owned state enterprises which report directly to the center. Nonetheless, it is notable that Henan's revenue and expenditure are barely half the national average.

<u>Center-Local Fiscal Relation</u>. Henan's relationship with the central government is governed by a four-year contract (1988-91), and the next contract which will take effect in 1992 has been negotiated, though has yet to be signed. In principle, Henan remits an amount determined by this contract each year (based on 1988 revenue, Henan's remittance was to increase by 5 percent annually, with 80 percent of any revenue collected in excess of the target being retained in the province). In 1990, under the contract Henan was due to remit Y 1.4 billion out of total collections of Y 8.4 billion. However, this amount was reduced by amounts (approved either at the annual budget or by supplementary allocation during the year) relating to additional subsidies for enterprise losses (including foreign trading corporations) and grain, disaster relief, and additional capital construction implemented through the local budget. In the final analysis, the central government transferred about Y 0.4 billion <u>to</u> Henan.

<u>Lower Levels of Government</u>. The provincial budget covers the activities of lower levels of government: there are 12 provincial municipalities, 5 districts, 105 counties, and 12 municipalities at the county level. Of this total, 56 counties and municipalities (almost half, typically those in the mountainous areas) have budget deficits that need support from the provincial government.

<u>Tax Reform</u>. Henan has not been selected as one of the provinces to participate in experiments with new tax-sharing arrangements between the central and local governments. Therefore, its next four-year contract (1992-95) will be similar in structure to that of the 1988 version. Concerning enterprise taxation, one small city, Nanyang, has been, since November 1989, an experimental area for new forms of contract that ensure better separation of tax and profit. Two particular concerns have arisen as a result of these experiments: the concerned enterprises have perceived an inequity in that they must now pay more tax (35 percent) than the effective tax rate for the area of about 24 percent; second, the termination of debt amortization as a deductible expense has met with considerable resistance from the enterprises. These factors have no doubt contributed to a situation in which the determination of the amount of post-tax profit to be remitted is characterized as "quite flexible."

---

real losses of the previous two years. In the 1991 budget, local government expenditure was projected to remain constant in <u>nominal</u> terms, with sharply lower transfers from the central government offsetting higher local revenue collection, in part flowing from the distribution of the collection of the new business tax (collected at the local level), and the new Investment Orientation Tax (see paras. 3.31-3.34). Detailed figures for the breakdown of central and local revenues and expenditures in 1991 are not yet available, but of the cash deficit of Y 21 billion, Y 18 billion was in central government, which implies that the budget overrun was split evenly between the center and localities.

Enterprises

1.42   The losses of the SOEs (Annex Table 9.6-9.9) impose a heavy financial burden on the Government and the banking system; indeed, the evidence is that the burden on the banking system from the SOEs is much greater than that imposed by the Government itself, and that it has been increasing over time. As noted above, the SOEs have made a progressively declining net contribution 18/ to the budget. It is notable, therefore, and surprising that there is reported to have been a marginal improvement in the SOEs' financial position vis-a-vis the government during 1990 (see Table 1.7). It seems

Table 1.7: CHINA: SELECTED INDICATORS FOR THE SOEs, 1984-91

	1984	1985	1986	1987	1988	1989	1990 Budget	1990 Actual	1991 Budget
Net flows from the enterprises /a									
In billions of yuan	81.7	69.5	56.7	52.3	46.7	35.5	29.6	39.7	41.0
In percent of GNP	11.7	8.1	5.8	4.5	3.3	2.2	1.8	2.3	2.1
Net domestic bank financing of state enterprises									
In billions of yuan	-	-	92.3	73.6	114.1	156.8	-	158.9	-
In percent of GNP	-	-	9.5	6.5	8.1	9.9	-	9.1	-
Memorandum Items:	(in billions of yuan)								
State enterprises with independent accounting /b									
Profit (post-tax)	85.2	94.4	87.8	100.5	119.0	100.0	-	-	-
Taxes paid	53.4	72.0	78.7	88.8	109.9	127.6	-	-	-
Losses	3.4	4.1	7.2	8.5	10.7	23.4	-	-	-

/a Consists of receipts from the taxation of the state enterprises and collectives, taxation of extrabudgetary receipts (for key energy and communications projects), and profits remitted to the Government, less subsidies to loss-making enterprises.

/b Medium and large scale enterprises with accounts distinct from those of the Government.

Sources: Data provided by the Chinese authorities; and staff estimates.

unlikely that this was due to a strengthening in enterprise performance (para. 1.43). Rather, it can be assumed that the Government reduced net flows to enterprises in the light of its own financial constraints and compelled enterprises to increase their remittances, which were concealed within the overall figures, not least by the growing inter-enterprise arrears.

18/ This net contribution is defined as the receipts from the taxation of state enterprises and collectives, the taxation of extrabudgetary receipts for key projects in energy and communication, less subsidies to enterprises. It is an incomplete definition, since it excludes the 10 percent regulatory fund, a tax on a portion of extrabudgetary funds introduced in 1989. It is not believed that this latter exclusion would fundamentally alter the picture.

1.43   Any efficiency gain can be discounted on the basis of the government's own statistics about the performance of the "budgeted" enterprises 19/ both in 1990 and in the first half of 1991. In 1990, their profits fell by 58 percent (and their total taxes and profits by 18.5 percent). In the first half of 1991, as production recovered, the rate of decline slowed, but profits still fell by a further 17.5 percent. Thus, efficiency, if defined narrowly in terms of financial returns and budget revenue, remains rather growth-determined in China, and this factor helps to explain the authorities' willingness to relax the austerity program.[15] It can thus be hoped that, as growth continues and retail sales pick up, the financial performance of the SOEs will gradually recover in 1992.

1.44   The enterprises have made demands on the banking system that have ranged from 3-5 times the total overall Government deficit. This is shown in Table 1.7. Net financing of the enterprise sector as shown in the table is defined as the increase in the specialized and universal banks' credit to state-owned industrial, commercial, and construction enterprises and urban collectives, less the deposits of these enterprises. It is less than the total deficit of the sector since it excludes foreign financing and other forms of domestic financing such as bonds. That such net financing of the sector rose sharply during 1988 accords with the generally expansionary monetary stance of the time, but it is significant that rapid expansion continued through 1989 at a time when monetary policy was supposedly more contractionary. By 1989 net bank financing of the enterprise sector had risen to 10 percent of GNP. Not only does this imply that the SOEs were utilizing an increasing share of the nation's resources--while producing a falling output share--but also it may explain why net contributions to the government were able to rise in 1990, as it is likely that SOEs were using bank credit to pay tax bills and meet contract payments. It is not unreasonable to add the rising deficit of the SOEs to the fiscal deficit, and conclude that the overall public sector borrowing requirement has been rising steadily since 1987, and may have risen from about 8 percent of GDP in 1987 to about 11 percent in 1990.

Medium-Term Fiscal Prospects

1.45   With the apparent decision to defer reform of the enterprise responsibility system and of the revenue sharing arrangements until the Ninth Five-Year Plan (see Chapter IV), the only way that the central government can avoid further declines in the revenue/GNP ratio--if that remains the government's intent--will be via annual discretionary measures such as the 1991 business tax rate increase. We would note, however, that the government has been quite proficient in recent years in introducing such measures to maintain revenue. It should, in addition, be noted that the government is very actively promoting price reform, and that, if this is instituted early, it could have a significant positive impact on both revenue and expenditure.

19/ These are a subset of SOEs which can be defined as those whose initial capital and major reinvestments are financed mainly by budgetary resources. Examples would be the iron and steel corporations and most energy enterprises.

1.46   On the expenditure side, although there has been a decline in the price subsidy bill 20/ in 1991, with, as noted, some prospects for this to continue, other components of the budget are unlikely to sustain reduction in real terms in the absence of significant changes in the services offered by the Government, in that nonsubsidy current expenditures have been a steady proportion of GDP since the mid-1980s. Wage pressure is evident at present, and since wage rates in the medium term are unlikely to deviate appreciably below the trend rate of inflation, avoiding growth in the wage bill seems unlikely. Interest payments are likely to increase as the burden of government debt grows and more attractive financial instruments are introduced to an expanding market. Capital expenditure, already substantially reduced in real terms will be needed to maintain the development effort. The bright spot, as noted above, is price subsidies, which can be expected to continue to reduce in importance, both by reducing the subsidy component in the budget.

1.47   While innovations in the securities markets may enable the Government to obtain a higher level of domestic financing, it should also be borne in mind that the Government will be competing for financial resources against an enterprise sector with large financing requirements. Therefore, in the absence of deeper fiscal reform, the only way to improve the fiscal situation will be to reduce the financial needs of enterprises through reforms designed both to reduce subsidies, and to limit enterprises use of bank credit.

F.   The External Sector

1.48   China's policy of opening to the outside world, its exchange and trade system reforms, and an improved climate for foreign direct investment, have resulted in an increasing integration of the economy to world markets, and a spectacular export drive. Moreover, China became a major player in international capital markets, although the growth of debt has been controlled well within affordable proportions. It was to be expected that the external sector would display considerable volatility during the last two years, in the light both of the depth of the austerity program, and the reaction of the outside world to the May-June 1989 events, but it is interesting that the major changes were recorded in the trade rather than the capital or services accounts.

The Current Account and the Structure of Exports and Imports

1.49   China's trade account has consistently lagged changes in other macroeconomic variables in the economy by about 6 months. Therefore, the impact of the "retrenchment program" did not result in an immediate improvement in the current account in 1989, but rather the slower growth trends evident from mid-1989 (see Table 1.9) had their impact in the following year. In 1990, the balance of payments was transformed from a deficit on both the current and overall account to a large surplus on all accounts. The more than $9 billion

---

20/   Price subsidies in 1990 were Y 38.1 billion, almost the same level as 1989, but 7 percent below budget, and are estimated to fall to Y 33 billion in 1991 on the basis of the grain, coal and transport price adjustments. Thus, price subsidies have fallen from 12.3 percent of expenditure in 1989 to 11.2 percent in 1990 and 9.3 percent of the 1991 budget.

surplus in the merchandise account reflected an 18.1 percent growth in export value while merchandise imports declined by 9.8 percent. This resulted in the resource balance improving by a remarkable 4.2 percent of GDP, which, as noted, served as one of the main sources of growth in 1990. In 1991, as the economy recovered, there was a sharp reversal in this pattern, with exports continuing to grow by 15.8 percent to $71.3 billion, but with imports rising sharply by 19.5 percent to $64 billion.

1.50   The structure of Chinese exports has continued the trend observed since the second half of the 1980s, with a declining percentage of primary exports, which accounted for about one fourth of total exports (see Annex Table 3.2), while manufactured exports represented three-quarters of export revenue. Among the latter, particularly rapid gains have been achieved by machinery and transport equipment, textiles, apparel and shoes, while the variety of products traded internationally has expanded by a large amount. In addition, a considerable share of the growth in export revenue now comes from trade carried out by town and village enterprises (TVEs [16]) and the large number of export-oriented joint ventures and wholly foreign-owned enterprises established over the years. Also, there is a regional dimension to China's export drive resulting from the concentration of exporting industries in the coastal areas. Indeed, Guangdong province alone accounts for more than 15 percent of the country's exports, being the recipient of about half of total foreign direct investment.

1.51   Indeed, export growth accelerated in 1990, and the question is whether this reflects the impact of the austerity program persuading producers to switch products to the export market, or the continuation of the earlier growth trend, with 1989 being a dip explained by other factors. Of the exports that registered large volume growth,[21] three categories explain most of the growth: machinery, chemicals, and products exported after inward processing. For the first category, it seems quite probable that the rapid jump in the growth of exports does indeed reflect in part the austerity program, as this was in particular for those goods such as TV sets and bicycles for which domestic demand was falling so heavily, although production capacity and the quality of the products has also had a strong impact. Exports of these two commodities, for example, grew by 54 percent and 50 percent in volume terms, respectively, although this category still represents less than 10 percent of the total.

1.52   For the other two categories, however, this is the continuation of earlier trends. Growth in the processing industry alone accounted for growth in exports of $2.2 billions, to reach a level of $10.5 billions (17 percent of the total), and the growth in chemicals was in particular for products such as pharmaceuticals. For these latter two commodities, the impact of the austerity program on product availability can be judged to be minimal. Overall, therefore, we would conclude from the export figures that the growth in 1990 primarily reflected the continuation of the upward trend in the last few years in response to the open-door policies, and to domestic reforms which have

---

21/   The value of oil exports grew by 20 percent in 1990, or by almost $1 billion, explained entirely by higher prices, and volumes fell by 1.6 percent.

improved China's competitiveness in these sectors, assisted by the strong, real, effective devaluation (para. 1.60). Therefore, the resumption of domestic demand is unlikely to have a very serious effect on the availability of export supply. More significant are likely to be the trade reforms introduced in January 1991 (see Chapter IV), which have placed exporting on a more level playing field by removing subsidies and mandatory planning of exports.

1.53   The almost 10 percent decline in imports during 1990 can be attributed to three main factors: the effect of the depressed domestic market; the tightening of administrative controls; and the large effective devaluation of the Renminbi. With respect to the latter two factors, it is significant that the volume of transactions on the foreign exchange adjustment centers (FEACs) rose by 53 percent, from $8.5 billion in 1989 to $13 billion in 1990, suggesting that access to the swap centers was encouraged, but also implying that the effective average exchange rate was even lower. At the same time, the exchange rate at the swap centers displayed remarkable stability, with the differential from the official rate narrowing to less than 10 percent. In 1991, imports grew by 19.5 percent, once again displaying the classic lag to a recovery in industrial output discussed above. From this we would conclude that the overriding factor in the import decline in 1990 was the impact of the depressed domestic situation.

1.54   The nature of the commodities to suffer from decline lends further credence to this. The biggest declines were suffered by textile fibers and machinery, steel, vehicles and petroleum, all of which would be expected to decline in the face of the depressed level of retail sales and construction, and grain, in response to the high domestic harvests. In terms of longer-term changes in the structure of Chinese imports, the share of imports of intermediate goods continued to decline from over half of total imports in the second half of the 1980s, to about a third in 1990. The share of manufactured imports, mainly capital goods, continued to rise from less than a third in the mid-1980s to over half of total imports in 1990. The share of consumer goods continued to be insignificant, with less than 4 percent of the total value (see Annex Table 4.2).

1.55   As on previous occasions, movements of the current account over the period 1988-90 were primarily related to changes in the merchandise trade balance, while the balance of services mimicked the merchandise account in a procyclical way. In 1990, the services account posted the highest ever surplus, as investment income and other nonfactor services (particularly tourism 22/) rapidly increased, recovering much more rapidly than had been anticipated, not least because of increased contact with Taiwan.

1.56   In terms of sources of foreign exchange, it is no surprise that exports have taken up a rising share in the last two years, but this is less dramatic than might have been expected (see Table 1.8). It seems clear that in drawing up the foreign exchange plan for 1990, the SPC assumed that tour-

---

22/   Tourism revenue reached $2.2 billion in 1990, practically equal to the highest ever level reached in 1988. However, tourism receipts explain only about 50 percent of the improvement in net services, the balance coming from other sources, particularly shipping and insurance.

ism, investment and loans would decline much more heavily than they did 23/ in response to the May-June 1989 events, and that this partly explains the very strong trade performance. That is to say, import plans were of necessity very conservative in 1990, as it was assumed that a large current account surplus was necessary to avoid external payments difficulties.

Table 1.8: SOURCES OF FOREIGN EXCHANGE, 1988-90
(Percentages)

	1988	1989	1990
Exports	77.4	79.4	81.6
Loans	10.6	9.5	8.4
Investment	6.1	5.7	4.9
Tourism	3.6	2.8	2.9
Labor Services	2.3	2.6	2.2

Source: Annex Table 2.1.

The Capital Account and the Overall External Balance: Recent Developments and Short-Term Outlook

1.57   The origin of capital inflows over the last two years has changed significantly, as the reduction of new longer-term capital inflows--resulting from the imposition of external sanctions after June 1989--has been partially compensated by a faster drawdown of existing commercial bank credits.   In 1990, net short-term capital drawdowns ($2 billion) more than compensated the decline in long-term funds.   China's overall external account balance in 1990 was therefore largely determined by the outcome of its current account. China's gross external reserves rose that year by almost $12 billion, to a level equivalent to more than eight months' imports. Even with the rapid recovery of imports, there was a further surplus of $12 billion in 1991, and reserves accumulation of $14 billion. It is expected that the current account will fall sharply in 1992 as imports grow in the face of rapid economic growth.

1.58   It should be noted, however, that preliminary balance of payments data for 1990 (Table 1.9) indicate a very large increase in the "Errors and Omissions" item, showing an unexplained balance of almost $4 billion (IMF definition).   Such a figure, which is more than twice previous levels, suggests a possible underreporting of imports or an overstatement of China's foreign exchange reserves derived from growing offshore deposits outside PBC

23/   In fact, investment and tourism revenue from developed countries declined sharply in 1989/90, but they have been replaced by very rapid growth in revenues from Taiwan, China. However, recovery in developed country investment and tourism is being seen in 1991.

and the Bank of China (BOC), and this deserves the attention of the PBC and the State Administration of Exchange Control (SAEC).

Table 1.9: CHINA: BALANCE OF PAYMENTS, 1986-91
($ million)

	1986	1987	1988	1989	1990	1991
Trade balance, customs basis	-8,401	-192	-3,169	-1,694	13,141	13,415
Exports FOB	30,942	39,437	47,518	52,537	62,063	71,911
Imports FOB	39,343	39,629	50,687	54,231	48,922	58,496
Services, net, IMF basis	1,427	1,737	1,094	923	2,558	2,787
of which:						
Travel receipts	1,531	1,845	2,247	1,860	2,218	2,639
Interest payments	909	1,189	1,622	1,658	2,016	4,103
Other current transactions	-360	-1,245	-1,727	-3,546	-3,702	-3,831
Current account balance /a	-7,334	300	-3,802	-4,317	11,997	12,371
Direct inv., net	1,425	1,669	2,344	2,613	2,657	3,340
M&L-term liab., net	4,851	6,131	6,781	6,023	6,249	3,108
Errors and omissions	580	-1,450	-1,094	45	3,213	-856
Memorandum Items:						
Gross reserves	11,994	16,934	19,135	18,547	30,209	44,308
In months of imports	3.4	4.7	4.2	3.8	6.8	8.3
Current account/GNP	-2.75	0.10	-1.01	-1.02	3.24	3.33

/a Current account balance after grants. Tables in Chapter VI use current account before grants.

Sources: Data provided by the Chinese authorities; and staff estimates.

Exchange Rate Management and External Competitiveness

1.59   In the past years China has maintained a dual exchange rate system, in which the official rate was administered as a managed float, while the parallel rate was determined by realized demand and supply in the FEACs by eligible participants. In practice, the exchange rate was adjusted infrequently. There were two large, discrete devaluations of the official exchange rate in December 1989 and November 1990 by 21 percent and 10 percent, respectively. Since April 1991, the SAEC has announced adjustments every two or three days, appreciating and depreciating by small amounts, apparently following the movement of a basket of currencies. Overall, the nominal rate has depreciated by about 3 percent since this practice was introduced. While these new developments might speed up the convergence of the two markets (and the unification of the exchange rate), it is important to maintain the competitiveness (in real effective terms) of the renminbi, particularly if the domestic rate of inflation were to exceed the rates of inflation of China's main trade partners.

1.60   Over the twelve months to June 1991, the real effective exchange rate depreciated by 12.5 percent, faster than the nominal depreciation given China's low inflation rate (Table 1.10). This brought the cumulative depreciation since November 1989 (the month before the first devaluation) to 31.9 percent on a real effective basis. This also goes a long way to explain why exports have been growing so rapidly in this period.24/ It is to be noted, however, that the exchange rate appreciated somewhat in 1991 with the rise of the US dollar.

Table 1.10: CHINA: EFFECTIVE EXCHANGE RATE, 1986-91
(1980=100)

		Real effective exchange rate	Nominal effective exchange rate	Exchange rate
1986	Q4	42.1	56.0	40.3
1987	Q4	39.5	52.4	40.2
1988	Q4	47.2	54.8	40.2
1989	Nov.	50.8	64.3	40.2
1990	Apr.	40.1	54.8	31.7
1990	Dec.	31.9	46.5	28.7
1991	Jun.	34.6	49.9	28.0

Source: IMF.

External Debt and Creditworthiness

1.61   China's external debt increased tenfold between 1980 and 1990 from $4.5 billion to $52.5 billion, growing especially fast between 1985 and 1988. The share of short term debt in total debt peaked in 1984 at 46.3 percent, but declined thereafter because of the mandatory 20 percent ceiling that was approved by the State Council in February 1989. Since then short-term debt has been used strictly for financing working capital needs. Total debt in 1989 remained at the same level of about $42 billion as in 1988, but the composition of short-term and long-term debt has changed. Medium- and long-term debt has increased by about $4.5 billion and short-term debt was halved to about $4.3 billion from $8.8 billion in 1988. China borrowed about a fifth of its medium- and long-term debt on concessional terms since 1985, from both multilateral and bilateral sources.

24/ Although this measure does not capture fully the effect of the transfer of transactions to the parallel market.

1.62   The ratio of total debt into GNP, a longer-term indicator of the
debt level, has increased from 1.5 percent in 1980 to only about 10 percent in
1990, a very low level by international standards. Similarly, debt service
projections indicate that the debt service/exports ratio peaked at 11.5 percent in 1991, and will decline thereafter to only 9.0 percent in 1995. This
indicates the creditworthiness of China compared to other countries. Even
though the market for medium- and long-term debt became very difficult for
China in the period following the May-June 1989 incidents, which affected the
confidence of China's lenders in its creditworthiness, lending to China picked
up in 1990 and by the end of 1990 total debt had increased by about $7.7
billion to $52.6 billion, of which incremental long-term debt was $8.3 bil-
lion.25/ Preliminary debt estimates for 1991 indicate that only a modest
increase appears to have been incurred, to a level of $57 billion.

1.63   The currency composition of China's external debt is dominated by
the US dollar, with a share of 40 percent, followed by Japanese Yen (34 percent), SDR (9.4 percent), and Hong Kong dollars (7 percent) in 1989. China
moved away in the mid-1980s from its high exposure to the appreciating
Japanese Yen, but still there is room for improvement in China's currency
risk. Overall, however, the strong efforts that China has made in the last
four years to bring its debt under control and to improve its management have
paid off, and this can be judged one area where macroeconomic management has
made major strides.

G. Conclusions

1.64   The period that has been the subject of this review began with the
5th Party Plenum, which sounded a strong note of austerity and reemphasis on
the role of the planning system. However, the out-turn has been very different indeed. China has been on the path of a rapid economic recovery with low
inflation and a strong external position. A combination of good policies and
good fortune came together to produce a very strong performance in the economy
in most sectors. Far from this being a result of the reemphasis of the role
of planning, the recovery came about because of the relaxation of controls,
reflected in highly expansionary monetary and credit policies, and because of
the good weather, and it was in the nonstate sector, agriculture and in
exports that most of the recovery was grounded.

1.65   The high level of inventories in the economy and the very strong
reserves position give some comfort that this recovery can be maintained without rekindling the fires of inflation. However, this has been a very strong
recovery indeed, and since the start of the fourth quarter 1990, industrial
output has been growing at an annual rate of over 15 percent, which will
clearly soon begin to put strains on infrastructure and input supplies if
maintained for too long. In addition, there are two other main reasons to
have concern about the dangers of inflation:

25/ It remains unclear to what extent this rapid growth of debt reflects
valuation adjustments as the Japanese yen has strengthened, as well as
improved recording of existing debt, as opposed to genuine new debt obligations.

(a) There is a very high level of financial savings in highly liquid
     form, and the events of summer 1988 demonstrated how quickly these
     can be converted into effective demand when inflationary expecta-
     tions change.

(b) There are clear signs of strong cost-push factors becoming more
     important, with real wage rises well in excess of productivity
     gains, and profit rates squeezed between rising costs due to these
     wage rises and price adjustments in the face of the sluggish market.
     It can be anticipated that producers will attempt to raise prices to
     restore profit levels as soon as the market recovers fully.

1.66   The danger, therefore, is that as the market continues to recover--
and retail sales are growing at around 13 percent--cost-push factors, vali-
dated by an easy credit stance, will once again force up prices. This situation could lead to a rapid change in price expectations, and to a consequent
move by consumers to convert financial into real assets. As was witnessed in
1988, the effect of this could be serious indeed.

1.67   This said, that is by no means the situation at present, and the
economy is much further from the production frontier than it was in 1978. It
was possible to predict the inflation of that year with some certainty, but it
is too early to say that at the present. Rather, the point is to learn the
lesson both of that experience, and of the earlier cycles, and take appropriate measures on a timely basis to counteract these tendencies. In terms of
short-term management, there are three key areas for attention:

(a) Adherence to a much tighter monetary and credit plan is critical,
     and cannot be expected to kill off the recovery at this stage.
     Thus, China must maintain a monetary and fiscal policy stance that
     is much more consistent with noninflationary growth than were the
     policies in 1990 and 1991, which would suggest limiting credit
     growth to about 14-15 percent per annum, in particular by limiting
     the access to credit of the SOEs. In addition, government should
     continue to exercise caution now in the rate of approval of new
     state investment projects, which have also been a major source of
     demand growth.

(b) While some recovery of real wages was to be expected in the after-
     math of the 1988 inflation and the 1989 austerity, this should not
     continue, and the government should set the example for this by the
     wage rises that it grants itself, and those which it approves for
     the large and medium SOEs.

(c) Government should monitor short-term developments carefully, and be
     prepared to take action to stabilize savings in the event of a
     change of expectations, as it did in the fall of 1988. This relates
     in particular to the use of interest rate policy, which has now
     proved its effectiveness in China, and the need to maintain the real
     value of savings accounts. However, it also relates to the import
     policy, and the comfort of the high reserves cushion. Thus, the
     timing is appropriate for a general relaxation of import licensing
     controls, not only for its intrinsic benefits, but also so that

selective imports can dampen any emerging supply bottlenecks which could kindle inflationary expectations. Indeed, the rapid growth of imports in recent months indicates that this may be beginning to occur.

1.68   But the government would also be advised to look at the experience of the last two years, and draw two other conclusions. First, it is clear that the capacity to manage the economy continues to require considerable strengthening. The 1991 monetary targets were revised several times as the year progressed, and it was clear that the rate of monetary expansion was not being controlled by the central bank. At the same time as monetary policy was exerting strong reflationary pressure, so too was fiscal policy, not because of a central decision to reflate, but because of overspending at the local level. It is also evident that, in 1990 especially, the separation of monetary and fiscal policies became less clear, as the role of "policy lending" to the SOEs increased. Given that a lesson of the past few years is that a stable macroeconomic situation is critical for the successful implementation of reforms, the continued strengthening of the institutions concerned should remain very high on the reform agenda, and should be seen to be an integral part of the reform itself.

1.69   Secondly, this period of retrenchment and recovery has seen much success for the Chinese authorities in controlling inflation, avoiding overheating, and in stimulating agriculture, but in other areas, it was much less successful. This is especially the case with respect to the management and restructuring of the SOEs, and this has been recognized time and again by Chinese leaders. While there has been some, perhaps temporary change in the relative proportion of production of intermediate and final goods, there has been very little, if any change in the enterprises themselves. This will entail a variety of measures in both reform and development policy, and especially in the areas of price, tax and ownership reforms, and these are the main subject of Chapters III and IV of this report. However, the design of such reforms should be based on a clear understanding of the success, failures and impact of past reform efforts, so it is to these issues that the next chapter is addressed.

ZONDERVAN LIBRARY
TAYLOR UNIVERSITY
500 W READE AVE.
UPLAND, IN 46989-1001

188312

II. CHINESE REFORM EXPERIENCE TO DATE

A. Introduction

2.1   It is now more than a decade since China launched its program of economic reform in late 1978. Much has been written and said about China's progress and experience since that time. This chapter is an attempt to examine the period of reform as a whole, to extract the essence of the Chinese reform experience and approach, and to assess the impact of the reform period on the Chinese economy. There are two main purposes for such an exercise. First, the length of the reform experience, and the availability of research results, now offer the scope to carry out such an assessment on a more rigorous basis. Second, now that the 1988-91 rectification program has been completed, China appears to have the opportunity and interest to enter a new reform era. In this regard, therefore, it seems appropriate to take stock of China's considerable reform achievements to date, to assess not only how far China has already gone along the reform road, but also how much further it has to go in order to have in place the new economic system for which it is striving. It is against this background, therefore, that in Chapter IV we assess how well China's current reform intentions address this unfinished agenda. Given the impossibility, and undesirability of listing the chronology of China's individual reforms, a reform matrix is included at Annex 1, which lists past reforms together with current stated intentions and Bank recommendations.

B. The Initial Conditions

2.2   It is clear that the initial conditions under which China entered its reform era were very different from those of other reforming socialist economies, and were such as to be in general favorable to the rapid achievement of economic gains. It sometimes seems to be the opinion of commentators both inside and outside China that it is only in the reform period that China has achieved any economic or social success. However, there were many well-documented achievements of the first 30 years of China's socialist system since 1949,[1] most importantly in health and education. Moreover, China was not impelled to enter upon its reform path because of deep macroeconomic crisis, which removed the need for a strong dose of deflationary policy to accompany the launching of reforms.[1] Indeed, the fiscal and external accounts were in broad balance at this time, and savings mobilization was already high. Rather, the launching of reform stemmed from two main factors:

(a)   dissatisfaction with the "extensive" growth model that had generated overall growth, but little if any improvement in productivity, and required increasing levels of investment to be maintained, thus preventing significant gains in personal consumption; and

---

[1]   For Central and Eastern European countries, stabilization measures are estimated to account for about half of the output losses that have followed the launching of their reform programs.

    (b)   a political rejection of the extremes of "leftism" associated in particular with the period of the "Cultural Revolution."

It should be noted, however, that even at that time and despite the excesses of that period, and the deaths of Mao Zedong and Zhou Enlai, there was no rejection of the socialist system per se, but rather a call for a radical reform away from the earlier approach to its implementation.

2.3   The initial economic conditions appear to have laid the basis for a situation whereby the immediate benefits of the reforms selected outweighed the immediate costs. In agriculture, where reforms were launched, the Commune system of socialized agriculture had achieved four of the five main goals for which it was established:

    (a)   It had developed rural infrastructure, especially in terms of irrigation facilities and use of improved seeds and fertilizers.

    (b)   It had created a rural management system, which not only served political and social needs, but fostered economic support systems, such as input supply and marketing.

    (c)   It had served to foster social aims, such as preventive medicine and attainment of universal education, through local (compulsory) funds mobilization for such purposes.

    (d)   It had diversified the rural sector from being a peasant agriculture on self-sufficient basis.

2.4   What it had not done was improve agricultural productivity and thus output, either in quantity, quality or variety. Grain output per capita was 283 kg in 1952, but had risen to only 317 kg in 1978. Moreover, agricultural productivity probably fell over this period (para. 2.55), not least because of the absence of alternative, off-farm employment, as well as the two problems of the incentive system: there were virtually no incentives for individual efforts,2/ and agricultural prices were kept intentionally low in order to generate a surplus for industrial investment. Thus, prior to reform, the agricultural sector was endowed with reasonable physical, marketing and human infrastructure, but without incentives. It was the sense of agricultural crisis that was perhaps as important as any other factor in creating the initial impetus for reform. Once individual incentives were introduced, and the role of the state was reformed, it was not surprising that the output response was rapid. It was improved output and productivity which were the aims (and, indeed, the result) of agricultural reforms. As will be seen, increased savings available for investment and the release of surplus labor were unforeseen but perhaps even more significant side-effects.

2/   The commune system incorporated an arrangement for awarding "work points" to individuals in relation to individual effort. In practice, however, measurement of effort proved very difficulty, not only because of intrinsic problems, but also because of the general ethos of egalitarianism in that period. See Perkins and Yusuf "Agricultural Development in China."

2.5   In the <u>industrial sector</u>, there are three key factors with respect to the initial conditions. First, China had changed from being an essentially rural, peasant economy in 1949 to one in which industry was very significant. The share of industry in national income had grown from 20 percent in 1952 to 49 percent in 1978. Of particular significance during this period was the first decade, and the 156 heavy industrial projects carried out with the assistance of the former Soviet Union. The second factor of critical importance was that by far the largest share of this industrial expansion was in heavy industry, and light industry was neglected, as would be expected in a Soviet-influenced approach. Heavy industry accounted for 57 percent of total output in 1978. The significance of this was twofold: first, it meant that there was a significant industrial base from which to build; but second, it meant that there were enormous opportunities for light industrial investment once investment decision making was decentralized.

2.6   The third factor was that almost all this early industrial development took place through large- and medium-sized state-owned enterprises, with only a relatively small share in smaller, local enterprises. Indeed, these SOEs accounted for 78 percent of industrial output in 1978. This is of course to be expected given the emphasis on heavy industry. But these large SOEs were burdened with excessive workforces and heavy social obligations and were managed in a largely administrative fashion, and this rendered them highly inflexible. Thus, when controls were released on small firm creation, the large SOEs were not able to squeeze out such firms or react rapidly to new opportunities. As with agriculture, the socialist system had laid a solid basis, but which lacked incentives, and thus was ripe for reform.

2.7   The third aspect relevant to the initial conditions is <u>provincial autonomy</u>. China after 1960 was never truly a centrally planned economy in the same sense as the former Soviet Union: there were only about 500 commodities under mandatory planning, compared with over 20,000 in the former USSR; and local governments always took the primary role in plan formulation and interpretation. This had three particular consequences for the initial conditions. First, it meant that local implementation capacity was rather well-developed, with officials well able to respond to improved incentives. Second, with obvious exceptions, there was significantly less pressure for provincial autonomy in China than in other reforming socialist economies, such as the USSR or Yugoslavia, made easier by the relatively high ethnic homogeneity of the Chinese population. Third, while the emphasis on regional autonomy had generated good government capacity, it had also bred serious inefficiencies, especially in agriculture. It therefoe offered enormous scope for gains from interprovincial trade.

2.8   Thus, China's initial domestic conditions in several key areas can be seen to have been ideal for reform. Unlike the case of many other socialist economies in transition, China's reform responded to socioeconomic pressures rather than deep crisis, and the absence of the need for major stabilization meant that "shock therapy" was not needed. China also had the good fortune of its historic ties to Hong Kong and the overseas Chinese community, which have played a critical role. Above all, it had a set of conditions whereby the economy and its system of government were well-situated to respond rapidly to improved incentives by increasing output. Of course, not all results would be positive and not everyone would be a winner from reform, as the stop-go pattern of reform in China has amply demonstrated. Moreover, it is clear that several of these elements were distinct to the Chinese case, possibly reducing the applicability of the lessons from this experience. It is important to bear these initial conditions in mind in assessing the gains from reform: it can be cogently argued that part of the returns to reform in terms of efficiency gains and output growth are the delayed returns to the physical investment of the prereform era, which could not be reaped at that time because of inadequate incentives.

C. China's Reform Style

2.9   Because China began its reform program at the particular point in its economic history noted, it was able to develop its own distinctive approach to economic reform. This is most frequently described as "gradual-ist," although this only refers to the time taken rather than the depth of reforms. Indeed, the transformation of the Chinese economy that has occurred in these relatively few years since 1979 can hardly be regarded as a gradual change. China has not developed a well-defined reform strategy, nor has it drawn up a clear reform blueprint. Pre-announced reforms have often been withdrawn--such as the price and wage reform plan of 1989--and at other times, deep reforms have emerged suddenly, as with the grain price reform of May 1991.

2.10   It can be argued that China's reform philosophy or strategy is indeed to not plan reforms, but to push forward reforms in a coherent way when the economic, political and social climate permits or demands it. This may itself be a response to the perceived failures of the planning system. It is generally agreed that a key reason why central planning fails--and must fail-- is that it requires too much information. Not only cannot this information be assembled and processed, much of it is unobtainable by definition. It can be argued with equal coherence that to draw up a comprehensive reform blueprint would require a similar amount of information, much of it unobtainable. China did not and could not have foreseen the response of the rural sector to the agricultural reform, and the easing of restrictions on entry to the industrial sector. Therefore, it is argued, it is better to use the Chinese approach which moves and adapts as responses and results become evident.[2] But throughout the reform period, four features of the Chinese approach can be traced as consistent themes in implementation; gradualism, partial reforms, decentralization and self-reinforcing reforms. It can perhaps be argued that these features, and especially the first three, were necessitated by the sheer size and diversity of China.

Gradualism and Experimentation

2.11   In almost all areas of reform, implementation has been spread over-time, often several years, and usually after experimentation.[3] Typically, such experiments take place in designated "reform areas," and after the results of trials are observed, they then spread to other parts of the

---

[3]   What the Chinese call "Feeling the stones to cross the river," in con-trast to the maxim coined by President Havel of the Czech and Slovak Federal Republic: "It is impossible to cross a chasm in two leaps."

country. Sometimes, this is the result of a well-publicized central government decision, and sometimes this happens "spontaneously," as other provinces copy the originating province. For example, the household contract responsibility system in agriculture began as an experiment in Sichuan province in 1980/81, and by the time it was formally endorsed by the central government in 1985, it had already spread throughout the whole country. Similarly, though less spontaneously, openness to foreign investment--and to foreign ownership of assets in general--started in a few areas and continues to be extended gradually over the whole country.

2.12   Sometimes, this gradualism is the result of the trial process. Other times it is opportunism frequently in response to rising fiscal pressures, and this is especially the case in price reform. In this area, there have been two attempts at formulating a comprehensive reform strategy, both of which have been abandoned. At other, sometimes unexpected times, progress has been rapid. The period from late 1989 to the end of 1991, when reforms in general were receiving less attention, perhaps saw the most radical changes in relative prices in China in the whole reform period (see paras. 1.29-1.31).

2.13   For some reforms, by their nature, gradualism is not possible, and an overnight change occurs. The central bank was established in 1984, and all its commercial transactions were rapidly transferred to the newly-created Industrial and Commercial Bank, although, of course, it took longer for the People's Bank of China to take up its new functions fully. The foreign exchange swap centers were all opened to domestic enterprises at the same time in 1988. But even in these areas, where arbitrage would suggest the impossibility of gradualism, the sheer size of the country and the inadequacy of the transport and telecommunications systems make gradualism possible.

2.14   The great advantages of this gradual approach, where it is possible, are clear[3]: severe shocks are avoided, trials permit mid-course corrections, institutional development can occur in line with the new systems, and economic agents can adjust slowly to the new conditions. China has thus been able to first bypass and later dismantle its administrative controls at the pace that market mechanisms capable of regulatory functions have emerged.[4] This has meant not only that severe dislocations have in general been avoided, it also has meant that China has been able to enjoy growth with reform. Of course, much of the reason that this has been possible has been the favorable initial conditions under which reform was launched.

2.15   But this approach has its drawbacks, and two in particular. The first is that some economic agents are unable to predict their future economic environment. In most areas of reform, the advantages of pragmatism override this,4/ but in other areas advance planning is important. This will be the case in the near future as China sets about reforming its import framework, for advance announcement of reduced protection will permit enterprises to adjust to the future set of arrangements. In such cases, there is a case for

_____

4/   Indeed, in some areas, pre-announcement is to be avoided. It was the _announcement_ of future price reform in 1988 which triggered inflation, not the reform itself. Similarly, in late 1990, a devaluation came to be known in advance, compressing the parallel exchange rate.

rapid implementation of the reform itself, but with adjustment to the new situation spread overtime.

2.16   Potentially more serious is the charge that gradual reforms can give time for those whose interests are threatened by reforms to re-group and either block progress along the gradual slope, or even reverse some reforms, and that failure to introduce reform rapidly will reduce the credibility of such reforms. This is clearly the fear of many policymakers in Central and Eastern Europe. There have indeed been such periods of reversal in China. The Communique of the Fifth Plenary Session of the 13th Central Committee in December 1989 clearly espoused a view that planning could solve the problems that had arisen during the course of reforms designed to address the short-comings of planning.[5] However, so far, each such reversal (or "one step back") has been temporary. It is clear that the new momentum of enterprise reform evident in 1992 is partly a conclusion of China's leaders that, during the rectification program, the instruments of planning failed to come to grips with the fundamental problems of the state-owned enterprise sector. Thus, while periodic reversals occur, the overall direction continues. The reasons why planners have failed to re-group effectively in China is discussed below (paras. 2.90).

Partial Reforms

2.17   Closely related to the gradual/experimental approach to reform has been the use of partial reforms within sectors, and one of the more interest-ing results of the Chinese reform experience has been the apparent success of this approach. This has perhaps been most obvious in the two-tier pricing system, under which state enterprises have been permitted to sell above-plan output at market prices. It has been estimated that in 1989, on average, 38 percent of an SOE's outputs were sold on markets, and 56 percent of its inputs were procured on markets.[6] This dual price system has been of partic-ular importance in the materials sector, for commodities such as coal, steel , timber, and cement, where differentials were sometimes very large indeed.[5]

2.18   The two-tier price system, like the partial reform approach in gen-eral, has two particular advantages. First, it has been a powerful instrument of the gradualist approach, providing an underlying assurance of continuity of supply, while creating a situation where market skills can be learned. Sec-ond, and most important, it has created a situation where marginal resource allocation decisions have been made on the basis of market prices. In almost all sectors, enterprises' output targets are such that enterprise managers have sufficient capacity to make decisions based on the market as to how much above-plan output to produce. Only in the state coal, crude oil and power sectors as well as transport does the command plan continue to leave little room for market-based resource allocation decisions.

2.19   This system has, however, had certain obvious drawbacks. The most important of these has been the incentive for leakage from the planned sector to the market sector, and the associated corruption this has engendered. One

---

5/   Coal minehead prices in 1989 were Y 30/ton in Shanxi, but Y 250/ton on a market basis in Guangdong.

explanation of the difference between the percentage of outputs and inputs under the planning system is that output leaving enterprises under the plan then gets diverted to the market, or else undergoes price adjustment. It is estimated that of output under the plan, one third arrives at its intended destination at the plan price, one third arrives at the intended location but with the price adjusted to the market rate, and one third gets diverted entirely. Clearly, the incentives for corruption in this have been realized and this not only has concerned policymakers in China, it was also one of the overt factors behind the May-June events of 1989. What remains unclear is why these price differentials have persisted for so long, without arbitrage eliminating them. One factor is clearly the undeveloped transport and information system, but beyond this, provincial protectionism and import barriers explain how such differentials can continue. This partial reform approach is one whose benefits appear rapidly, but whose costs increase overtime. Thus, if used as a transitional device, the approach has merits, but it has severe drawbacks as a long-term system. As discussed later (paras. 2.82-2.83), integration of the domestic market remains one of the major challenges.

Decentralization

2.20   One of the features of China's initial conditions discussed above (para. 2.8) was the presence of a capable, in-place decentralized administration. This became a critical element in China's reform approach. As the central government released control, provincial, municipal, county, township and even village administrations were ready to respond. This decentralization element of the reform approach is controversial in two ways: first, governments at local levels have frequently replaced reduced central planning with increased local planning; and at times, the decentralization ran ahead of other reforms, so the local response was reacting to distorted relative prices, leading to inappropriate local investments, as in, for example, over 100 car assembly plants each with a capacity of less than 5,000 vehicles per annum. But in general, and taken over the period, the unrelenting pursuit of economic development at the local level has clearly been a tremendous force for good and for progress as, for example, through the creation of so many new jobs in the township and village enterprises.

2.21   Moreover, decentralization has not just been to local governments, but to actors in all spheres of economic activity: to enterprises in making production and marketing decisions; to foreign trade corporations in selection of export products; to farmers in selecting crops; and, most important, to individuals, to a large extent with respect to purchases, though to a much lesser extent with respect to employment. Of course, this form of decentralization is how markets get created, for it is the absence of concentration of decision-making that makes markets work, and thus the decentralization of decision-making that is at the heart of market creation. In China, the key to market creation without severe disruption has been twofold: as noted earlier, via gradual change which releases administrative controls only as markets develop; and via judicious balancing of markets and local governments. By decentralizing administrative power to lower levels of government, other forms of economic decentralization have been made more effective by local governments. For example, for most consumer goods, the government decentralized price controls to local governments in 1986, leaving it to them to decide when to release controls entirely, depending on the state of local market conditions. This moved rapidly in the dynamic South, with its many small firms, but more slowly in the North-East, where state firms dominate. The direction of causality is open to debate, but the results seem to be positive in general.

2.22   Such decentralization has its dangers. Some conservative parts of China have moved slowly in some areas, such as price decontrol in the North-East, and public ownership in Shanghai. It has also created a tendency towards overheating, as local development aspirations have forced a more rapid growth of credit than desired at the center. Thus, while the microeconomic effects appear to have been positive, it is less clear that the macroeconomic impact of decentralization has been wholly desirable.

2.23   Perhaps the greatest advantage of the decentralization approach has been to create interest groups in favor of further reforms, and to foster a climate for reform initiatives and "spontaneous" reform at the local level. This comes in two forms. First, many central reforms are "enabling," in the sense that they remove central prohibitions. Trade reform, for example, began in the mid-1980s with the removal of the prohibition on the creation of local foreign trade corporations: by 1990, 6,000 had been created, where only 15 existed before. Second, as noted earlier, local reforms frequently spread, often from experiment in one area, and are later sanctioned nationally. This was the case in agriculture with the spread of the household contract responsibility system in 1981/82, and appears to be being repeated in the case of social security systems at the present time. This is often the result of arbitrage pressures, when one province moves faster than a neighbor. This not only helps to build up increased confidence and interest in reforms, it also creates innovative approaches to reform.

Self-Reinforcing Reforms

2.24   The fourth characteristic of China's approach to reform has been the self-reinforcing nature of reform: "Once a crack is opened in the monolith that is the centrally planned economy, natural forces take over and force the crack open ever more widely."[7] It can thus be seen with the benefit of hindsight how reforms in one area lead naturally to reforms in other areas, and indeed force those reforms by creating pressures for change, and this seems to refute the thesis that the gradualist approach permits the rise of counter-vailing forces. The initial agricultural reforms created surplus savings and labor, which created pressures for decentralization of enterprise creation authority in rural areas, spawning the massive expansion of township and village enterprises (see para. 2.60-2.62). The creation of nonstate firms in turn created pressure of competition on the state-owned sector, forcing the state to relax control on the SOEs. This itself compelled the state to restructure its own sources and uses of revenue, and to reform the financial sector.

2.25   The key to the successful linking of one reform to another requires the appropriate response of policymakers. It would be possible, of course, for the pressure emerging from one area to be met with counter-pressure rather than a complimentary reform. For example, competition from TVEs was met in 1989 by an initial attempt to restrict availability of credit for these enter-prises and to close some of them administratively. Some of this did occur for a time, but it was short-lived, and soon attention returned to how to solve the more serious problems affecting the SOEs. There is no clear way to ensure that the response of policymakers will be appropriate, but two factors seem paramount: the dynamics of the reform process create opportunities for government to push forward with new reforms; and second, attempts to reverse reforms and reintroduce planning soon reveal those limitations again--just as attempts to solve the SOE problem in 1989/90 via planning have had little impact on restructuring and have instead fostered new interest in market-based solutions to these issues.

D. China's Major Reform Steps

2.26   As noted earlier, this is not the occasion for a detailed review of individual reforms in China, a subject on which several books have already been written, and many more will come.[8] Nevertheless, it seems appropriate to consider briefly the main steps that were taken in each major reform area, and how they linked to others, not least so that the discussion of future reform priorities in part "F" can be seen against the achievements of the past. The discussion that follows is divided into nine major sectoral areas, rather than chronologically. While it is useful to have this kind of periodic overview--and for the Chinese to put together the sort of document seen in the reform plan that accompanied the Eighth Five-Year Plan--the emphasis of China's reform approach will continue to be on individual interventions at the sectoral level, rather than the formulation of grand, cross-sectoral comprehensive blueprints, and we have already discussed the strengths and weaknesses of this approach. It does seem likely that the approach will be more <u>balanced</u> than in the past, with an absence of emphasis on a leading reform sector, and with coordinated reforms in different areas, but this will remain well short of a blueprint approach.

Major Reform Turning Points

2.27   There are different ways to define turning points in economic and political history. However, in this context, we are primarily concerned with key decisions taken by the Communist Party and the Government of China with regard to reforms. These decisions then became important reference works,[9] and bear rereading for what they do and do not say about what is permitted after such decisions have been taken. The first of these is, of course, the decision of the 3rd Plenary Session of the 11th Central Committee of the Communist Party of China,<u>6/</u> the Communique of which officially launched the reform program, and spawned the agricultural reforms and the beginning of the opening up to the outside world. Reforms in urban areas were only on a very limited experimental basis until the Third Plenary Session of the 12th CCP, which adopted the "Decision on Reform of the Economic Structures" in October 20, 1984. It was this document that launched the acceleration of

---

<u>6/</u>   The Communist Party holds a Congress about every five years, and elects a Central Committee. This Central Committee meets in plenary session about ten times between Congresses, to make important decisions. The last (13th) Congress was in November 1987. Since then eight plenary sessions have been held, and the next (14th) Congress is scheduled for the last quarter of 1992.

reforms in urban areas in 1985, and especially the two-tier price system, and decentralization of enterprise management.

2.28   Despite these two milestones, the reform lacked a theoretical background and basis in socialist principles--it being based on Deng Xiaoping's principle of "seeking truth from facts," the basis for pragmatic decision-making--but this came in October 1987 in the Report of Government to the 13th Party Congress "Advance Along the Road of Socialism with Chinese Characteristics." This adopted the theory of the "Primary Stage of Socialism," which provided the theoretical basis for Deng's approach, by showing the acceptability of multiple forms of ownership and of economic systems during the early period of socialism that China would be likely to be under until well into the 21st Century. This also spawned the important guidelines of "the state regulates the market, and the market guides the enterprises," which remains the fundamental principle for China's "planned commodity economy." Finally, the adoption of the "Outline of the Eighth Five-Year Plan and the Ten-Year Development Program" is very significant, as it includes a clear description of China's reform approach for the coming period, and sets out reform intentions in a wide range of areas, as further discussed in the next two chapters, marking the first occasion when the Plan has focused on policy issues as the key to development. However, it is likely in the future that this turning point will be seen to have been overtaken by the 14th Party Congress scheduled for the last quarter of 1992, which can be expected to take major decisions to guide the next phase of reforms. Each of these four documents/decisions should be regarded as part of the enabling framework which has permitted the central and local governments to move on to define specific reform moves, which are addressed in subsequent paragraphs.

Rural Reforms

2.29   These are listed first, not only because this is where the reform started, but also because these remain the most significant of all the reform efforts. As noted, China began the reform period with socialized agriculture operating on a reasonable technical basis, and at the heart of the reform was a return to individual, household agriculture with the break-up of the communes. With the return of the land to individuals on a long (15-25 year) lease basis, farmers had to agree to turn over a percentage of output to the state, and in some areas, the particular crops (especially rice in the south) were specified, and thus the phrase "Household Contract Responsibility System." This was accompanied by a 25 percent (average) real increase in relative agricultural prices. Together, these improved incentives elicited a very rapid output response (para. 2.52), and generated large cash savings. Pressure for permission to utilize these for industrial use grew, resulting in the formal decision in 1984 for local authorities to create township and village enterprises.

2.30   Much has been written about the growth of rural industry,[10] and this remains the key to much of China's success in the 1980s (see Part D). But why did this mushrooming of rural industry occur, apparently without positive policies, and as a result essentially of an enabling environment? We would offer three main reasons:

(a) As suggested, the agricultural reforms created a surplus available for investment and released a pool of labor eager and available for new sources of employment.

(b) The initial industrial conditions had, by having neglected the light industrial sector, and as a consequence of the socialist pricing system which favored light industry, created major opportunities for entry of small firms into this sector, where rapid, very high profits could be made.

(c) Local governments were heavily committed to local economic development and played a key facilitating, and even sometimes entrepreneurial role in fostering such industries.

In the South, the role of overseas Chinese is also relevant, while in provinces with large rural industrial sectors, such as Zhejiang and Jiangsu, domestic factors are paramount.

2.31   These are, in essence, the only two reforms of significance, and it was not until 1988 and 1991 that new reforms were launched, on the pricing/marketing side. In 1988, it was in the prices of nonstaples (sugar, eggs, vegetables and pork) that the price reform was successfully launched, and abandoned only after an attempted widening. But this approach--of converting product subsidies into wages--was the basis for the important grain and oilseeds price reform of 1991 (see Table 1.5). These have been accompanied by the introduction of wholesale and futures markets in grain, and together, these indicate that China is slowly moving to a situation where markets will dominate agriculture.

Foreign Direct Investment

2.32   It is sometimes forgotten that it was in the area of foreign direct investment that the first industrial reforms were made, with the passing of the joint venture law in 1979, and the opening of the first four Special Economic Zones in 1980. Since that time, FDI has poured into China (para. 2.66). The importance in Chinese terms of this was that it represented a major break with the autarkic principles of the pre-reform era, recognizing that China could not rely on its own resources alone to catch up with the rest of the world in terms of technology. Thus, the importation of foreign technology and management techniques and their financing by overseas capital became a key strand of Deng's reform approach from the outset. Nevertheless, the early approach, focussing solely on export-oriented industries, severely limited the volume of FDI. Major modifications were introduced by the "22 Articles" in October 1986, which paved the way the following year for the opening up of the foreign exchange swap centers, which removed the most serious constraint, which had been China's attempt to force joint ventures to achieve self-sufficiency in foreign exchange. These "Articles" were further improved in 1990, when regulations were introduced to limit administrative interference with the operation of joint ventures.

2.33   It would have been surprising if the opening of China to FDI would not have been successful, given the size of its market and the cheapness and quality of Chinese labor. But the role of overseas Chinese communities, and of Hong Kong and Taiwan in particular cannot be over-emphasized. Fully three-quarters of all foreign investment in China originated in Hong Kong, of course much of it being by non-Hong Kong residents but rather channelled, but this is of no matter. The turning point for this was the adoption of the "one country, two systems" policy, which led to the signing of the Sino-British accord in Hong Kong in 1986, which has in turn permitted a remarkable integration between the economies of China and Hong Kong.[11] While the regulations have been an important and appropriate enabling environment, it is the Hong Kong factor that explains, in our view, most of the great success of the open door policy.

Commercial Reforms

2.34   One of the earlier reforms in China that appears to have been repeated in other reforming socialist economies has been the effective privatization of the commercial sector. This began in 1982 and, by 1985, 75 percent of all state-owned commercial and service companies had been sold or leased to private owners, and entry was permitted for any newcomers. The state sector remained important in three main areas: wholesaling of a wide range of products, especially agricultural; retailing of commodities under price controls and under the ration system; and operation of major commercial outlets employing large numbers of people, such as department stores. In addition to these formal retail channels, local governments have fostered the emergence throughout the country of "free markets" for food and consumer goods, especially clothing, frequently by providing basic facilities such as covered market stalls. Again, we have seen here the combination of the initial conditions of neglected consumption and facilitative local government.

2.35   It is no surprise that this proved a popular and successful reform, as it has in other countries, where improved commerce has been an early reform result. But two parallel results of this reform seem to merit mention. First, the private commercial system has provided a demand for backward linkage to the emerging new industrial sector, not least in alternative transport systems to deliver small quantities of goods to these outlets. This spawning of nonstate services seems set to continue in the 1990s, and indeed is now recognized by policymakers as a key source of future employment creation. Second, this area of reform has served as much as any to create a constituency in favor of the preservation and continuation of reforms, especially among the younger generation. It seems likely that this reform also had such instant results in China because the state commercial system had never been as all-encompassing in China as in other countries, and private commercial skills never completely disappeared, especially in rural areas.

State-Owned Enterprise Reforms

2.36   There have been many detailed reforms related to the SOEs, but they really come down to two basic changes in the system. First, in 1983/84, the system of profit remittance to the central government was changed to one whereby enterprises paid income taxes, and shared profits with their supervisory authority, with an increasing role for local industrial bureaus in this, compared with the earlier dominance of central ministries. This was accompanied in 1984 by incentives to generate those now retainable profits by the lowering of plan targets and permission to sell above plan output on markets, together with the further decentralization of plan formulation and implementation. This led to investment hunger and very rapid industrial expansion in 1985, so the system became more structured from 1986 onwards, as the agricultural contract responsibility system was applied to the SOEs under the enterprise contract responsibility system, which fixed profit remittance, retention rates, investment targets, etc., usually for a three-year period. By 1988, over 90 percent of all SOEs, accounting for over 50 percent of industrial output, were operating under this system, and by the end of 1991, most had signed a second contract.

2.37   Further innovations have been made, such as the Bankruptcy Law in 1987, the Enterprise Law in 1988, the use of enterprise groups and leasing of enterprises, but these are merely codification or variation of these two basic changes. Contrary to many general impressions, important efficiency gains have been achieved in the state sector (see Table 2.3), as well as in the nonstate sector. What these have amounted to is this: gradually changing the focus of SOEs from concern with meeting output targets to one of meeting financial targets, by specifying the latter targets as the main performance criteria of the contracts, and by offering incentives for attaining and exceeding such targets. The key to ensuring that such gains have come via efficiency improvements has been the role of competition, not only from new nonstate enterprises, but also from other SOEs given the size of the market in China. On the positive side, more gains have been made via this route than is frequently acknowledged. The key difficulty, as we discuss more below (para. 2.73-2.75) is that the system is primarily one of positive inducements, without clear negative consequences of failure.

2.38   In short, China's enterprise reforms can be summed up in this way: it has been the "marketization" of such enterprises, as contrasted to the "privatization" approach of many other countries. Can state-owned enterprises operate fairly and effectively in the market? That is at the heart of the assessment of China's future (para. 2.89).

Financial Sector Reforms[12]

2.39   Like most other socialist economies, China operated an essentially monolithic banking structure, and this has been one reform area where a classic sequencing of reforms over time has been planned and followed. The first step, in 1984, was to separate central banking from commercial banking, by creating the Industrial and Commercial Bank to take over the latter functions, leaving the People's Bank of China to focus mainly on central banking. This was extended in 1987 by the creation of two new universal banks to introduce slightly more nonprice competition into the banking sector. At the same time, financial innovations were encouraged, first by decentralizing authority to create nonbank financial institutions beginning in 1987, and secondly, by forming new capital markets, essentially for secondary trading of government bonds in 1988/89 and more recently, for trading in shares, beginning officially in 1991. This gradual deepening of the financial sector--at times ahead of the central institutional capacity to supervise and manage it--has been rapid and logical.

2.40   These financial innovations were necessary and "forced" by the change in the respective roles of the state and enterprises and individuals with respect to savings. The enterprise reforms meant that no longer would most surpluses be channeled via the government, but rather they would be retained by enterprises for investment, or passed on to workers in the form of rising wages and bonuses, who then needed somewhere to lodge their financial savings. It was this rapid financial deepening of the economy which also explains why China was able to sustain monetary expansion of close to 20 percent per annum throughout the decade of the 1980s without either revealed or repressed inflation.[13]

2.41   These financial innovations took place extremely rapidly in the mid-1980s, with little change since then. The commercial banking system remains 100 percent state-owned and operated, with a considerable share of total (especially working capital) lending influenced by the state through direct intervention to support its industrial policy, and seemingly only a relatively small proportion of total lending decided by banks on purely commercial grounds. Further reform in this area, then, also remains one of the major items on the unfinished agenda (para. 2.77).

Fiscal Reform

2.42   Many would argue that China has never had, and continues not to have, a tax system, but rather it has a revenue system. It should first of all be noted that China has always operated a decentralized taxation system, with the central government relying on provincial taxation bureaus to collect their taxes. The main changes that have taken place have been less concerned with a fundamental restructuring of sources of revenue, but rather changes in the way it has been collected and shared. In particular, the first big change has already been noted: profits began to be retained at the enterprise level, instead of being remitted almost in total to the state. This, of course, relieved the state of most of the burden of funding enterprise investment (see para. 2.64). The second big change came from the introduction of the fiscal contract responsibility system, the third of the four contract systems. This was introduced over a few years beginning 1985-86, when contracts were signed between the central and local governments, specifying the taxes to be handed over to the state, those to be shared and--in what proportions--and those to be retained.7/ Similar arrangements had always been in place but the contract system formalized them.

2.43   These contract systems, together with the high initial reliance on profits taxes, meant that central revenues were bound to be squeezed, as the former did not take account of inflation, and the profitability of enterprises was reduced in the face of competition. However, after the initial rapid decline in revenues following the measures noted above, the central government

---

7/ A common misconception is that all taxes are subject to sharing. In fact, a significant proportion (about 40 percent) are collected by local finance bureaus on behalf of central government, about 50 percent are collected and retained; and about 10 percent gets handed over for redistribution. In fact, transfers from the center exceed amount handed over from shared revenues. Taxes from centrally-owned SOEs are handed over to the state, as are certain other taxes, such as the salt tax and the extrabudgetary tax.

was able to introduce minor tax adjustments, especially on indirect taxes, to permit revenues to remain reasonably buoyant. China's tax or revenue system remains very unusual, however, with its reliance on contracted tax payments, layered indirect taxes and near-total absence of personal taxes, together with the absence of any centralized tax collection system. This is a second area where two major reforms occurred early (in 1986-88) with only minor adjustments since.

Foreign Trade

2.44   In contrast to fiscal and financial reforms, the foreign trade area has seen evolutionary, gradual change, very much exemplifying the "Chinese model"[14] Not only has it progressed gradually as opportunity has arisen, it has also involved partial reforms and has seen the "two steps forward, one step back" phenomenon. From its opening position of a system of about 15 foreign trade corporations operating under a near total mandatory trade plan, China rapidly moved to decentralize authority to create foreign trade corporations, while simultaneously reducing the scope of the trade plan, and permitting retention of foreign exchange at the local level. This rapidly spawned 1,500 new FTCs by the end of 1987, when the next two innovations were launched: sectoral reforms, whereby certain sectors (garments, electronics, and agricultural sideline products) were essentially forced from planning (and subsidy) and given high retention, and the institution of the fourth contract system, providing for the sharing of foreign exchange between central and local governments and the level of "support" from the center. Further power to create FTCs was delegated, and the number reached over 5,000 by 1990.

2.45   The third wave came in January 1991, when the second round of trade contracts was put in place, which eliminated central subsidies for exports and increased local retention of foreign exchange, which has increasingly been traded on the official parallel market. Over the last five years, a series of devaluations has gradually corrected the over-valued exchange rate and eliminated all but 7 percent of differentials between the official and parallel rates, with more than one third of all transactions now taking place at the parallel rate. The results of all this in terms of export performance are well-known (para. 2.80), and have permitted a rapid increase in technology imports. However, the emphasis of trade reform has always been on export promotion to finance "modernization" imports, and the import sector has never been seen as a source of competition. Now, however, with China once again seeking to resume its seat in the GATT, the fourth wave of trade reform can be expected to focus on liberalizing the import regime and making it more transparent.

2.46   It can thus be seen that the successful trade reforms have been driven by the desire to increase foreign exchange earnings to finance technology and materials imports. China has succeeded in this because of competition in the export sector, constant improvement in export incentives, and openness to foreign traders, especially from Hong Kong. In this regard, it has mirrored the Korean export experience a decade earlier. One final similarity should be noted: while import liberalization was left to last, imports of raw materials and other inputs for exports have been open from the start, especially in the assembly industries of electronics, toys and garments.

Social Sector Reforms

2.47   China has left social sector reforms to last. The reason for that seems to be twofold: first, by keeping the enterprise-based social safety net in place, it has postponed, or possibly avoided, many potential social problems; second, China continues to be very concerned about growth of large urban areas, so has resisted major labor reforms. Thus, within the labor area, the main reform has been a preparatory one: the introduction of the labor contract system, whereby all new workers in SOEs since 1986 have been on contract not permanent status, and can theoretically be fired, and this system covers about 20 percent of all state workers. The wage system has seen greater reliance on bonuses, but, on a national basis, the biggest change has been the growth of employment in nonstate enterprises, where rewards are usually on a piece-rate basis, and where the nonwage benefits (housing, pension, health) generally do not exist, or are far less significant. Thus, the main change has not been to the basic state system, but in the development of a parallel system.

2.48   It is only very recently that the government has begun to move on a national basis with respect to areas such as housing, social security and health financing, having largely focused on experiments so far. The difficulty is to move from a system of nonwage benefits tying the worker to his enterprise, to one where rewards are essentially monetary, with such social facilities and services being made available to the worker through other mechanisms, both public and private. Given its potential for creating social instability, this is an area where the Chinese government is moving very cautiously indeed, as these reforms will also serve to loosen the state's control over labor mobility.

2.49   This brief overview of the main steps in China's reform hopefully displays many of the characteristics of Chinese reform discussed earlier, from gradual (trade), to decentralized (enterprise), to partial (price) and self-reinforcing (financial). It also shows a clear trend throughout towards marketization of the economy, and the gradual evolution of arm's length, rules-based systems, although there remains a considerable way to go. What we can also see is that reforms have made least progress, the more they can be seen to affect the state-owned enterprises in any adverse way, and most progress where the opposite is the case. Thus, the challenges appear greatest in enterprise reform, and in financial and fiscal reforms. However, before we address future reform priorities, it seems appropriate to review the impact of reforms to date, as an indicator of how far reforms have come.

E.   The Impact of Reforms

2.50   Reform is not an end in itself: it is employed as a mechanism to foster development, and especially gain in efficiency, so that economies can enjoy growth and have a quality of growth that permits individuals to enjoy the benefits of growth. Fortunately, after more than 12 years of reform, and building on research results, we are now able to begin to assess quantitatively what has been the impact of China's reform. We look here at measures in four areas that seem most pertinent: output and consumption; gains in productivity; the changing role of the state; and openness to the outside world. As we shall see, these results are impressive indeed, and a powerful source of justification for China's approach. They do not prove that China could not have done better with some alternative policies, perhaps avoiding some pitfalls. Such a contrafactual argument can always be raised and will be partially true. But the numbers show a strong response to reforms, in particular in terms of achieving its main goal: to generate rapid economic growth on the basis of efficiency gains and opening to the outside world, through a growing role for the market.

Gains in Output and Welfare[15]

2.51   China has had a strong growth performance for most of the period since 1949, and even during the Cultural Revolution. This is not surprising considering that the state has seen to it that over 30 percent of GNP has been invested every year. During the period 1965-80, real GNP grew by about 6.4 percent per annum, with the gross value of industrial output rising by 10.3 percent and of agriculture by 3.1 percent. What we will see in the reform era is thus an _acceleration_ of growth and welfare gains, rather than their introduction, for it bears repeating that the purely economic gains of the prereform period were impressive, even if obtained at enormous cost, physical, political and social. The reform era itself saw most rapid gains in 1982-88, with significantly lower growth in the two tails, although 1991 has seen a strong recovery, as discussed in Chapter I.

2.52   At Table 2.1, we show various indices for the change in GNP and output over the reform period. With GNP growing at over 9 percent per annum--

Table 2.1: OUTPUT GAINS IN THE REFORM ERA
(average growth rates per annum)

	1979-89	1982-88
Gross output value	10.7	13.1
Agricultural output	6.0	6.8
Industrial output	12.5	15.3
of which:		
SOEs	8.1	9.8
Collectives	19.0	23.1
(TVEs)	29.9	38.2
Private	-	222.6
Other	-	45.7
GNP	9.1	10.9
of which:		
Primary	5.3	6.4
Secondary	10.5	12.4
Tertiary	11.1	13.3

Source: China Statistical Yearbook and Xiao, op. cit.

and per capita GNP at 7.8 percent per annum--there was a remarkably sustained increase in output over this period. Moreover, this growth in output was relatively balanced, especially during the early period, for agricultural performance also responded well to the reform, as noted. It is also not surprising, given the nature of reforms, that the tertiary sector saw the most rapid growth over this period. Indeed, the share of transport and commerce in national income fell from 13.6 percent in 1965 to 10.1 percent in 1980, but had risen to 14.8 percent by 1988.

2.53   But while output had grown during the prereform period, there had been relatively modest gains in private consumption per capita. Indeed, real wages saw little if any improvement over the period prior to 1979, with more increase in household income coming via growth in employment. At Table 2.2,

Table 2.2:   CONSUMPTION INDICATORS, 1978 AND 1988

	1978	1988	1988 as % of 1978
Cloth (m/person/yr)	8.0	12.2	152
Housing space (m/person)			
Urban	4.2	8.8	210
Rural	8.1	16.6	205
Wristwatches	8.5	47.0	553
Bicycles	7.7	30.4	395
Food (kg/person/yr)			
Pork	7.7	14.9	194
Poultry	0.4	1.8	438
Eggs	2.0	5.8	291

Source: China Statistical Yearbook.

we show various indicators of consumption in 1978 and 1988, showing how basic consumer goods and housing improved in availability over this period. Perhaps an even stronger indication of the real change in living standards is possession of major durable consumer goods. To take the three most startling examples: in 1981, there was less than 1 color television set per hundred urban households, but by 1990, this number had risen to 59; there were 0.2 refrigerators per hundred households in 1981, and 42.3 in 1990; and for washing machines, the figure rose from 6.3 per hundred to 78 per hundred households. Thus, the rapid growth in output translated into a very significant change in the standard of living in China over this period. That this was possible was because the reform era has seen intensive rather than extensive development, and thus rapid gains in total factor productivity.

2.54   These welfare gains are reflected in sharp reductions in the measured incidence of poverty during the reform era. A recent Bank report [16] found that the proportion of the population below the poverty line in China declined from 28 percent in 1978 to under 10 percent by the middle of the 1980s. However, no additional gains were made after 1984, as poverty in China is overwhelmingly a rural phenomenon, and the gains reflected the early gains from agricultural reforms. By 1990, some 11.5 percent of the rural population and 0.4 percent of the urban population remained in poverty. This meant, however, that over 160 million people had emerged from poverty during the reform era.

Table 2.3: ECONOMIC GAINS DURING THE REFORM ERA
(Percent growth per annum unless stated)

Productivity Indicators			
	1980-88	1980-84	1984-88
State Sector			
Growth	8.49	6.77	10.22
TFP growth	2.40	1.80	3.01
Use of materials	4.31	3.72	4.90
Collective Sector			
Growth	16.94	14.03	19.86
TFP growth	4.63	3.45	5.86
Use of materials	9.70	8.30	10.85
Agriculture			
Output growth	6.12	7.71	4.13
TFP growth	6.44	9.52	2.60
Land under cultivation	-0.13	-0.38	0.12
Use of fertilizers	6.75	8.20	5.33
Convergence of Returns			
(Ratio of nominal marginal returns		1980	1988
in collective industry as % of state)			
Labor		48.5	55.4
Capital		168.7	153.7
Materials		95.4	100.7

Source: Statistical Yearbook of China and Jefferson et al (op. cit).

Productivity Gains

2.55   Several of the studies have cited begun to provide reliable estimates of gains in total factor productivity during the reform period, incorporating re-estimates of the value of China's capital stock. Some of the results are summarized in Table 2.3.8/ These show very strong gains in TFP over the reform period, in all sectors of the economy. We have already noted that the first half of the reform period focused on agriculture, with industrial reforms coming later, and the TFP gains reflect this, with TFP growth accelerating noticeably in industry after 1984. In agriculture, by contrast, productivity gains were rapid for a while, but then fell off, as most gains from increased effort were by then achieved. It is also of interest to note that TFP explains most growth in agriculture--land area fell, though use of fertilizers grew rapidly--but extensive growth (meaning greater use of inputs) continued to be the most important factor explaining industrial growth.

2.56   These gains in factor productivity are in stark contrast to the prereform era. Various estimates have been made which indicate that productivity was stagnant during the 1957-76 period. Indeed, one study showed a decline in combined agricultural and industrial TFP of -1.41 percent during 1957-65 and a gain of only 0.62 percent per annum during 1965-76.[17]

2.57   These changes in TFP overtime are supported by more conventional measures of efficiency gain. The accumulation/national income ratio (the Chinese equivalent of a capital-output ratio, given the absence of GNP data before 1978) rose from 3.79 in the first decade (1953-59) to 4.30 in 1960-69, and to 5.39 in 1970-78. However, from 1978-88 it fell to 2.38, despite the surge in investment during the reform era. It is only during the slower growth performance of the rectification program of 1989/90 that the capital-output ratio has again risen.

2.58   Other results show that the reform in China is beginning to make the economy behave in ways similar to market economies. One of the distinctive features of the socialist system is that the inability of factors of production to move between alternative uses means that the government can fix the price system so that profits are a matter of administrative decision, and can vary widely between sectors, and the returns to factors of production in different uses can be very divergent. Evidence of equalizing profit rates and convergence of returns is a sign of effective marketization.

2.59   In 1980, profit rates in industry ranged from 7 percent to 98 percent: by 1989, the range had fallen to 8-23 percent, which is much more normal. In 1980, returns to labor in collective industry were only 48 percent of those in the state-owned sector, while this same ratio had risen to 55 percent by 1988. In contrast, returns to capital, which were 69 percent higher in the collective sector in 1980 were only 54 percent higher by 1988. Thus, reforms are not only serving to generate productivity gains, they also appear to be improving resource allocation. This, it must be assumed, is the direct result

---

8/   These results, based on survey data, confirm earlier results from Chinese researchers. They found TFP growth of 3.39 percent per annum during 1980-84, and 4.46 percent during 1984-88, although such growth turned negative during the 1989/90 rectification program, and results for the 7th FYP period were below those for the 6th. See Li Jingwen et al "Analysis of Economic Growth in China," Institute of Quantitative and Technical Economics, Chinese Academy of Social Sciences (1991).

of the rapid growth in competition, especially between state and nonstate industries.

The Role of the State

2.60   The primary purpose of reform in a centrally-planned economy is to change the role of the state from one of planning and directing economic resources directly, to one where the state manages the policies which direct the resources.   The impact of reform on the role of the state is shown in a variety of indicators in Table 2.4, and these show how fundamental this change

Table 2.4: CHANGING ROLE OF THE STATE

	1978	1984	1989
Output of state-owned enterprises as % of total	77.6	73.6	56.1
Gov't revenues as % of GNP	34.4	26.4	20.9
Extrabudgetary revenues as % of GNP	9.7	17.1	16.8
Financing of investment (1981)			
Budget	28.1	23.0	8.3
Loans	12.7	14.1	17.3
Foreign investment	3.8	3.9	6.6
Other	55.4	59.1	67.8
SOEs as % of total	69.5	64.7	61.3
Financing of SOEs Investment			
Budget	37.7	39.0	13.4
Loans	n.a.	15.4	20.9
Foreign investment	n.a.	2.2	10.2
Other	n.a.	43.5	55.6
Bank deposits as % of GNP			
Total	31.6	47.6	56.8
Enterprise	10.3	19.2	19.5
Urban savings	4.3	11.2	23.6
Rural savings	4.3	5.4	4.5
Treasury & government	9.7	7.1	5.8

has been. The first, and perhaps most dramatic change has been in the structure of output. In 1978, 78 percent of all industrial output came from the SOEs, operating entirely under the planning system. By 1989, the share of SOEs in total industrial output had fallen to 56 percent. This was not the result of privatization--for the effect of change in ownership of SOEs during this period was negligible, as it mostly occurred in the commercial sector-- but rather the growth of the nonstate sector. This should thus be seen as one of the results of the gradual approach: that small, incremental changes (in this case, via differential rates of growth) can over time add up to major structural reforms. Among these, we may note the growth of output of township and village enterprises, individual enterprises and joint ventures in particular, as shown in Table 2.5 and Chart 2.1.9/

Table 2.5: SHARES OF INDUSTRIAL OUTPUT OF
NONSTATE INDUSTRY
(percentage)

	1985	1990
Total collective	32.1	35.7
of which:		
Township	7.8	10.4
Village	8.4	12.3
Urban collective	15.9	13.0
Individual enterprises	1.9	5.4
Others, including joint ventures	1.2	4.4
Total nonstate	35.2	45.5
excl. urban collectives	19.3	32.5

2.61   What this shows very clearly is that since the inception of urban reforms, the share of nonstate industry in the total has expanded enormously by virtue of very rapid growth rates. SOEs have been growing fast as well, but at only half the pace of nonstate enterprises. In fact, despite their low base, nonstate industries account for more than half of the total growth in industry over the 1985-90 period. If this result is linked back to the productivity figures of Table 2.3, then it can be seen that part of the explanation for the rapid growth of total TFP is the relative growth of collective industry, where TFP gains have been particularly rapid.

2.62   This can be seen on a regional basis as well, as demonstrated in Chart 2.2. This traces gains in total factor productivity at the provincial level with the share of nonstate industry in total industrial output in different provinces. As can be seen, there is a generally close relationship between high-productivity provinces such as Zhejiang, Jiangsu and Guangdong, and the high share of nonstate industry, which in the extreme case of Zhejiang reached 68 percent in 1989. In contrast, provinces with very low shares of

---

9/   While all collectives and TVEs are defined as "nonstate," many would also fall under the definition "publicly owned." While many TVEs (the "Wenzhou" model) should be seen as akin to private enterprises, others (the "Suzhou-Nanjing" model) are closer to local state enterprises, with the role of the entrepreneur being critical in the former, and local government in the latter. See Byrd and Lin, op. cit.

Chart 2.1: OWNERSHIP SHARES IN INDUSTRIAL OUTPUT

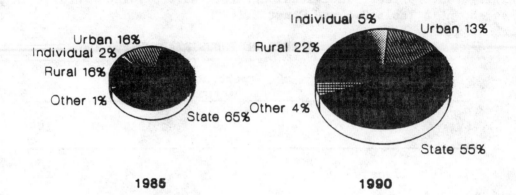

Urban = Urban Collectives; Rural = Rural Collectives & TVEs.

Other = Foreign Joint Ventures & all other.

Source: China Statistical Yearbook 1991.

nonstate industry, especially those in the North-West of China, had the lowest productivity. The only significant outlier is Shanghai, where the state sector appears to be most productive, perhaps as it is in Shanghai where much of the state's final goods production (automobile, bicycles, electronics, cigarettes, processed food) is located.

2.63   The reforms of the budget system and decline in the role of budgetary financing show up very clearly in the fiscal statistics. About one third of GNP used to pass through the budget in 1978, but this had fallen to only 21 percent by 1989, with the fall in budgetary revenues being more than compensated by increases in extrabudgetary revenues, 80 percent of which belong to enterprises in the form of profits. The main change that this has brought about is with respect to the structure of government spending and the financing of investment.

2.64   The change in the budget has meant that investment is now financed primarily from retained profits and bank loans. This is especially the case for the state-owned enterprises. In 1978, when they were remitting profits to the center, about 40 percent of their investment came from the budget: by 1989 this had fallen to only 13 percent, with most of this change coming after 1984. While the state continues to influence investment very heavily through its approval system and via the banking system, it no longer has any significant direct financing role, especially in the productive sectors, for almost all of the budgetary investment is in infrastructure.

2.65   The corollary of the declining influence of the state in the financing of investment is the rising importance of the banking system in mobilizing

Table 2.6: STRUCTURE OF GOVERNMENT EXPENDITURE, 1978-90
(percentage)

	1978	1984	1990
Current expenditure	56.5	71.2	79.7
of which:			
Defense	(13.7)	(9.3)	(7.6)
Culture, education, health	(9.2)	(13.6)	(16.2)
Administration	(4.0)	(7.1)	(8.1)
Subsidies	(9.3)	(21.1)	(25.2)
Development expenditures	43.5	28.8	20.3

Source: Statistical Yearbook of China.

savings. Not only has the use of bank loans for financing investment risen, but it has been made possible by the rapid growth of personal and enterprise deposits, although this does raise some of the key issues for the future (paras. 2.76-2.77). In 1978, savings deposits were only 8.6 percent of GDP, since when they have more than tripled to 28 percent in 1989, and enterprise deposits have about doubled as a share of GDP, with the corollary being a decline in treasury and government department deposits. Indeed this overall marketization and financial deepening of the Chinese economy is one of the more noticeable features of the reform period.

The External Sector

2.66   The fourth area of impact has been in the external sector, and in ways that distinguish China's reform effort from earlier socialist reform experiments. The key result has been that China has become a much more sig-nificant participant in the world economy. This has been an area of reform where decentralization of decision-making has been the primary factor behind the change. There are four aspects in which the impact can be seen: trade, technology, foreign exchange arrangements and foreign direct investment.

2.67   Perhaps trade is the most significant of these in many ways, and this is shown in Table 2.7. It should perhaps be noted that, even in 1978, trade was relatively high in China, as by this time the program to import western technology was already under way, but via the planning system. How-ever, since 1978, trade has consistently grown at rates well above GDP growth, so that by 1990, trade had risen to the equivalent of 31.3 percent of GDP, making China, by this measure, the most open of all large countries, and with

Chart 2.2: Regional Development and Non-State Industry

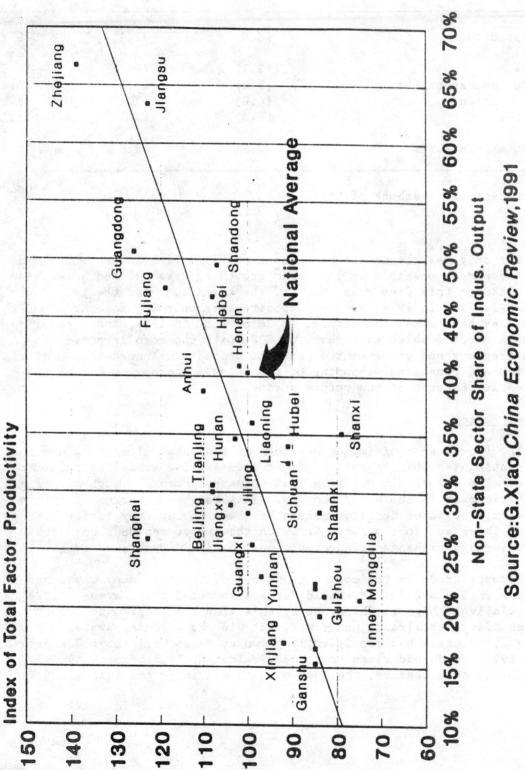

Table 2.7: TRADE IN THE CHINESE ECONOMY, 1978-90

	1978	1984	1990
Exports			
$ billion	9.75	26.14	62.09
Y billion	16.76	58.05	298.58
% of GDP	4.7	8.4	17.1
Imports			
$ billion	10.89	27.41	53.35
Y billion	18.74	62.05	257.43
$ of GDP	5.2	8.9	14.2
Trade as % of GDP	9.9	17.3	31.3

Source: China Custom Statistics.

a degree of openness more than twice that of India, Brazil, USA or Japan.10/ Note also that with the exception of the two retrenchment programs--1982/83 and 1990/91 11/--a trade deficit has been recorded every year. While no doubt some part of this growth in exports is the result of planning, more than half of all exports by the end of the 1980s fell outside any sort of planning, so these can be regarded as the result of the strong export incentives China has had in place.[18]

2.68   Of all such incentives--including foreign exchange retention, tax rebates, and direct subsidies on planned exports--the most important has been use of the exchange rate and foreign exchange markets. The exchange rate, which at the time was almost irrelevant for the determination of trade, was only Y 1.72/$1 in 1978, but stands today at Y 5.38/$1, despite there having been only less than 30 percent more inflation in China than in the United States over the period, and thus we have witnessed a very strong real effective exchange rate depreciation in China. In fact, taking 1980 as 100, the real effective exchange rate index at June 1991 was only 34.6. Thus, with the reduction of trade planning and the aggressive use of the exchange rate, it seems reasonable to attribute a considerable share of the growth in trade to this factor. However, not all of this exchange rate change has been strictly "managed," since, as noted earlier, one of the reforms has been the introduc-

10/ Although it would not alter the conclusion, care should be taken in using these statistics. GNP may be somewhat underestimated, and trade statistics include the full value of exports based on processing of imported inputs, which tends to exaggerate the true role of trade in the economy.

11/ Trade surpluses have occurred in the two years following the main stabilization efforts of 1981 and 1989.

tion of the parallel foreign exchange market. In its first year, turnover on the parallel market was only $4 million, but this rose rapidly to an estimated $18 billion in 1991, accounting for about one third of all transactions. It has been the growth in this market which has forced the realignment of the official rate since 1987, to the point where the differential, which was close to 100 percent in 1988, is now less than 10 percent, and unification of the rates under a market-based system seems to be under active consideration.

2.69   One other factor about the growth of trade in China has been its impact on the level of technology in the country. About one third of all imports over the last ten years have been of machinery and equipment. In other words, each year China has imported the equivalent of about 3 percent of GDP in capital goods, accounting for about 7.5 percent of all investment, and about 15 percent of all investment in equipment. It can be assumed that this has had a marked impact upon the equipment manufacturing industry, in China, and thus, while modernization and upgrading of equipment remains a priority, it can also be safely assumed that there is a wide range of Chinese industries where the vintage of capital equipment is not the primary issue in terms of competitiveness.

2.70   The fourth area of openness has been the impact of reform on foreign direct investment, which was the very first of the urban reforms. According to official statistics, there have been contracts signed over the period 1978-90 for over 29,000 joint ventures, with a contracted value of $45 billion. About half of these are in operation, with an investment value of about $22 billion. This translates in the last few years to annual direct foreign investment of $2-3 billion, which is of the same order as inflows of either official borrowing (World Bank, ADB, Japan, etc.) or commercial borrowing. More important, as many of these investments have been export-oriented, especially in the southern provinces of Guangdong and Fujian, this has been the other major explanatory factor behind China's export growth, as the economies of China, Hong Kong and Taiwan have been more closely linked. Indeed, some 70 percent of all foreign investment originates in Hong Kong, and over one third of all trade. To put this in a global perspective, China is the destination for about 10-15 percent of all direct foreign investment in low- and middle-income countries, and is exceeded in Asia only by Singapore.[19]

2.71   Thus, the reforms have led to a situation in which China has been a major player in world markets, both through its own trade links and the integration of its manufacturing sector through direct foreign investments, and this distinguishes China's reform efforts. However, as discussed below, this effort on the export sector has proceeded faster than and has not been the result of import liberalization, which remains high on the unfinished agenda.

F. Reform Priorities

2.72   We have seen from the preceding five parts of this chapter that China has come a long way in its economic reform, and that the economic impact has been measurably strong. However, it takes no more than a reread of the first chapter of this report to see that many problems remain, and, while progress has been great and the overall economic performance of the last decade remarkable, it seems clear that much indeed remains to be done. Indeed, this follows from the Chinese approach to reform, which expects the reform process to last a long time. The rest of this section therefore is concerned with the main items on the unfinished agenda. In terms of the major priority areas, it seems to us that there are six of particular importance. These are: the state-owned enterprises; the financial sector; public finance; trade; prices and markets; and the role of the state. In this chapter, we will only concern ourselves with the major unresolved issues, leaving the details to be addressed in Chapter IV. While actions in each area are distinct, it is reform of the SOEs that is the key constraint, and the main obstacle to be overcome.

The State-Owned Enterprises

2.73   Many incentives have changed for the state-owned enterprises, and their focus has shifted considerably away from achieving output targets and providing social services towards making profits and improving efficiency. Nevertheless, while the role of the nonstate enterprise sector has changed dramatically, the fundamental structure of the relationships between the state and the SOEs, and between the SOEs and their workers remains unchanged. Enterprises remain subjected to administrative interference in day-to-day operations, the negative consequences of failure remain unclear (in contrast to the positive rewards for success), and workers continue to be assigned to enterprises administratively and to be bound to those enterprises through the housing, health, education and social security systems. China's state-owned enterprises therefore continue to display many characteristics of public enterprises throughout the world, not least in making losses, funded both via the budget, and, in a less open way, through the banking system.

2.74   However, China requires that the publicly-owned enterprises must remain dominant in China's society (see paras. 4.16 and 4.16). Therefore, the reform priority in the state enterprise sector relates not so much to the issue of privatization, as to the regulatory and competition framework. Three areas seem to be paramount in this regard:

(a)   In terms of ownership, property rights remain vague, and there continues to be the need for new institutional mechanisms to separate the roles of government as regulator, owner and manager of enterprises.

(b)   The regulatory and legal framework remains largely undeveloped-- there is no company law for example--which makes the development of an arm's length trading system difficult.

(c)   The SOEs continue to be protected from the full impact of domestic and foreign market forces. Nonstate enterprises have less than equal access to credit; they are restricted from entry to sectors where they would threaten SOEs; foreign investment is not permitted to compete with existing SOEs; and trade is restricted. Finally, bankruptcy remains extremely limited, and while the use of mergers is gaining, it is being carried out in a largely administrative fashion.

2.75   The challenge is therefore to create a framework whereby public enterprises are operating within a clear system of regulation and are subject to the full force and consequences of competition, so that they behave much as private enterprises would in the same situation. Progress in this aspect will both be key to and closely linked to progress in the financial sector. While there are several reform experiments underway or planned in this area, it is not at all clear what Chinese policymakers are trying to achieve, or what concept of the future Chinese SOE they have in mind. While in such areas as price reform and the tax system, the final goal seems clear, it is in the area of SOE reform that new thinking seems most needed.

Financial Sector Issues

2.76   Dramatic change was introduced to the financial sector in China in the first years of urban reforms, but, aside from some encouraging developments in capital markets, reform in this area seems to have stalled since 1988. At the heart of the problem is the excessive use of the banking system by the state to meet its own economic aims, via the use of directed lending and "policy" lending. This effectively prevents the banking system from performing its key role of allocating savings to their priority uses. Furthermore, if the state is directing resources towards, for example, the covering of SOE losses, this could be storing up enormous portfolio problems for the banking system.

2.77   Associated with this remains the continued relative weakness of the central bank in China, both in its ability to regulate and supervise the financial sector and to formulate monetary policy and implement it via the use of indirect instruments. Instead, monetary policy appears still to be heavily influenced by, inter alia, provincial leaders, and is implemented largely by use of direct credit controls. This suggests three key areas for priority development in the financial sector:

(a) Development of alternative methods of financing for government policy objectives, including the budget itself and capital market developments.

(b) Continued strengthening, both in terms of technical capability and status, of the central bank in formulating and implementing monetary policy and in carrying out its regulatory/supervisory functions.

(c) Further efforts to increase the use of indirect instruments of financial control, such as the interest rate structure and use of open market operations via new instruments such as short-term treasury bonds.

Although the financial sector has yet to face a serious crisis, portfolios of banks deteriorated during 1989-91 through a combination of heavy lending (made possible by very high savings) and the weak economy. While the recovery should bring some relief, this still poses a threat to the long-term success of the Chinese approach to economic reform, and short-term action in these three areas is most urgent.

Public Finance

2.78   The second of the three strands of macroeconomic management development in China relates to public finance. As with the financial sector, this
underwent one massive reform--the shift from profit remittance to corporate
income tax--but only minor change since. China continues to have a revenue
system rather than a tax system, and it is one that is bound by contracts. As
such, it is tied inextricably to the old economic system that links the state,
enterprises and workers. It thus perpetuates the old economic system and will
need dramatic overhaul if it is to promote a new economic system. This would
seem to relate to three aspects in particular.

   (a) Taxes are contracted (both at the enterprise and at the provincial
        level) and taxes will have to be clearly separated from such con-
        tracts.

   (b) The tax system is heavily based in the state production enterprise
        system--this being the primary tax collection point--and will have
        to be diversified with greater reliance on personal income tax and
        final sales point taxes, in line with progress in converting nonwage
        into wage income.

   (c) The indirect tax system cascades and makes incentives very unclear
        and will need to be replaced by more transparent, rules-based sys-
        tems, such as value-added taxes.

2.79   Finally, it must be noted that one third of all public expenditures
are for price and enterprise subsidies, at the expense of infrastructure
investment and social expenditures, although the solution to this lies primarily in the area of price and enterprise reform. The growing pressure on the
budget seems to be lending some urgency to the attention given to fiscal
issues, which take time to implement once reforms are formulated. Therefore,
this too appears to merit acceleration.

External Sector

2.80   It was observed earlier that great progress has been achieved not
only in expanding trade, but in making exports responsive to economic signals
on an aggregate basis. And yet two factors about the trade regime continue to
be of particular importance. First, external trade continues to be dominated
by foreign trade corporations of various kinds, and participation of production enterprises directly in trade is limited. Second, as suggested, the
import regime continues to offer a high degree of protection to domestic
industry, and thus imports continue to be regarded primarily as a source of
embodied technology. This protection is provided by an opaque and unpredict-
able system of import licensing, and by an uneven tariff structure, albeit
with apparent frequent exemptions to reduce the anti-export bias. This would
suggest two primary areas of focus for future trade reform.

   (a) Reform of the import regime, by moving to a system of management by
        indirect control, under a lower level of protection effected by
        tariffs rather than licenses and administrative barriers, and with
        transparent control mechanisms.

- 64 -

(b) Continued efforts at institutional reform of FTCs, through further reduction of their effective monopsony and greater entry to export markets for production enterprises.

2.81   It is logical that the existing import regime has been accompanied by a foreign direct investment system that, while offering good incentives, restricted the competitive impact of foreign enterprises, and, in order to achieve this, developed a complex and lengthy approval process. Similarly, therefore, efforts in this area would have to be directed towards further opening of the domestic market, and improved efficiency and transparency in the approval process. With a very strong trade balance, and about nine months of imports in foreign exchange reserves, this would seem a most opportune time to launch such reforms.

Prices and Markets

2.82   In terms of reform progress, we stressed that more than half (perhaps two thirds) of all transactions were now carried out at market prices. Moreover, a key factor is that most marginal resource allocation decisions are made at market prices. However, this implies that at least one third of all transactions are at controlled prices and many of these remain subject to the materials allocation system. In theory, this need not matter, as the state should be able to adjust for this in other ways. For example, low coal prices reduce the attractiveness of investment in coal for local governments, and reduce available financial surpluses at coal mines for reinvestment. Theoretically, and in practice in the prereform situation, the planning system could compensate for this with fiscal transfers, but the state no longer has the fiscal resource control to do this. The result is unbalanced investment, and unfair interprovincial income distribution, in addition to obvious microeconomic consequences such as wastage of energy.

2.83   Price reform in these areas, in the sense of new price formulation systems, especially in raw materials and grain, will require not only lifting of controls or adjustment of fixed prices, but development of market infrastructure, such as transport and storage facilities, and information systems. It will also require price sensitive consumers, so a major accompanying reform will need to be the conversion of price subsidies into wages. Thus, reforms in these areas would need to focus on:

(a) Removal of remaining price controls for most commodities, usually preceded by price adjustment, and accompanied by market infrastructure investments. Priorities seem to be in energy, transport, certain raw materials and in grain. This would need to be accompanied by the development of regulatory mechanisms and institutions to guard against abuse of monopoly powers.

(b) Conversion of remaining consumer price subsidies--especially for grain--into wages, so that state procurement and distribution can be gradually eliminated.

It appears that, with recent price adjustments, there are no longer any "sacred cows" in pricing. Given the continued favorable demand-supply balance in most markets, there continues to be plenty of scope for rapid movement in this area at the present time.

The Role of the State

2.84   Much has already changed with respect to the role of the state, as it has fostered the growth of nonstate enterprises, and yielded control over prices, revenues and materials. Much of what has already been mentioned in this section is concerned with continued progress in this direction. Other elements that have been mentioned imply things that the state will have to do more, such as indirect macroeconomic management and development of a legal framework. In short, the role of the state and of planning will have to continue to evolve. The third chapter of this report is allocated to a discussion of this issue in the context of an assessment of the Eighth Five-Year Plan.

2.85   Over and above this, there are two other key areas where the role of the state will have to change dramatically and where little concrete progress has been made so far. First, social services of one kind or another continues to be provided primarily by the enterprise sector, especially housing, health insurance and pensions. Also, by virtue of the gradual reform process, and emphasis on development of new enterprises rather than radical reform of existing enterprises, the state enterprise system has continued to offer protection against unemployment. Here, there is a new role for the state, either in direct provision of such services, or by creating a framework for nonstate, nonenterprise based systems, such as private pensions and health insurance. It is only by removing this burden from enterprises that true enterprise reform can begin, and yet the state will have to directly promote appropriate solutions.

2.86   Finally, an area where virtually no significant progress has been made has been in the labor market. Most workers continue to be assigned jobs, and movement between geographical areas remains highly restricted. Movement between enterprises within one geographical area is even difficult, because of nontransferability of accumulated nonwage benefits and housing. These factors are compounded by a set of antiemployment-creation policies, such as low interest rates and low energy prices, coupled with bias against labor-intensive sectors such as service industries and private enterprises. These suggest three areas of primary focus:

(a)   Conversion of nonwage benefits into wages and separation of services provision from enterprises.

(b)   Gradual relaxation of labor allocation systems, both vocational and geographical.

(c)   Continued attention to removal of antiemployment policies, especially those that encourage high capital/labor ratios, such as low input prices and interest rates, and policies that discriminate against TVEs.

G. <u>Some Tentative Conclusions</u>

2.87   The discussion of this chapter has been concerned with the way that China has gone about its reform program, and the impact on the economy of these reforms. It is clear that the Chinese approach has worked well in the initial conditions under which it was launched. This is not to say that the outcome was <u>optimal</u>, and it must be accepted that other measures could have made the results even better. For example, it is now generally accepted in China that stronger monetary management in 1988 and more rapid price reform in 1990 would have improved matters. It must also be stressed that one of the key features of China's initial conditions was the absence of a need for harsh stabilization measures, and no simultaneous external shocks, such as the collapse of the CMEA which has so strongly affected the countries of Central and Eastern Europe. This said, five key features of the Chinese reform experience do seem to be key elements of success, which may have some more general applicability, irrespective of the issues related to the gradual approach, and to the special conditions that are unique both to China and its approach to reform.

Five Key Features

2.88   At the start of the reform program, China had a large and relatively well-developed industrial system, but was nevertheless fundamentally a rural economy. Moreover, as the discussion of initial conditions suggested, the agricultural sector was highly repressed, and was thus ripe to respond to reforms. These factors supported the appropriateness of the decision to use <u>agriculture as the entry point</u>. Not only did agriculture respond rapidly--as it has in other countries such as Vietnam--but this generated the rural savings and surplus labor necessary to launch the next phase of reform, and created a constituency for reform.

2.89   The second element that seems to have been of particular significance in China was the emphasis on <u>marketization instead of privatization</u>, and on the role of growth of the nonstate sector in diversifying ownership patterns. The spectacular growth of nonstate enterprise has served two key functions.

    (a) It created economic growth and generated employment opportunities, thus bringing out significant gains from reform.

    (b) It generated competitive pressure on state-owned enterprises, forcing change in their behavior, even though this process remains far from complete.

This process is one that can be regarded as "privatization from below," in that, within just a few years, 45 percent of industrial output is now from nonstate industries. More generally, this emphasis on creation of new nonstate industries suggests the possibility of creating a competitive framework in which state enterprises can be made more efficient without recourse to direct privatization programs.

2.90   The gradual approach to reform runs the risk that the losers from reform can regroup either to oppose further change or even attempt reversal.

Of course, this same factor can also work in the opposite direction, as reform skeptics can be won over when the pace of reform is gradual, and benefits start to emerge. The particular problem in a socialist system is how to change the interest of the bureaucracy and the Party. Bureaucrats, especially at the national level, are among the major losers from socialist reform, with loss of power, prestige and, in particular, nonwage income. Nevertheless, China seems to have had some success in reorienting the bureaucracy. The reforms created pressure on the planners because they reduced central revenues and the profitability of state enterprises. Although to some extent, this caused part of the bureaucracy to seek to protect their profits and interests, it also redirected the interest of the bureaucracy towards ensuring that their enterprises were oriented towards profit-making. This has seen setbacks at times, but the periods of resurgence of planning theology, as in 1989/90, have proved short-lived as even planners have found it hard to preserve their interests through such methods in the face of past reforms. We can observe in 1992 a recognition of the failure of planning solutions to achieve significant restructuring of state-owned enterprises during the previous three years. Thus, the use of decentralization and promotion of nonstate industry generated a reorientation of the interest of the bureaucracy away from planning goals towards economic performance. This coincided with the interests of the Party, which saw its political interests geared increasingly to the achievement of economic success.

2.91   The fourth element of the Chinese approach that is distinctive has been its emphasis on export development and more generally its entry into world markets. The big contrast between this approach and that of other countries has been the postponement of import liberalization to late in the reform process, although it has had the result of a relatively high level of importation of advanced technology. This has been possible for two reasons: first, the size of the domestic economy has made it possible to generate competitive forces, especially among smaller enterprises vying for export business; second, while China had been closed to import competition, it has been very open to influence from outside in its export industry, and especially from Hong Kong entrepreneurs, who have been permitted to impose rigorous export design and quality control standards. The unique relationship between China and Hong Kong may reduce the replicability of this element of the strategy.

2.92   The fifth key factor in the Chinese approach has been the role of the state in maintaining social stability. By using the gradual approach, and by not subjecting the state sector to major shocks, China has succeeded in avoiding severe social costs during its transition. The Chinese effort has focused much less on changing old enterprises and more on generating new opportunities. Moreover, by postponing social reforms to the end of the reform process, this has given the opportunity to develop over time the institutional framework for a new social security system. What remains to be tested is whether China can now move beyond this approach to address the more fundamental issues of the state enterprise sector and the dismantling of this social system--and indeed the issue of whether the state wishes to carry out this aspect of reform. Nevertheless, it is clear that this approach has avoided some of the serious social consequences that could have undermined the case for further reform.

Sustainability

2.93   A key question in considering the Chinese approach to economic
reform is whether this approach is sustainable over the medium to long term,
or whether it is simply postponing problems that will later "come home to
roost." Three potential issues for the future need to be addressed:

(a)   The danger of future insolvency of some large banks, as they acquire
an increasingly weak portfolio by funding the losses of the state-
owned enterprises, with limited capital bases and small loan loss
provisions. It is further argued by some that this problem will
worsen as the influence of nonstate industry rises, which would
result in the squeezing out of such enterprises from resources.

(b)   The argument that so long as state-owned enterprises remain dominant, they will never be able to achieve efficiency at internationally competitive levels, so that so long as this position is maintained, China will always be a highly protected economy, and the
benefits of present reforms will fade away to lead to stagnation
until this issue is addressed.

(c)   That social tensions will mount in two directions. First, that
increasing provincial autonomy and self-sufficiency will increase
further the growing regional disparities in China, leading to
increasing conflicts. Second, that the fight against poverty in
China is showing fragile gains, with many persons only just above
the poverty line. With reforms and further difficulties for the
central government, the present social safety net could collapse,
pulling millions back into poverty.

2.94   In other words, these arguments suggest that the gradual approach
has limitations, and that China will eventually approach these limits. This
argument is based primarily on the recent experiences of the formerly socialist countries of Eastern and Central Europe. These are serious issues, and
the possibility of such a collapse--forcing China into its own "big bang"--
should not be dismissed out of hand. Moreover, it must be recognized explicitly that China's reform is indeed one which does not have successful
historical precedent. But two important factors must be stressed as sources
of reassurance:

(a)   Over the existing reform period, China has generally responded to
the problems arising out of the reform experience by introducing new
reforms and by deepening existing reforms. Thus, we can see incremental reform movement over the entire period of the reform era,
albeit at varying speeds. This gives reassurance that, as new problems emerge, so they too will be met by incremental movement, so
that, as with the past ten years, deep crisis simply will not occur.
For example, this could result in incremental reforms which restructure existing SOEs, such that these reforms in turn correct on an
incremental basis the genuine portfolio problems of banks.

(b)   The gains of the reform era have been "intensive" rather than
"extensive," as measured by the strong productivity gains that have

been registered, and China has succeeded in maintaining the momentum
of GDP growth even during periods of adjustment. These productivity
gains are not restricted to the new industries, but have been
recorded also in the existing SOEs. This suggests that the economic
results of the Chinese approach to reform may be qualitatively different from the experiences of some others that tried such an
approach, and we would suggest that this could lend credence to
sustainability, and to the possibility that China will grow out of
its problems. The secret to this success has been China's use of
"marketization" and the vigorous development of the nonstate sector,
which has been unique to the Chinese approach, and is in marked
contrast to the Hungarian experience of the 1970s.

2.95   The key to sustainability thus rests, in our view, not on any theoretical or philosophical issues about the ultimate level of efficiency that
publicly-owned enterprises can achieve, but rather on the solutions that China
will develop towards the unfinished agenda. In particular, this relates to
solutions to the problems of the financial sector and the state-owned enterprise sector and its environment. If appropriate incremental reforms are
instituted, stressing growing "marketization" and a continued associated
increase of competitive forces via growth of the nonstate sector and trade
reform, then the remarkable experience of the past decade lends hope that the
Chinese approach can indeed lead to a sustainable pattern of growth with
reform. The question is how well future policy will address the unfinished
agenda, and this is addressed in the next two chapters of this report.

III. CHINA'S DEVELOPMENT PLAN, 1991-95

A. Introduction

3.1   The preparation of the Eighth Five-Year Plan, 1991-95 (8th FYP) and Ten-Year Program, 1991-2000, offers the opportunity to examine not only the Chinese Government's stated intentions for economic policy over the coming period, but also the evolution of the planning process in China. Within the Chinese economic system, there are three distinct aspects to planning: the formulation of medium- and long-term (five and ten year) plans, and corresponding annual plans; the instruments of planning, or more generally, the planned economy, and notably the use of output targets, the materials allocation system, and the use of other administrative means of management, such as price and credit controls; and the formulation of plans for the role of the state, such as government investment programs or policy reform programs. In assessing the 8th FYP, it is necessary to consider all three aspects of planning in China, and to place any such assessment more generally within the framework of the rapidly changing economic system.

3.2   This chapter attempts to carry out such an assessment. First, it is important to see the current plan in the context of how planning has been evolving in China since the First FYP was formally adopted in July 1955. Then, we discuss what seem to be the key roles for planning in China in the 1990s, and assess how the present proposals fit into that structure, which raises some of the key economic policy issues addressed in the plan. This leads naturally on to some conclusions about the future of planning and plan formulation in China.

B. The Evolution of Planning

3.3   There are three quite distinct phases in the history of economic plans in China.1/

   (a) The Soviet Period. The first two plans, covering 1953-57, and 1958-62, reflected Soviet influence and style. The Second FYP included the period of the "Great Leap Forward," with its mass programs of communization in agriculture, and massive investment in heavy industry, with well-known consequences. The Second FYP was followed by a period of adjustment and consolidation, which many Chinese economists regard as a "golden age" of the Chinese approach to planned economic management. Both plans were relatively detailed, and most targets achieved.

   (b) The Pre-Reform Period. The Third and Fourth Plans covered the period of the Cultural Revolution, and were, in the end, essentially irrelevant to the unfolding economic situation. The period included the one year, 1968, when it was impossible to formulate an annual

---

1/   For a good description of China's early experience in planning, see Liu Suinian and Wu Qungan "China's Socialist Economy; An Outline History 1949-84" (1986) and Nicholas Lands "Chinese Economic Planning" (1978).

plan because of the chaotic political situation. Nevertheless, this can be typified as a period of "planning as propaganda," in which the plans were intended as means to mobilize the population, rather than as guides to specific policies and priorities. The Fifth Plan, formulated immediately after this in 1976, was essentially in the same mold, but with elements of the Soviet period in that it aimed once again for massive levels of investment to accelerate development.

(c) The Reform Period. The present plan is the third since the reform process was launched in 1978. These plans have attempted to make realistic assessments of the economic situation, and to draw up a framework for the country's overall development strategy. Nevertheless, they have continued to include many output and investment targets of the sort traditionally included in Soviet-style economic plans. A clear contrast, however, between this period and previous periods is that while past plans were generally underfulfilled, especially during the Maoist era, the reform period has seen plans overfulfilled; while planners have sought to be more realistic, they have consistently underestimated the impact of economic reform.

3.4   In the Sixth Plan period, which came on the heels of inflation following the 1977-79 expansion, very modest targets were set and the plan aimed to create a program of slow steady growth. Yet, targets were achieved by the third year, not long after the Plan itself was promulgated in late 1982.[2] This was a combination of lack of information following the chaos of the Cultural Revolution, together with a genuine desire to send out a message of modest growth and an equally genuine inability to estimate the impact of reform.

3.5   The Seventh Plan for 1986-90 was prepared in elaborate detail, with many years of officials' time put into its preparation.[3] The results of the 7th FYP are presented in Box 3.1. Perhaps two particular features of this should be stressed as lessons for the future:

(a) Although the five year outcome was remarkably close to the aggregate target, the projected pattern was entirely reversed, with rapid growth for three years followed by harsh stabilization, while the Plan called for two moderate years followed by acceleration. This was not least because macroeconomic policy, especially credit expansion, was not governed by the planning process.

---

[2] A consistent feature of Plans before the 7th and 8th is that they were approved well into the Plan period. The first FYP for 1953-57 was approved in July 1955.

[3] See Carol Hamrin "China and the Challenge of the Future" for an excellent description of the various working groups and investigation teams that were set up, and Wang Huijiong and Li Poxi "China Towards the Year 2000" for some of the output.

Box 3.1: THE 7TH FYP AND ITS OUTCOME

1.   The Seventh Plan set a target average annual real growth rate in GNP of 7.5 percent which, while high by the standards of the rest of the world, was a reasonable target for China in the light of the previous five years. However, given the need to control the expansionary impulses in the economy, the plan proposed slower rates of growth in the first two years while the last three were expected to feature faster growth accompanied by accelerated reform, consistent with achieving the average growth target of 7.5 percent. The tertiary sector was designed to grow faster than other sectors. The plan focused on reducing investment and output of low-tech industries and improving the growth of exports and imports. Given infrastructural bottlenecks, energy conservation was touted as a goal.[1]

2.   Unlike the 6th Plan, which saw growth through productivity improvements, in the 7th FYP, growth came through demand-driven growth that intensified shortages in bottleneck areas and contributed to inflation. Following the tight macropolicy in 1989 and first half of 1990, the average annual rate of growth for the plan period averaged 7.6 percent-- almost exactly the plan target. Grain output hit a record high in the last two years, and production of the major nonstaple foodstuffs was on a continuous rise over the period. As a result, the gross output value of agriculture (GOVA) grew a little bit higher than planned. The strongest performance was shown by export industry, which expanded at an annual rate of 19.2 percent, but the gross value of industrial output grew overall by a remarkable 13 percent. A major factor in China's achievements in these areas was the dynamic performance of the rural industrial sector which took advantage of reduced entry barriers in many sectors and increased its real value of gross output by over 182 percent over 1985-90, absorbing in excess of 15 million workers over the same period.[2]

MAJOR INDICATORS OF 7TH FYP
(Y billion)

	Value (target)	Growth Rate (target)	Value (outcome)	Annual Growth Rate Growth Rate (outcome)
GNP	1,117	7.5	1,740	7.8
NI	935	6.7	1,430	7.5
GOVIA	1,677	6.7	3,123	11.0
GOVA	353	4.0/a	738	4.6
GOVI	1,324	7.5/a	2,385	13.1
Light	661	7.5	1,179	14.1
Heavy	663	7.5	1,205	12.2
Public finance				
Revenue	257	6.7	324	11.8
Expenditure	257	7.1	340	13.2
Fixed inv.	297	3.7	445	12.5
Ext. trade /a	83	7.0	486	14.3
Export	38	8.1	233	19.2
Import	45	6.1	254	9.8

/a In $ billion

Price Indexes, 7th FYP
(previous year = 100)

	1986	1987	1988	1989	1990
Cost of living	106.5	107.3	118.8	118.0	103.1
Retail price	106.0	107.3	118.5	117.8	102.1

Note: (1) GOVIA figures for targets are in 1980 constant prices.
      (2) GNP and NI figures for targets are in current prices (1985 prices).
      (3) Annual growth rates for outcomes are based on 1980 constant prices, while values are in terms of current prices (1990 prices).
      (4) Public finance and total investment figures are in current prices.

Sources: 7th FYP, SSB Communique on Completion of 7th FYP, and Annual Plan documents.

3.   The pace of development during the 7th FYP also had a distinctive regional bias (discussed further in Part F), the results of which are displayed in the following table. The coastal provinces, which were given various advantages (in addition to their natural advantages) in terms of freedom from central planning, tax retention and openness to the outside world. Clearly, this was reflected in output growth over the 7th FYP, with the coastal provinces growing much faster compared to the older cities or the "unreformed" areas. Interestingly, minority areas continued to exert strong growth performance, reflecting perhaps their continued high access to investment financing resources.

REGIONAL GROWTH RATE, 1985-90
(percentage growth in GVIAO at current prices)

Beijing	117	Guangdong	203
Shanghai	90	Jiangsu	153
Tianjin	117	Shandong	179
		Fujian	178
Liaoning	112		
Henan	138	Xinjiang	153
Heilongjiang	118	Ningxia	144

Source: China Statistics Abstract, 1991.

4.   If judged by the aims, the outcome was also a demonstration of some of the fundamental problems in the economy. The annual growth rate of fixed investment was almost four times as high as the target, and that of industry and government expenditure twice. This could be attributed, to a large extent, to the lack of determination of the government to deal with the fundamental problems which were at the root of the excessive growth and macroinstability (investment hunger, poor performance of the state sector, soft budget constraint, and inability of the macroeconomic management system when faced with the robust growth of the nonstate sector).

[1] See Barry Naughton, "China's Experience with Guidance Planning," Journal of Comparative Economics, 1990.

[2] Output of rural industry (township, village and individual enterprises) is estimated at Y 182 million in 1985 and Y 614 million in 1990 using Statistical Yearbook 1990 and Statistical Abstract 1991. Real output is derived by using industrial output price deflators given in Table 1.3 of the Appendix.

(b)   The Plan continued to have many quantitative output targets, including for commodities where the state no longer had a position of dominance, or the planning instruments--in terms of material allocation or investment financing--to influence the outcome. However, the Plan did not include a policy framework to influence the achievement of those targets, nor, in general, any particular program for the use of indirect economic levers. Perhaps as a consequence of this, planners at the local level in particular, resorted to "secondary" mandatory planning and materials allocation to attempt to achieve their targets.

3.6   That such an elaborate exercise as the 7th FYP should have an outcome so divergent from expectations throws doubt on the credibility and value of the entire plan formulation process in China.[1] Does this mean that it has become irrelevant to the realities of the economy? It is clear that the plan formulation process remains of critical importance to the formulation of overall economic policy. Indeed, reversal of a trend back towards mandatory planning (following the Fifth Plenum of the 13th Central Committee in December 1989) to a renewed emphasis on economic reform appears to have coincided with discussions of the draft 8th FYP in the fall of 1990. Moreover, the Plan itself remains a significant influence in the Chinese economy, since it provides the macroeconomic framework for the period, and it outlines policies towards the state-owned sector, which still dominates production. Of increasing importance is the indication it provides of the future policy framework (see Chapter IV).

3.7   This evolution of the planning process towards the macroeconomic framework and policy planning mirrors the reduction in the scope of mandatory planning. It is estimated that the share of industrial production under the mandatory plan has declined from 70 percent in 1979 to an estimated 16 percent in 1990, with only 9 percent falling under the state plan. Similarly, the proportion of investment financed by the government budget directly has fallen from 28 percent in 1981 to only 8 percent in 1989, with the share financed by enterprises and especially banks rising to mirror this change. These trends may even underestimate the true decline of mandatory planning, as there has also been a general decline in the level of fulfillment of plan supply contracts between the mid-1980s and the late 1980s.[2]

3.8   As the economy continues to change and as the scope for direct determination of outcomes by the state continues to fall, it is obvious that the old style plan has less and less relevance. Therefore, in assessing the new plan, the question to be addressed is how well it has incorporated the lessons of the past, and how well it fulfills what can be regarded as the new role of planning in the framework of the reformed planned commodity economy.

C.   Role of the Plan in the 1990s

3.9   From the above discussion, we can conclude the Plan should no longer be primarily a set of arithmetic targets, or a framework for the allocation of materials or budget resources. As noted, the state no longer has the capacity to control investment financing or materials allocation. However, there are three functions within the economy that the government is uniquely equipped to

- 74 -

deal with via the planning process,4/ each of which is highly relevant to
China and to the 8th FYP.

(a)   The Economic Framework. Only the government can address its
      economic intentions, and most governments have staff resources
      assigned to analyzing future directions for the economy. If such
      frameworks are coordinated with actual government intentions and
      actions, they become powerful information tools for the rest of the
      economy. This is especially so if such frameworks are accompanied
      by statements outlining economic policies designed to achieve the
      aims of the economic framework. Good examples of this are provided
      by the planning experience of South Korea and Japan during the 1970s
      and 1980s.[3] This is relevant in China to the issue of the pace of
      development in the 1990s and the use of industrial policies to
      adjust the economic structure (paras. 3.28-3.35).

(b)   Correcting Market Failures. As the Chinese reform proceeds, and
      more and more transactions are determined by the market, an increas-
      ing role of the state will be to correct for market failures.
      Traditionally, this means providing[4] for the production or control
      of commodities that provide externalities or are essentially public
      goods or natural monopolies. The classic examples are such goods as
      parks and roads, and externalities such as pollution. The state can
      do these things because it has the power to tax, the power to pro-
      scribe, the power to punish and (in some cases) lower transactions
      costs than the private sector.5/ In the course of gradual and
      partial reform, market failure can be expected to be rather a
      serious problem in China, and one which has as yet received
      relatively less attention. It can thus be expected that the state
      will have a critical role to play in regulating the market as its
      role increases. This would be to foster competition, to regulate
      against or combat monopoly and to prevent the erection of barriers
      to trade. Two particular issues in China are that the market may
      not generate sufficient employment opportunities given market rigid-
      ities and constraints, and that it may generate a distribution of
      income which is not compatible with Chinese equity consideration
      (paras. 3.38-3.58).

(c)   Planning for Bottlenecks and the State Sector. The state in most
      countries retains responsibility for the provision of economic
      infrastructure, and planning is necessary to avoid bottlenecks,
      given the lumpiness of such investments. However, when the state is
      also responsible for many production decisions, infrastructure can
      be interpreted as an "input" to such plans. This calls for a
      different sort of sector planning once production decisions are

---

4/   The two unique features of the State that relate to these three issues
     are that the state has universal membership, and the state has power of
     compulsion--see Stiglitz (1991) "The Economic Role of the State."

5/   For example, state social security systems have much lower administrative
     costs than private pension plans.

decentralized, as planners have to attempt to anticipate the
decisions of others. The clearest example is the provision of transport, to which Chapter V of this report is dedicated. However, it
applies more generally to investment decisions that remain within
the government's purview, and thus is relevant to policies towards
the state-owned enterprises (para. 3.56-3.61).

3.10   These three critical functions of the state, which would call for a
continued strong if re-directed planning function, can be seen to be the same
areas where our review of the most recent past plans found major shortcomings.
The following sections therefore examine the 8th FYP in the light of these
three roles.

D.   The Macroeconomic Framework and Development Policy

3.11   The "Outline of the Ten-Year Programme and of the Eighth Five-Year
Plan for National Economic and Social Development" was adopted by the 7th NPC
on April 9, 1991. It differs from past plans, in one substantial way, in that
it is an outline, not a detailed plan, and so it does not contain the many
tables of detailed targets familiar from past plans. Instead, it aims to set
out the main tasks and priorities for the decade of the 1990s and the instruments to be used to achieve those tasks, including investment and economic
reforms. This, in itself, is a reform and one that is to be welcomed. Unlike
the 7th FYP, which underwent an elaborate preparation process, with huge
expenditure of officials' time (para. 3.5), the 8th FYP was prepared quite
quickly over about 9 months in 1990, with a relatively compact preparation
team. While the Plan takes a long term view, it is heavily influenced by the
recent economic past in China, and in particular, by two factors: the severe
instability of 1988 resulting from overheating; and the economic difficulties
of the SOEs during the rectification period.

3.12   Planning authorities characterize the Eighth Plan as one which
incorporates an awareness of market conditions and demand-supply balances,
moderates growth objectives to take account of real and fiscal bottlenecks,
features a revamped industrial policy to restructure industry, and acknow-
ledges the need for enterprise and market reform to achieve plan targets.
Notwithstanding the claims about a significantly different plan strategy, the
Eighth Plan bears an uncanny resemblance to its predecessor.

3.13   Like the 7th FYP, the new plan was formulated during a period of
policy-imposed recession and proposes an initial two years of slower growth to
be followed by a quickening of the pace of growth in the last three years.
Also as with the 7th FYP, growth targets are expressed in real terms although
there is no explicit discussion of the expected rate of inflation (para.
3.14). The average annual target real growth rate of GNP for the period is
6 percent, suggesting a lowering of the growth total below the 7.5 percent
targeted, and achieved, during the Seventh Plan. This rate of growth has two
origins. First, it is derived "in accordance with the goal of quadrupling
1980 GNP by the year 2000." As such, this is reminiscent of earlier targeting. However, it is later stated clearly that a moderate growth rate (by
Chinese standards) has been adopted in order to achieve demand-supply balance
and to control inflation. It is also hoped that such growth would derive from
efficiency gains, rather than by extensive developments. Thus, the Plan

emphasizes technical upgrading projects and projects annual labor productivity growth at 3.5 percent.

3.14   The projected sources of growth are very similar to those of the 7th Plan (in terms of projections if not outcome), with agricultural, industrial and tertiary sector output projected to grow by 3.5, 6.5 and 9 percent respectively. This implies two things in particular: first, agriculture would have to perform significantly better on a relative basis (ie. compared to industry) than in the 7th FYP period, with the GVIO:GVIA ratio at 1.86 instead of the outcome of 2.85; and industrial growth would have to be half the rate of 1986-90. The first of these is reflected in a strong emphasis on agricultural investment and agricultural services development, while the second is reflected in the emphasis on restructuring and renovation, rather than development of new enterprises.

3.15   The outline also provides other macroeconomic indicators, although with less elaboration. There is no explicit inflation target, but the Plan aims to limit credit expansion to 12 percent, which, given the 6 percent growth rate, implies a 6 percent inflation target. Within the credit target, loans for fixed investments are targeted to grow much faster (at 15.3 percent) than loans for working capital (11.7 percent). This implies that with only 8 percent of loans outstanding for fixed investments, this share would still be below 10 percent in 1995. There are no indications of monetary policies to be used to achieve this target, implying a continued reliance on administrative controls. In the same paragraph, the Plan notes the intention of reducing the fiscal deficit, by containing expenditure growth to 5.7 percent a year, while increasing revenue by 6.1 percent, given large recent deficits and the coming debt repayment peak. As this is apparently a target for nominal revenue and expenditure, it would imply continued decline in revenue and expenditure ratios to GNP. Since it is clear from other statements that the government's intention is in fact to raise "the two proportions"--the share of revenue in GNP and the share of central government in total revenue--this would seem to indicate an area where greater attention is warranted in future planning. It is quite possible that the public finance plan has been drawn up under a zero inflation assumption.

3.16   The Plan has a separate section on the external sector, and has qualitative targets for export growth, focusing on diversification of exports and increasing value-added, as well as policies for improving the institutional framework. There are, however, no quantitative targets for exports, or for the balance of payments. One of the strongest trends in the 1980s was the growth of trade at higher rates than the growth of GDP, together with moderate but steady growth in external borrowing. While it can be presumed that trade will continue to expand as a share of GDP (as it did in 1991), there is no statement of intent to this effect.

3.17   In terms of expenditure categories, various consumption level indicators are given, and two important quantitative targets: real wages are projected to grow at 2 percent per annum and farmers' income by 3.5 percent, while the total value of retail sales is projected to be 61.1 percent higher, which implies nominal consumption growth at 11 percent per annum, and real growth at 5 percent. Fixed investment, however, is only projected to grow by 5.7 percent per annum. Consistent with the emphasis on intensive rather than

extensive development, expansion investment is targeted to be limited to
2.1 percent growth and investment in new machinery to 9.8 percent per annum.
As will be seen in Chapter VI, these targets do not seem quite consistent,
especially in the light of the very large opening external surplus, so it
would seem likely to us that consumption will grow considerably faster than
the implied 5 percent, and indeed, faster than GDP.

3.18   There are two main conclusions to be drawn from a consideration of
this macroeconomic framework. First, it is clearly a realizable framework on
the basis of recent experience. Indeed, it would seem to err very much on the
conservative side, as have the last two plans, and there is every reason to
believe that growth would tend to be nearer the 7.5 percent mark of the last
plan than the more moderate growth projected by this plan,6/ and the rapid
expansion in 1991 would seem to support such a conclusion. Second, however,
while it is a somewhat more comprehensive framework than in previous plans, it
falls short of being a full description and analysis of expected macroeconomic
trends and policies, and, as such, continues to be of only limited information
benefit to the rest of the economy. In addition, we are already seeing a
repeat of the outcome of the 7th Plan: the framework calls for moderate growth
in the first year or so, but GDP grew by 7 percent in 1991, which considerably
undermines the credibility of the Plan's framework.

Development Strategy and Sectoral Priorities

3.19   The Plan describes the future development strategy on two levels.
At the general level, it focuses on major tasks and important targets; and it
describes sectoral priorities and programs as "department targets." In terms
of overall development strategy, the outline focuses on six priority sectors:
agriculture; basic industries; adjustment of the processing industry; electronics; services; and defense. It is on the basis of the structural adjustment and modernization of those sectors that the 8th FYP seeks to modernize
the economy overall, and cater for the changing needs of citizens. In
addition, the plan stresses the links between sectoral policies and policies
with respect to regional development, science, technology and education,
social services, and reform and "opening to the outside world." As noted
earlier, however, the plan is only an "outline" at this stage, so unlike
earlier plans, it does not contain tables of detailed targets for individual
subsectors. These may be published later--they are known to have been pre-
pared---or such details may be left to annual plans. However, we do know that
the priorities are reflected in investment allocations.7/

6/   Indeed, the government has recently revised its targets for the rest of
      this decade to about 10 percent per annum. This revision occured after
      this report had been initially issued.

7/   For example, state investment in energy is expected to rise from 30 per-
      cent of the total in the Seventh Plan to about 35 percent under the pre-
      sent plan, and transport and telecommunications are also expected to
      receive larger allocations of investment, with the share rising from
      15 percent under the previous plan to about 18 percent under the Eighth
      Plan (see Chapter V).

Table 3.1: 8th FYP OBJECTIVES AND TARGETS

Objective	Units p.a.	Average 1981-90	Actual 1990	Average 1991-95	Target (Average) 1995	1996-2000	2000
GNP (1990 prices)	Y bln.		1,740		2,325		3110
GNP growth	%	8.96/a		6	6	6	6
Population	Y bln.		1.143				
Population growth	%		1.25	1.25	1.25	1.25	
Labor Productivity	%		0.8	3.5	3.5	3.5	3.5
Urban Unemployment	%				<3.5		
Urban Employment			139.9				
Per capita	%			5	5		
Consumption growth							
Sectoral growth targets							
GVAO	Y bln.		738		878		
GVAO growth	%			3.5	3.5		
GVIO	Y bln.		2,385		3,270		
GVIO growth	%			6.5	6.5		
TVE output level	Y bln.		843		1,400		
Tertiary industry growth	%			9	9		
share of GNP			25				33
Energy cons.per Y 10,000 of GNP	std.coal tons		9.3		8.5		
Retail sales	Y bln.		825.5		1,330		
Revenue and Expenditure							
Revenue growth	%			6.1	6.1		
State Fixed	%			5.7	5.7		
Investment	Y bln.		445.1	2,600/a			
of which:	%			5.5	5.5		
by SOEs	Y bln.		292.7	1,700/a			
of which:							
CC /b	%			2.1	2.1		
CC /b	Y bln.		170.3	840/a			
TT /c	%			9.8	9.8		
TT /c	Y bln.		82.8	550/a			
Growth of expend. on agric., educ, defense, key projects, ST /d	%			5.7	5.7		

/a Items marked with asterisks refer to five year totals.
/b CC refers to capital construction investment.
/c TT to technical transformation.
/d ST refers to Science and Technology.

3.20   At the general level, there are six main strategic areas of focus to the development strategy, that are supportive of the general targets described earlier:

(a) Agriculture is re-emphasized as the most important sector of the economy, but with a new recognition of both the need for investment (especially in water conservancy) and the provision of agricultural

services, as well as a recognition of the key role of TVEs both in
supporting agriculture and in strengthening the rural economy;8/

(b) In industry, there is a clear emphasis on the perceived need to
balance development of basic industries with expansion of processing, and an implied analysis that it was the excessive growth of
processing industries relative to basic industries that led to the
problems of overheating in 1988;

(c) Efficiency improvements, especially in processing and in energy use
are thus seen as the key, rather than expansion of processing, and
this explains the tilted investment target;

(d) Electronics is the sole industrial subsector singled out at this
level, it being seen not only as a key product industry, but also as
the key process industry for improving technical efficiency in other
subsectors;

(e) Construction is identified as an important sector primarily in terms
of its relationship to housing and the achievement of the targets
for expanded availability of housing per person; and

(f) The tertiary sector is mentioned almost in passing, with its share
of GNP being targeted to rise from one quarter to one third (see
paras. 3.50-3.53 for a fuller discussion).

3.21   These general development principles are clearly consistent with the
macroeconomic strategy outlined, in that they follow logically from a desire
to avoid rapid growth of the economy through high levels of investment by new
facilities, focusing instead on avoiding bottlenecks and increasing the
efficiency of existing facilities. At the same time, such a strategy recognizes that, as incomes rise, so too does the demand for various urban services
and for improved quality of products. It is therefore to be expected that the
rest of the plan would outline the program, policies and projects to be put in
place to achieve the aims of this strategy. Reform policies are addressed in
Chapter IV, and the following sections focus on how the investment program and
industrial policies are to be used in this regard.

Investment Priorities and Financing

3.22   The long section of the Plan describing 'Department Tasks' covers
twelve separate areas, and is the part of the Plan which most closely
resembles traditional five year plans. Each section contains quantitative
targets--such as 500 million tons of grain in the year 2000--and gives some
indication of the policies and priority investment programs to achieve the
targets. Many of the priority investments to be implemented during this
period are identified, but it is not clear which such projects are to be
funded from the budget, and which are identified for priority funding from
other sources.

8/   The output of TVEs is projected to grow by about 11 percent a year in
real terms.

3.23   Since 1984 the investment system has been changed in a number of respects. The project approval process has increased the authority of local governments to approve investments below specified levels. At the same time, declining revenues have forced the central government to focus its investment expenditure on a few priority sectors such as energy and communications. Another result of the tighter budgetary revenue situation is that state investments are increasingly made in the form of credit allocations through the banking system rather than as straight budgetary allocations.[5] The creation of six State Investment Corporations in 1988 was meant to enhance the implementation of the state investment plan. Furthermore, in order to control total nonstate investment and its specific use, investments made out of local funds had to be deposited in the Construction Bank for six months before being used. Nonplan investments, other than those in energy, construction, transport and communication, schools and educational facilities, were subject to the construction tax.[6] With the exception of the construction tax, however, most measures featured extensive reliance on administrative controls.

3.24   The 8th FYP proposes investment of about 32 percent of GNP, implying total investment of Y 2,600 billion during the plan period. Of this amount, state investment will constitute about Y 1,700 billion--spread among "capital construction" (i.e., new capital stock investment) of Y 840 billion, "technology transformation" (upgrading existing plant and equipment) to the tune of Y 550 billion, and purchases of planes, ships, etc. (Y 310 billion). Capital construction of the SOEs is expected to grow at only 2.1 percent whereas their technology transformation will rise at 9.8 percent, indicating the priority given to restructuring existing state enterprises rather than setting up new ones. Capital construction projects are largely funded through the state budget whereas technical updating is funded out of the depreciation funds of enterprises as well as extrabudgetary funds.

3.25   Plan authorities estimate that central government will account for about Y 500 billion or 60 percent of the Y 840 billion projected for Capital Construction (CC) under the Eighth Plan. This share is higher than that under the Seventh Plan and reflects three factors:

(a) the creation of Capital Construction Funds financed by higher prices for oil, coal, transport and electricity. Although in principle these are extrabudgetary funds, the resources will effectively be controlled and directed by the central government;

(b) the introduction of the Investment Orientation Tax (IOT) to be levied on all investment (see paras. 3.31-3.34) which will both direct investment into preferred activities as well as generate revenue for the government; and

(c) increased budgetary direct investment.

3.26   The plan document is silent about how it is intended to fund the state investment program, and it is clear that there is no specific plan in this regard. Even the Y 500 billion of state capital construction investment alone will greatly exceed available budgetary revenues, which have provided only about Y 40 billion per annum for investment financing in recent years.9/ As is discussed further in Chapter IV, there are at present no proposals for serious fiscal reform during the 8th FYP period.

3.27   While the Ministry of Finance speaks of the need to arrest the decline both in total revenue as well as the center's share in the total ("the two proportions"), the stated targets belie this statement. The plan projects an annual rate of growth of revenue at rates similar to the present of 6.1 percent (apparently in nominal terms), and expenditure growth at a slower rate of 5.9 percent to reduce the deficit. This implies that the proportions will continue to fall, and that there will be an increasing reliance on industrial policy to guide investment lending by banks, and investment spending by enterprises. It also would suggest relatively little attention to this aspect of the plan, as falling revenues would be met with revenue measures to stem the decline, as has been the case in the last few years.

Use of Industrial Policies

3.28   Since 1989, China has been operating with what it refers to as a detailed industrial policy as a guide both for investment approval policy and for credit allocation. This was first approved in March 1989, and modified in July 1990. This is essentially a targeting policy, consisting of long lists of industrial subsectors and individual industrial products that fall into high, low and nil priority classifications, with the latter meaning no new approvals or credit. This policy has been a major instrument of economic management during the economic retrenchment program, as it was used to select investment projects for cancellation during this process. However, the policy suffers from three major defects:

(a)   It was highly administrative in nature, as it incorporated no economic instruments to effect the policy, and it was not linked to price, trade, fiscal or financial sector policies.

(b)   It was based only on present demand/supply balances, with little forward projection for future demand patterns.

(c)   It was essentially reactive not proactive, acting mainly as a deterrent against investment in low priority areas, but with little beyond exhortation for high priority areas.

3.29   This said, the policy was effective during the retrenchment program, and did provide some useful guidance to provincial-level planners faced with the need to administratively review and cut back investment. It thus served a function at that time, but once the economy had recovered from the "emergency" situation of 1988/89, the policy began to outlive its usefulness.

3.30   Guidance of investment via industrial policy is an important feature of the Eighth Plan, and this is a prime example of the Plan as a framework for decision making by others. While the policy will continue to consist

---

9/   This is not the same as the budget for capital construction, as the above numbers are on an ex post, national accounts basis.

essentially of target sectors and priority industries, which are being reviewed at the present time with a view to their simplification, several other features of such policies are now recognized:10/

(a) The key priorities should only be identified at the broader level, as, for example, the emphasis on basic industries, and there should only be a limited number of "priorities" if this is to be a meaningful concept;

(b) The main task for the administration in industrial policies is to create a favorable, competitive environment for the industrial enterprises, instead of pursuing "tilting" policies and using administrative instruments, and that as reform progresses, such administrative tilting policies can be removed;

(c) In strengthening infrastructure, the most important steps are to correct price distortions, both to remove investment disincentives and to generate investment funds;

(d) A major task identified for planning authorities is to identify enterprises operating below scale for merger, and to formulate adjustment programs for 'sunset' industries; and

(e) The need to identify major policy reform issues that can assist the industrial restructuring process.

3.31   Together with this recognition that industrial policy is much broader than the simple identification of high and low priority subsectors has come the use of more indirect instruments of implementation, and in particular, to supplement the administrative controls on investments with the use of taxation to influence its direction and volume, for which purpose, the govrnment introduced the Investment Orientation Tax (IOT) on April 16, 1991. The Investment Orientation Tax (IOT hereafter) 11/ schedule consists of a positive list of activities subject to one of three tax rates (0, 5 and 30 percent) on the value of capital construction. Any capital construction activity not explicitly mentioned in the regulation is subject to a 15 percent tax rate, and all technical transformation investment in activities that are not explicitly zero rated is subject to a 10 percent tax. In addition to the IOT, the preexisting "Table of State-Banned Development Projects" continues to prevent any investment in certain sectors. Only activities that are explicitly zero rated or exempted are not subject to the tax. Zero-rated items are primarily priority sector activities, while "fixed asset investments made by

---

10/   This section is drawn from the background papers prepared for the mission by the counterpart team, as the Outline does not describe the industrial policies explicitly.

11/   See Decree No. 82 of the State Council on Interim Regulations of the People's Republic Of China on Regulatory Tax Levied in Accordance with the Orientation of Investment in Fixed Assets. The Tax came into effect from 1991, and in the 1992 budget is projected to raise Y 3 billion.

Sino-foreign joint ventures, cooperative ventures and foreign enterprises" are granted a blanket exemption from the IOT.

3.32   Clearly, the IOT represents a significant new comprehensive tax instrument that attempts to achieve many objectives. It is first and foremost a means to strengthen the government's ability to define and implement industrial policy by discouraging investments below a certain scale and in certain lines of activity altogether. Since investment approval limits have in the past encouraged inefficient-scale investments by lower levels of government, this may be seen as a corrective tax. Secondly, it increases central control over the direction of investment by giving the government a more potent means of influencing the flows of extrabudgetary resources. Given the larger context where the center has seen its control over total resources decline, this may be seen as a way of reasserting central influence through indirect means. It should be noted, however, that it remains unclear how the tax revenue will be divided between the center and the localities.12/ Thirdly, it may be viewed as providing the government with a mechanism to control the volume of total investment and to moderate the appetite of enterprises for investment funds by raising the cost of capital. Fourth, despite uncertainties as to sharing arrangements, it creates a new source of revenue to the center, providing a much larger tax base than the extrabudgetary construction tax that it replaces. Given the scope of the tax and the many effects it is likely to generate, it also promises to be administratively challenging.

3.33   The IOT is a second best solution to the problems it seeks to address. It is an attempt to use one instrument to solve problems created by incorrect price signals, absence of fiscal instruments to control extrabudgetary resources, local protectionism and underpricing of capital. The obvious first observation to make is that this is a tall order for one instrument, and is very much a second best to more direct attention to these same issues, through price, tax, trade, commerce and interest rate reforms.

3.34   The other major observation is that by designing it as a positive list, many anomalies are bound to occur, and administration may become very heavy. The encouraging feature of the tax is that it is an attempt to use tax policy to replace administrative controls. However, as has been shown from recent experience with industrial policy, such instruments are most effective as deterrents. Therefore, consideration should be given to recasting this as a simpler, negative list of activities to which the tax would apply, or alternatively, as a much broader based positive list. However, even more important are two other factors with respect to the tax. Government should recognize that this is a second-best solution to the problem of investment incentives, which should therefore be temporary, until such time as the more fundamental reforms can be put in place; and secondly, use of an economic instrument such as this should replace administrative methods of controls (such as the imposition of policy lending on banks) and not merely be an overlay.

12/ The central authorities claimed that all the revenues would belong to the center, although this was disputed at the provincial level.

3.35   The macroeconomic framework, the development strategy and the formulation of policies to achieve those aims must be regarded as the critical elements of the Plan in the future if it is to perform its key function as a guiding framework against which others can formulate their own future plans. This review of these three aspects of the 8th FYP would suggest the following in broad terms;

(a) The framework appears to be sensible and realistic, but suffers from rather incomplete coverage, from a lack of exposition of macro-economic policies, and, more important, from a continued divorce between the framework as formulated and actual economic policy. Thus, the rapid growth being experienced in the first year of the Plan, and which is itself the consequence of the government's policy stance, significantly reduces the usefulness of the policy framework.

(b) Similarly, the development strategy as formulated seems to be sensible and to be consistent with the overall aims and targets. What is much less well developed, however, is any analysis of the policies necessary to achieve these strategies. For example, the aim is to bolster 'basic' industries and to restrict processing industries, but there is no related discussion of the pricing issues that give rise to such policies, nor the respective roles of central and local governments both in creating the present situation and in solving it in the future.

(c) The prospective role for industrial policy in the future and the proposed instruments of that policy are a clear advance on the past. With all the existing distortions in the economy there is a clear role for the state in correcting some of these. However, the balance of such policies will need to continue to shift in favor of a role for identifying and removing such distortions, with less emphasis on administrative counter-measures or over-laying distortions. This appears to be the intention of the planning authorities and it is hoped this trend will continue.

3.36   It is also clear from this discussion that further efforts in the area of investment system reform will be needed in the coming period. This is discussed further in Chapter IV (paras. 4.43-4.45). It is understood that the government is considering aligning the investment approval system more closely with the industrial policy, by liberalizing approval procedures for basic infrastructure projects and projects in industry which meet "efficiency" criteria, while tightening up, and centralizing certain other approval procedures, as was done in August 1990, when projects in various sectors—including automobile assembly—became subject to central approval regardless of project size. It is our view that the financing system also merits continued attention and reform (paras. 4.84-4.85).

3.37   While further rationalization of the approval procedures is sensible, it must also be recognized that in the area of productive investment, this is a form of correction for market failure and should be regarded as a transitory mechanism. The distorted price structure, undeveloped domestic market, trade protection, and soft budget constraint on enterprises mean that

administrative control of investment will continue to be necessary, for other-
wise there would continue to be sub-economic size investments. However, as
reforms in these four areas in particular proceed, so it should be possible to
relax or remove those administrative controls, leaving such investment decisions increasingly to the enterprises and financial institutions. This, in
turn, would permit increased attention in planning authorities to the new
roles of the state described in this chapter. A related aspect of investment
system reform that will continue to merit attention relates to center-local
relations, and the clarification of responsibility for investment in infrastructure by the various levels of government.

E. Planning to Correct Market Failures

3.38   As discussed earlier [para. 3.9(b)], correcting for market failures
is a new issue for Chinese planners, and one that will be of increasing importance over time. Although the 8th FYP does not discuss the issues in this
form, it lays particular stress on two particular aspects of market failure in
the Chinese context: regional development and employment generation. The
first reflects factor endowments, the lack of integration of the national
economy, and 7th Plan policies that favored coastal provinces; the second
reflects major imperfections in the labor market, and in particular, rigidities which increased the cost of labor [8].

Regional Development Issues

3.39   The pattern of regional development in China is the result of a
complex set of policies--notably center-local fiscal relations, pricing policies which act against raw material producing provinces, and planning policies
which give different degrees of autonomy in policy and decision making to
different provinces--in combination with fiscal compensation in the form of
state investments and subsidization of social services such as health, education and food distribution. The slant of such policies has varied greatly
over the various plan periods. [9]

3.40   More recently, since the Open Door policy was announced in 1979,
development strategy has featured a strong coastal bias. This found explicit
expression in the Coastal Development Strategy adopted by the CCP in 1988 and
in the Seventh Plan which described China in terms of Coastal, Central and
Western Regions and proposed a strategy that emphasized external trade and
technology import for the coastal regions (expansion of special economic
zones, open coastal cities, consumer goods and high-value industries), while
advocating focus on raw material production, technology upgrading and
agricultural development for the Central and Western regions. This strategy
was largely implemented by relying to a greater extent on local authorities to
use the freedoms provided by economic reforms and reduced mandatory planning
to fashion local development. This has resulted in differential rates of
economic growth, conflicts over access to resources, and tendencies towards
provincial protectionism. However, it is also clear that the strategy has
contributed significantly to the rapid growth rates of industrial output and,
especially export production in the last few years, not least by unleashing
entrepreneurial capacity and attracting investment and management expertise,
especially from Hong Kong.

3.41   Table 3.2 provides an indicator of shifts in regional emphasis by comparing the shares of state investment in the three regions during the Sixth

Table 3.2: PROVINCIAL ALLOCATION OF STATE INVESTMENT, 1981-90

Region	Province	1981-85 Volume	1981-85 Share	1986-90 Volume	1986-90 Share	% change
c	Beijing	24.374	4.6	60.582	4.8	6.0
c	Tianjin	18.366	3.4	33.491	2.7	-22.2/a
c	Hebei	24.931	4.7	48.426	3.9	-17.2/a
c	Liaoning	34.135	6.4	93.286	7.5	16.5/a
c	Shanghai	34.37	6.4	84.278	6.7	4.6
c	Jiangsu	24.198	4.5	61.881	4.9	9.0
c	Zhejiang	12.653	2.4	32.391	2.6	9.2
c	Fujian	10.302	1.9	25.681	2.1	6.3
c	Shandong	29.371	5.5	81.464	6.5	18.3/a
c	Guangdong	39.109	7.3	99.812	8.0	15.9/a
c	Guangxi	8.023	1.5	20.326	1.6	8.0
c	Hainan	-	-	6.669	0.5	-
	Coastal Total	259.832	48.74	648.287	51.86	6.4
m	Shanxi	19.468	3.7	39.289	3.1	-13.9
m	Inner Mongolia	12.479	2.3	21.157	1.7	-27.7/a
m	Jilin	12.771	2.4	29.091	2.3	-2.9
m	Heilongjiang	31.496	5.9	60.917	4.9	-17.5/a
m	Anhui	13.562	2.5	30.279	2.4	-4.8
m	Jiangxi	9.672	1.8	19.028	1.5	-16.1/a
m	Henan	22.106	4.1	47.26	3.8	-8.8
m	Hubei	21.171	4.0	41.088	3.3	-17.2/a
m	Hunan	14.238	2.7	30.071	2.4	-9.9
	Central Total	156.963	29.4	318.18	25.5	-13.6
w	Sichuan	28.3	5.3	68.338	5.5	3.0
w	Guizhou	7.465	1.4	15.038	1.2	-14.1
w	Yunnan	11.07	2.1	20.983	1.7	-19.2/a
w	Tibet	1.755	0.3	2.412	0.2	-41.4/a
w	Shaanxi	12.969	2.4	29.201	2.3	-4.0
w	Gansu	8.778	1.6	19.271	1.5	-6.4
w	Qinghai	5.253	1.0	9.301	0.7	-24.5/a
w	Ningxia	3.008	0.6	6.898	0.6	-2.2
w	Xinjiang	13.547	2.5	27.543	2.2	-13.3
	Western Total	92.145	17.3	198.985	15.9	-7.9
	Nonregion specific	24.108	4.5	79.402	6.4	40.4/a

and Seventh Plans. Under the Sixth Plan, which followed the open door policy and therefore already featured the coastal strategy, the 12 provinces that constitute the coastal region received almost half (48.7 percent) of total state investment, while the central region received about 30 percent and the west about 17 percent. In the Seventh Plan period, the share allocated to the coast increased by over three percentage points to about 52 percent, while the share of nonregion-specific investments rose by almost two percentage points. This reallocation came at the expense of the central region (whose share declined by four percentage points) and the west (decline of 1.4 percentage points). Investment shares therefore tend to support the rhetoric of the coastal strategy, reinforcing the advantages of greater use of market forces in these areas. Within the coastal region, some provinces (Shandong, Liaoning, Guangdong) have received the bulk of these investment increases while others (such as Tianjin and Hebei) have experienced sharp declines in their shares. Nevertheless, coastal provinces as a whole have had an increase in share of total investment, largely at the expense of central provinces such as Hubei, Jiangxi, Inner Mongolia, Shanxi, and Heilongjiang.

3.42   The issue of whether the coastal strategy and the different pace of economic reform in different provinces has increased regional disparity has been the subject of some analysis recently,[10] which is as yet inconclusive. However, two things are clear.

   (a)   The provinces with the highest rates of growth in recent years--
         Guangdong, Jiangsu, Hainan, Fujian, Shandong, Zhejiang--have been
         those favored by the coastal strategy and, more importantly, given
         the greatest latitude in economic reforms.

   (b)   There is a perception among Chinese officials that regional dispari-
         ties have increased over the period of the 7th FYP.

3.43   The 8th FYP has a large section devoted to regional policy, but whereas the 7th FYP had a clear emphasis on regional policy as an instrument of the overall development policy through the accelerated development of coastal areas, this is not the case with this Plan. Rather, the regional policy component of the plan is a clear compromise in that it has policies for development in coastal, inland, minority and poor areas, and, in this sense, advocates an absence of regional favoritism, and instead a set of regional development strategies tailored to the needs of the regions. While the coastal strategy remains important, it is clear that these areas are no longer to be given administrative or financial advantages over other provinces.

3.44   The strategy for the inland provinces calls for them to specialize in natural resource based industries. In some instances this will require the relocation "in a planned manner" of industries from coastal to inland regions. For example, cities like Shanghai are looking for ways to switch from the textile industry which may be better located in cotton-growing provinces such as Henan. The coastal region will continue to provide access to new technology and generate the surpluses needed for development of the interior provinces. The Pudong zone in Shanghai is the most important manifestation of this strategy. Box 3.2 illustrates how this strategy is manifested in the five-year plans of two important Chinese provinces: Henan, an interior province that has hitherto served as an important natural resource base, and Jiangsu, a coastal province that has developed rapidly on the back of the TVE sector that has seized the opportunities made available by economic reforms.

3.45   However, the outline does not specify the instruments that are to be used in this process. It recognizes the need to correct distortions that have led to "the present irrational situation characterized by regional separation, market blockade and pursuit of regional self-sufficiency." It, however, does little to recognize the causes for this situation. Moreover, the proposed solution of "relocating" industries has a clear suggestion of the use of planning mechanisms to solve the problem. The experience of, for example,

Box 3.2: DEVELOPMENT PLANS IN AN INTERIOR AND A COASTAL PROVINCE

Background. Both Jiangsu and Henan are populous provinces with 1990 populations of 67.7 and 86.5 million, respectively. Both are important sources of national output of grain and cotton. However, the two provinces differ in important respects including the fact that per capita GNP in Henan is approximately half that in Jiangsu. Structural differences are also significant: Jiangsu sees itself as a "processing economy" with a relatively large industrial base (with an increasingly significant TVE sector) and a stock of skilled labor that is dependent on other provinces for important raw materials and energy. Henan, on the other hand, is rich in resources (including energy) but feels the need to develop its industrial base in downstream activities. The cotton textile industry provides a good illustration of the difference in level of industrialization of the two provinces. While Henan produces 15 percent of the national output of cotton, its share in the production of yarn is only 6.8 percent while its share of cloth production is less than 6 percent. Jiangsu, on the other hand, produces about 10 percent of China's cotton output but has a higher share of yarn production (14.7 percent) and cloth production (14.6 percent). Finally, the central plan has remained a significant instrument of policy in Henan given the importance of coal, crude oil and cotton to central procurement. Plan procurement prices for these items have served to transfer resources out of Henan, stunting its development potential.

Table 1 indicates the growth targets for the two provinces. It indicates Henan's Eighth Plan slogan of "One High and One Low" which symbolizes the province's intention to achieve output growth higher than the national target and to control population growth rates to a level lower than the national target. Jiangsu's targets for GNP, NI and population are close to the national targets, although GVIO growth is pegged at a higher level.

Table 1: EIGHTH PLAN TARGETS IN HENAN AND JIANGSU

Growth rates	Henan	Jiangsu	China
GNP	6.5	6.0	6.0
NI	6.0	5.0	5.0
Population	0.98	1.2	1.25
GVIO	8.0	8.0	6.5
GVAO	3.5	3.0	3.5

Source: State and Provincial Planning Commissions.

The two provincial plans do not suggest any significant difference in provincial development policy and appear to support the contention of the center that, rather than an explicit regional bias, this plan features an emphasis on integrating markets as a means of promoting development of lagging regions. Henan is in the process of forming a trading zone with five neighboring provinces (Shanxi, Anhui, Hunan, Hubei and Jiangxi) to reduce interprovincial barriers while Jiangsu is focused on integrating its economy more closely with the proposed Pudong Development Zone in particular and with Shanghai in general. Both Henan and Jiangsu stress the role of industrial policy and this is seen to be consistent with central guidance. Henan's development plan focuses on the development of downstream industries in petrochemicals, nonferrous metals, electronics, machinery, food processing, and textiles as a means to capture value added that is currently lost to other provinces such as Jiangsu. Jiangsu stresses the achievement of grain and cotton output targets as well as the development of transport and energy infrastructure which are seen as bottlenecks on further development.

In the area of reforms, Jiangsu intends to promote industrial restructuring by encouraging the development of ten large enterprise groups but has few other initiatives. Surprisingly, Henan, an interior province that, by the admission of provincial authorities, has not pushed reforms in the past, appears to be more active now. Experiments are designed to improve the enterprise CRS system, to separate profits and taxes, to promote shareholding, and reforms to the rural household responsibility system, social security, etc. are also in experimental process.

European countries with similar regional policies merits study in this regard, for it has been very expensive in terms of budget resources, without being noticeably effective.

3.46   Instead, the government should be looking to the positive aspects of the implementation of the coastal development strategy to address most of the issues involved in growing regional disparities, to the extent that they are growing. The areas of the country that have lagged behind are in the central area and in the northeast. These can be characterized as follows:

   (a)   They are producers of raw materials or of major capital goods. In the former, prices are held low, and in both, the level of the mandatory plan remains relatively high.

   (b)   They have been given fewer freedoms to set economic policy, including policies toward the outside world.

   (c)   Their industrial sectors are dominated by state-owned industries, and in particular, those still managed centrally.

   (d)   They tend to be self-reliant for their fiscal revenues, although losing profits of SOEs to the center.

The potential benefits to the inland provinces of planned relocation would seem to be very small in comparison with the potential benefits from having the center address those few key issues. In this sense, the development plan is of less critical interest to the inland provinces than the reform plan, which is addressed in the following chapter.

Employment Creation and the Services Sector

3.47   Absorbing a large number of new entrants to the labor market is one of the major tasks facing planners in the Eighth Plan period. China's labor force has been growing faster (2.5 percent per annum) than the population as a result of the age structure, and the size of the employed labor force is expected to rise from its current level of 570 million in 1990 to 640 million by 1995, adding 20 million to urban employment and swelling rural employment to 470 million. About 7 of the 20 million additional urban workers are expected to be the result of in-migration from rural areas.

3.48   Planners estimate the extent of surplus labor (open and disguised unemployed) in China in 1990 at about 29 percent of the total workforce.13/ The Eighth Plan target is to reduce the extent of surplus labor to about 23 percent by 1995 (Table 3.3). This implies that an additional 88 million jobs have to be created during the eighth plan period--absorbing 68 of the 70 million new entrants while also reducing rural disguised unemployment by 20 million. Urban open unemployment, which is critical to political stability, is expected to rise from 4 to 6 million, with the unemployment rate

_____

13/   For comparative projections in this area, see World Bank (1992) "China: Strategies for Reducing Poverty in the 1990s", report No. 10409-CHA, esp. pages 49-56.

Table 3.3: LABOR AND EMPLOYMENT UNDER EIGHTH PLAN
(millions)

	1990	1995
Total employed labor force	570	640
Urban	150	170
Rural	420	470
Surplus Labor	164	146
Urban unemployed	4	6
Urban underemployed	20	20
Rural underemployed	140	120

Source: SPC.

expected to rise from its current 2.7 percent level to no more than 3.5 percent in 1995.

3.49   Significantly, urban disguised unemployment is expected to remain unchanged, suggesting that there will be little or no attempt to improve industrial efficiency by reducing overstaffing and featherbedding. Moreover, given the problems with the statistical coverage of the floating population, the unemployment estimates must be taken as an underestimate of the actual rate of open unemployment in China.

3.50   The magnitude of the employment creation task that faces China cannot be exaggerated and the realism of the targets can only be assessed against China's own performance in recent years. China's employed labor force increased from an estimated 402 million in 1978 to 570 million in 1990, a growth of 168 million in 12 years implying a rate of growth of 2.5 percent per annum. Before the effect of the retrenchment policies slowed employment growth, agricultural employment grew by 1.3 percent per annum while nonagricultural employment increased at 6.3 percent annually over the period 1978-88. Overall employment grew at 3 percent per annum, exceeding the rate of growth of the labor force and allowing some rural to urban labor transfer.14/ The average annual rate of employment growth over the period 1980-89 in the primary, secondary and tertiary sectors has averaged 1.4, 5.5 and 8.6 percent, respectively. This indicates a significant shift towards service sector employment relative to rates of 2, 6.3 and 2.5 percent over the period 1957-79.[11] As Table 3.4 indicates, the employment elasticity of GNP has been highest in the tertiary sector and lowest in the primary sector which is known to feature sizable underemployment.

14/ See Judith Bannister, China's Population Changes and the Economy, in Joint Economic Committee Study Papers, 1991.

Table 3.4: EMPLOYMENT ELASTICITY OF GNP BY SECTORS,
1980-89

	Primary	Secondary	Tertiary
Employment growth	1.4	5.5	8.6
GNP growth	5.4	10.7	11.15
Elasticity	0.26	0.51	0.77

3.51   If the targeted growth rates for the primary, secondary and tertiary
industry are achieved, the employment creation target should be
attained.15/   Table 3.5 provides illustrative calculations. More than half
the projected new jobs are in the service sector. The key question is whether
the projected 9 percent growth in the service sector can be achieved, and the
policies needed to achieve it.

Table 3.5: POSSIBLE EMPLOYMENT GROWTH, 1991-95

	Labor force 1990 (millions)	Planned sector growth 1991-95 (%)	Employment growth 1991-95 /a (%)	Labor force 1995 (millions)	New job 1991-95 (millions)
Primary	340	18.8	4.9	357	17
Secondary	122	37.0	18.9	145	23
Tertiary	105	53.9	41.6	149	44
Total	567	34.0	14.8 (2.8 p.a.)	651	84

/a Sector growth and elasticity from Table 3.7.

3.52   As noted, overall economic growth is expected to average about
6 percent, while the service (tertiary) sector is designated to grow at
average annual rates of 9 percent. Of the 18 million new jobs that are to be

15/ It should be noted in addition that China's elasticities of employment
     creation bear a close resemblance to those of other economies. For exam-
     ple, for South Korea, Taiwan and Singapore over the period 1960-70,
     employment elasticities in industry were 0.5, the same as China's, and at
     a relevant stage of their development. Evidence from Latin America sug-
     gests an elasticity for the tertiary sector of close to unity.

created to absorb urban labor growth, 12.5 million are expected to be in service sector occupations.16/ Recent years have seen the rapid growth of employment in the service sector (at rates in excess of 5 percent) although the share of this sector in total employment in China (21 percent) remains well below the levels in other labor abundant countries such as India (38 percent) and Indonesia (40 percent).17/ Similarly, the share of the service sector in GDP in China is well below levels for a wide range of countries, as shown in Table 3.6.

3.53   Nevertheless, service sector GNP growth over the period 1980-89 has been very rapid, averaging 11.15 percent while, correspondingly, the secondary sector grew at 10.7 percent and the primary sector averaged 5.4 percent, reflecting partially the low base from which it started. The share of the service sector in real GNP has risen from 21 percent in 1980, to 23 percent in 1985, and 24 percent in 1990, but much more rapidly as a share of nominal GNP, as real wages have increased. As Table 3.7 indicates, the service sector has rapidly increased its share over the period at the expense of both the primary and secondary sectors. The present plan's projections for the high growth of the tertiary (service) sector extend its resemblance to the Seventh Plan. The service sector is targeted to grow faster than the primary and secondary sectors, raising its share in nominal GNP from 27 percent in 1990 to 30 percent in 1995.

3.54   Although the policy framework to support this growth has not been spelled out, the authorities indicated that favorable policies towards this sector are being designed and will be announced in 1992.18/ In May 1991, the State Council formed a Tertiary Sector Development Office to design policies to facilitate service sector development, and this group recently submit-

---

16/   SPC staffers estimate that a one percentage point increase in tertiary industry share of GNP will provide employment for 15 million. Increasing tertiary share from 27 percent in 1990 to 31 percent by 1995 as planned will therefore provide 50-60 million jobs. These calculations are consistent with those in Table 3.4.

17/   While some service sector activities are classified under industry in China, this does not significantly affect the estimate of the sector's share of employment. Moreover, in such an international comparison, unrecorded service sector workers in China are less numerous than in India and Indonesia and would tend to offset any bias due to misclassification. See "China: Reforming the Urban Employment and Wage System," Report No. 10266-CHA, World Bank, 1992. It should be noted that the measurement of service sector GNP is subject to problems of coverage and classification which also affects the accuracy of growth estimates for the sector. See "China: Statistical System in Transition," Report No. 9557-CHA, World Bank, 1991, for a detailed discussion of the methodological issues involved in GNP measurement in China.

18/   In fact, just as this report was being finalized for publication, the State Council and the Central Committee of the Communist Party of China issued its "Decision on Speeding Up the Development of the Tertiary Industry," on June 16, 1992.

Table 3.6: SHARE OF SERVICES IN CURRENT GDP
IN SELECTED COUNTRIES, 1965-90

	1965	1990
India	34	41
Indonesia	31	39
Thailand	45	47
Turkey	41	48
Mexico	59	59
Brazil	48	48
Yugoslavia	35	48
Korea	37	46
Japan	46	56
United States	59	69
Low income (except China/India	37	39
Middle income	45	50
China	17	20

Source: World Development Report, 1991

Table 3.7: SECTORAL COMPOSITION OF CHINA'S GNP, 1979-90

Year	Total	Primary	Secondary	Tertiary
1979	100.0	31.5	47.9	20.7
1984	100.0	33.0	44.6	22.4
1988	100.0	27.3	46.9	25.7
1990	100.0	27.5	45.3	27.2

Source: Statistical Appendix, Table A2.10.

ted its proposals to the State Council for approval. In the short term, this
group is putting forward policies that favor employment generating tertiary
industry, and service industries which "promote the market," as well as policies to promote the "socialization of public facilities." However, it is
expected that tertiary sector promotion will be primarily delegated to local
governments. In particular, it is expected that the TVE sector, which has
hitherto been concentrated in light industrial manufacturing, may have a
greater focus on service sector activities. This is suggested by projected
rates of growth of tertiary sector output of TVEs of 15 percent per annum,
compared to secondary sector output growth of 11.4 percent.[12]

3.55   Perhaps the most important policy action is to create an "enabling"
environment that supports private initiative in the provision of business and

consumer services. Policy actions in this area will have to focus on developing the institutional capacity and the regulations to guide market based development. Among the key steps in this area would seem to be the following:

(a) Licensing systems for the service sector should be rapid and efficient, especially for retail and personal services, including open and efficient systems for enforcing zoning, health and hygiene regulations.

(b) Creation of institutional arrangements for the provision of access to credit (at commercial rates) for small-scale and individual enterprises in the service sector.

(c) An aggressive program of removal of service provision from government and state-owned enterprises, with the consequent divestiture or contracting of such services to small and individual enterprises.

(d) The provision of vocational educational training skills and the creation of certification agencies to provide the essential labor skills needed, especially in such areas as office technology, repair and consumer services.

F. Planning for the State Sector

3.56   The third strand in planning is that of planning for the state sector, and especially for the provision of infrastructure to relieve or prevent bottlenecks, and this is addressed in the case of transport in Chapter V. However, in China, production continues to be dominated by state-owned enterprises, so the question becomes a wider one than merely the provision of infrastructure. It is to be noted, however, that the SOEs' share of industrial output has fallen dramatically from 65 percent in 1985 to 55 percent in 1990, with the share of individual enterprise and joint ventures rising from 3 percent to 10 percent, and this is paralleled by a rise in the share of light industry from 47 percent to 50 percent.

3.57   Such changes notwithstanding, significant structural problems remain. State enterprises have experienced declining profitability in the face of increased competition. Between 1985 and 1990, the proportion of SOEs that were unprofitable increased from 10.7 percent to 31.5 percent. Pretax net profit of SOEs as a proportion of sales revenue declined from 24 to 10 percent correspondingly. In large part, it must be acknowledged, this is the result of the strong recession of 1989/90, but it also reflects the effects of competition in shrinking profit margins, relative price changes and structural inefficiency in the state industrial sector.

3.58   The 8th FYP and ten-year program envision a continued key role for the state-owned enterprises as the "backbone" or "core" enterprises. The emphasis is on technology, investments and on enterprise reform to "revitalize" the SOEs, and to make "the overwhelming majority become socialist commodity producers," which means state-owned enterprises operating within a market framework. As discussed further in Chapter IV, it is in this sense that China

<u>Table 3.8</u>: PERFORMANCE OF INDUSTRIAL SOEs IN CENTRAL BUDGET

	1985	1988	1989	1990
Proportion of loss-making SOEs	10.7	12.2	16.3	31.5
Net pretax profit as % of revenue	23.8	18.7	15.8	10.4
Retained profit as % of net profit	18.3	18.5	16.7	15.3

Source: China Statistics Abstract, p. 87.

is maintaining its socialist stance, as the plan defines the essence of socialism as being the continued "dominance" of the SOEs.<u>19</u>/

3.59   The latest government initiative ("Eleven Measures to Revitalize the Medium and Large SOEs") defines some additional instruments to revive these-enterprises (see Box 3.3).<u>20</u>/ Among the measures are some that will impact favorably on efficiency by improving the economic environment for the SOEs. These include measures to reduce the share of mandatory quotas (item 2), the granting of direct foreign trading rights for enterprises (item 7), and efforts to reduce the burden of ad hoc levies and administrative interventions on enterprises (item 9). The attempt to adjust depreciation rates would also be a useful policy if it were applied in a nondiscriminatory way and with reference to the economic rate of depreciation of the assets. Other measures, such as those providing preferential interest rates and allocations of working capital, will have the effect of replacing an explicit subsidy to loss-making firms with numerous hidden subsidies, which should be avoided as it would reduce the visibility of the problem. Recent statements have also emphasized the need to restructure unviable enterprises or shut them down, if necessary.

<u>19</u>/ It should be noted, however, that more recent statements have taken a more moderate approach, closer to "market socialism". This question is likely to be revisited during the 14th Party Congress in late 1992.

<u>20</u>/ A recent decision by the State Council replaces the existing Production Committee with a Production Office headed by a Vice-Premier. The new Office has wide ranging powers to put this set of "revitalizing" policies into effect through its authority to set production targets (along with the SPC), influence material distribution, "coordinate" different sectors, "guide" enterprises on improving management, technical renovation, etc. This implies a strong reliance on administrative measures to address the problems of the SOEs. It should also be noted that the "Eleven Measures" were endorsed and extended by the Eighth Plenary Session of the 13th Central Committee, but this did not materially affect the main measures to be adopted, although it gave further impetus to the initiative. In June 1992, this office was renamed the "State Council Economic and Trade Office".

Box 3.3: ELEVEN MEASURES TO REVITALIZE SOEs

1. Preferential treatment regarding retention of revenue from over-stocked goods and allocation of earmarked bank credit for renovation.

2. Reduction of mandatory plan quotas for selected enterprises with additional revenue to be earmarked for technical renovation.

3. Higher depreciation rates for selected enterprises (total revenue Y 3 billion) not subject to energy and transportation tax or budgetary regulation fund.

4. Higher retention rates on technical renovation fund for selected enterprises involved in new product development.

5. Y 40 billion increase in working capital for some enterprises--provided by local and central government and enterprises themselves (?).

6. Preferential interest rates on loans for enterprises in priority activities.

7. Granting foreign trading rights to some enterprises.

8. Double guarantee for 234 enterprises.

9. Reduce and clear debts of enterprises. (?) (chain debts)

10. Form enterprise groups--100 pilot enterprise groups.

11. Reduce enterprise burden--eliminate ad hoc levies, reduce inspections and many meetings.

Source: China Daily, May 1991.

3.60   These policies also illustrate the prevalence of the view that investment and better technology is a panacea for the most diverse problems. These attempts to "revitalize" industries and enterprises abound with calls to increase investment and improve product quality, reflecting faith in capital-intensive solutions.

3.61   This issue of industrial restructuring, especially of SOEs, is a complex one, beyond the boundaries of this report, but is raised here as a prime example of a planning issue for the future. While the task of restructuring SOEs must depend on improved market signals, it may also benefit from an activist role for the state, in areas where markets either fail or do not (yet) exist. The experience of Japan is useful in this regard and suggests a role for the government and industry cartels in managing declining industries and in switching factors to more profitable activities. It is instructive that such intervention typically <u>assisted</u> rather than <u>resisted</u> the process of structural adjustment and focused on training and redeploying labor and scrapping or mothballing equipment and plant, thus assisting industries and workers through the necessary adjustments.[13] While the management of declining industries is a major feature of policy in Japan, industrial restructuring has focused also on "modernization," "upgrading" and "structural improvement" of small and medium enterprises. It should also be stressed, however, that at all stages, the door was gently but firmly shut on nonviable enterprises and industries after all organizational solutions were found to be inadequate.

G. Conclusions and Issues for Future Plans

3.62   This chapter has reviewed the evolving role of planning in China, and has assessed the 8th Plan in the light of the role of the state in a reformed economy. In general, the present plan can be considered an advance upon past plans, in that it focuses on the macroeconomic framework and on policies--especially economic system reforms, as discussed in the next chapter--which are to be adopted to achieve the aims and targets of the plan. Nevertheless, in terms of the three roles for planning that have been suggested, the assessment would suggest three areas in particular where efforts would seem to be warranted.

(a) The Macroeconomic Framework. While certain indicators about expected macroeconomic trends are presented, it is less than clear how such indicators have been derived. For example, the overall growth rate of 6 percent is <u>substantially</u> below the level of the 1980s, despite the fact that efficiency is expected to improve. However, 6 percent is the level necessary to achieve the target of redoubling 1980's GNP by the year 2000, so the suspicion remains that this is a <u>target</u>, rather than a macroeconomic assessment. Moreover, the absence of a framework for the external sector, or for monetary and fiscal policy reduces the usefulness of the framework that exists. As with the case of the 7th FYP, the first two years of the plan is seeing expansion, and government policy to that end, which is well above the planned level. Therefore, more effort is required to integrate the process of macroeconomic assessment and policy formulation into the planning process, or else such frameworks will continue to be of little use in their main function as a source of information to the nongovernment sector. Notably, if the plan analysis had called for a moderate initial growth period in 1991-92, this should have been reflected in tighter monetary policies and a less aggressive expansion of public investment. More generally, the key role of the state is to foster a climate of macroeconomic stability within which economic agents can operate. The 1980s saw periods of quite severe instability in China and of "stop-go" policies, and one of the challenges for the planning authorities in the 1990s will be to improve macroeconomic planning and coordination and to strengthen the instruments of macroeconomic management, as discussed more in the following chapter.

(b) The Policy Framework. The continued decline in the role of materials allocation and in the availability of fiscal resources for capital investment mean that the plan will have to be increasingly concerned with policy formulation, and especially policies for market

failure. While some progress has been made in this area, we
observed in two major policy areas--employment generation and
regional income generation--that the plan has made more progress in
problem identification than in identification of solutions or policies. Rather, such issues are also being addressed as a targeting
issue--as with employment--or via planning solutions. For example,
the role of the tertiary sector as a potential source of new employment was identified, but without clear indications of policies to be
used to promote it. Increasingly, it will be the responsibility of
planning authorities to find solutions to these market failures that
are more compatible with the use of markets or which correct the
distortion rather than overlaying additional distortions in attempts
to correct them. In addition, the planning authorities will also
have to move forward in the area of planning the policy framework.
Examples of policy areas where central actions may be appropriate
are:

(i)   improving the functioning of industrial markets, either by
       removing restrictions such as licensing or by moving to elimi-
       nate monopolies or provincial protectionism;

(ii)   planning for the opening up of domestic industry to foreign
       trade, and for the impact of reduced protection and greater
       openness on the structure of production;

(iii) establishing the new legal framework that will gradually
       replace administrative management of the economy. This relates
       in particular to the relative absence of legislation governing
       the enterprise sector, especially with regard to accounting,
       auditing and property rights; and

(iv)   fostering institutions for technological development and
       absorption. Instead of planning for technological upgrading of
       individual enterprises, the planning authorities should instead
       focus on creating institutions involved in "technological
       extension services," and on systems of standards, testing and
       certification.

(c) The State Sector. The Plan continues to have large elements of
     targeting of outputs that are outside the state sector, and so long
     as this continues, large parts of the plan will be irrelevant.
     Therefore, those parts of the Plan concerned with sectoral issues
     will need to focus increasingly on planning for those sectors that
     remain primarily under state control, such as economic infrastruc-
     ture, and sector planning will have to be increasingly concerned
     with analyzing the demand of others for such economic services, and
     not simply the demand of the state sector for inputs. Of particular
     importance in this regard is "investing in people" and the role of
     the state in provision of education, whose share in government
     expenditure will need to rise in the future.

3.63   This means that while the 8th FYP has made progress, it falls far
short of providing the sort of planning framework appropriate to the needs of
the reformed Chinese economy, and it will probably prove ex post, to have been

of little more relevance to actual events than was the 7th Plan. Nevertheless, some of the improvements are encouraging and are in the right direction, and during the process of carrying out this analysis it was evident that many of the staff in the planning authorities recognized its weaknesses and the need for further planning system reforms, and for the further integration of the planning process and the reform process, as discussed in the following chapter.

IV. THE REFORM PLAN

A. Introduction

4.1   In Chapter II of this report, we assessed the impact that China's reform has had on its economy, and the major areas where more attention seemed to be necessary. We concluded that the approaches to reform in the 1990s, including both reform design and speed, were likely to be key determinants of the performance of the Chinese economy in the coming decade. Moreover, with the official completion of the 1988-91 rectification program, there is a new emphasis on economic reform by Chinese leaders, as shown most clearly in recent speeches by Deng Xiaoping, and by the decisions of the recently concluded Fifth Session of the Seventh National People's Congress.

4.2   The preparation of the development plan and reform plan offers an opportunity to assess the government's current reform intentions. Indeed, it should be stressed that it is itself a significant reform that the 8th FYP consists fundamentally of a development strategy and accompanying set of macroeconomic targets, and a reform plan, or more generally a policy framework to achieve these targets, and this is a very welcome change of approach. However, care should be taken in assessing this plan, as it remains very much a strategic outline, and much remains to be worked out in terms of details, timing and sequencing. The reform should thus be regarded as a statement of reform intentions at the time of plan preparation, not as a fixed blueprint for action. The reform program in China is very much an evolving process, and, as we have seen, the relative stress on reform issues can change quite rapidly. This said, the recent debate has been concerned essentially with the speed of reform implementation, with as yet, little indication of changes in design.

4.3   This is not to say that reforms did not continue during the rectification program, and these are reviewed briefly in paras. 4.4-4.11. Although these are perhaps less deep reforms than might have been desired, it is notable that the government felt able to move on reform issues at all during this period of retrenchment, and to move on certain areas--such as grain and transport pricing--that had scarcely been touched in the previous 35 years. However, these reforms were essentially ones which were supportive of the aims of the retrenchment program, notably measures to reduce government price and trade subsidies. The success in overcoming inflation and the overheated economy created ideal conditions of stability within which to launch a bold program of reform, especially to tackle the more deep-rooted issues that generate improvements in economic efficiency. The question to be addressed in assessing the policy framework for the 1990s is the extent to which the government is signaling its intention to seize this opportunity.

B. Reform in 1989-91

4.4   Reform measures introduced in 1989-91 may be grouped into two categories. The first is the continuation of reforms that started before the austerity policy was adopted. This included experiments with the separation of profits and taxes for SOEs, and with the tax-sharing system between the center and provinces for their fiscal relationships. These experiments were extended to 1,800 SOEs and 27 cities. There were also some improvements in the contract responsibility system of the SOEs when the second round of contracts were negotiated in 1990 and 1991, and by now over 90 percent of these contracts have been renewed. However, the improvements were primarily related to performance indicators, and fell far short of the goal of separation of profits and taxes, that could render greater autonomy and independence for the SOEs. In Shenzhen and in other major cities, limited experiments with joint-stock enterprises continued, and some existing SOEs were converted into joint-stock enterprises.

4.5   Stock exchanges were established in Shenzhen and Shanghai, with counters in some smaller cities, with active trading of part of the issued shares of a very limited number of listed companies, including joint ventures. The trading was originally highly restricted and localized. Shanghai inaugurated a Western-style open stock exchange in 1990, with Shenzhen following in May 1991. It was the initial intention that these would only serve as experiments in the localities concerned. However, more recently it has been decided to permit enterprises from anywhere in China be listed on the Shanghai exchange, and from the whole of South China in Shenzhen. However, the number of listed companies remains extremely small (less than twenty, relatively small companies in each). The related development was that in December 1991 the first "B" shares were issued in Shanghai, which are for holding by foreigners. The year 1991 also saw an expanded role for foreign banks in China, with new branches opening in Shanghai, Pudong and Hainan, with similar spheres of operation to the present branches of foreign banks in the special economic zones.

4.6   Since 1988 foreign exchange adjustment centers (FEACs) have been operating at provincial and subprovincial levels all over China, with a national center in Beijing. One major limitation to the impact of the FEACs was that local governments and enterprises, both Chinese and foreign-invested ones, did not have the liberty to trade outside the adjustment centers in their locality, while only central government organizations and local governments were able to trade foreign exchange at the national center. In 1990, local rates and the national average rate were quoted publicly to provide traders at each local center information about rates at other centers, and this created a gradual tendency towards a unification of rates at the many local adjustment centers of the nation. As noted in Chapter I, the volume of transactions on the FEACs rose dramatically in 1990 and again in 1991.

4.7   Another round of foreign trade reform was formulated to replace the existing contract system that expired at the end of 1990. Two major measures increased the separation of foreign trade enterprises from government control and helped to foster competition among foreign trade enterprises. The first was the abolition of export subsidies from central budgetary sources.1/ The second was to unify the retention ratios of foreign exchange earnings of all localities. In the past, the large differential in retention ratios among foreign trade enterprises was the main source of rent-seeking behavior in the foreign trade sector. Artificially high retention ratios represented a partial devaluation of the Chinese currency for foreign trade enterprises in

---

1/ Import subsidies had been mostly removed in earlier reforms.

specific localities, and this tended to compensate their low efficiency and penalize other highly efficient enterprises that were unfortunately located in low retention ratio areas.2/ By unifying retention ratios, a major area of administrative intervention in the operation of China's foreign trade enterprises was removed, and this can be classified as a reform to "level the playing field."

4.8   The other reform area that saw renewed emphasis and expanded experimentation during this period was in social reform. In particular, there has been a renewed emphasis on both housing and social security. In those two cases, we see a classic demonstration of China's new reform style (see para. 4.63), in that there have been national guidelines on the approach to these two areas of reform approved by the State Council in the latter half of 1991, followed by reform experiments designed and implemented at the local level. Thus, the housing reform decision at the national level emphasized inter alia the adjustment of rents, and the creation of new institutions to generate funds for housing construction and purchase. Beijing Municipality has emphasized the former, doubling housing rents in January 1992, while Shanghai has focused on the latter, introducing a forced savings scheme designed to emulate Singapore's Provident Fund.

4.9   The second group was reform measures that served or formed part of the austerity policy. The most notable of these was the aggressive use of indirect instruments of monetary policy, including interest rates, in reducing inflationary pressures in 1988/89. The impact of the index-linked deposits introduced in 1988 on retail sales and savings in 1989/90 clearly demonstrated the power of this indirect policy instrument. Although the austerity policy began with a heavy reliance on administrative means, the success of monetary policy in suppressing aggregate demand and inflation gained in importance, and this shift towards indirect means of macroeconomic management should be seen as an unexpected reform achievement in the austerity period.

4.10   Various price adjustments were made in 1989-91 at the same time as the government attempted to stop excessive fluctuations in market prices by imposing administratively set ceilings or controlled price ranges, and these were listed in Table 1.5. The price reform program has two elements: price adjustments are when the government adjusts by administrative fiat the level of prices for commodities or services subject to price control; and price liberalization is when government price control (or guidance) is lifted, leaving prices to be determined by the market. During the first phase of price reform in 1984-87, the emphasis was on price liberalization, and most consumer goods are now regulated by market forces. However, during that period, prices of intermediate goods and of government-provided services (such as transport and housing) were largely unchanged, and it has therefore been in this area that most emphasis has been placed during the rectification program. These price adjustments have served three useful purposes:

2/   The new retention ratios are somewhat complex. The basis, however, is that 20 percent of foreign exchange earnings have to be surrendered at the official rate, and the central government has a right to buy a further 30 percent at the FEAC rate, except in those sectors that maintain higher ratios, such as electronics.

(a) They reduced the gap between the market price and planned price of the same product under the two-tier price system by raising the planned price.

(b) The relative prices of raw materials and services, which had been kept at an artificially low level, were raised.

(c) Within certain sectors, relative prices of related products were distorted by the plan and by dissimilar characteristics of the two-tier system each was subject to, and the price adjustments corrected irrationality in relative prices. An example of this is the relative rise of railway freight rates compared to trucking in 1990.

4.11   While the price adjustments did not render the price system more market-oriented, and the frequent use of administrative adjustments might be seen to have delayed the more urgently needed market liberalization, they were compatible with the anti-inflationary aim of the austerity policy, by reducing fiscal pressures. At the same time, they represented improvements in the price system that reduce obstacles to a more genuine price reform at a later date, in particular by reducing differentials in the two-tier price structure.

C. The Reform Plan

4.12   The reform plan which comes as an integral part of the 8th FYP and the Ten-Year Development Program focuses on six main areas, and these are described in paras. 4.18-4.57 below. First, however, it is important to attempt to understand the guiding principles of the reform strategy, in order to see how these specific reform proposals fit into that strategy.

The Guiding Principle of the "Integration of Plan and Market"

4.13   The general objective of the reform plan is described as being to "initially establish a new system based on the socialist planned commodity economy and an economic operating mechanism which integrates the planned economy with market regulation."[3/] The question of the relative roles and meaning of the plan and the market in China has caused great debate among Chinese economic circles in the last two years, and great confusion among outside observers. The reform plan and related background documents attempt to clarify this concept, and bring some specificity to what has appeared to be a compromise generalization.

4.14   First, it is stressed that the differences between "plan" and "market" are not the same thing as the differences between capitalism and socialism. "Planning" in socialist countries has come to be associated with mandatory allocation of resources, while "market" is associated with private ownership of property and with Western-style democratic institutions. It is these stylizations that the Chinese model is attempting to reject and redefine. In the reformed Chinese economy, the role of planning is essentially a macroeconomic regulation function, and especially of ensuring "balance" and

---

3/ Decision of the 7th Plenum of the 13th CCP.

stability in economic development, while the role of the market is in micro-economic resource allocation.

4.15   Therefore, planning will essentially deal with drawing up medium- and long-term plans for the economy at the aggregate level, and develop policies and operate indirect economic instruments to ensure balance between the major sectors and ratios, notably overall supply and demand, the proportion of various sectors such as industry, agriculture and services, fiscal balance, the external accounts and the price level. However, in a few sectors, specifically "those products and construction projects vital to the national economy and people's livelihood," it is envisaged that the system of command planning and allocation of resources by administrative means should have a larger role to play. This said, it is the clear intention that even this level of mandatory planning should be conducted on a more reasonable basis than the past, with the emphasis on the placement of contract orders for commodities rather than a command plan. Market regulation would therefore guide the majority of production activities at the microeconomic level.

4.16   What must be clearly understood, however, is that "socialist" refers to the public ownership of the means of production. While China is prepared to tolerate and experiment with various forms of ownership, there is currently no intention to alter the situation in which the state or collectives dominate ownership, and there is therefore no discussion in any of the documents of the concept of privatization of SOEs. Rather, there are a set of proposals for how the ownership, regulatory and management functions can be separated more effectively, and how the state can exercise its ownership function in a more rational and "arm's length" way. This insistence on the role of public ownership continues to distinguish the Chinese approach to economic reform from the approach in Eastern and Central Europe more than anything else.

4.17   Therefore, this concept of the meaning of "planned commodity economy" and of integrating planning and market must be seen as the core of the reform effort in China, and each of the specific reform measures discussed in the following paragraphs must be seen in the way that they contribute to the achievement of this target. For example, how well reforms in finance and taxation contribute to the aim of equipping the planning authorities with the necessary regulatory instruments, and how well the price reform proposals would strengthen the ability of the market to allocate resources rationally.

Enterprise Reform

4.18   The future of the large- and medium-sized state-owned enterprises continues to dominate the thinking of policymakers in China, and enterprise reform is at the very heart of the reform program. This is the area where all other reforms--price, fiscal, finance, investment, planning, labor and trade--come together. The Eighth Plenary Session of the 13th CCP in December 1991 renewed the emphasis on further enterprise reform, and on the "revitalization" of the SOEs, not least through efforts to "push the enterprises to the market." The declared aim of the reform is to create a dynamic and efficient system of management and budget constraints for SOEs while preserving the nature of their public ownership. Five main reform approaches have been identified.

(a) <u>Contract Responsibility System</u>. This system, which was implemented in 1988 for three years, is being renewed with minor changes, such as adjustments to the contracted base and remittance ratios and substituting profit with a more comprehensive index as the main target of the contract. The second contract for the SOEs will last for another three to four years and it means the basic enterprise system would not be changed before the Ninth Plan period. By late 1991, over 90 percent of contracted enterprises had negotiated and signed these new contracts.

(b) <u>Separation of Taxation and Profits</u>. This experiment is being extended to a larger number of SOEs and is being accelerated in 1992. With the separation, contracts between the enterprise and the government are made on an after-tax basis, so that taxes have to be paid first before any repayment of principle of loans, or profit remittance. To compensate for higher taxable income, enterprise profit taxes are lowered to 33 percent under the experiments, which also serves the purpose of lowering the gap in tax rate between SOEs and other types of nonstate-owned enterprises. This change is designed to be tax-neutral. Every province now has designated a city where this system is to be tried out during the 8th FYP period, and it is being applied at the national level on a sector-by-sector approach.

(c) <u>Joint-Stock Enterprises</u>. Experiments with the conversion of SOEs into joint-stock enterprises are continuing, and are to be conducted on a larger, but still limited, scale. The forms of joint-stock enterprises include the issuing of shares to legal persons (enterprises), employees and to the public, as well as a combination of these. A company law for limited companies will be introduced in 1992/93 by the government, which will give a uniform legal framework for the various forms of joint stock enterprises.4/ This would permit trading in shares held by enterprises. However, this is not expected to be a generalized form for enterprises, as it is considered that "conditions are not ripe to translate this into reality," so 8th FYP activity in this regard will essentially be preparatory.

(d) <u>Enterprise Groups</u>. The government has encouraged leasing and sales of small SOEs and mergers, contracting, and take-overs among other larger SOEs. These have been undertaken in earlier years as an alternative to bankruptcy as well as a genuine attempt to allow property transfer. In the process, some enterprise groups have been formed. However, they generally lack clarity over ownership rights and they are not governed by a set of well-defined regulations or legislation. The new initiative of the reform plan for the 1990s is to set up a different type of enterprise group. The government has begun to form 100 such groups at the national level from among large central and local SOEs. Each of them is being empowered to engage

4/ In fact, several regulations on the management of joint stock companies, and issuance of shares were approved by the State Council on May 15, 1992.

in industrial, trading and even foreign trade and finance activities that will not be restricted by present regulations, or by the administrative jurisdiction of ministries and local governments. They are also being dissociated one by one from their present administering authorities in the government, so as to become fully independent and competitive. These enterprise groups will remain publicly owned, but with a joint-stock ownership system that allows shareholding by government organizations, enterprises outside and inside the group, employees and outside individuals. It has also been suggested that after the completion of the formation of the 100 national enterprise groups, local governments will be encouraged to form more localized enterprise groups in the same way. It is to be noted that each group has one "core" enterprise around which others will be linked either "closely" or "loosely."5/ While, to date, each such enterprise is a large or medium SOE, the possibility that this would be a collective or a TVE has not been ruled out.

(e) Restructuring and Bankruptcy. The government recognizes the problems that derive from the present structure of the SOEs, including product mix, technology, internal organization, plant size, etc. Many such enterprises inefficiently produce goods that no one wants to purchase. Renewed efforts are being made, especially via the Production Office, to reorient these enterprises towards new products and markets, and by subjecting them to merger via enterprise groups. However, after proving unwilling to resort to bankruptcy in the rectification period, this is now recognized again as one instrument of enterprise reform, albeit only to be used as a last resort.6/ The Economic and Trade Office has a target of declaring 2,000 SOEs bankrupt in 1992, and it is understood that about half this number suspended operations in the first quarter of 1992. It is clear, therefore, that restructuring rather than bankruptcy will be the policy to be stressed.

Ownership Reform

4.19 As noted earlier, ownership reform does not refer to privatization of public enterprises. Rather the authorities recognize three challenges in ownership reform: finding better ways to represent the state ownership function and separate ownership from management; diversifying state ownership in order to dilute sectoral or provincial interests; and promoting alternative ownership forms. These have received different degrees of attention in the plan.

5/ This is similar to the Western concept of economies of scale and of scope. "Close" links are in the same sector, vertically or horizontally, while "loose" links provide economies in management and finance.

6/ "For the sake of the workers and administrative staff, we should try to have unsuccessful enterprises shift to a different lin eof production or merge with others, rather than suspending operations or closing down." Report of the Work of Government delivered by Premier Li Peng to 5th Session of 7th NPC on March 20, 1992.

4.20   The first challenge may be taken up by the institutional development
of holding companies and investment companies. Six state investment corporations were set up in 1988 under the SPC, but they are yet to assume the functions of investment agents on behalf of the central government. In the eyes
of the government, the present time is still one for the preparatory stage of
checking the assets of SOEs, and for defining their property rights and financial responsibilities. No attempt is planned to extend the number of investment companies to beyond the existing six, but there is to be an attempt to
convert them into holding companies whose role and functions are yet to be
defined.

4.21   However, in a less planned manner, mainly because of the inadequate
financing ability of the central government, a considerable number of the key
investment projects approved under the Development Plan will take the form of
joint-stock companies. Central and local governments, large SOEs and individuals are eligible as shareholders of these companies. Although such a method
does not fully separate investment functions from the government, it allows
large SOEs to assume the role of investors and to cross sectoral and provincial boundaries. Participation by individuals would provide the basis for a
later conversion of the companies into ones that would be listed in stock
exchanges for their shares to be publicly transferrable.

4.22   The 100 national enterprise groups that can operate across sectoral
and local boundaries are also another institutional development that serves to
diversify state ownership. Given their right to invest in new projects and in
other enterprises, the core enterprises of these groups may evolve into holding companies representing diversified local, sectoral and individual interests.

4.23   As for the development of alternative ownership forms, the Chinese
government has already promulgated regulations governing collective and private enterprises. These nonstate-owned enterprises will be promoted further
in the 1990s alongside with foreign-invested enterprises, but the reform plan
is essentially silent with respect to changes in the policy framework for
these enterprises.

Price Reform and Market Development

4.24   The Chinese government has decided, on the basis of the failed comprehensive price reforms of 1985 and 1988, not to attempt any further comprehensive reform of a "shock therapy" style. Price reform will therefore proceed in steps, with the government paying more attention to its possible
impact on economic and social stability. Nevertheless, it will be a major
focus of attention during the first half of the 8th FYP. In general, price
reform is seen to provide a mixed or dual management system, in which a few
strategic and important products and services are still to be priced by the
government while the rest will be freed, subject only to market forces. The
reform in the 1990s is to reduce further the scope of government pricing and
to put into place the mixed system in the second half of the 1990s. It
includes the following:

    (a) Adjustment of Prices of Important Raw Materials. This means the
         raising of the planned prices of these products, including coal and

oil, so as to narrow the gap between planned prices and market prices with the aim of eventually merging the two prices and abolishing the two-tier price system. Indeed, as noted earlier, this is the area that has seen particular progress in the last two years. Prices of some raw materials, e.g., oil, are to be adjusted to approach international prices. However, no schedule is set for the abolition of the two-tier system, nor for removing the partial planning control over prices of these products.

(b) <u>Adjustment of Prices of Infrastructural Facilities and Urban Services</u>. Partly this is in order to reduce or remove government subsidies, and partly it is hoped that the increased revenues from price adjustments would provide capital for investment in these sectors, as described further in Chapter V.

(c) <u>Adjustment of Agricultural Procurement Prices</u>. This refers to price increases for those products still under government purchase arrangements, like foodgrains, edible oils, cotton, sugar, tobacco and silk cocoons. An average 18 percent increase in grain prices for 1992 was announced on April 1, 1992. For foodgrains and edible oils, there will also be a similar rise in their selling prices to urban residents under the government rationing system to "do away with the irrationality of selling prices lower than state purchasing prices." It is hoped that by mid-1990s they will approximate market prices, and there are signs that this target may be reached sooner. The prices of grain to consumers were raised 45 percent on April 1, making the total adjustment 144 percent in one year. This equalizes procurement and selling prices, although it does not cover the heavy distribution costs, although deeper experiments in moving to a market system are being launched in Guangdong and Hainan.

(d) Besides the above three categories of products and services that will continue to be subject to government control, prices of the rest, including consumer durables that are still under some form of pricing regulation, are being gradually liberalized, starting with those that had been liberalized earlier, but were temporarily "deliberalized" in 1989.

4.25   Progress in price reform is also, by necessity, being accompanied by reforms of the domestic trading system, particularly in the case of trade in capital and intermediate goods. The trading system in China includes two parts, the system of distribution that is being transformed gradually from administrative redistribution into allocation by markets, and the trading enterprises that have operated within the system.

4.26   Reform in the distribution system has proceeded quite rapidly. Consumer goods are mostly allocated through markets and even raw materials and intermediate goods that have long been under strict planning controls have over 50 percent of transactions being conducted in markets. The next reform is to set up specialized markets for trading in large volumes and in futures. These include the national trading centers in agricultural products in Zhengzhou, in nonferrous metals in Shanghai, and other more localized markets like those in Suzhou, Shenyang, and Shenzhen. More will be set up to substitute the former planned distribution networks and the present ad hoc trading fairs, with properly managed permanent trading centers or specialized markets that handle futures. To avoid unnecessary fluctuations in these markets, the Ministry of Materials is beginning to experiment with active trading via government-controlled buffer-stocks of industrial goods to balance market demand and supply. The recently set-up State Reserve of Food Grains has also given the government a means to stabilize prices at grain trading centers.

4.27   Most agricultural products (in number) have already been taken out of government's direct pricing and distribution controls. Even foodgrains and edible oils are traded in markets for production over and above the amount contracted for government procurement. However, four cash crops--cotton, sugar, tobacco and silk cocoons--are still under exclusive pricing and distribution control of the government. It is planned that the central government will first stabilize its procurement amount and allow local governments to use the surplus for intergovernmental barter trade. This is certainly far from being market exchange, but it is a significant breakthrough that might lead to further erosion of central government's monopoly of these cash crops, paving the way for some degree of allocation by market forces.

4.28   In the past, relatively little attention has been paid to the reform of the trading enterprises, but this is beginning to change. At present, the Chinese market has been demarcated administratively into three segments, those managed respectively by government's commerce, materials allocation and foreign trade departments. Trading enterprises are also defined administratively as commercial enterprises, materials allocation enterprises and foreign trade enterprises and their operations are strictly restricted to only one of the three segments. The recent reforms that allow trading enterprises greater autonomy and more market sales have taken place mostly within each segment.

4.29   Since 1990, the Ministry of Materials has begun an experiment with comprehensive trading enterprise groups. The two enterprise groups chosen in Suzhou and Shenyang were originally materials allocation enterprises, but the experiment, which was approved by the central government, granted them additional scope of operation, including trading in consumer goods, that had previously been restricted to commercial enterprises, as well as finance and other services. They are also promised rights to engage in foreign trade and direct foreign investment.

4.30   These experimental enterprise groups are structured as joint-stock companies. For instance, the Suzhou one has more than one third of its shares subscribed by 58 national and local SOEs, including branches of state banks. As such, they are not directly controlled by any one government department. The aim of the experiment is to use the enterprise groups to break down the present market segmentation. The above experiment is also accompanied by the engagement of many materials allocation enterprises in border areas to begin actually participating in foreign trade, and the forming of joint ventures with foreign companies and foreign trade enterprises to overcome the restriction on foreign trade.

4.31   This experiment with comprehensive trading enterprise groups will become part of the central government's scheme of 100 enterprise groups. It will add a new dimension of reform of the trading system to the scheme. The reform in this area is not well-planned and coordinated, but could neverthe-less begin a chain reaction to liberalize the highly segmented market, and be instrumental in breaking the monopolistic grip of the central ministries over the three segments of the market.

Macroeconomic Management

4.32   A key target of the reform plan is to establish a macroeconomic regulation system "which combines direct and indirect regulation with the emphasis on the latter, and central and provincial regulation with the empha-sis on the former" (Chen Jinhua, 1991). The role of planning was discussed earlier (paras. 4.13-4.17), reflecting the declining role of mandatory plan-ning and growing role for guidance plans and policy planning. The following paragraphs discuss the other key reforms in the area of public finance, bank-ing and investment.

4.33   It should also be noted that a major strand of the reform program is to increase the role of the legal system, and a wide range of economic laws and regulations are scheduled to be implemented to standardize and codify reform measures. These include laws on planning, budget, banking, investment, company law, pricing, markets, labor, wages, auditing, monopoly and illegal competition, social security and management of state assets. All these are to be formulated within the Eighth Plan period.

(a) Public Finance

4.34   No major changes have been proposed to the enterprise contract responsibility system or the fiscal contract system, and therefore no major taxation reforms can be expected, although the tax system will continue to be developed. The only exception to this could be with respect to the large- and medium-sized SOEs, where it is intended, as noted, to speed up the separation of taxes and profits, lowering the tax rate to 33 percent. The value-added tax will be extended to industrial production and wholesale trading. This is intended to broaden the tax base and to distribute tax burdens more equitably. A special consumption tax will be applied to a selected number of commodities to enforce governments' industrial and consumption policies, and the coverage of the resources tax will be broadened with the aim of reducing waste in the use of scarce natural resources.

4.35   All these represent individual attempts to improve and reform the tax system. A more concerted effort is said to be going to be given to apply-ing a uniform tax rate to enterprises of different ownership forms that are at present under widely different rates of profit or income taxes. The same is said of the proposal to separate the collection and management of taxation. However, neither has been substantiated with concrete steps and explicit time-tables. Without a coordinated framework for reforming the taxation system, the introduction of new taxes or enlarging the scope of existing taxes look more like efforts primarily aimed at increasing revenues to meet fiscal needs of the government, and it is not clear how they can fit within the contract responsibility framework, until the separation of taxes and profits is put into effect.

4.36   The government will adopt several measures to strengthen its control over revenue collection. One is to remove part of the power of local governments in cutting or exempting taxes. The other is to increase the central government's supervision over tax collection. Unfortunately, the latter falls short of the development of a national tax service by the central government. Nevertheless, they represent steps toward the establishment of a more standard, less arbitrary tax system under central administration. Another reform measure in this area is the adoption of a double budgeting system at the central and provincial levels of government. The capital budget is separated from the current budget, and the government aims to attain a balance in current incomes and expenditures. This "double budgeting" system was introduced in the 1992 budget presentation as a first step, although this was essentially a presentational change.

4.37   The more significant public finance reform relates to the fiscal relationships between central and local governments. This is often regarded as one of the most difficult areas of reform, as fiscal relationships have political implications. Any change to the existing pattern will involve a redistribution of revenues between the center and localities that would change their respective capacity in investment and economic control. The present fiscal contract responsibility system is not a uniform system, as provinces are assigned different contract amounts or ratios of remittance or subsidies. Either the contracted amount or the ratio is a product of negotiations that is inevitably arbitrary in nature.

4.38   There have been proposals to replace the present fiscal contract responsibility system with less arbitrary and more predictable arrangements. However, this system is tied in with the enterprise contract responsibility system, as revenues from enterprises, either in the form of profit remittance or taxes, are used as the base for the calculation of revenue-sharing under the fiscal contract. In fact, in the discussion about the fate of the fiscal contract system in Fall 1990, provincial authorities used the signing of the second round of enterprise contracts as a reason against its abolition. Despite the obvious shortcomings of the fiscal contract and the central government's determination to raise its share of fiscal revenues, opposition from local governments was successful in extending the term of the present fiscal contract system for one more year until the end of 1991, and it seems unlikely that the fiscal contract system would be completely abandoned during the 8th FYP period. The alternative for the reform is the experiment with a tax-sharing system, a method of "getting enterprises to divert taxes and. profits into different channels," which involves identifying different taxes which will "belong" to the central and local governments, respectively, and those which are still to be shared, such as product taxes. It will be tried out in a number of provinces and municipalities, including notably Zheijiang, Xinjiang and Tianjin from 1992, and will be for national application in the second half of the 1990s.[7]

7/   In May 1992, the State Council approved "Measures to Experiment with the Tax Separation System."

(b) Banking Reform

4.39   Reform in this area lies in two areas: the strengthening of the macroeconomic regulation functions of the central bank and the setting up of a competitive and efficient commercial banking and insurance system. Regulation by the central bank through more indirect means such as the use of reserve money management, base discount rate and open-market operations will be increased, although direct controls are unlikely to be abandoned in the near term. This is to be strengthened through the passing of various laws and regulations, including a banking law. In addition, the branches of the PBC will have reduced rights to issue credit to the rest of the banking system.

4.40   Commercial banks are being asked to "explore" a separation of policy lending and commercial lending. However, there is no suggestion that this should go beyond accounting and application of different appraisal methodologies. The main thrust of reform in the coming years will be the gradual setting up of proportional management of assets and liabilities and an assets risk management system.

4.41   The revival of the Bank of Communications (BOCOM) in 1987 and the creation of the CITIC Industrial Bank in 1988 introduced new competitors for the specialized banks. In 1991, BOCOM formed a subsidiary insurance company that became the second insurance company, and poses the first direct challenge to the monopoly of the People's Insurance Company. Other insurance companies of a specialized or local nature will also be set up to enhance the degree of competition and specialization in the insurance business, but "state organs are forbidden to engage in insurance."

4.42   While there appear to be few intended structural or institutional changes to the state banking system during the period of the Plans, a process of financial deepening is being pushed forward. This should be seen as part of the process of "pushing enterprises to the market" by increasing the direct reliance of enterprises on the capital market for financing, rather than relying on banks for such financing. The interbank market and FEACs, which at present operate only at the provincial level, under the guidance of local PBC branches, will be linked up in national networks. More bonds and stocks will be issued, and there are to be experiments with investment funds. There will be an expansion of the number of housing finance facilities to accompany housing reform, albeit primarily within existing institutions. Retirement insurance funds have also begun to be set up to supplement the social security reform. Stock exchanges may be established in cities other than Shanghai and Shenzhen and might be partially open to overseas investors, through the expanded issuance of the recently introduced "B" shares, the dividends and sale proceeds from which can be exchanged for foreign exchange in the FEACs.8/ The sales of treasury bonds will continue to be partly handled by commercial banks and even nonbanking institutions, as was initiated in 1991, and the range of maturities may be extended to include treasury bills of less

---

8/   There continues to be considerable variation in the degree of enthusiasm for development in shares and stock exchanges. While some regard it as the most important direction, others remain dubious and concerned about unleashing the forces of speculation.

than one year. Treasury bonds held by enterprises may follow the example of those held by individuals and be permitted to be traded on the secondary market.

(c) Investment System

4.43   The investment system has already been radically reformed during the past decade, so the coming period will see smaller changes. However, three changes are envisaged. First, the continuing decline of budget finance is foreseen, although there will continue to be a large state investment program. Therefore, the state will continue to impose a high volume of "policy lending" on financial institutions and provincial governments.

4.44   Secondly, the government will reform its control over investment in two ways. The first was discussed in Chapter II, the introduction of the Investment Orientation Tax. Second, the present system of approval authority will be revised from its present one of limits by project value (or production capacity addition) to one whereby power and management are determined for different industries according to the industrial policies. Thus, low-priority projects of all sizes would have to be approved centrally, while high-priority projects of any size could be approved locally.

4.45   It was already noted that the six investment corporations may become holding companies. The plan also notes the intention to set up specialized long-term investment banks charged with fund-raising through bond issues for long-term investment in the State's priority projects. It is not clear how these two proposals would coexist. Finally, although not included in the reform plan, there continues to be discussion about the conversion of the People's Construction Bank of China away from its present main role of channeling budget funds towards becoming a national development bank.

Social Sector Reforms

4.46   To facilitate and in response to enterprise reform, which aims to create a system of independent, efficient and competitive enterprises, including SOEs, the traditional system of permanent state employment with a uniform national wage system has to be reformed. Enterprises, government departments and public organizations will each have their own wage systems. The wage system of enterprises will gradually change from a uniform grading system to one based on job and skill requirements. It is intended that the present level of nonwage benefits will be converted into wages, but the change will be coordinated with the progress of reforms in price, housing and medical insurance.

4.47   Housing reform has been experimented with for some time and there is now a major initiative to extend it to the whole nation, and with a lot of progress in this particular reform area in recent months. However, as presently being implemented, it will not turn subsidized housing into fully-fledged commercial housing for fear of social instability. The core of the housing reform being implemented in the short term is to raise the present low rental to one that would cover the costs of maintenance, management, depreciation, interest payments and property taxes. The whole process is being put in place in stages and full completion is scheduled to take ten years. At the same time, publicly owned housing may be sold to state employees at a discount, but the offer of a discounted price will give the government or enterprise a claim to part of the ownership. It is hoped that 20 percent of the present housing stock can be commercialized during the 8th FYP. To facilitate house purchases, various schemes of housing savings, bonds, mortgage loans, and insurance are being introduced and expanded. The government is also encouraging the establishment of housing funds and housing cooperatives for the development of private housing. In addition, there is a suggestion for experimentation with saving banks for housing. Shanghai has put forth a more complicated housing reform proposal.9/ However, it includes compulsory purchases of bonds and obligatory provident funds, both representing forms of forced savings.

4.48   The other area of reform that converts nonwage benefits into wages is the social security reform, and a set of national guidelines was published in October 1991. The proclaimed direction of the reform is to move away from the present enterprise base system to a national system funded by contributions from the state, enterprises and individuals. As a first step, old-age pension insurance is being introduced in Jiangxi, Guangdong, Shanghai, Dalian and Qingdao. Unemployment insurance will also be experimented with in a larger number of cities, while comprehensive social security reform will be introduced first in Special Economic Zones like Hainan and Shenzhen. In the meantime, most cities have introduced some form of pension pooling for contract workers. It is anticipated that these social sector reforms will begin to be implemented relatively early in the plan period.

External Sector Reform

4.49   A new round of foreign trade reform was completed in early 1991, involving the abolition of all export subsidies and most of the import subsidies, and equalization of retention ratios. The new foreign trade reform is based on contracts of 3-4 years' duration. During the terms of the contracts, it is difficult to expect any drastic alteration to be made to the contracts, and thus to the contractual relationship between foreign trade enterprises and the government. The contracts preserve the exclusive right of the enterprises to engage in foreign trade, but this also turns round to restrict their scope of business only to the foreign trade area. Within the confines of the contract system, but probably as a potential threat to the preservation of the system, is the encouragement given to the formation of foreign trade enterprise groups that will be multiproduct, multifunction and internationalized in nature. These enterprise groups will also be the model organizational form to be adopted by joint ventures of foreign trade enterprises and industrial, agricultural and other enterprises, and industrial enterprises that are granted direct trade rights in the overseas market. Interestingly, the reform plan makes no mention of any kind of reforms in the import regime.

4.50   However, while the broad institutional arrangements seem relatively fixed in the short-term, there are signs of movement with respect to incentives. The Chinese government has launched a renewed effort to resume its

---

9/   See IBRD Report No. 9222-CHA, "Urban Housing Reform: Issues and Implementation Options" for a fuller discussion, esp. paras. 2.10-2.14.

seat in the GATT, negotiations for which began in mid-1986, but which have been stalled since June 1989. Recently the Minister for Foreign Economic Relations and Trade signalled 10/ the government's intention to reduce the scope of import licensing by two-thirds, to reduce tariffs further (tariffs on some 225 items were reduced in January 1991) and to make all import regulations transparent by publishing them. As noted, this area was not included in the plan, and clearly represents a major push to complete the GATT negotiations successfully.

4.51   In the area of exchange rate policy, 1991 has already seen the practice of a managed floating rate system. The Reform Plan says that this should lead to "favorable conditions for the abolition of the dual exchange rate." In the meantime, as noted, it is hoped to remove barriers to the creation of a national market basis for the adjustment centers.

Rural Reform

4.52   The Chinese government plans to further deepen rural reform in the coming decade. Along with "revitalization of SOEs," agricultural development was the second major focus of the 8th Plenary Session of the 13th CCP. There are two major areas of reform that may be considered as part of the reform deepening process.

4.53   The first is to establish a two-tier management system for agricultural production that would combine both centralization and decentralization. The individual household contract responsibility system will be retained as the decentralized part of the management system. There is no dispute about it and no attempt to alter it, with the exception of a highly restricted call for collective farming in areas that demand an appropriate level of scale production, and when the farmers themselves voluntarily opt for it.

4.54   However, in many parts of the country, a gradual change in the contract responsibility system has been underway in the last few years. In these localities, farmers are now allocated two or three types of plots. One is allocated equally for everyone in the village community, similar to the private plots they were given during the People's Commune period. This type of plot is fixed and will not be open to reallocation. It is subject only to the agricultural tax. The second type is the "responsibility" plots that may be reallocated. These are contracted to individuals or individual households or via contracts that are open for bidding. Those taking up the contracts are required to pay, in addition to agricultural tax, grain in kind to fulfill the government's procurement quotas, and contributions to collective expenses that are administered by rural cadres. When there is a third type of plot, they are open for bidding, and the income from these contracts constitutes a main source of revenue for collective expenses in villages.

4.55   This change in the contract responsibility system is a further example of the "bottom-up" approach to reform, in that it has been carried out mostly at local (or local cadres') initiative, and has become quite extensive in the countryside. By imposing obligatory contributions to collective

_____

10/   People's Daily, January 16, 1992.

expenses by farmers taking up plots under contract (with the likely sanction of taking away the plots from farmers who do not pay the contributions), local cadres are given a mechanism to extract payment in kind or in cash from farmers for fulfilling their procurement assignment from the state, and for building up once again collective organizations and/or a collective economy at the village level.

4.56   One of the reasons given for the two-tier rural management system is to provide farmers better services in the rural sector. It is now considered that this can be achieved without a recollectivization of land or a collective rural economy that is tied to collective control over land. Examples within the Agricultural Experiment Zones show that farmers can be organized together through cooperatives on a share-capital basis to develop specialized services in the countryside without the need for land collectivization, and the emphasis in this regard has clearly shifted of late to the provision of collective services funded through village taxation schemes, such as the one described above, through cost recovery, or through central funding.

4.57   The other area of reform in the rural sector is with respect to the distribution system for agricultural products. Wholesale markets--some including futures contracts--at national, regional and local levels have been set up recently and will be increased further. The government plans to set up reserves of cotton, edible oils, sugar, pork, wool and rubber in addition to that of foodgrain formed in 1990, to be used as the resource base for government's intervention in wholesale markets to maintain price stability. It also plans in the first few years of the 8th FYP to abolish procurement contracts for sugar and oil and remove restrictions on their sale. Towards the end of the 8th FYP, it hopes to decontrol prices of all agricultural products other than foodgrain and cotton. Sales in agricultural products will then be determined by market forces.

D.   The Implied Shape of the Reformed Chinese Economy

4.58   The reform plan for the 1990s as described above is an ambitious program of reform across the entire spectrum of economic policies. As noted earlier, while the recently renewed emphasis on reform may alter the speed with which these changes are put in place, it as yet does not seem to question the basic design as set out in the Plan. However, beyond the general slogan of "planned socialist commodity economy," no clear description is made of the sort of economy that is being designed. Indeed, one of the characteristic features of government policy during the last three years has been the absence of any clear vision for the end-target of reform, and the ad hoc nature of decision-making. The preparation of the plan in a relatively comprehensive version permits us to interpret the implications of the plan, if fully implemented over the ten-year horizon.

4.59   The various reform plans in the six areas described have three common themes:

(a) To reduce the reliance on administrative means of economic management by the government and to increase the use of indirect instruments.

(b) To develop the nascent market into a unified and competitive one.

(c) To reform the state-owned enterprises, including by the formation of enterprise groups that are relieved of administrative controls and constraints and enjoy economies of scale and scope.

When these three themes are applied to each of the main reform areas, we get the sort of picture described 11/ in Box 4.1.

4.60   The key question to be addressed is how far this plan would go towards creating a vital, efficient economy. It seems to us that the ultimate difference between the implied future Chinese economy and a "Western" market economy is revealed in three areas: ownership of large-industrial enterprises; the role of the banking system; and the role of the external sector. Enterprises would continue to be state-owned, and subject to government influence. In view of this, and of the government's view of the banks' role as supporters of the government's industrial policy, banks would be expected to maintain a high level of policy lending; and because of the nationalistic nature of Chinese socialism, it appears that policymakers find it hard to assign a role for the external sector as a source of competition, instead of merely a source of capital, technology and demand for exports. While some softening has been seen in import policy in recent months (para. 4.50), this appears to be motivated more by concerns governing international relations than a different attitude to the role of the external sector.

4.61   In short, the fundamental difference between the Chinese reform approach and other reforming socialist economies has little to do with speed or with the design of most institutions or the role of prices, but it comes down as noted (para. 4.15) to the fact that China has no intention at present of changing the socialist aspect of the economy in terms of public ownership, even though it would continue to be diluted as other forms of ownership grow, and would continue to be subject to improvements in the way such ownership was represented. Rather, the question should be whether, within the framework described, the reform plan goes as far as it can to incorporate efficiency-enhancing measures, and whether there are further steps that can be taken to reduce administrative management and interference. This is discussed in sections F and G. First, however, the plan as it stands raises issues related to timing, sequencing and style, and with respect to its links to the development plan.

E. Timing, Sequencing and Reform Style

4.62   From the above description and interpretation of the reform plan, it can be seen that in general its contents are encouraging and appropriate, and could be expected to continue to generate the sorts of efficiency gains enjoyed during the past decade (see Chapter II). If our interpretation is correct of the sort of economic system that would result from the full

---

11/ This is drawn up on the basis of the framework suggested in Gelb and Gray "The Transformation of Economies in Central and Eastern Europe": World Bank Policy and Research Series #17.

Box 4.1: THE FUTURE CHINESE POLICY FRAMEWORK

1. **Macroeconomic Management**

   - Planning is based on macroeconomic framework and on the formulation of sectoral priorities.
   - Tight fiscal budget with revenue on a broad base, but divided between central and local taxes, and central expenditure focused on key service and infrastructure.
   - Strong central bank uses indirect instruments of monetary control to prevent inflation.
   - Exchange rate policy and tight debt management to maintain external balance and creditworthiness.
   - Exports are unsubsidized, but imports continue to be subject to strict licenses and high tariffs.

2. **Price and Market Reform**

   - Most domestic prices determined by unified competitive markets with state fixing a few, such as electricity, coal and grain, but with full cost recovery.
   - Mandatory materials allocation disappears and is replaced by widespread system of wholesale markets backed up by government buffer stocks.
   - Housing, pension and medical benefits are converted into wages, and these services are provided by services, enterprises and/or the state outside the SOEs.
   - Wages more market determined, subject to aggregate growth limits.
   - The financial system deepens, with new institutions, but major banks remain state-owned, operating two "accounts", for policy and commercial lending.
   - Interest rates are key instruments of monetary management, but commercial rates cross-subsidize policy rates.

3. **Enterprise Structure and Private Sector**

   - Most major enterprises remain state-owned, but become joint-stock enterprises, with state shares vested in holding companies, and banks and individuals also as owners. Enterprise property rights defined by law.
   - Entry of collective and private enterprises to all sectors is free and encouraged.
   - Land use rights become classified as a "commodity" and can be transferred on basis of long lease.
   - Most housing becomes property of individuals or joint-stock housing corporations owned by enterprises, banks, government and individuals.
   - In place of bankruptcy, nonviable enterprises are absorbed by use of mergers and workers are retrained.
   - Investment needs of state enterprises come from profits and banks, but subject still to state direction.

4. **Role of the State**

   - Broad legal framework replaces the administrative framework to manage economic relations.
   - State manages the economy by indirect levers and guidance plans, plus the allocation of policy lending to implement industrial policy.
   - State investment focuses on provision of economic and social infrastructure.
   - Current expenditure focuses on providing the social safety net, education and training and price and enterprise subsides disappear.

---

implementation of the plan, it should certainly contain sufficient incentives to generate the pace of development being sought.

4.63   Yet there is a long way from the reform measures proposed to reach a full implementation in practice. At least in the Eighth Five-Year Plan period, partly because of the inflexibility of the contract responsibility system in major areas, fundamental changes in the areas of enterprise reform, public finance and taxation, may not take place unless present intentions are

changed.12/. The various reform measures to be implemented in the next
five years, especially price adjustments and more immediate reforms like those
in housing and social security and the more seemingly unrelated attempt to
create independent enterprise-groups that break through existing institutional
constraints, may be regarded as preparing for fundamental reforms to be
launched in the second half of the 1990s. In terms of timing, the plan itself
is relatively silent on specific steps. In some cases, this is because of the
nature of the plan as a general document, but in other cases, such as tax-
sharing for example, this reflects the absence of any detailed design. In the
recent calls for accelerated reforms and greater opening, there has been
little or no discussion of which reforms should go faster.

4.64   In general the cautious and gradualist approach to reform, in many
cases to be preceded and guided by relevant legislation and regulations, is an
improvement in reform style over the previous reform period. One of the particular features of this reform style is that the central government will
increasingly focus its reform efforts on the design and publication of central
guidelines, leaving the "when, where and how" for local governments to decide
upon within those guidelines. Nevertheless, without adequate attention to
sequencing issues, serious issues can arise which can halt reform progress,
just as in 1988 inadequate attention to monetary issues led to the slowdown of
price reforms. In addition, the extensive use of contracts as a vehicle of
reform itself can become an obstacle to later reforms. It breeds arbitrary
negotiations between the government and economic agents on the basis of narrow
vested interests, and the fixed tenure of the contracts could cause the government to miss opportunities for speeding up the pace of reform in response
to changes in the economic environment.

4.65   This would lead us to recommend four aspects of the reform plan
which deserve early attention by the government:

(a)   The present macroeconomic conditions continue to offer opportunities
      for advancing reforms, and many reforms are ready and should be
      implemented in the very near future, especially in pricing, housing
      and social security (see Matrix 4.1).

(b)   The reform plan offers many principles for reform, but the govern-
      ment is much less clear on specific reform intentions, and should
      increase attention on the practical steps to the implementation of
      reforms--regulations, laws, training, new reporting forms, etc.

(c)   The biggest threat to economic reform progress in the recent past
      has been economic instability. The macroeconomic framework of the
      8th FYP calls for more steady, inflation-free growth which would
      create a much more appropriate backdrop to reforms. A feature of
      the recent debate on accelerating reforms has also been a call for
      raising the rate of growth. While adequate growth is necessary to
      permit enterprise restructuring, rapid reform and growth of 10 per-

---

12/   As noted elsewhere in the report, the reform momentum has been building
      rapidly since Spring 1992, although this remains to be converted into
      explicit reform plans.

cent or above would be likely to generate inflation, and such high growth is not to be recommended.

(d) If the experiments and trials of the 8th Plan are to lead to concrete results, they must be carried out on a more methodical basis. Baseline data sets need to be established in reform trials and in control (nonreform) areas; reporting timetables need to be established and monitoring criteria established. Finally, each reform trial should have a specific period for the experimentation period, after which concerned officials should evaluate results to determine next steps and formulate designs for nationwide implementation.

F. Links with the Development Plan

4.66   The development plan and the reform plan should be mutually and explicitly supportive. The reform plan should create the policy framework that will facilitate the achievement of the main targets and strategies of the plan, and the development plan should create the right macroeconomic framework to support reform. In addition, of course, some reforms need investments of various kinds to ensure their success, notably those related to market development.

4.67   The development plan calls for a moderate pace of economic growth and lays great stress on balance. If more even-paced, balanced growth can be achieved, without the swings of the last decade, this will lay the perfect foundation for the further deepening of reforms. This said, achieving stable, balanced growth itself depends critically on reforms to strengthen the ability to manage the economy through indirect economic levers, and to improve the enterprise control system, notably via hardened budget constraints. Similarly, the development plan is supportive of reforms because of the emphasis of the investment program on the building of economic infrastructure, especially in agriculture and transport, and this infrastructure is critical to the development of markets in general and to interprovincial trade in particular.

4.68   There are four aspects in which the reform plan can be seen to be supportive of the aims and objectives of the development plan:

(a) Price reforms will generate financial resources to assist investments in energy, agriculture and in transport, and this is the strongest direct support to infrastructure reform and development.13/   Indeed, it would appear to be a sine qua non for the successful achievement of the plan's targets.

(b) Leveling the playing field in trade, foreign investment, and tax rates will assist in reducing income disparities and promoting regional development. Of course, the natural comparative advantage of coastal areas would suggest that these areas would in any event

---

13/   See, for example, the discussion of the Railway Investment Fund in paras. 5.32-5.33).

do better than interior regions, but these coastal areas have also enjoyed advantages in incentives in the recent past.

(c) Investment system reforms will contribute to the government's aim of raising incentives for high priority sectors (by reducing adminis- trative barriers) and will further discourage low priority sectors.

(d) Public finance and banking reforms are designed to strengthen the ability of the government to manage the economy, and thus to improve the overall macroeconomic framework within which the plan will be carried out.

4.69   However, in general it is the financial difficulties facing the public sector that are framing reform design. In particular, there are four key areas of the development program where the reform plan has little to say, or offers no help:

(a) Financing the Plan. The plan continues to suffer from the fact that the investment plan has a large unfinanced gap. This can be addressed either through public finance reform, to generate addi- tional fiscal revenues, or by investment system reform, to adjust investment responsibilities. Neither is proposed, so a large volume of "policy lending" remains.

(b) Nonstate Enterprises and the Service Sector. Aside from general statements about encouraging diversified forms of ownership, the plan has little to say about TVEs, except some things that indicate that some incentives may be reduced. In particular, this affects the service sector, which is a key to the achievement of the plan targets. The development plan had little to say, and the reform plan is silent on this sector.

(c) Regional Development. Although the reform plan has encouraging things to say about market development in general, it does not address the question of interprovincial trade, and of fiscal and regulatory reforms to facilitate this aspect of development policy.

(d) Efficiency Enhancing Reforms. The reform plan is essentially prep- aratory so far as the 8th FYP is concerned, and, therefore, little can be expected in terms of efficiency gains from the reform side, and we already expressed skepticism about the efficiency impact, especially on SOEs, of recent development measures.

4.70   Overall, therefore, while the reform plan has elements of a support- ing framework for the aims and objectives of the plan, these are weak in key areas. In particular, what is distinctive about this plan is its emphasis on infrastructure and on the development of the services sector, and it is here that more attention of the reform designers is needed, especially with respect to investment system reform and nonstate enterprises. This goes to reinforce the discussion of Chapter III, that policy planning is an area where continued efforts and reorientation of the planning system will be necessary.

G. Specific Reform Areas

4.71   This reform plan is the most detailed and comprehensive that has yet
been drawn up. In Chapter II, we attempted to assess progress in the different reform areas, and from this to assess the reform priorities for the coming
decade in six main areas of economic policy. In Matrix 4.1, we bring together
the conclusions from Chapter II in these six areas, together with the Plan's
statement of intent, and our consequent suggestions for continued attention to
reform design or reform speed. To take contrasting examples, the price reform
proposals seem to be well-designed, but unnecessarily extended, while the
financial reform proposals seem as yet inadequate in terms of scope.

4.72   Within this group, there are three that merit particular attention,
in terms of the extent to which the present proposals do not seem as yet to
match up to the assessment of Chapter II: enterprise reform, and especially
questions related to ownership reform and enterprise groups; financial sector
reform, and the related issue of investment system reform; and external sector
reform, and the issue of "opening up to the outside world." These three areas
are addressed in some depth in paras. 4.74-4.89.

4.73   We raise these observations so that they can be taken into consideration as the reform program evolves. For the reform plan should not be seen
as an end in itself or as something set in stone, but rather as an evolving
reform program that is adjusted in the light of experience and of economic
conditions. Indeed, the strength of the past reform style in China has been
its pragmatism, and the willingness of policymakers to act flexibly as opportunities rise.

(a) Enterprise Reform

Ownership and Management

4.74   It has been repeated many times that enterprise reform and the hard-
ening of enterprise budget constraints lie at the very heart of China's reform
program, and that it will be the success or failure of efforts in this area
that will ultimately determine whether China will succeed in building its new
economic system with a high degree of economic efficiency. But given that
this is regarded as the most important area of reform, the government has
surprisingly little to say about it, and plan statements display a clear
ambivalence in this area. For example, the government has emphasized the role
of the market in regulating the SOEs in the future, and yet the recent decisions include measures such as higher budgetary allocations for working capital, more rapid depreciation rates, and exemption on taxes, all of which
reduce the strength of market forces and make the ties between government and
these enterprises even closer. Moreover, the continued reluctance to rely on
bankruptcy 14/ reveals the dilemma of the absence of negative incentives
within the socialist framework of public ownership and the public duty to
provide employment.

14/ See footnote "5."

4.75   While the reform plan has much to say about the framework within which enterprises will operate--especially pricing, the provision of social services, investment financing and industrial policies--it is notably reticent on the question of ownership reform. While it makes the welcome reiteration that nonstate forms of ownership are welcome, it has much less to say on the form in which the state will continue to exercise its ownership function. The present system of administrative representation continues to be the key obstacle for the achievement of improved efficiency in enterprises, and to the creation of factory directors who truly take responsibility for profits and losses. The key issues are raised in a general way in the reform plan, such as via the conversion of enterprises into joint-stock companies, the formation of holding companies and, perhaps more important, the separation of profits and taxes so that the ownership function can begin to be translated into financial return targets. What is called for is an aggressive program of trial reforms within the next few years to find ways in which the public ownership function can be exercised in a more economic, less administrative way.

4.76   Such a program would seem to call for coordinated actions and reform experiments in a number of sectors. It is to be noted that some local governments--notably those in Shanghai, Hainan, Shenzhen and Shenyang--are already beginning to address these issues and to institute experiments, but this is an area where a national framework could be very helpful, but where, as yet, it is lacking. The key areas of focus would seem to us to include:

(a)   The development of laws and regulations, notably a company law, not least to define clearly the property rights of the government, enterprise managers and shareholders.

(b)   The development of a set of regulations and systems, not least being clear guidelines for accounting standards and auditing requirements, especially with respect to enterprises which issue shares to the public.

(c)   The launching of experiments in the creation of new institutions to represent the public ownership function. This would include the use of holding companies which could take over the functions of representing the government as owner (and, in particular, take over from the industrial ministries and bureaus).

(d)   The conversion of several major state-owned enterprises into joint-stock companies, with the ownership of such enterprises diversified between a government holding company, workers and provincial governments.

(e)   The launching of institutional development programs in two main areas: in the central government, to develop skills to regulate markets, especially with respect to antimonopoly; and in local government, to convert industrial bureaus from being administrative regulators, to performing consulting functions, such as market information, technology development and restructuring advice. Clearly, such experiments would be most appropriate in those areas where holding companies are to be established.

4.77   Of course, all this presupposes action in other areas, such as housing and social security reforms. But even so, the actions that are needed to
prepare the way for ownership reform are so extensive that postponing even
these preparations pushes implementation very far into the future. The recent
experience of Central and Eastern Europe suggests that even with a strong
will, the technical difficulties (especially of valuation in a half-reformed
system) are enormous and cannot be left to the end of the reform process.
This is an area where well-designed and controlled experiments deserve the
earliest attention, especially in those locations, such as Shanghai, where
financial innovation is also proceeding.

4.78   There is no doubt that there are large incremental efficiency gains
to be achieved in China's state-owned enterprises, or that there is scope for
such gains within the framework of public ownership through better means of
representing such ownership. Nevertheless, international experience casts
doubts on the ability of the SOEs to attain the same level of efficiency as
private enterprises, so long as they remain dominant. That is to say, the
systems to achieve this have yet to be devised and this remains the fundamental reform design challenge in China. What is being suggested here is that
the key to moving towards such an end lies in institutional reforms to separate regulation, ownership and management, while at the same time removing
restrictions to the role of the nonstate sector as the essential source of
competition to the SOEs.

Enterprise Groups

4.79   As noted earlier, an essential defect in the enterprise control
mechanism in China is that it has developed several positive inducements to
reward good performance, and notably the contract responsibility system, but
it has found it much more difficult to devise clear negative incentives to
harden the budget constraints of poorly performing enterprises. In some
cases, such as enterprises whose prices are held below market levels, actions
on these other fronts will first be required. But for others, the problem
ultimately remains the softness of budget constraints given the unacceptabil-
ity of bankruptcy. The Chinese solution to this is the use of mergers, for it
may be that the threat of takeover, and of loss of management status can be,
within a socialist framework, at least as powerful as the threat of bankruptcy. Given, in addition, the need to improve economies of scale and scope,
and to break down administrative and provincial barriers, the Chinese have
developed a key role in enterprise reform for enterprise groups.

4.80   The importance to be attached to the enterprise groups is that they
will be freed from most of the administrative restrictions and controls
imposed by the planning system on SOEs, and this may make them a viable chal-
lenger to the contract responsibility system, which defends the status quo.
Unlike previous experiments in enterprise reform that often started with small
enterprises, the 100 national enterprise groups will be chosen from among the
biggest and most efficient SOEs in the nation. The greater autonomy and business diversification that they will enjoy would allow them to use their economies of scale and scope for rapid expansion, taking over or coopting other
enterprises into the group by legitimate means such as mergers, takeovers,
leasing, contracting and even purchase. Their respective share in the
national economy is already quite sizable, and there is a high probability

that it would be increased further. Their mere size and scale would enable them easy entry into most sectors and regional markets in China. The experiment, if followed by the formation of similar enterprise groups at the local level, could bring a dramatic change to the present enterprise system, currently preserved by the contract responsibility system, and could create a need for speeding up other institutional reforms.

4.81   However, the fact that most of the enterprise groups are to be formed from existing large state-owned enterprises, and will be given special policy privileges, will further enhance their monopolistic positions vis-à-vis other enterprises. International experience has shown that, in the absence of competition, monopolistic enterprise groups may not be under pressure to improve their efficiency and rationalize their investments, and their special relationship with the government can facilitate the persistence of soft-budget constraints in them. It will therefore be critical to ensure that there is no exclusivity between such groups, and rather that competition between them should be encouraged. In particular, nonstate enterprises should also be permitted to compete with such groups within their market niches, and nonstate enterprises should be permitted to become leading enterprises of such groups. More generally, successful nonstate enterprises should be permitted and encouraged to take over inefficient or poorly run state-owned enterprises.

4.82   Finally, those groups that are formed as comprehensive trading enterprises will be dissociated from any direct government administration. The state will only exercise its right of ownership through the authority of a board of directors and its control over the appointment of the senior managerial staff of the enterprise groups. This leads to the important issue of corporate governance. As individual shareholders will be in the minority and institutional shareholders similar to pension funds in the West are yet to be born, the main burden of supervision lies with the government, which is also the largest shareholder. In other words, the comprehensive trading enterprise groups and other independent enterprise groups will not eliminate the problems of government-SOE relationships, but transform it into a more delicate issue of corporate governance and the new role of government as majority shareholder, which demands a more comprehensive reform in the area of public ownership, as previously discussed.

    (b) Financial Sector Reform

4.83   As discussed in Chapter II (paras. 2.76-2.77), financial sector reforms, and especially those related to the banking system, appear to have become "stuck." Partly, no doubt, this is due to nonmovement on the question of SOE reform, for so long as SOEs are required to continue to operate with inflated workforces, but with inadequate budget funding, and so long as people continue to save at such high levels, the banks are bound to be compelled to lend to the SOEs, even to cover losses. Thus, the key issue facing the banking system is so-called "moral hazard": the banks cannot be expected to be responsible for that part of their lending which is dictated by government, although financed with individuals' and enterprises' deposits. At the same time, it would not be realistic to say that all such lending should come directly under the budget. The difficulty is to find nonbudgetary ways of financing deserved investments without prejudicing the function of banks as banks. As noted, the reform plan has little to say about this directly, and it only discusses experiments in separating "policy lending" from commercial lending in terms of accounts. This may require different approaches, depending on whether we are referring to the financing of production enterprises, or projects, such as roads and airports, of high economic but not (necessarily) viable financial merit.

4.84   One approach to the latter issue is raised briefly in the reform plan, and this deserves renewed attention, and it could address two issues in one. First, the plan mentions the possibility of creating specialized investment banks that would issue bonds to finance key investment project. At the same time, mention is made in another part of the plan of the possibility of converting the State Investment Corporations (SICs) into holding companies. What should be considered urgently is to combine these two approaches: The SICs could be converted into specialized investment banks, issuing bonds guaranteed by the government to finance the priority projects that are at present forced upon the commercial banking system. This would create a real rationale for the SICs--which is lacking at present--and would relieve much of the pressure for policy lending from the banking system.

4.85   The question of financing for the SOEs raise the question of capital market development, for the problem in general requires that the market, and not banks of the type China has at present, should be the source of funding for these enterprises. Moreover, for the stability of savings, it seems appropriate to diversify the range of instruments available in financial markets, and not least via those instruments that are more closely connected to physical assets. This, then, is a powerful argument for two types of institutional development within capital markets.

(a)   The use of bonds and securities issued by enterprises, but subject to some form of ratings agency.

(b)   The continued development of well-regulated institutions such as trust and investment corporations specializing in enterprise lending.

However, one word of caution in terms of reform sequencing: it seems most unlikely in the short term that stock exchanges and stock markets could contribute significantly to this issue of efficient mobilization and allocation of financial savings, if the experience of other countries is a guide. This would suggest that the relative emphasis being placed on this aspect of the capital market compared with these other issues is misplaced.

4.86   Finally, the government has one key role it could play. The financial sector has an inadequate range of financial instruments available at present, not least with respect to facilitating indirect management by the People's Bank. Simultaneously, the government is compelling the banking system to cover the operating losses of enterprises. It would be a better result for the financial system as a whole--and for the transparency of government decision-making--if the government were to diversify its range of domestic debt instruments, especially via short-term treasury bills, and finance these losses via the budget, rather than through compulsory bank loans.

(c) External Sector Reform

4.87   Reforms in the external sector have been deep and wide-ranging.
Indeed, it can be cogently argued that it has been China's approach to the
role of the external sector in reform that has distinguished its economic
performance from that of other socialist countries, and that the external
sector has served as the catalyst to successful gradual reform. With each
step in reform of the external sector, including 1989's reform of the joint
venture law and the new 1991 trade contracts, the external regime has become
more rational and appropriate.

4.88   But one area remains to be addressed: the role of the external
sector as a source of competition. On the contrary, foreign investment policy
continues to stress that outside involvement is not welcome in those areas
where sufficient capacity--regardless of quality--is deemed to exist. Moreover, nothing is said about the further liberalization of the import regime,
and the replacement of the present strong quantitative restrictions by tariffs. The external sector can not only serve to provide a source of economic
growth and of foreign exchange to purchase improved technology, but also as a
source of competitive pressure to generate efficiency in those enterprises
producing for the domestic markets. This pressure can be provided equally by
imports or by foreign investment, but in the case of the latter it can only
serve its full effect if joint ventures are also subject to competitive pressure from imports.

4.89   This is most obvious in the area of import competition, which should
be seen as a integral component of overall competition policy. As noted earlier (para. 4.50), there are signs of movement in this area. And yet, it
seems clear that movements in policy towards the role of imports are not motivated by real belief that imports have a greater role to play in generating
efficiency, but rather by political motives to resume China's seat in the GATT
and avoid measures being imposed on China's exports. While the end-result may
appear to be the same, it has different implications for the considerations
that will be applied with respect to management of the trade system. This is
an area where further work and effort is needed to convince policymakers of
the benefits in terms of economic efficiency gains of actions in this area.

H. Conclusions

4.90   There has been a strong, positive impact of reform in the Chinese
economy in the last decade, and, as was argued in Chapter II, such reform
policies have translated into efficiency gains. It is also clear that China's
leaders intend to maintain the momentum of reform in the 1990s. Moreover,
even as the economy now stands in its half-reformed state, it seems likely
that China could continue to enjoy satisfactory rates of growth for quite some
time, given the present savings propensity in China, and the likelihood that
this will continue.

4.91   It seems to us less likely, however, that the strong cyclical pattern of the 1980s can be avoided, and that major efficiency gains can be
achieved without further reforms. Indeed, it would be our contention that
these two goals cannot be achieved without further, deeper reforms. The issue
then, is not whether China can achieve its broad goal of redoubling 1990s GNP

Matrix 4.1: REFORM PRIORITIES AND THE REFORM PLAN

Reform priority	Reform plan intention	Bank suggestions on timing or design
Enterprise Reform		
1. Property rights remain vague and no institutional mechanism for separation of ownership and management.	1. Extension and "perfection" of the contract responsibility system.	1. Separation of taxes and profits is a key step in enterprise reform, that should be implemented as soon as possible for all SOEs.
2. The regulatory and legal framework remains undeveloped.	2. Separation of taxes and profits, with contracts on an after-tax basis, to be tested in 8th FYP and implemented in 9th.	2. Ownership reform not addressed aggressively enough. Launch reform experiments for conversion of large SOEs into joint-stock companies and formation of holding companies to represent owner.
3. SOEs not subject to adequate competition from nonstate enterprises or from imports and FDI, and bankruptcy not used.	3. Experiments with conversion of SOEs to joint-stock companies.	3. No program to reform existing ownership institutions. Launch experimental program to reorient industrial bureaus to consultancy functions.
	4. Formation of 100 enterprise groups crossing administrative and provincial boundaries.	4. Accelerate regulatory framework, especially on accounting standards and antimonopoly regulation.
	5. Restructuring of enterprises with ultimate threat of bankruptcy.	5. Proceed with enterprise group program, but permitting nonstate enterprises to participate.
	6. Formation of "holding companies" to be owner of state assets.	6. Improve legal framework protecting rights of nonstate enterprises.
Financial Sector		
1. Need for alternative methods of financing policy objectives, especially via capital market.	1. Call for "exploration" of separation of policy and commercial lending in banks.	1. Need alternative approaches to problem of moral hazard. Finance government priority projects via bond issues, and push SOEs to direct access to capital market.
2. Strengthening of central bank in regulatory capability and strength and in policy formulation.	2. Strengthening of central bank by passing regulations and training, to emphasize use of indirect instruments.	2. Technical strengthening of PBC urgent and not to be delayed.
3. Increased use of indirect instruments of management.	3. Expansion of NBFIs, especially in insurance, and extension of interbank market and FEACs to national basis.	3. In capital market, extension of bond markets has highest priority, and stock exchange, while useful should not be regarded as a panacea.
4. Issue of deterioration of banks' portfolios.	4. Increased role for stock exchanges, operating at national level.	4. Banks should increase loss provisioning and write-offs.
Public Finance		
1. Need to replace contracts with tax systems, both at the enterprise level and provincial level.	1. Government aims to deepen experiments with separation of taxes and profits, especially for large and medium SOEs, reducing tax rates to 33 percent.	1. As noted, accelerate the separation of taxes and profits, especially for SOEs.
2. Need to diversify the tax base beyond enterprises, especially via income taxes and final sales point taxes.	2. Experiments with tax-sharing arrangements between central and local governments.	2. Tax-sharing experiments need to be pursued aggressively so that a new system can be ready by 1994.
3. Indirect tax system lacks transparency, not least due to exemptions, and needs to be replaced with a VAT.	3. Strengthened tax administrations and in particular central control over exemptions.	3. Increased attention is merited for new tax system, especially income taxes and VAT.
	4. Introduction of "double-budgeting" systems.	

Matrix 4.1 (cont'd)

Reform priority	Reform plan intention	Bank suggestions on timing or design
External Sector		
1. Need to reform the import regime, essentially by moving from direct control to indirect control via tariffs.	1. Reform plan silent on import regime, but recent MOFERT statements indicate intention to reduce licensing and publish regulations.	1. Timing seems appropriate for rapid movement on import liberalization, which could assist fiscal problems, although analysis needed urgently.
2. Continued institutional reform of foreign trade corporations, opening up trade to production enterprises.	2. Encouragement to formation of foreign trade enterprise groups, and unification of exchange rate.	2. Further opening of export markets to producers seems warranted.
3. Open domestic market further to joint ventures and SEZ enterprises.	3. Development of Pudong area, and extension of Shenzhen SEZ.	3. Need for change in attitude and regulations towards access to domestic market for foreign enterprises.
Prices and Markets		
1. Adjustment to market levels of remaining distorted prices--energy, transport, raw materials, grain--followed by removal of most price controls.	1. Program to adjust these major prices "as circumstances permit" to eliminate two-tier differentials, and price controls to be retained only on a few key commodities such as power.	1. Price reform program very much in line with assessed priorities, but current market conditions suggest some acceleration possible.
2. Conversion of price subsidies into wages and consequent reduction of state distribution.	2. Rapid development of wholesale markets and new system of distribution of materials that bypass ministerial constraints.	2. New market channels are well-designed and need investment backing.
	3. Rapid program of conversion of price to wage subsidies and no agricultural distribution by state except grain and cotton by 9th Plan.	3. If price reform proceeds, so can dismantling of distribution channels, including for grain and cotton, but government can retain buffer stock.
Role of the State		
1. Continued shift away from direct to indirect control of economy, and of the role of planning from investment and enterprise planning to policy planning.	1. Extension of FYP to cover policies and replacement of direct controls with indirect instruments, reduction of mandatory plan, and replacement of investment controls with IOT and industrial policies.	1. Direction and policy broadly appropriate. Main issue is institutional mechanism for financing investment (see finance section).
2. Conversion of nonwage into wage benefits, and establishment of systems outside enterprises, especially in housing, social security and health care.	2. Housing reform to be accelerated and completed over 10 years, via rent adjustments and new financing mechanisms to encourage home ownership.	2. Housing reform should be accelerated with more emphasis on rent reform and on creation of joint-stock housing corporations to manage existing stock and less emphasis on commercialization and compulsory provident funds.
3. Removal of antiemployment policies, and gradual relaxation of labor allocation system.	3. Creation of pension pooling arrangements and experiments with health insurance.	3. Social security needs clear national framework and national administration if it is to achieve pension transferability.
	4. Extension of labor contract system.	4. Labor mobility issues are not addressed yet and will be an increasingly important issue as floating population inevitably increases.

by the year 2000, but in what way this will be achieved. It certainly can be achieved by high rates of savings and investment being maintained while the economy fluctuates dramatically around its trend growth; or it can be achieved by relatively stable growth, with a gradual improvement in economic efficiency, which permits greater gains in average welfare at the same level of income.

4.92   The areas of reform where the program is weakest are in just those two areas which would contribute more to these goals: the absence of strong fiscal and banking reforms to strengthen macroeconomic management, and the absence of a clear, aggressive strategy to address the issue of SOEs' efficiency. We have indicated in this Chapter the sort of reforms that could be advanced in these areas, and we attempt to illustrate in Chapter V the sort of impact that, in our judgment, this could have on the economy.

V. THE PLAN FOR THE TRANSPORT SECTOR

5.1   This Chapter reviews the Eighth Five-Year Plan for the transport sector, and aims to analyze how this sector is expected to develop and reform during the 8th FYP, transport being identified as a major bottleneck to economic development, and to illustrate how Plan objectives and instruments are applied in the sector. The Chapter focuses on Plan directions and priorities (Section B), financing objectives and approaches (Section C), and sectoral and institutional reforms (Section D). The chapter also includes a brief background section, focusing on the Seventh Plan, and a closing section with main conclusions.

5.2   As noted in Chapters III and IV, the 8th FYP intends to continue the trend of investments and reforms set in motion over the last two five-year plans. While the process will continue to be gradual and no radical departures from recent past directions are envisaged, it will have significant implications for the transport sector, as new investments in transport transform the quality of the system, economic development changes the structure of transport demand, and the 8th FYP places more emphasis on competition, decentralization, interprovincial trade and small enterprises' role in the provision of services.

5.3   Transport has long been one of the main bottlenecks in the economy, serving not only as a constraint to the achievable rate of growth, but also as an impediment to efficiency gains through greater integration of the national market. As such, the plan for the transport sector should be seen very much in the light of the reform and development objectives outlined in the previous two chapters, and as its analysis can provide an example of the sort of planning that is to be encouraged in China.

A. Background

Achievements of the 7th FYP

5.4   The 7th FYP (1986-90) targeted and achieved a substantial improvement and expansion of China's transport system, but such developments were insufficient to make up for several decades of underinvestment in the sector. Selected sectoral reforms were initiated and helped to improve the management of the transport system and to make better utilization of the system's facilities.

5.5   Thanks to the new investments, and to increased efficiency in the use of existing capacity, total freight turnover reached 1,825 billion ton-km, or an increase of 43 percent during the Plan period, while total passenger turnover reached 561 billion pass-km, representing an increase of 27 percent during the period (see Statistical Appendix Tables 15.2 and 15.3). Traffic growth would have been even stronger if transport demand had been fully met; this was not possible due to transport bottlenecks, severe in some routes and for some commodities such as coal.

5.6   Total investment in transport during the 7th FYP amounted to Y 85.7 billion (in constant 1987 prices). While this represented a

substantial 73 percent increase over the previous plan, such level of investments was insufficient to catch up with a longstanding, accumulated deficit in
transport sector investment (see Table 15.4). In relative terms, only in
ports did new capacity come close to meeting existing demand and relieving
users from excessive wait.

5.7   Implementation of reforms during the Plan was either more limited,
or measures made effective later, than originally foreseen, especially as
regards pricing. Despite this, some difficult and noteworthy structural
changes were initiated, particularly in breaking up the integrated monopoly of
air transport services and facilities (Box 5.1), and in launching experiments
with decentralization and financial autonomy in ports. Institutional and
decentralization reforms also spread to other transport modes, and allowed
more private individuals and collective enterprises to provide passenger and
freight transport services on roads and inland waterways.

Box 5.1: ORGANIZATIONAL REFORMS IN AIR TRANSPORT AND PORTS

Air Transport

        Despite rather rapid growth of air transportation in China, averaging 20 percent each year during the 1980s,
China's civil aviation system has not been able to keep up with the even faster growing demands of its modernizing economy. The government regarded its centralized system, run by the Civil Aviation Administration of China ("CAAC"), as a key
barrier to development of air services. In 1984, it decided to break up CAAC.

        Up to that point, CAAC acted as an integrated monopoly, owning and operating all aircraft, airports, routes, air
catering services, pilot, maintenance and service training facilities. CAAC also selected air routes and negotiated
arrangements with outside entities, such as travel agencies, foreign airlines, and freight companies. The decentralization of CAAC was intended to separate the operational from the regulatory functions of a civil aviation system, ultimately
allowing CAAC to evolve into a purely regulatory body, similar to the US Federal Aviation Administration ("FAA").

        The first step in the decentralization process was to break off CAAC's regional divisions into separate airlines
and do away with provincial and local air administrations all together. Eight airlines came into existence from this
stage: Air China (Beijing), China Northwest Airlines (Xian), China Southwest Airlines (Chengdu), China Eastern Airlines
(Shanghai), China North Airlines (Shenyang), China Southern Airlines (Guangzhou), China United Airlines, and China
Xinjiang Airlines (Urumqi). Almost immediately following the initial breakup, new, more localized airlines also began
operations, independent from CAAC, such as Shanghai Airlines.

        As autonomous, profit-making entities, the seven CAAC-originated airlines are responsible for their financial
performance and perform a combination of services: passenger and cargo transport, air catering services, hotels and
guesthouses, restaurants, advertising, and ground maintenance functions. The airlines must also finance any aircraft purchases they wish to make, although CAAC still tightly controls aircraft purchases for the entire system. Very little
direct competition has affected these airlines as yet, but that time is soon approaching, particularly as several different airlines vie for access to major Chinese cities as well as Hong Kong.

        Airports have also been detached from CAAC. By letting localities decide on and build their own airports, China
hopes to speed up their expansion because, at present, China still lags far behind. With almost four times the population
of the US, China only has one-fourth the number of airports and many of those airports cannot handle wide-bodied planes.

        The need for rapid expansion of China's civil aviation system is obvious; the old system could not handle the
necessary pace of change. The initial results indicate an increase in competition, as two or three regional airlines
offer services on many trunk routes. While tariff rates are fixed, consumers are starting to show their preferences for
those airlines which have better quality service. On several routes, competition will soon intensify as several different
airlines vie for access to other major Chinese cities as well as to Hong Kong and other international destinations. Over
time, domestic and international tariffs should be deregulated.

        The safety, operational and financial performance of the regional CAAC airlines merits scrutiny over the coming
years, especially given the tendency of airlines in other parts of the world to consolidate and create larger companies.
This consolidation process, now underway in the US, for instance, is offsetting the initial surge of new airlines which
entered the market after deregulation passed in 1978, although there is still more competition, at least in the trunk
routes, and lower prices than before deregulation. The complexity of the technology and huge sums of money needed to
purchase equipment in the air transport industry requires government to stay involved to ensure competition and prevent
uneconomic fragmentation of the industry. Improvement of basic infrastructure, such as air traffic control, navigation
and approach control systems, is still urgently needed throughout China and deserves full government attention. Designing
CAAC's role in a modernized Chinese air transport system must continue to be considered carefully.

Ports

        The first and most substantive port reform was the decentralization and increased autonomy for Tianjin port, in
1984. Under this process, Tianjin Port Authority (TPA) was put under the primary responsibility of Tianjin Municipality,
rather than the Ministry of Communications. TPA was authorized to: (a) retain the income tax and the profit remittance
due from its subordinate enterprises, and to utilize the funds for capital expenditures instead of paying them over to the
State; (b) raise the ceiling to Y 10 million per investment project without requiring approval from the central government; and (c) retain the foreign exchange generated by its subordinated enterprises for application to the purchase of
imported plant and equipment. In addition, the TPA was empowered to set up and independent import company to purchase all
major equipment needed, thus enabling the port to bypass the state foreign-trade companies. TPA has used its increased
managerial and financial autonomy to make a speedy expansion of the port to reduce ship delays, step up penalties for
cargo lying in the port area, and institute bonuses for personnel handling unpopular cargoes such as cement.

        Decentralization of other ports followed later, but the conditions were more restricted, especially as regards
financial autonomy. These ports were: Shanghai, Dalian, Yantai, Qingdao, Lianyungang, Nantong, Huangpu and Nanjing. The
contract agreements between the central governments and the ports expired in 1990. The agreements were then renewed on
the same terms, for two more years, despite requests by the ports to have their terms equalized with Tianjin.

5.8   Although implemented later than originally envisaged, hefty tariff increases in railways, 113 percent for passengers (1989) and 31 percent for freight (1991),[1] coupled with earlier adjustments in 1985, removed some of the major tariff distortions, and paved the way for future selective restructuring of the rail and other transport tariffs.

The Transport Network and Its Utilization

5.9   China's transport network is small by international standards. Chart 5.1 compares the density of China's land transport networks both in relation to population and to area, with those of other relevant countries.[2] To account for China's large desert areas, only arable areas are considered. Of the 12 countries in the graph (including China and five other developing countries), China has the smallest network when both population and areas are considered together. A comparison limited to railways shows that only the former Soviet Union had a smaller system relative to area, but relative to population it was much bigger than China's. The smallness of the network is the result of historic underinvestment. This situation worsened in the last ten years. During the period 1980-90, investments in transport infrastructure represented only about 1.4 percent of GNP (Table 15.4) compared to about 2-3 percent for countries such as Korea, India and Brazil.

5.10   The high freight intensity--ton-km per unit of GNP--that characterizes China, as well as most other centrally planned economies, continued during the period of the 7th FYP. In 1990, China moved 5.1 ton-km per dollar of GNP, which placed it highest in the world and three times as much as India or Brazil (see Table 15.1).[3] China could carry this traffic thanks mainly to the high utilization of its railway track capacity, at a rate about 3 times higher than US railroads (Table 15.6). While recent and future transport price adjustments will constrain demand, distortions in industrial location and other structural factors determining the high freight intensity will only change slowly. Thus, it seems unlikely that substantial reductions in freight intensity can be achieved within the next five to ten years.

5.11   Conversely, the mobility of people in China is among the lowest in the world. In 1990, average annual intercity travel in China was about 550 km per person, which compares with 4,570 km for the USSR, 23,580 km for the US and 10,560 km for Germany.[4] Low mobility is in part the result of saturated transport capacity; in 1989, express passenger trains had at least 30 percent more passengers than seats available. This problem threatens to frustrate government objectives to increase interprovincial trade and to allow citizens better access to markets and services.

B.   The Eighth Five-Year Plan (1991-95)

Objectives and Principles

5.12   Investments in transport under the 8th FYP will focus on high return projects designed to relieve bottlenecks for key commodities such as coal, to reduce congestion, and to improve and extend the network in areas where there is already proven transport demand. In contrast to previous Plans, the 8th FYP is more "indicative," and neither a complete list of Plan investments, nor the investment ceilings in the various transport modes, was available in 1991,

Chart 5.1:

International Comparison of Transport Networks

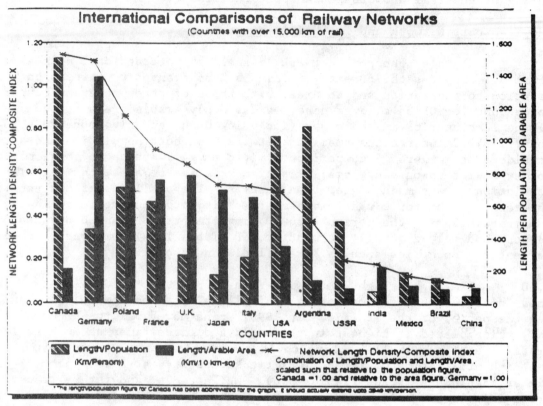

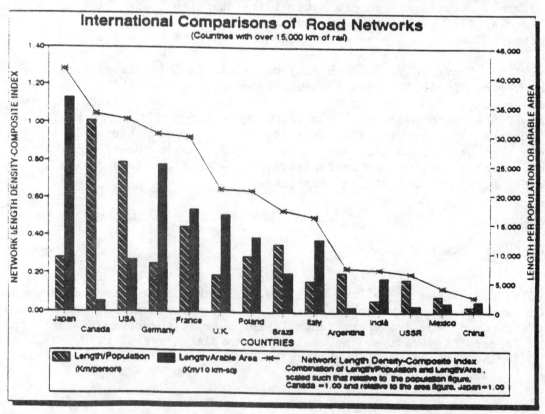

the first year of the Plan. Only the railways' plan and total ceiling had been approved, but investment priorities for all modes had been laid out.

5.13   Transport demand projections assume that, in line with GDP growth estimates and past experience of transport elasticity to GDP, transport turnover for freight (ton-km) and passenger (pass-km) will grow by about 47 percent during the five-year period. The 8th FYP investments are intended to help meet the need of the increased demand and are expected to contribute to industrial productivity improvements by reducing transport costs, diversifying and generally improving the quality of transport services.

5.14   Plan priorities indicate that while transport, and railways in particular, will receive higher allocations than in the past, total sectoral investments would still not reach international levels. This would require, some 2.5 percent of GDP, representing an investment of about Y 260 billion (in 1990 prices) during the 8th FYP, which appears unlikely. Yet, even if such a figure would be about double the proportion of GDP that has been invested in the past, it would not allow the sector to make up for a history of under-investment. This signals the need for conducting careful analysis of proposed plan investments, and the use of analyses as refined as possible to ensure that priorities are correctly identified--by mode, location, design standards and timing.[5] It also lends further urgency to the need for government attention to the needs of the transport sector for investment financing.

5.15   Together with the planned, key projects, designed to relieve bottlenecks and congestion, smaller investments and operational management improvements, assisted by modern technology, can make a substantial contribution to stretching the use of existing facilities and equipment. This is possible in all transport modes, but appear especially attractive in aviation, where the recent, large purchases of aircraft have provided additional capacity but flying hours are restricted due to lack of modern support facilities, and in river transport if fleet can be modernized. Investments should be accompanied by reforms of pricing, to make it an effective tool for managing demand and improving allocative efficiency, and by institutional measures to improve sectoral, agency and enterprises' productivity, and the Plan does contemplate reforms in these areas.

5.16   Outstanding transport bottlenecks from past underinvestment mainly affect bulk commodities such as coal, fertilizers and grains. Coal is the key commodity in China's transport system, as it represents some 40 percent of total ton-km carried on the railways system. These commodities are primarily served by rail and river transport. An example of the effect of such bottlenecks is the diversion of coal from railways to trucking, at substantially higher costs; in Shandong, a coastal province and a major consumer of coal, the average market price for "outside plan" steam coal, transported by truck, is reported to have reached Y 200/ton, compared to Y 115/ton if capacity existed to carry this coal by rail. The priority assigned to railway investments is primarily to relieve such bottlenecks, and to expand capacity to transport the increased output of these commodities.[6]

5.17   An additional important objective of the 8th FYP is to increase market integration and to foster interprovincial trade. This will lead to a substantial increase and diversification of the traffic flows, particularly of consumer goods and of intermediate products. Such flows increasingly will be carried by the roads, and by local railways. It is envisaged that provincial and local authorities will have a substantially greater control than in the past over investment decisions, and in the financing and management of such links (see Box 5.2).

<u>Box 5.2</u>: TRANSPORT DEVELOPMENT AND MARKET INTEGRATION

The expected key role of transport development in supporting the 8th FYP priority to accelerate market integration may be illustrated by an example from Guangdong Province Transport Study (GATS).<u>1</u>/

In this province, light industry is expected during the 1990s to have the largest growth of any sector, with an average annual growth rate of 12.5 percent, compared to 7.5 percent for heavy industry, and 3.0 percent for agriculture.

In the past, Guangdong's light industry was concentrated in Guangzhou, the province's capital, with lesser intensities in other population centers. Since 1980, light industry has grown rapidly and became diffused throughout the Pearl River. Access to Hong Kong appears to be the principal criterion for the location of industry, and rural townships appear to be favored with higher growth in value of industrial output than cities. New technology from Hong Kong, as well as from other sources, will be the key factor in the projected high growth rate for this sector. Thus, light industry development typifies the need for market integration, for the necessary provision of materials as well as technology, and for adequate access to domestic and external buyers.

Road transport, with its ability for fast delivery, careful loading and unloading, and door-to-door services, is particularly suited to light industry, and the construction of modern highways could, therefore, be expected to influence economic growth. Local railways, managed independently and generally responsive to local demand needs, can be important complements.

An example of the impact of improving transport facilities and services on market integration and economic growth may be taken from Eastern Guangdong. Presently, this region is poorly connected with the center of the province, and, consequently, with Hong Kong. A proposal to build two new connections from the center to the East, a coastal expressway and a local railway to the Meixian Prefecture, would change this. The GATS study estimated that the growth of economic output between 1990 and 2000 (about three quarters of which would be in light industry) would be greatly influenced by these two investments. In the Eastern Guangdong corridor, economic output, if the expressway and railway are built, would be expected to be about 30 percent higher than without these investments.

<u>1</u>/ This box draws heavily from Guangdong Province Comprehensive Transport Study, Transportation Division, Country Department III, Asia Regional Office, World Bank, July 7, 1991.

5.18   There are no indications that the Plan intends to bias the composition of the transport investments in favor of specific regions, but rather, investments are to be selected on the basis of economic needs. Removing the main transport bottlenecks will require increasing capacity in a number of key, saturated links between interior, coal-producing areas and the coastal consumer areas. Plan objectives to encourage interregional trade, however, will require the development of more intra and interprovincial highways, and substantial improvements of trucking services, both through investments and through restructuring of the industry.

(a) Main Modal Priorities

Railways

5.19   Diversion of nonbulk freight, and of short-distance passengers, mainly to the road, has been taking place steadily over the last 40 years (Chart 5.2), and this will continue in the future. However, bulk commodities and long-distance freight and passenger transport needs will continue to be more cheaply served by the rail (and water transport where available). The railways' main priority is to continue to relieve coal transport bottle-necks,[7] which will be done by increasing capacity of existing lines (through double-tracking, electrification, and improving signaling and telecommunications), building new lines, and upgrading motive power and rolling stock. Other investments will include the expansion of local railways, and the establishment of fast passenger services in key corridors (see Box 5.3). Overall, 8th FYP rail investments are estimated at Y 116 billion and will therefore continue to be the main call on investment resources for the transport sector.

5.20   While the general structure of the program appears to reflect economic priorities, all key investments should be carefully analyzed through network-wide analysis, complemented with individual feasibility studies. Special attention should be paid in the analysis to the justification of new line construction, especially those intended to serve frontier regions. In the case of new lines to serve enclave mining and or industrial operations, appropriate analysis should assess the economic return of the complete investment package, including the railway line, the industrial/mining investments and any complementary transport investments.[8]

Highways

5.21   The Plan anticipates that highway traffic will on average continue to develop at the high annual growth rates of the 1980s (15.5 percent for freight and 14.0 percent for passengers). Over the next five to ten years, even though the railways will continue to require higher levels of funding, roads, more than any other mode, will play a crucial role in the logistical support required by light and high-tech industry, and for the projected increased exchange of commodities stemming from the 8th FYP's objective to promote development of intra- as well as interprovincial trade. To meet this demand, 60,000 km of new road are expected to be built, of which half are within the national trunk road plan of the Ministry of Communications, which covers Class I and II roads, as well as expressways. Provincial roads, including trunk as well as county and rural roads, will comprise the bulk of the new mileage to be built during the Plan. The Plan will also give priority to the construction of the national road system, and this will include 500 km of expressways and some 3,500 km of roads exclusively for motorized traffic, with a view to avoid the congestion caused by the high proportion of slow-moving, nonmotorized traffic and to provide fast road connections among major cites.[9]

5.22   The plans of Henan Province provide an illustration of provincial road development projected for the 1991-95 period. The province plans to build 3,500 km of new roads, representing an 8.1 percent increase over the 43,000 km network in 1990. This will include 200 km of single carriageway

Chart 5.2: Traffic Volumes in China

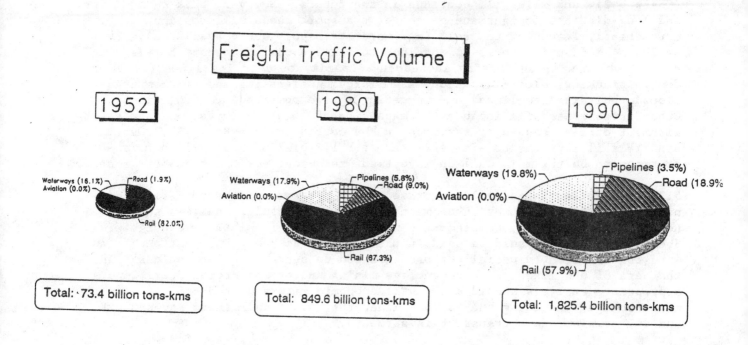

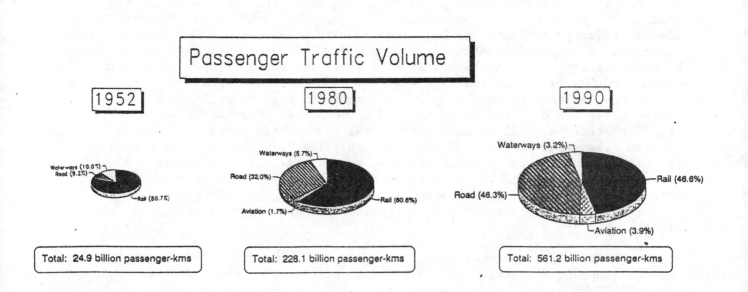

Box 5.3: GROWING ROLE FOR LOCAL RAILWAYS

From the time of their first development in 1958, local railways were seen by the government as a means to enlarge China's national rail network. Now, 30 years later, with rapid modernization severely straining China's transport system, China is actively exploring a variety of less centralized means of expanding its transport network. As part of this effort, local railways are again being consciously promoted.

The growth of the local railways in the last decade signifies the renewed importance placed on them. By 1990, local railways represented almost 8 percent of the total Chinese rail network, covering approximately 4,400 km. By the year 2000, the government expects another 6,000 km to be built. The new emphasis on local administration of railways reversed a previous trend, which dominated up until 1980, where the government regularly incorporated many of the local railways into the centralized system.

As indicated by the name, local railways are developed, financed and operated by local governments and enterprises, rather than by the State, although the Ministry of Railways may lend technical advice. Turning away from its previous policy of heavily taxing profits or subsidizing losses, the government's economic reforms now only require local railways to remit a 3 percent business tax on gross revenues, less than the 5 percent rate now charged to the State railways.

Due to their smaller size and the looser regulations governing them, local railways generally operate quite efficiently and flexibly. Among their many advantages over more centralized forms of transportation, they can mobilize more quickly the local population for work, local land for construction, and the local governments for funding. Also, local railways do not need to conform to the strict design standards of the Ministry of Railways, and they are allowed to employ used rails and equipment.

Local railways are allowed to set their own tariffs. These are higher than the State rates, despite greater efficiency of the local railways, because the national railways' rates cross-subsidize the types of traffic generally carried by the local railways.

Because local railways handle mainly light traffic over short distances, their total traffic is a small proportion (about 1 percent) of total China railways traffic. However, the 121 percent growth in local rail freight traffic in the last ten years (measured in ton-km), which is greater than the 74 percent growth of local rail length—and than the 86 percent growth of traffic in the national rail system—over that same time period, testifies to the strong desire for this service.

As China modernizes, more short-distance freight and passenger traffic will probably move to the highways as they are considered more efficient for short distances. Long-distance passenger traffic will most likely move more towards airline travel. Rail is seen, instead, as most efficient for medium- to long-distance freight transport. Thus, connecting the local railways to the national rail system is essential for their long-term success. Presently, approximately two-thirds of the local railways are sufficiently standardized that they are compatible with the national network. Efforts to maintain a high level of standardization must continue.

Decentralization reforms in other forms of transportation and in other countries should be watched, analyzed and when appropriate, followed. In China, many new, independent airlines are starting up following the decentralization of the Civil Aviation Administration of China (CAAC). In Japan, the government has recently privatized its nationally owned rail corporation. And, in the US, smaller railways are growing. China's local railways should certainly be capable of growing and adding to the national rail network, perhaps in a manner similar to these other reforms.

expressways and 100 km of paved roads with separate lanes for nonmotorized traffic. An additional 3,500-4,000 km will be upgraded or improved. The total road investment by the province will amount to Y 4.85 billion, of which about 43.5 percent is for expressways and other high standard roads. This appears as a balanced road development program, one that initiates a prudent development of modern facilities but which gives preference to maximizing road access and coverage throughout the province. However, there is no evidence that an appropriate financing plan has been devised to fund these investments.

Inland Waterways

5.23   Demand for inland waterways freight grew at 9.2 percent annually during 1980-90, while passenger demand grew at a rate of only 3.3 percent during the same period, as some of this traffic was diverted to roads. Freight traffic by waterways is heavily concentrated on four key routes: the Yangtze river system (53 percent); coastal shipping (20 percent); the Grand Canal (14 percent) and the Zhujiang system in southern China (13 percent). The 8th FYP will focus on improvements to the Yangtze system, both the trunk line and tributaries, as well as improvements to the Zhujiang system. These investments are designed to enhance China's waterways good potential for increasing their contribution to serving bulk, long-distance traffic, which presently are underutilized.[10]

Ports

5.24   Substantial investments during the 1980s provided large increases in capacity in all major ports. By the end of the 7th FYP most of the heavy congestion caused by the large increases in foreign trade and consequent port traffic--annual growth of 9.8 percent over the 1980 decade--had been eliminated, and ports were handling very large volumes, led by Shanghai with nearly 150 million tons (Table 15.7). However, as trade continues to grow, more will need to be done, and so the 8th FYP envisages the construction of 180 new berths (100 in deep water and 80 medium-sized), mainly for coal, containers and roll-on/roll-off operations. (There are about 1,100 berths at present at the major ports.) Total port investments during the 8th FYP are estimated at about Y 10 billion.

5.25   While construction of new port capacity during the 8th FYP will be required given the projected increases in exports and imports, investments in new infrastructure need to be carefully analyzed. First, because port efficiency in Chinese ports is generally below international standards--particularly as regards handling of containers--there is obvious room for extracting higher throughputs from existing facilities. Second, expansion of the rail and especially of the road networks is allowing shippers more choice in port selection, inducing competition among the ports which may result in readjustments in demand among them, and in improving utilization of their infrastructure. Therefore, comprehensive master plans, including analysis of potentially competitor ports, need to be conducted for proposed new port developments.

Civil Aviation

5.26   For the 8th FYP, the Government forecasts a continued high growth in air traffic, growing at possibly twice the rate of the economy; this is based on the experience during 1980-90, when the average annual growth rates were 19.0 percent for freight and 18.8 percent for passengers. During the last five years, more than 40 airports were built, renovated or expanded, and airlines added more than 100 aircraft to their fleets. In the 8th FYP, emphasis will not be in construction, but mainly in renovating and expanding some 20

airports that today handle about 80 percent of the passengers and cargo transported by air. In addition, the three major airports at Beijing, Shanghai and
Guangzhou will be provided with the most advanced facilities and support
equipment, while other trunk route airports will also be modernized. Consistent with the projected growth in demand, large purchases of aircraft are also
envisaged, probably reaching some Y 20 billion during the Plan period.
Investments in en-route navigational aids and air-traffic control are essential to improving utilization of aircraft and airports and the investment
program should accord them high priority.

C. Financing of the Plan

Key Directions

5.27   Financing of the transport component of the 8th FYP has two main
aims: (i) to redress the perennial underfinancing of transport investments;
and (ii) to achieve this objective without causing excessive strains on the
central governments's budget.

5.28   The first of the two aims requires an increase in real terms of the
total allocation for transport. As noted in the preceding section, although
full Plan details and sectoral ceilings were not available at the start of the
Plan in 1991, indications are that the Plan does, indeed, give the transport
sector a high priority and envisages an increase in investments in real terms
over the previous Plan. However, the 8th FYP is more an instrument to guide
provincial (e.g., highways and ports) and enterprise (e.g., railways) investments than to allocate central government resources. Thus, it proposes that,
through increased tariffs and user charges, enterprises and state and local
governments should secure themselves a significant part of the financial
resources, with the central government generally providing a minority share of
the key investments.

5.29   In addition to its direct financing for key investments, the government will use its new Investment Orientation Tax (IOT) to guide investments
in all sectors, including transport (see paras. 3.31-3.34). For example, the
IOT, as applied to new expressways, is zero for the construction costs of the
road itself, but may vary from 5 percent to 30 percent for ancillary investments such as administrative buildings or toll booths, signaling the priority
the government allocates to new transport capacity, and discouraging investments which are not considered directly productive.[11]

5.30   The mix of central, state and local governments and other financial
sources will vary among and within the transport modes. This chapter will not
examine all transport modes, but will be limited to the railways, as the largest revenue-earning entity and with the highest level of investments, and the
highways, as the fastest growing transport infrastructure component.

Financing for the Transport Modes

5.31   The 8th FYP intends to continue reforming the way railway investments are financed, the general direction being more accountability and more
use of internally generated funds. Such evolution started during the 6th FYP
when in 1984 Government ceased to provide grant capital funds for the railways

and began to finance railways investment with loans from the Treasury, as well as onlending of funds from the World Bank and Japan, at interest rates of between 3 and 4 percent. Subsequently, the Government exempted the railways from a 55 percent corporate tax, to enable it to increase cash generation to fund future investments, and limited the railways' contribution to the treasury to a 5.3 percent business tax on gross revenues. The 8th FYP intends to drastically reduce the funding from the State, and replace it by increased user contributions, through higher railway tariffs. A Railway Investment Fund (RIF) has been created to channel the additional internally generated resources. The provinces will finance most of the local railways development, which during the 8th FYP will be larger than in the past.

5.32   As noted in Chapter III, the Railways Investment Fund is one of the six Investment Funds to be created during the 8th FYP. Creation of the RIF is a positive initiative. The railways needs to make substantial investment during the Plan. The railways already generate a large net operating surplus, and have potential for substantially increasing revenues while correcting distortions in transport pricing. In this situation, the railways ought to be able to generate all the cash required for their investment needs, without recourse to government investment subsidies. Preliminary estimates prepared by the Ministry of Railways indicate that during the five-year period the Fund could generate an additional Y 15-25 billion, over and above net operating revenues at current tariffs, representing 13-22 percent of total financing required for the 8th FYP.

5.33   The operating rules for the Fund had not been established at the start of the Plan period. As such rules are developed, it would be important for certain key features to be incorporated:

(a)   The level of funding to be earmarked for the Fund should be carefully assessed. The RIF may not need to collect all the funds required for the investments during the period, yuan for yuan. A proper financial package ought to be devised to fund the Railways' investment plan, including internally generated funds and debt financing, both domestic and foreign.

(b)   Utilization of the Fund's moneys ought to be carefully scrutinized, including proper investment analysis of the projects to be funded, and auditing of the use of the funds.

(c)   The level of the RIF's resources, as compared to the railways' investment needs should be closely monitored, particularly if there is the potential for generating more funds than can be economically justified. This situation is unlikely to happen in China at least during the 8th FYP, but the setting up of the Fund should consider such an eventuality for the longer term.

5.34   Financing for local railways development is solely with provincial funds, but the sources may vary from province to province. In the case of Henan province, 8th FYP local railway development will be financed through a mix of the province's capital budget, funding from prefectures and counties, and loans from users, such as coal and electricity companies. The government has also been developing a new concept of "joint-venture" railways. These would be for trunk railways linking to national system, but serving specific localities. While they would operate at full cost-recovery tariffs, they would need development finance, and central government funding would be mixed with funding from those who would benefit from the new railways, either via local government contributions or via enterprises. Experiments in this type of venture have begun in Guangdong and could provide a useful additional channel for raising funding for the sector.

5.35   In the case of highways, the central government budget will contribute 50-60 percent of total financing, covering roads included in the national road network, and for selected provincial roads in poor areas. The proportion in the latter case will vary from province to province, with the Western Provinces and Tibet reaching higher percentages (up to 100 percent) and the richer coastal provinces receiving a lower government share. The remainder of the costs for these roads, and the full cost of other roads, will be financed mainly with provinces' own funds, domestic loans from the State Communications Investment Corporation (SCIC) and foreign loans from multilateral and bilateral sources. Provincial funding, in turn, includes the province's budget and earmarked user charges. An example from Henan province is given in Table 5.1.

Table 5.1:   FINANCING OF 8th FYP HIGHWAY PROGRAM
HENAN PROVINCE
(Y billion)

User charges	
Maintenance fee, vehicles /a	2.80
Maintenance fee, tractors /a	0.20
Surcharge tax on freight /b	0.30
Tolls (2 bridges)	0.15
Provincial budget	0.25
Central government (MOC)	0.60
Foreign loans	0.60
Total	4.90

/a   The maintenance fee consists of a tax of 15 percent on the revenue of passenger and freight companies, and of Y 130/ton of capacity for own-account vehicles, including a proportional fee for private passenger cars. Total receipts amount to Y 5.1 billion for vehicles and Y 0.35 billion for tractors, are earmarked for the Energy and Communications Investment Fund, but the province only expects the amount shown in the Table to be returned by the Central Government for use in transport investments.

/b   The surcharge, to be paid by the owners of the freight, is Y 0.02/ton-km. Collection of this surcharge started in 1991.

5.36   While the sharing of highway investment costs between the center and provinces is a good policy generally, road financing is becoming increasingly critical, and there is a need for studies and consequent improvements in three areas:

(a) Formulation of a structure of road user charges that is economically efficient, provides the necessary resources, and is cost-effective to operate. For example, beyond generic product taxes, China levies no additional road user tax on motor fuels, which is considered as the most efficient way to charge road users and which is commonly used in other countries, nor does it levy an annual fee on vehicle ownership, which is considered an appropriate complement to motor fuels, especially for large trucks with heavy axle loads. For example, motor fuel taxes and annual ownership taxes, respectively, as percentage of total road user charges, amount to 65 percent and 13 percent in the USA, 49 percent and 22 percent in India and 39 percent and 22 percent in Japan.[12]

(b) Preparation of guidelines for setting up toll roads and toll rate structures. Guidelines are needed as provinces are increasingly resorting to tolling as a cost recovery and financing device, and there is increasing evidence that tolls are being established where traffic levels are too low. Setting up of tolls is leading to high road design standards resulting in high construction costs and to diversion of traffic to lower quality roads, thus negating the benefits of the better roads.

(c) Analysis and reformulation of the financial flows between user charges, central and provincial governments, and the road authorities, to ensure that fund arrive in time and at adequate levels to finance the roads maintenance and investment plans.

5.37   The financing of highway maintenance will become increasingly critical and needs to be paid closer attention. A recent study[13] concluded that under present criteria for allocation of maintenance funds, during the period 1990-2000 there would be shortfall of at least 30 percent in the amount of funds available to carry out maintenance at an adequate standard.

Role of Investment Corporations

5.38   A potentially important source of finance for transport infrastructure projects is the State Communications Investment Corporation (SCIC), one of the six investment corporations created in the 7th FYP. The SCIC has been operational since mid-1988. Its intended main business is to serve as intermediary for the provision of financing for projects in all transport modes, and to ensure that high standards of project economic, financial and technical analysis are used in project selection, appraisal and implementation. Its main sources of financing are central government funds allocated to it by the State Planning Commission, earmarked taxes on purchase of motor vehicles (30 percent of total revenues, the remainder going to the MOC) and fees on loading/unloading of cargo at the ports. SCIC funding for revenue-earning entities is on a loan basis, but it makes equity contributions in other cases (e.g., SCIC lends funds for construction of new berths, but provides grants for marine works).

5.39   With only about two years of operations, the SCIC is still looking
to define and assert its role better. In principle, an investment corporation
such as SCIC could make an important contribution to helping establish high-
level standards in the whole project cycle and to raising finance through
bonds. Its main problem appears to be its small size, with only about 100
staff, to cover a broad spectrum of transport projects, and to conduct a variety of business activities. It seems unlikely, given such staff limitations,
that SCIC can have the ability to conduct detailed analysis of projects in a
variety of modes, and to be able to have a level of economic and technical
expertise equal to or higher than the planning departments of the various
transport agencies. There is also an apparent duplication of functions, as
all projects receiving SPC financing are reviewed by China's International
Engineering Consulting Corporation (CIECC). Thus, it would seem important to
conduct soon an assessment of the SCIC, particularly on how best to focus its
work in relation to its stated objectives and to the size of the organization;
such review ideally should be done in the wider context of examining the performance of all state investment corporations, and of possible duplication of
efforts with entities such as the CIECC. Moreover, this further strengthens
the argument raised in Chapter III about the possible conversion of the SICs
into investment banks or corporations.

Box 5.4: THE BANK FOR PUBLIC WORKS, MEXICO

There is little experience in other countries with investment corporations for
public works, with which to compare the SCIC. One relevant to China is the Bank for Public
Works, Banobras, in Mexico. Banobras serves as an intermediary for external funds going to
Federal, state and municipal governments, where Banobras' main role is to transfer resources
but not to assess the projects these funds support; it acts as a development bank, mobilizing external and domestic funds, and relends them mainly for urban infrastructure projects,
for which Banobras conducts investment analysis; and it serves as a fiduciary for several
trust funds. Banobras loans bear interest rates that, as a minimum, cover the cost of its
funds. The experience with Banobras has been mixed. Its financial position is satisfactory, mainly because its large number of operations as intermediary where it derives a commission without bearing any risks. Its development banking function, the most relevant to
SCIC, requires expensive overhead for the whole project cycle, from assessment of the projects, to disbursements, monitoring and collection. Banobras does not enjoy special salary
or benefits advantage that would allow it to recruit the highly-qualified, above-average
personnel necessary to take a lead role in its development banking function and to provide
guidance in the evaluation and implementation of investment projects.

Use of Bonds

5.40   In the 7th FYP, experiments with bond financing were made for various transport investments. For example, bonds were issued to help finance the
Jimei highway bridge in Xiamen, Fujian Province. The experiment failed
because the bonds had short maturities of three years, and the toll revenues
were not enough to repay the bonds within three years. Henan Province issued
five-year bonds, at 3.6 percent interest paid at maturity to help improve and
pave provincial roads, but only transportation companies purchased bonds as a
way to contribute to the Province's road improvement efforts. Such attempts
to introduce bonds with short maturities--apparently on the assumption that
there would be no demand for longer term bonds--are not useful for the financing of long-term infrastructure investments. As a result of these and other
similar experiences, the 8th FYP does not envisage the use of bonds for

financing infrastructure. However, bonds might have a potential to mobilize savings to finance a few, high quality, high utilization facilities, where tolls, or other charging methods could generate enough revenues to repay interest and principal if maturity were to be longer term, for example, over ten years. As noted, the issue of such bonds could be coordinated by the SCIC or its successor.

Role of Small Entrepreneurs and Joint Ventures

5.41   Given the generally high cost of transport infrastructure investments and the still monopolistic nature of most transport services in China, the private sector will not become an important source of financing in the near future. Yet, private operators increasingly are taking a role in the provision of trucking and shipping services, and this role is likely to be expanded under 8th FYP policies to promote the services sector and further develop the collectively-owned town and village enterprises (TVEs). Their further involvement in trucking, which offers the largest potential for management and investment by small enterprises, requires, however, a drastic industry restructuring to establish the notion of common carriers as opposed to the prevailing industrial and commercial enterprises' practice of owning and operating trucks to meet their own transport needs.

5.42   At the same time, foreign direct investment may contribute financing for ancillary facilities through joint ventures, in practically all transport modes, following the experience of Tianjin and other ports [14] or, exceptionally, for large infrastructure projects such as a proposed 180-mile toll road in southern China. In the latter, a private investor and external commercial loans would contribute most of the financing. [15]

D.   Sectoral and Institutional Reforms

5.43   The 8th FYP intends to continue the gradual process of sectoral and institutional reforms initiated in the previous plan, aimed to enhance economic efficiency in the use of transport assets and resources. [16] The context of such reforms will be somewhat different, however, as: (i) structural changes in the economy lead to a higher proportion of manufacturing relative to raw materials, requiring more diversified transport services; (ii) further development of the road system and of aviation services will start to create the potential for competition among modes, at least for selected routes and commodities; (iii) collective enterprises--mainly the town and village enterprises (TVEs)--and private individuals will play a larger role in the provision of road and shipping services, and will normally offer such services at market-determined prices; and (iv) barriers to interprovincial trade start to fall. These gradual, but key changes affecting the operations of the transport system will lead to more competition and less central control.

Pricing and Competition

5.44   Earlier studies of the Chinese transport system noted that inadequate pricing was a major factor distorting utilization of the modes and inducing excessive demand, especially for railways. As already noted, significant corrections were introduced during the 7th FYP. Funding for the Railways Investment Fund will require additional, substantial tariff increases.

Implementation during the 8th FYP of a new costing system will allow the railway to properly cost services and propose tariff adjustments which full reflect costs for the various services it provides.

5.45   Similar efforts for assessing the cost structure are underway in ports and should allow a restructuring of tariffs. At present, there is too little differentiation in prices to reflect differences in costs and to encourage efficiency. For example, shipping companies earn a fixed price per ton shipped, and ports also charge a fixed fee per ton handled, irrespective of the size and form of the shipment, with the result that no one has an incentive to implement cost-modernization in cargo handling. As a first step, private boats should be permitted to set their own tariffs, and for administered tariffs the range of flexibility around posted prices should be increased to give shipping companies and port authorities greater leeway to reflect cost differences in their fee schedules.[17]

5.46   Trucking tariffs, currently some five to ten times those of the railways, are aberrantly high, but this is more the result of an inefficient industry organization, management and inadequate vehicles than of government-imposed rates. Substantial reforms of the trucking sector are essential to bring down road transport costs and rates, thus setting the conditions for increased road-rail competition. As noted below, the government has given indications that it plans to tackle this issue during the 8th FYP. As with the services sector in general (paras. 2.50-2.53) the most important steps are to establish an efficient licensing procedure and access to credit for small operators.

5.47   There is great scope for an increased role for TVEs in China that will allow a growing share of transactions, both in manufacturing and in services, to be operated outside the Plan. This will also apply to transport services, and will result in a gradual but sustained increase in the tonnage of goods, and number of people, being moved at fully commercial prices.

5.48   While current transport bottlenecks prevail, hampering the movement of coal and other key commodities, there is little scope for systemwide competition. For such key commodities, the government allocates traffic to the transport modes and, in the case of coastal shipping, it decides which commodities will go to which port; over the medium term, it will be necessary to continue to search for optimal rationing and routing rules base on economic efficiency. Increasingly, however, more freedom should be given initially for movements of other commodities, and, as the bottlenecks are removed, for the bulk commodities.

5.49   Changes in the factors mentioned above are creating the conditions for some competition among transport modes, at least in some routes and for the haulage of mainly light industry products. The construction of expressways and provincial roads will play an essential role, although the benefits will be constrained until the trucking sector modernizes. The experience in the industrial world is that the availability of modal choice to shippers is the foremost factor for government and public acceptance of deregulating and decontrolling transport services. In turn, deregulation and decontrolling has led to diversification of services and in prices, giving the shippers more choice, generally at lower prices.[18]

5.50   Benefits from competition in the construction of transport facilities, such as roads, in the form of lowering costs and encouraging a commercial orientation for the construction industry are widely acknowledged, and the Government would like to enhance this competition during the 8th FYP. Competitive bidding for civil works is gradually being extended, even in projects solely financed with local funds. For example, in the Kaifeng-Zhengzhou expressway in Henan province, that will be financed by province's and central government's funds and where works started in early 1991, contractors were selected through competitive bidding. The bids received were about 10 percent below what would have been paid if provincial construction companies had been assigned the work under average costs of works. This competition in civil works needs to be continued, and extended to the procurement of engineering services.

Sectoral Restructuring

5.51   Sectoral restructuring during the 8th FYP should focus on trucking, because: (i) trucking is, in relative terms, the most backward subsector in China's transport system, as shown by operating costs abnormally higher than in the rest of the world; and (ii) the diversification of transport demand and the needs of agriculture and light industry for door-to-door transport of breakbulk cargo, and the growth of China's road network urgently calls for increasing the efficiency, lowering costs and prices, and improving the quality of services of road transport.

5.52   The trucking industry's main problems are organizational and technological.[1] The first is characterized by a very small common carrier sector, as the large majority of trucks and services are by own account, that is, industrial, agricultural and commercial concerns meet their transport requirements by owning and operating their own trucks. This situation is partly a reflection of the lack of reliable commercial trucking services-- mainly operated by provincial and local governments--and partly the traditional business culture of self-sufficiency among China's large companies. One consequence of this organizational structure is low load factors for the vehicles, as trucks only carry the companies' supplies and products, and often carry no loads on the return trips. The latter problem is mainly the small capacity of trucks, normally 5-6 tons, mostly manufactured in China, which are highly inefficient for intercity transport.[19] The combined effect of these factors is high operating costs and, in the case of commercial trucking, very high tariffs. The government has expressed its intention to give priority to reforming the trucking industry during the 8th FYP.

5.53   The major organizational reforms already undertaken in the aviation sector should be consolidated during the 8th FYP, in particular by encouraging greater competition among the regional airlines, including on international routes. In addition, it would be appropriate for China to study the various ways aviation support services, such as air traffic control, air navigation

---

[1]   The World Bank is collaborating with the provincial government in Henan to study the trucking industry in more depth and to prepare a policy framework for its future development. This should be completed in 1993.

aids, and meteorological information, are operated in other countries and whether further restructuring of CAAC would therefore be warranted.

Decentralization, Autonomy and Economic Contracts of Modal Enterprises

5.54   The 8th FYP will continue the efforts initiated during the last two five-year plans to devolve planning, investment and management responsibilities from the central to the provincial and local governments and to the transport sector enterprises.

5.55   One of the most successful decentralization reforms in transport in the 7th FYP was in the ports, and is exemplified by the case of Tianjin Port (see Box 5.1). The 8th FYP does not envisage any significant expansion of its autonomy, or extension of it to other ports. However, in light of the successful experience of Tianjin, and the interest of other ports to follow the same path, the Government should consider revising the Plan's position on port reform. The Government, through the appropriate central agencies, such as the Ministry of Communications, should retain a key role for investment planning, and endeavor to improve analysis of the port system and of individual ports. At the same time, the government should encourage a greater market orientation, especially to give port managements progressively more leeway with regard to operational and commercial decision-making. Successful experiences from other countries indicate the need to provide greater management autonomy in such matters as organization, staffing and salaries, ability to contract work out, equipment and investments. Such experiences also point to the importance of letting individual port managements market their services and make agreements with port users, e.g., leasing, concessions, special discounts and other agreements which affect prices and costs, and of letting them have the choice of rendering services directly or through third parties. The central authorities role during the transition would be to provide advice and to monitor progress.[20]

5.56   The encouragement for the development of local railway lines (Box 5.3) fits well with government's policy of decentralization. These lines are managed independently from the national railways, although there is coordination in a number of areas. Some of the most successful reforms in railways in other countries are in the management of local lines, where local management can be smaller, more effective, and have a better knowledge of the demand and of the services required. This was, for example, the experience in the US during the 1980s [21] and there is a growing number of recent cases in other countries. In Thailand, since 1989, high-quality passenger services in three branch lines have been operated on a pilot basis by individual, private operators, rather than by the central railways, leading to important increases in traffic, mostly diverted from the road.[22]

5.57   The essential role being played by China's railways justifies the government's approach of attaching priority to improving economic and financial policies with respect to the railways, with less emphasis on organizational issues. This implies a focus of reforms during the 8th FYP on setting up and management of the Railways Investment Fund, implementing costing changes and tariff restructuring to put in place cost-based tariffs, and on completing and implementing comprehensive computer-based models to prioritize investments system-wide. However, changes in the structure of demand, and in

the development of competition from roads and other modes, should induce the
management to think strategically of the impact of such changes on its organization. Most major railways in market economies are evolving an organizational structure which focuses on market segments served, and on the policies
and investments needed to serve these segments; these railways are moving away
from the traditional, production-led form of organization, and are adopting a
market-oriented approach. Changes in this direction are taking place in the
national railways of Britain, France, Sweden, Finland, and Japan, among
others. In such railways, the tendency broadly is to divide the organization
into passenger and freight lines of business, with related revenue and cost
reporting. Depending on the specific circumstances of the railway, the broad
freight line of business may be further subdivided into the various major
commodity and/or customer segments, and the passenger line of business into
intercity passengers segment as well as a series of separate commuter services.[23]

5.58   The first round of contracts between the state and the enterprises,
economywide, began in 1985, is now being completed. Signing of second round
contracts started in 1990 and is expected to be completed soon. Contracts in
the second round will need to be more detailed and with more precise targets,
and be more incentive-driven and encourage decentralization, than were first
round contracts, which generally targeted bottom line financial results, and
in the case of transport, aggregate levels of traffic. One significant change
envisaged in the contract for the railways is to allocate payroll amounts--
from the center to the various enterprise levels--based on output, that is,
ton-km and pass-km produced, (appropriately adjusted to compensate for dis-
tricts' differences in type of traffics, line saturation, etc.) rather than on
the level of staffing as was in the first contract. Such change should allow
the railways to streamline the system of bonuses which supplement staff salaries, to reward increases in productivity rather than continuing to be auto-
matic additions to salary.

5.59   The second round of contracts will also need to make a start on
economywide reforms envisaged for the provision of social services. This is
important for all large enterprises, including the railways, where some
1.5 million staff out of its total labor force of 3.3 million work in the
provision of services to staff, such as housing, health and education. The
Ministry of Railways intends to gradually start raising the charges to staff
for the social services it provides, and to include compensatory payments.
This is a necessary first step for future reforms, which eventually should
lead to enterprises such as the railways bowing out altogether of direct provision of social services.

Intermodal Transport

5.60   The 8th FYP investments and reforms in individual modes will be
insufficient to make the best use of the system until intermodal transport is
modernized, particularly for the movement of containers and other unitized
cargo. This implies not only physical investments for intermodal transfers,
but improvements in the management, organization and commercial documentation
in transport and related agencies, such as customs. Some 450 intermodal
transport companies exist in China today, mostly serving domestic traffic and
offering station-to-station, rather than door-to-door services. Less than

50 percent of the containers move beyond the port, thus severely reducing the benefits of containerization. Of the domestic container traffic carried by rail, less than 6 percent moves door-to-door.[24] Key constraints hampering improvements in container movements have been identified by Chinese authorities, notably: loading and unloading equipment, storage facilities are inadequate and management information systems for organizing and following-up container movements need to be developed.

5.61   Improvements of intermodal transport would need to be selective and focus initially on routes and commodities where the potential is greatest. One approach would consist of identifying priority container corridors that are strategically important in order to provide faster, more reliable and cheaper transport services for exports, and, based on this, to formulate an intermodal transport plan for those corridors, including investments, organizational and documentation improvements.

E. Conclusions

5.62   The 8th FYP reaffirms the view that transport bottlenecks are a key constraint to economic development and endeavors to tackle this problem by allocating to this sector an albeit slightly higher proportion of central government investment than in previous plans, and by encouraging higher extra-budgetary investments.

5.63   In contrast to previous plans, the 8th FYP is more indicative, and, at the beginning of the Plan in 1991, sectoral and subsectoral allocations and identification of key projects had not been finalized. Available indications were that practically all modes would see higher investments, and this appears as a sound decision given the high economic costs of current bottlenecks, longstanding underfinancing for transport and the projected further integration and diversification of the economy, all of which point to the need for more diverse transport services.

5.64   In view of the fact that most transport bottlenecks countrywide stem from coal and other bulk commodities hauled over long distances where the railways offer the lowest costs, the Plan sensibly allocates to this mode the highest share of investments. But the plan also envisages substantial expansion of the road network in all provinces, and continued improvements in ports, inland waterways and aviation. Demand for the latter had the largest increases during the 7th FYP and the current Plan envisages significant investments in equipment and infrastructure.

5.65   Plan directions to modernize and introduce new technology appear to be well conceived, as such efforts will be limited and will be directed to the use of cost-effective designs rather than wasteful, overbuilt facilities. Special interest will be focused on railway and highways construction oriented to allowing faster transport services, such as expressways and faster speed railways, but only for a few key links and with prudent design standards. This is the case, for example, with planned faster railway speeds of up to 160 km/hr (which can be achieved with modern but conventional technology) and only a limited number of new highway expressways, including some initially to be built with two lanes only.

5.66   While the overall direction of transport investments appear to be appropriate, increasing efforts should be put into analyzing investments systemwide and to both broaden and refine the use of cost-benefit analysis, for which studies and appropriate tools have recently been developed or are being tested. The railways, in particular, should be particularly careful with plans for construction of new lines, which are long-life investments. The railways are key to providing the capacity needed for the millions of tons of coal and other bulk commodities which are essential for China's industrial development. Yet, China's high transport intensity relative to its national product, will have to fall gradually over time, in part as a result of increased energy conservation and efficiency.

5.67   The Plan envisages a substantial increase in enterprises', provincial and users' participation in the financing of new investments. This approach should enhance accountability and cost recovery. A Railways Investment Fund, to be financed through incremental tariff increases, is expected to provide some 13-22 percent of total Plan railway investments; local railways will be further developed and will be financed by provincial and other local resources. Provinces will also bear the brunt of developing their road systems, as cost-sharing with the central government (on average 50-50) will be limited to the national road network and selected rural roads in high-priority, poverty-stricken areas.

5.68   Improving cost recovery and financing needs to be given priority in all modes. While recent large tariff increases for rail services, both freight and passenger, corrected some of the most serious underpricing, more is needed both for economic efficiency and for mobilizing resources. The focus should be more on structure than on level of tariffs. During the 8th FYP, studies on costing will be completed for railways and ports which should allow the government to implement new costing systems and restructure tariffs. Improving cost-recovery and financing in highways has not been a priority in the past, as the road system was not a major factor in China's transport system. However, this is changing rapidly following substantial expansion of the network during the 7th FYP and further developments envisaged in the current Plan. The government should assign priority to modernizing its system of road user charges and financial sources for road construction and maintenance, as well as issuing guidelines for appropriate use of tolls.

5.69   Despite these various initiatives, however, it is not clear that there will be an adequate level of financing for the transport sector. As both domestic and international trade increase, the consequences of transport investment falling behind could be severe. The government will therefore need to monitor progress with the transport plan and intervene as appropriate. If such intervention proves necessary, three main avenues would seem appropriate: (a) as price and enterprise reforms ease budget pressures, infrastructure investment allocation could be increased; (b) transport price adjustments could be accelerated to generate higher surpluses in the sector; and (c) the government could authorize, with government guarantees, increased issuance of long-term bonds for the financing of transport investments.

5.70   Competition among transport modes, at least for some commodities and where the system has some slack capacity, has good potential for increasing during the 8th FYP, and to lead to more commodities being transported outside plan prices and modal allocations. This increased competition will result from four main factors: the diversification of the economy, with more light agro- and light-industry products; the further development of road and air transport; the larger role of township and village enterprises (TVEs) in the provision of services; and the reduction of barriers to interprovincial trade.

5.71   The most urgent sectoral reform is in road transport services for freight. Trucking costs and rates are aberrantly high (five to ten times those of the railways), mainly as a result of inadequately small trucks, and inadequate trucking industry organization, which lacks commercial trucking services and forces industrial companies to rely on their own truck fleets. Trucking offers a good potential for involvement by TVEs, but such potential can only be fully realized if the trucking industry organization provides adequate conditions for entry and competition, as well as access to credit which does not happen at present.

5.72   The second round of economic contracts between the state and the enterprises will coincide with the start of the 8th FYP. Such contracts are a key vehicle for promoting increases in efficiency, but the first round of contracts were too general. It appears that the second round will be more focused but may still also fall short of setting adequate, well-defined productivity targets.

5.73   In summary, the 8th FYP appears to give the transport sector the increased priority it requires and, within budget constraints, attempts to remedy longstanding neglect of the sector. The Plan does not fully identify all projects from the beginning, and this offers an opportunity to ensure that new, major investments are subject to rigorous economic analysis. Sectoral and institutional reforms will continue gradually, and the priorities for reforming costing and pricing are correct. It is however, essential that such reforms are effectively implemented during the Plan period, as they are vital to ensure a more efficient use of the system, to improve cost recovery, and to help transport enterprises and infrastructure enhance self-financing for capital and current expenses. An early start to reforms in the organization of the trucking industry is needed to improve road transport services, facilitate entry by small entrepreneurs such as town and village enterprises, and to promote competition.

VI. SCENARIOS FOR THE CHINESE ECONOMY

A. Introduction

6.1   The first five chapters of this report reviewed recent economic developments, China's development strategy, the results of past reform efforts and prospects for reform in the future. In reviewing these issues, we found that there were uncertainties in three areas in particular:

(a) It was unclear what would happen to inflation in the short term, and thus whether China would continue to enjoy inflation-free, moderate growth, or whether the economy would once again overheat and return to an inflationary upswing.

(b) The medium-term macroeconomic policy framework was not fully explicit, and consequently, it was unclear what would be the policy stance over time, particularly in the light of the fact that the current economic policy was at variance with the policy as stated in the framework, in that the framework called for moderate growth, while the actual policy was encouraging a rapid expansion. This is compounded by recent statements calling for accelerated growth.

(c) While the reform plan put forward a relatively comprehensive program of steady change over time, we found it wanting in certain key respects, particularly those related to the improvement of macroeconomic management via indirect economic levers, and the framework for improved management and performance of the state-owned enterprises.

6.2   It therefore seems appropriate to consider a range of possible outcomes for the economy over the coming period.1/ It should be stressed that these are not forecasts for the economy. Rather, they are consistent scenarios that we would associate with any particular set of policies. Therefore, while not being forecasts, they are intended to illustrate quantitatively the possible consequences of different policy choices over the next few years. This should be helpful in assessing alternatives and in sequencing and timing reforms.

6.3   China's macroeconomic prospects have been considered under three separate policy frameworks. The base case assumes that China makes good progress with a wide range of economic reforms, on a somewhat accelerated schedule in comparison with the program set out in the reform plan, as this seems to be the present intention. In particular, this assumes reasonable progress with the policy framework for the SOEs, and improved policy for the financial

---

1/ These scenarios have been constructed by using a RMSM-X model, a new standard projections model of the World Bank. The structure of the model and the assumptions for the various scenarios are provided in the Annex. It should be noted in particular that these scenarios were drawn up prior to the very strong growth statistics for the first half of 1992 being available, and this goes to reemphasize that these are not to be regarded as forecasts.

sector and public finance to improve macroeconomic management. It should be noted that this base case assumes growth performance somewhat better than the relatively modest 6 percent target of the 8th Plan. The rapid reform case assumes even more acceleration and development of the reform program, along the lines suggested in Matrix 4.1, and this has consequent impact in terms of high efficiency. The slow reform/economic cycles case assumes poor macroeconomic management in the short term, leading to a new bout of overheating and inflation and related slow progress on reform.

6.4   In the base case and the rapid reform case, we have not attempted to model the fluctuations around the trend that would be bound to occur, and thus the scenarios portray a steadiness that is most unlikely to happen. However, this is because these are scenarios not forecasts, and are meant to illustrate changes in fundamentals. The slow reform case, in contrast, does have fluctuations around a trend, but that is to illustrate the fundamentals of such a case, reflected in a repeat of the strong macroeconomic cycles of the 1980s. However, it will be seen that the range of differences in the economic growth performance between these scenarios is not so large: rather, the key distinctions are reflected in the degree of efficiency improvement, and consequently, in the level of welfare.

Table 6.1: THE BASE CASE, 1989-2000

	1989	1990	1991	1993	1995	1997	2000
GDP growth rate (%)	4.6	5.6	7.0	7.5	7.5	7.5	7.5
Total consumption growth rate (%)	6.5	2.2	7.4	10.3	8.2	8.9	8.5
Incremental capital output ratio	9.60	7.10	5.00	4.87	4.80	4.60	4.40
Investment/GDP (%)	38.4	36.6	35.7	36.5	36.0	34.5	33.0
Inflation (GDP deflator)	9.0	5.1	4.1	6.0	6.0	6.0	6.0
Imports growth rate (%)	7.8	-12.8	12.5	16.9	8.8	8.5	8.5
Exports growth rate (%)	7.8	12.6	15.9	7.6	7.8	8.0	9.4
Current account balance ($ m)	-4,460	11,935	12,236	-1,511	-5,918	-8,924	-10,328
Current account balance/GDP (%)	-1.1	3.2	3.3	-0.3	-1.0	-1.3	-1.0
Total Debt ($ m)	44,847	52,554	57,197	68,078	82,221	95,837	112,902
Total Debt/GDP (%)	10.6	14.2	15.4	14.9	14.4	13.5	11.4
Direct foreign investment ($ m)	2,613	2,660	3,340	3,753	4,217	4,738	5,643
Total debt service/exports (%)	9.8	10.3	11.5	9.2	8.6	8.3	7.7

Source: Mission estimates.

B. The Base Case

6.5   The results of the base scenario are shown in Table 6.1. As noted, the key assumptions for this scenario are that the reform program is implemented on a somewhat accelerated schedule, permitting further improvements in macroeconomic management and in the enterprise control mechanism. The recovery of 1991 continues, and the economy is then able to repeat the growth performance of the 1980s, with average growth around 7.5 percent per annum. This would mean that the target of redoubling GNP by the year 2000 would be achieved one year ahead of schedule. More importantly, with efficiency gains, this could be done at a growth rate of investment below this rate (in fact, below the planned growth of 5.7 percent) as the capital-output ratio would gradually fall from 7.1 in 1990 to 4.9 in 1995 and 4.4 in the year 2000, when the investment rate would be down to 33 percent of GDP. The sectoral growth pattern is, however, expected to be somewhat different than in the recent past. Industry is expected to show more moderate growth, at about 6-8 percent in GDP terms, while the services sector, and especially transport, finance and information services, are expected to be the leading source of growth, at around 9 percent per annum.

6.6   One particularly positive result of this scenario relates to consumption growth. The plan's projections look for 3 percent per capita gains in consumption over the period. However, the economy is almost certain to generate much better results than this, for two reasons. First, the very high trade surplus of 1991 can be expected to be eliminated during 1992-93, via growth of imports at very high rates, after which they level off on a basis of affordability (i.e., a balance of payments constraint). Second, government consumption declines slightly in real terms, and quite sharply as a share of GDP. The consequence of this is that total consumption is able to grow <u>faster</u> than GDP, at an average of 8-9 percent per annum in this scenario. To some extent, of course, this is to compensate for very low consumption growth in 1989/90.

6.7   Given the very strong external picture at the start of the plan period, with a current account surplus of 3.3 percent of GDP and reserves at 9 months of imports of goods and services, it is no surprise that the external sector does not prove to be a constraint. Indeed, if we were to construct a scenario simply on the basis of today's situation, with growth in imports based on general economic growth, it would be virtually impossible to eliminate the current account surplus for many years with any "reasonable" set of elasticities. However, the Chinese economy is not entirely "reasonable" and so it can be observed that imports which grew at almost 20 percent in 1991, are projected to continue to grow strongly in 1992, at about 21 percent in nominal terms. After this burst of import expansion to eliminate built-up unsatisfied demand, imports and exports settle into a pattern of growth at about 10 percent per annum in value terms. While this rate of export growth is below the level of the 1980s, it seems more reasonable given world trade prospects, and the much higher base from which China is now operating. Imports of capital goods are projected to be above average, reflecting the priority attached to technical transformation projects in the Plan, and import liberalization is expected to permit growth in consumer goods imports to satisfy the projected high level of consumption demand. Nevertheless, the current account deficit stays in the range of 1-1.3 percent of GDP throughout the decade, and while external debt grows, it actually falls as a share of GDP, and debt service ratios stay well under 10 percent.

6.8   Given the present high level of reserves, it seems reasonable to project that the ratio of reserves to imports will gradually fall to about four months' equivalent by the end of the decade. This requires relatively modest additions to the level of reserves, and so the net external financing requirement barely exceeds the current account deficit. In the base case, about $4 billion of this amount is expected on average to come from foreign direct investment and thus the net external borrowing requirement is about $6 billion per annum on average over the course of the decade. This is lower in real terms than the average level of net borrowing during the 1980s, which was about $5 billion per annum. The distribution of such borrowing between official and private sources is expected to be a bit more favorable to China than the last decade, as more and larger sources of official financing are now available, notably already committed additional Japanese credits, and access to Asian Development Bank ordinary resources, expected to rise to $1 billion per annum on a commitment basis by 1993. Thus, just over half of the external financing requirement is expected to come from official sources, and the balance from private sources, compared with the 40-60 split to date. However, it should be noted that we are still talking of very large absolute sums to be borrowed, and over the decade China will probably be among the largest international borrowers among developing countries.

6.9   On the fiscal and monetary accounts, the plan projects a slow reduction in the fiscal deficit, which restricts the government's use of credit. Therefore, the monetary authorities would be able to achieve the targeted ceiling on growth of money supply at about 12 percent per annum, without crowding out the private sector. In the Chinese context, however, 'private sector' includes the state-owned enterprises and we are projecting a gradual improvement in their performance, and therefore a reduction in their demands on the banking system, permitting a slow growth in credit, and a higher share of such credit for nonstate enterprises. Inflation control is assumed to remain a priority for the government--hence the lower rate of growth than in the 1980s--and inflation is expected to be in the 5-6 percent range over the period. Any sign of a return to double-digit inflation is expected to generate the sort of firm policy response that was witnessed in 1988/89.

6.10   Overall, therefore, this scenario would suggest bright prospects for the decade ahead if the requisite reforms to improve both macroeconomic performance and the efficiency of the SOEs are put in place. The natural tendency of the economy towards high savings and investment guarantees the achievement of the growth target, and the strong opening position permits major welfare gains to be achieved, especially given incremental efficiency gains as reforms proceed. This scenario, therefore, is based very much on the experience of the 1980s and the sort of growth performance and efficiency gains that were generated in that decade through the stimulus of improved incentives generated by reforms. It assumes, however, some "learning by doing," so that the mistakes in macroeconomic management are not repeated. The difficulty with this scenario lies in two respects:

(a) It assumes that the government will be able to move relatively quickly with the necessary enterprise and macroeconomic reforms; and

(b) While this reform package delivers substantial economic benefits, the economy still displays a considerable degree of inefficiency even in the year 2000.

It is these two issues that are the focus of the two alternative scenarios.

C.   Scenario 2:   Slow Policy Change/Macroeconomic Instability

6.11   In this scenario, we assume that the government still carries out reforms, but only on a rather gradual schedule. This means that the effects of reforms are not felt at the beginning of the decade. In particular, this derives from reform intentions in three major areas: tax reform, financial sector reform, and state-owned enterprise reform. As we argued in Chapters I and IV, without further reforms in these areas, it is not clear how the government can improve macroeconomic management capability, or the responsiveness of enterprises to such signals. In the absence of improvement in this area, which entails the strengthening of both the management and the impact of indirect economic levers, there is no reason to believe that the economy will be able to avoid repeating the cyclical pattern that we have observed in the 1980s. Indeed, there is clear evidence of growing amplitude in these cycles: the upswing of 1987/88 was the strongest of the decade, and it consequently took a downswing of the magnitude seen in 1989/90 to eliminate inflation. This said, Chinese downswings yield growth rates better than many other economies' upswings, so this does not imperil the basic targets, but rather it suggests the likelihood of continued tendencies towards instability.

6.12   Indeed, there continues to be concern in China that the economy could move quite rapidly back towards overheating and inflation in the short term, as was discussed in Chapter I. This would pose the biggest threat not only to the achievement of the economic targets of the decade, but more importantly to the success of the reform program. It thus bears repeating that the current calls in China for accelerating economic growth towards 10 percent per annum would not create a climate conducive to reform, and would be likely to lead directly to the sort of stop-go cycle witnessed in the 1980s and illustrated in this scenario. A key underlying assumption is that growth above 9 percent causes inflation pressure through bottlenecks.

6.13   The results of this scenario are shown in Table 6.2. The strong recovery that began in mid-1990 continues through 1992, and causes serious overheating by 1993, when inflation is around 15 percent and GDP growth around 9 percent. This causes the authorities to slow credit sharply once again, and the economy again goes into a downswing in 1995-97, with 4.5 percent average growth, while inflation falls back to under 5 percent. This permits the brakes to be released again in 1998, and again too quickly, so that we get another peak in the year 2000.

6.14   As we have observed in the last few years, this strong cyclical pattern raises the rate of inflation, which would average 9-10 percent per annum in this scenario, as the size of the credit expansion in the booms cannot be totally recouped in the downswings. This, of course, has a second consequence: the pace of price reform is dependent in China on the overall rate of inflation, as the government has clearly indicated that it will make progress on price reform dependent on moderate price rises.

6.15   The consequence of slow progress on price reform would be reflected in the absence of significant efficiency gains, and consequently in the level of investment required for the output target. As a consequence, consumption (welfare) gains are not much higher than GDP growth, and no higher after the initial boom in 1991/92, associated with the import boom. While investment as

Table 6.2: THE SLOW REFORM SCENARIO, 1989-2000

	1989	1990	1991	1993	1995	1997	2000
GDP growth rate (%)	4.6	5.6	7.0	9.0	5.0	5.2	8.2
Total consumption growth rate (%)	6.5	2.2	7.4	10.1	1.9	6.7	8.2
Incremental capital output ratio	9.60	7.10	5.00	4.00	9.70	4.85	6.10
Investment/GDP (%)	38.4	36.6	35.7	38.0	38.8	37.8	36.6
Inflation (GDP deflator)	9.0	5.1	4.1	15.0	7.0	3.0	12.0
Imports growth rate (%)	7.8	-12.8	12.5	18.6	0.7	5.2	8.2
Exports growth rate (%)	7.8	12.6	15.9	6.9	7.1	7.2	7.5
Current account balance ($ m)	-4,460	11,935	12,236	-4,177	-4,786	6,983	-14,004
Current account balance/GDP (%)	-1.1	3.2	3.3	-0.9	-0.8	1.0	-1.5
Total debt ($ m)	44,847	52,554	57,197	67,618	80,856	89,998	116,323
Total debt/GDP (%)	10.6	14.2	15.4	14.6	14.0	13.3	12.0
Direct foreign investment ($ m)	2,613	2,660	3,340	3,613	3,907	4,226	4,754
Total debt service/exports (%)	9.8	10.3	11.5	9.3	8.9	8.6	8.3

Source: Mission estimates.

a share of GDP falls to about 33 percent in the base case, it remains in the 36-38 percent range under this scenario.

6.16   On the external side,2/ the instability of GDP growth is of course mirrored in the balance of payments, which moves from surplus to deficit and back again several times. This has two consequences for external debt. First, the instability means that on average the authorities must have a higher level of foreign exchange reserves to be able to always have a reasonable cover, so we assume that reserves cannot fall below six months of imports. Second, the macroeconomic instability and absence of rapid reform--especially of price reform--deters foreign investors, and as a consequence, foreign investment does not rise from its present level in real terms. Both of these factors necessitate a relatively higher level of external debt, although it stills remains within reasonable proportions, with debt service around 9 percent of exports, and total debt averaging 14 percent of GDP.

2/   The issue in terms of downside risk that we have not attempted to project is that of a serious deterioration in export markets, and especially the removal of MFN status for China in the United States. This is for two reasons: first, the probability of this occurring is judged to be low on the experience of the last two years; second, we consider that the impact of such a step would be felt primarily through a reduction in the capital goods' import level in China, and thus in the pace of modernization, rather than in creditworthiness indicators, as China would be sure to react to such an event with tightened import restrictions.

6.17   Thus, in this scenario, there is no serious doubt that the basic plan targets can be achieved, but the projections show quite vividly the impact of continued instability in the absence of reforms to strengthen economic management capability and to generate efficiency gains, which puts welfare gains in this scenario some 40 percent below those of the base case.

D. Scenario 3: Accelerated Reform

6.18   In Chapter II, we examined how past reforms have had a strong impact on productivity gains since 1979. In Chapter IV, we reviewed current reform intentions, and identified several areas where we believed efficiency could be enhanced further through accelerated reforms. The difference between this scenario and the base scenario is thus essentially one of speed of reform implementation. However, we did note above (para. 6.10) that although the base scenario saw considerable economic achievements, it still left the economy with a high degree of inefficiency. Therefore, the distinguishing element of the accelerated reform scenario is that efficiency-enhancing reforms--notably price reform, trade reform, nonstate sector development, and financial sector (especially banking and capital market) reforms--are brought forward and improve the efficiency of investment. This is reflected in somewhat higher growth, but also lower investment rates and capital-output ratios.

6.19   This generates economic growth very close to the frontier of infrastructure capacity at about 8.5 percent per annum after 1992. However, under this scenario, the investment/GDP ratio would fall to close to 30 percent, a more "normal" ratio. This is made possible by a rapid decline in the capital-output ratio to finish the decade at 3.5, which is much closer to efficient levels.3/

6.20   There should be other, perhaps less obvious gains that can be measured. China imports raw materials, and wastes so much energy that its petroleum exports have been falling, and may become negative in the absence of price reforms. It seems reasonable to assume that correction of low prices for energy and raw materials would not only induce declines in demand and improvements in efficiency, they would also improve domestic supplies. Therefore, under an accelerated reform case we can project higher petroleum exports, and a lower elasticity of demand for imported raw materials. This, in turn, permits a higher level of capital goods imports, which has a further positive impact on modernization and thus on efficiency. Price reforms would also remove certain anti-export biases in the economy, by reducing the relative profitability of domestic and external markets. If this were combined with trade reforms, this could be expected to raise the level of exports.

6.21   There could be additional external effects, which are the opposite of those described in the slow reform case. First, the greater stability expected permits the present excess level of reserves to be reduced even fur-

---

3/   Alternatively, it could be that the increased efficiency makes resources available to improve the quality of investments, for example, through enhanced environmental controls, in which case, the I/O ratio would not fall so far. The current scenario is drawn to demonstrate the resource gain, not its use.

ther over the decade. Second, the improved policy environment should attract more foreign investment, and we are projecting that this would grow by about 8 percent a year, averaging about $5 billion. Both of these factors mean a relative decline in external debt over the decade, despite improved creditworthiness. The debt/GNP ratio would be only 9 percent in the year 2000, and debt service would fall from 11.5 percent in 1991 to 7.3 percent in 2000.

6.22   The results of this scenario are shown in Table 6.3. As can be seen, GDP is projected to grow steadily over the decade, as the government

Table 6.3: THE ACCELERATED REFORM SCENARIO, 1989-2000

	1989	1990	1991	1993	1995	1997	2000
GDP growth rate (%)	4.6	5.6	7.0	8.5	8.5	8.5	8.5
Total consumption growth rate (%)	6.5	2.2	7.4	12.4	10.4	10.0	9.7
Incremental capital output ratio	9.60	7.10	5.00	4.40	4.10	3.90	3.60
Investment/GDP (%)	38.4	36.6	35.7	37.4	34.9	33.2	30.6
Inflation (GDP deflator)	9.0	5.1	4.1	6.0	6.0	6.0	6.0
Imports growth rate (%)	7.8	-12.8	12.5	16.9	9.7	9.4	9.4
Exports growth rate (%)	7.8	12.6	15.9	7.9	8.1	9.1	9.8
Current account balance ($ m)	-4,460	11,935	12,236	-831	-5,056	-7,967	-9,355
Current account balance/GDP (%)	-1.1	3.2	3.3	-0.2	-0.9	-1.1	-0.9
Total debt ($ m)	44,847	52,554	57,197	67,040	77,576	88,414	99,713
Total debt/GDP (%)	10.6	14.2	15.4	14.5	13.2	11.9	9.4
Direct foreign investment ($ m)	2,613	2,660	3,340	3,824	4,460	5,202	6,553
Total debt service/exports (%)	9.8	10.3	11.5	9.1	8.5	8.1	7.3

Source: Mission estimates.

would desire, and improvements in economic management mean that cycles can be largely avoided. However, the key figure is the gain in consumption of over 10 percent per annum as a result of the efficiency gains. This means that while GDP is doubled over the decade, incomes are much more than doubled. It is to be noted that in this scenario we do not project any increase in the rate of inflation above the base case of 5-6 percent rate, associated with the higher growth rate. This is because it is assumed that the accelerated reform would strongly impinge upon fiscal and financial areas, which would reinforce the effectiveness of macroeconomic management under conditions of rapid growth.

6.23   The external sector is, on the whole, stable, but continues to expand as a proportion of the total economy. Exports grow at over 12 percent per annum (in value), and imports at about 14 percent. Of particular note, the composition of imports is different in this scenario from the low case.

The greater openness and higher consumption rate is reflected in increased consumer goods imports as well as the higher level of capital goods.

E. Conclusions

6.24   It must be repeated that these are merely scenarios, but we consider that the storyline underlying the scenarios is reasonably strong and coherent, and that they serve to illustrate the possible impact of different policies. This estimated impact is not based on economic theory, but rather derives from the experience of the last 12 years of reform in China. The highly decentralized economy is likely to continue to show instability unless instruments of macroeconomic management are improved, and economic reforms have proved their power to generate real productivity gains, especially when they foster the development of the nonstate sector. It is therefore our clear presumption that a slower pace of reform will generate a scenario more like Scenario 2, and that more rapid reform would generate a picture more like Scenario 3.

6.25   This said, there can be little doubt on two things. First, the basic GDP target is very achievable, and the Chinese economy will continue to show its tendency for high growth under most conceivable scenarios. Indeed, the potential for growth above this rate, without inflation, is clear and desirable, although moving to rates around 10 percent would be imprudent. Second, the economy will continue to have moderate external debt and continue to be highly creditworthy. Thus, on two basic counts, the future is bright under all scenarios. But that is not really the question. The scenarios suggest that there are policy choices to be made that can significantly affect the level of welfare of the Chinese people over the next decade. The report has suggested a set of reform and development policies that we believe could have a major impact on the level of efficiency and on the pace of employment creation in China over the next decade, and significantly change the face of the economy.

END NOTES

Chapter I

1. The cyclical nature of the economy and its performance in 1988/89 are discussed in detail in IBRD "Between Plan and Market," 1990.

2. See Chen Yuan, "Strengthening of Macro Control is a Requirement of the Deepening of Reform: Seeking Truth," 1991, #9.

3. See M. Blejer et al., China: Economic Reform and Macroeconomic Management, IMF Occasional Paper 76, Washington, D.C., January 1991.

4. For a fuller analysis of changing savings functions see IBRD, "Macroeconomic Development Under Decentralized Socialism": Report #7483, 1989, especially pp. 101-113.

5. The age profiles of wealth, income and savings in China show a pattern consistent with the life-cycle hypothesis of saving. It has also been shown that the level of pensions is not sufficient to maintain the consumption level of retirees without drawing from previously accumulated savings, being a powerful incentive to increase savings during their working age. See "Saving and Wealth Accumulation of Chinese Rural and Urban Household: A Cross-Sectional and Comparative Study," Yan Wang, MacNamara Fellowship Program, IBRD, October 1990.

6. See J.B. Stepanek, "China's Enduring State Factories: Why Ten Years of Reform Has Left China's Big State Factories Unchanged," in China's Economic Dilemmas in the 1990s: The Problems of Reforms, Modernization and Interdependence, Joint Economic Committee, Congress of the United States, Vol. 2, April 1991.

7. For a discussion of possible evidence pointing to the existence of upward bias in measuring China's real industrial output growth during the past decade, see T.G. Rawski, "How Fast Has Chinese Industry Grown?", mimeo, March 1991.

8. In some sense this a similar argument made by Hinds for the unworkability of decentralized socialism in Eastern Europe when there is no "interested party" to represent the owners of capital in enterprises. See "Issues in the Introduction of Market Forces in Eastern European Socialist Economies", in S. Commander, op. cit., pp. 121-154.

9. "Inflation in China: Patterns, Causes and Cures", op. cit., p. 155.

10. See IBRD, "Between Plan and Market," pp. 17-18.

11. Derived from Yun-wing Sung in "China Review," op. cit.

12. See Ma Kai, "Retrospect of China's Price Reform in 1990," in China Reform, Vol. 4, #1.

13. For a fuller discussion, see IBRD, op. cit., and forthcoming China Department Working Paper. "Reforming Intergovernmental Fiscal Relations."

14. "As central government requirements increased in mid-1980s, they threatened to crowd out the new decentralized investments that were fueling China's economic growth. At this point, the government, unwilling either to reduce its own borrowing or to crowd out decentralized investment, instead shifted to a much more expansionary credit policy. This shift was the proximate cause of inflation," B. Naughton, "Why Has Economic Growth Led to Inflation?," AEA Papers and Proceedings, AER, Vol. 81, No. 2, May 1991.

15. This point is cogently argued by Hsueh and Woo in "China Review", op. cit.

16. Evidence from Jiangsu suggest that about half of provincial export revenues were generated by TVEs in 1990. See China: Economic Development in Jiangsu Province, IBRD, Washington D.C., June 1991. At the national level, rural enterprises in 1990 exported about $13 billion worth of goods, almost 21 percent of China's total. See "The Performance of China's Economy," L. Zinser, in China's Economic Dilemmas in the 1990s, op. cit., p. 117.

Chapter II

1. See World Bank's "China: Socialist Economic Development," 1981.

2. See McMillan and Naughton "How to Reform a Planned Economy: Lessons from China," Oxford Review of Economic Policy (1992), and Lindblom "The Science of Muddling Through" (1959).

3. See World Development Report 1991, "The Challenge of Development," Box 6.2, p. 117.

4. See Yusuf (1991) "The Case for Gradualism," mimeo.

5. See World Bank "China: Between Plan and Market."

6. Figures from a CASS Survey quoted in MacMillan and Naughton, op. cit.

7. MacMillan and Naughton, op. cit.

8. Among these, two are particularly recommended: Carl Riskin "China's Political Economy," and the Chinese University of Hong Kong "China: Modernization in the 1980s," the latter being the closest to a textbook as we have seen. For an excellent shorter review, see Dwight Perkins "Reforming China's Economic System," Journal of Economic Literature, June 1988.

9. The first three documents referred to in this section have been reproduced in "Major Documents of the People's Republic of China, 1978-88", China Foreign Languages Press, 1991, and the fourth in "China's Economic Structure Reform" July 1991.

10. See Byrd and Lin "China's Rural Industry" and Anthony Ody "Rural Enterprise Development in China, 1986-90," Staff Discussion Paper No. 162.

11. See Yun-Wing Sung "The China-Hong Kong Connection" (1991).

12. See Fernando Montes-Negret "Financial Reform Priorities," World Bank Discussion Papers (forthcoming).

13. Several studies have purported to estimate a high degree of repressed inflation in China, but they ignore the fact that rapid institutional development and financial deepening has reduced velocity. See Feltenstein and Ha "Measurement of Repressed Inflation in China," Journal of Development Studies (1991).

14. For a thorough review of trade reforms, see Nicholas Lardy "Foreign Trade and Economic Reform in China, 1978-90" (1992), and World Bank "External Trade and Capital" (1988).

15. While many statistics used in this section are available in various government publications, those selected are drawn heavily from other sources, notably: Geng Xiao "What is Special about China's Economic Reforms?" World Bank Socialist Economies Research Unit, Research Paper 23; Chen, Jefferson and Singh "Lessons from China's Economic Reform"; and Jefferson, Rawski and Zheng "Growth, Efficiency and Convergence in China's State-Owned Industry." These papers were drawn up as part of an ongoing World Bank-Chinese Academy of Social Sciences Research Project: "Industrial Reform and Productivity in Chinese Enterprises."

16. World Bank (1992) "Strategies for Reducing Poverty in the 1990s", Report No. 10409-CHA.

17. See Perkins, "Reforming China's Economic System," Journal of Economic Literature, June 1988; and Chen, Jefferson, Rawski, Wang and Zheng, "New Estimates of Fixed Investment and Capital Stock for Chinese State Industry," China Quarterly, 1988.

18. See Nicholas Lardy "Foreign Trade and Economic Reform in China, 1978-90" (1992), Chapter 3.

19. See Zafar Khan "Patterns of Direct Foreign Investment in China," World Bank Discussion Papers #130, and Yun-Wing Sung "The China-Hong Kong Connection: The Key to China's Open-Door Policy" (1991).

Chapter III

1. China's recent experience with planning is well discussed in Barry Naughton's "China's Experience with Guidance Planning" Journal of Comparative Economies (141, 1990). In particular, he points out that "since the central government could not provide credible projections of its own behavior, the entire planning exercise was undermined."

2. See William A. Byrd, <u>The Market Mechanism and Economic Reforms in China</u>, M.E. Sharp Inc., 1991. Byrd notes that given limits on monitoring such activity, producers and commercial intermediaries have a number of avenues to capture the arbitrage profit implicit in the two-tier price system--inflation of input output coefficients, extracting side payments, levying service fees, etc. He suggests that, largely as a result of shortfalls in plan-allocated inputs, the level of plan fulfillment for several major industrial producer goods in 1987/88 fell to below 95 percent whereas earlier periods had seen levels of close to 100 percent.

3. For a discussion of these, see World Bank "World Development Report 1983" and World Bank "Finance and Investment."

4. Providing for production does not mean they must be produced by the state. See Stiglitz (op. cit), p. 40.

5. See Peter Harrold, "Investment System Reform in China: The Role of the State Investment Corporations," and Peter Dittus, "The State Investment System of China: Development Issues and Options," World Bank background papers, 1989. Also see Wang Jiye, "The Investment System" in Nolan and Fureng (eds.), <u>The Chinese Economy and its Future</u>, 1990.

6. The extrabudgetary construction tax applied at a 10 percent rate on investment out of retained earnings financed outside the state budget. See <u>Resource Mobilization and Tax Policy: Issues and Options</u>, World Bank Report #7605-CHA, 1989.

7. For more on the fiscal situation, see Chapter I. Also see Blejer and Szapary, "The Evolving Role of Tax Policy in China," <u>Journal of Comparative Economics</u>, 14:1990; Naughton, "Why has Economic Reform led to Inflation?" AEA Papers and Proceedings, May 1991; and "Prime Taxation Reform in China's Public Finance" in JEC Study Papers, 1991.

8. See World Bank "China: Reforming the Urban Employment and Wage System," Report No. 10266-CHA.

9. See Cannon, "Spatial Inequality and Regional Policy" in Cannon and Jenkins (eds.), <u>The Geography of Contemporary China: The Impact of Deng Xiao Ping's Decade</u>.

10. See Fuh-Wen Tzeng, "The Political Economy of China's Coastal Development Strategy: A Preliminary Analysis" in <u>Asian Survey</u>, March 1991.

11. See <u>China: Socialist Economic Development</u>, Volume 1, p. 74.

12. See "The Prospect for TVE Development in the 8th FYP Period" in <u>Economic Forecast and Information</u> (English translation in RMC Economic Research Monitor, July 1991).

13. See R. Dore, <u>Flexible Rigidities: Industrial Policy and Structural Adjustment in the Japanese Economy 1979-80</u>, 1986.

Chapter V

1. A major reason for the delay was government fears of further igniting inflation, which was double-digit most of the time from 1987 to 1990.

2. Since China relies heavily on the railways, the countries selected for comparison are those having the largest railway systems.

3. The high transport intensity is caused by several structural factors: low energy efficiency, demanding a large amount of coal; a large heavy industrial sector; a small service sector; suboptimal location of industry, stemming from long-standing, systemic distortions in prices of transport and raw materials; and from past industrial and regional development policies.

4. <u>A Study of the Soviet Economy</u>, IMF, World Bank, OECD, EBRD, Vol. 3, February 1991.

5. Further, the flexibility built in the 8th FYP should be used to economic advantage, notably to allow engineering design, and therefore investment costs, to be determined by economic analysis rather than by definition at the formulation of the Plan. This approach should allow to enhance the effective utilization of Plan funds for transport. This is especially important regarding Plan's objectives for introduction of modern facilities; decisions in roads on establishing tolls, control of access and on number of lanes, or, in railways design speed of fast train services, should be made as result of, and that prior to, the conduct of economic studies.

6. A recent, comprehensive study of coal transport has developed a model that allows to assess the optimal location, type, capacity and type of energy and energy-related transport investments, optimal coal routings and optimal use of mining technologies. Source: <u>China, Coal Transport Study</u>, Asia Region, World Bank and State Planning Commission, China, draft report, June 28, 1991.

7. On almost 26 percent of China's railway network lines (13,841 km), coal constitutes over 40 percent of the freight tonnage carried. Of these heavy coal lines, 48 percent were running at capacity at the beginning of the 8th Plan. Pricing reforms, energy system approaches (e.g, more mine-mouth power plants) and technical measures such as more coal washing are being studied and may reduce transport demand but are not expected to lead to significant reductions in rail capacity bottlenecks.

8. The need for careful analysis of future railway capacity expansion, particularly of new lines, is especially important in light of recent experiences in centrally planned economies. For example, the Soviet Ministry
of Railways predicts that railway freight traffic will decline by 12 percent through 1991; similarly, during 1989 and 1990, railway traffic in
German Democratic Republic, Poland and Rumania dropped by about one
third. In all these cases, the main reason appears to be structural
changes in the economy, rather than the (temporary) economic downturn.
Because China has already implemented substantial economic reforms and
transformation of its structure over the last 10-15 years, the situation
in China and the CPEs is not fully comparable. The situation is also not
comparable due to the higher share of railways in total traffic in other
CPEs, for example, in the former Soviet Union 90.9 percent in 1988.
China has already diverted much short-distance traffic to the road, and
the railways modal share was 57.9 percent in 1990. (Source: A Study of
the Soviet Economy, International Monetary Fund/The World Bank/
Organization for Economic Cooperation and Development/European Bank for
Reconstruction and Development, February 1991).

9. Altogether, during the 8th Plan, 60,000 km are expected to be built,
aiming at a network of 1.1 million roads by 1995. Emphasis will be given
to the construction of the national road system, expected to consist at
full development of 110,000 km, divided in some 70 main roads. During
the 8th Plan, 4,000 km of national roads will be built, including some
500 km of expressways and an additional 3,500 km of roads exclusively for
motorized traffic (Classes I and II roads). These priority roads are
selected from 30,000 km of heavily trafficked, highly congested roads.
Key 8th Plan projects include: Beijing-Guangzhou; Beijing-Shanghai;
Beijing-Harbin; Lianyungang-Lanzhou; Shanghai-Nanjing; Haikou-Sanya; and
Kaifeng-Zhengzhou-Luoyang.

10. Traffic densities on these routes range from 17.1 million ton-km/km for
the Changjiang main stem to 3.4 million ton-km/km for the Grand Canal.
These densities are substantially lower than in other major waterways of
the world. For example, the Rhine has 29 million ton-km/km, the
St. Lawrence Seaway about 54 million, and the Lower Mississippi about 76
million. Source: China: Water Transport Study, World Bank, 1987.

11. For example, in the recently started construction of the domestically-
financed Kaifeng-Zhengzhou Expressway, in Henan Province, highway
authorities have been asked to identify the investment components
according to the IOT categories, so that taxes will be paid accordingly.

12. Source: Ian Heggie, "Pricing, Cost Recovery and Accountability for Roads
in Developing Countries: An Agenda for Reform," World Bank Discussion
Paper, Draft Version, March 20, 1991.

13. Road Funding Study, Ministry Of Communications, June 1991.

14. In Tianjin, for example, a foreign venture with a Japanese company provides chassis for the movement of containers and another with a Hong Kong
subsidiary of a Dutch company for the construction of bonded warehouses
within the port. The latter may serve as a model for future bonded warehouses in other ports. See, "Ports," by Paul Jensen, in China Business
Review, November-December 1989.

15. <u>Engineering New Record</u>, Vol. 220 #25, June 23, 1988.

16. Based on experience elsewhere with key transport reforms, the 8th Plan's gradualistic approach seems to be a realistic one. For example, deregulation of transport industries in the US took about 20 years (or 10 years if the count is started with the collapse of the Penn Central Railway in 1970, which triggered faster action), and deregulation of the bus industry took 13 years in the United Kingdom. See <u>The Politics of Deregulation</u>, M. Derthic and P.J. Quirk, Brookings Institution, 1986.

17. <u>China: Water Transport Study</u>, World Bank, February 1987.

18. For example, in the United States, although railways, trucking and airlines were privately-owned, they were severely regulated until the late 1970s, with prices, routes and commodities fully under the control of the federal government. Many such regulations are still in effect in Western Europe, and are expected to be drastically reduced, but not totally eliminated, when the Common Market takes full effect in 1992.

19. For a detailed analysis of China's automotive policies and operations, see "China, Industrial Organization and Efficiency Case Study: The Automotive Sector," World Bank, confidential draft, June 20, 1991.

20. "Port Administration: Should Public Ports Be Privatized?" Zvi Raanan, draft Working Paper, World Bank Latin America Region, March 1991.

21. J.F. Doe. Update as of October 1986 in <u>New Railroads Formed to Take Over Lines Abandoned or Spun-off by Major Railroads</u>. Bureau of Economics and Business Research. College of Commerce and Business Administration, University of Illinois, Champlain, Illinois, 1986.

22. See "Privatization in Transport: Contracting-Out the provision of passenger railways services in Thailand." Hernan Levy and Aurelio Menendez, Economic Development Institute Working Paper, 1990.

23. "The Changing Role of Railways in Central and Eastern Europe: New Investment Priorities." Lou Thompson, Draft Working Paper, World Bank, 1991.

24. Mission notes. Discussions during Round-Table on Intermodal Transport, June 5, 1991.

A RMSM-X MODEL FOR CHINA

Table of Contents

A. Introduction

B. The RMSM-X Model for China

    B.1 Consistency Framework

    B.2   Behavioral Structure

C. The Debt Module

D. Closing the Model

A. Introduction [1]

1.   The RMSM-X (Revised Minimum Standard Model - eXtended) is a macroeconomic model with an elementary economic structure. The World Bank's country operations divisions use the results of this model for several macroeconomic reports, such as Country Economic Memoranda, Country Strategy Papers, and creditworthiness assessments. The present Annex is an outline of the RMSM-X model for China, used to develop the projections presented in Chapter VI of the main report. This model shares a common accounting framework with models developed for other countries, that ensures economic consistency among economic sectors.

2.   The RMSM-X macroeconomic model has four components; a consistency framework, a projections module, a debt module, and a module to produce standard tables. It was developed to use "Javelin Plus" software, which is a financial planning and analysis program. Javelin Plus is a variable based software, unlike Lotus 1-2-3 which is space-based, where information is entered directly into the cells of the spreadsheet. The model has a central database with different "views". Data or formulae can be changed in any "view", which will be reflected in other views. For data base management, including transfer of data, Javelin Plus has a useful import building block option, which can be used, for example, to interact with the Bank's Debt Reporting System.

B. The China RMSM-X Model

3.   The historical data required by the RMSM-X fall into seven groups that are linked together through the Model: National Accounts, Balance of Payments, Debt tables, Fiscal Accounts, Monetary tables, Trade and an additional worksheet consisting of the data required by the RMSM-X model but not available in other sectors. Whenever data in any of the tables are updated, the model automatically recalculates and generates new projections.

4.   The RMSM-X model for China includes four sectors. Government (non financial public sector), Private (non financial private sector), Monetary and Foreign sector. Government includes both central government and local governments, but excludes State-Owned Enterprises. The Monetary sector consists of the Peoples Bank of China (PBC), and the banking sector.

B.1.   The Consistency Framework

5.   The RMSM-X model is based on the flow of funds methodology which assures consistent projections. In a flow of funds model, each source of funds for one sector is also a use of funds for another sector. This system of double entry accounting portrays income, expenditure, savings and investment in such a way that consistency among sectors is achieved by requiring the budget constraints of all economic sectors to be satisfied simultaneously. Each sector must satisfy one of the following budget constraints:

          Sources of Funds   =   Uses of Funds

    or

          Current Income + Accumulation of Liabilities
          = Current Expenditure + Accumulation of Assets

---

[1]   This Annex is essentially a technical presentation of the model, and does not attempt to describe the economic forces underlying the assumptions or the outcomes of the three scenarios, as these were presented in Chapter VI of the main report.

or

$$\text{Current Income} - \text{Current Expenditure}$$
$$= \text{Accumulation of Assets} - \text{Accumulation of Liabilities}$$

or

$$\text{Net Savings} = \text{Net Accumulation of Wealth}$$

6.   Since we have chosen four sectors for China, there are four budget constraints. In addition there is one overall budget constraint representing the national accounts. In a flow-of-funds framework, sources of funds must equal uses of funds, therefore one equation out of five is linearly dependent on the rest. Thus, if we balance four budget constraints, by definition the fifth one will automatically be satisfied. All these budget constraints are of identical form. They can also be written as:

$$\text{Current Sources} = \text{Current Uses}$$
$$\text{Capital Sources} = \text{Capital Uses}$$

This separation of current account and capital account, which is sometimes referred to as "above" and "below" the line, focusses on how different sectors finance their current and capital expenditure (savings).

7.   There are three stages in building a consistency framework. The first step is identification of total flows in each sector. The next step is to disaggregate each flow based on factor ownership. For instance, interest payments on bonds is a use for the government and a source for private sector. In Table 1 this relationship is reflected by entering interest payments in the column of the government and the row of the private sector. The third step is the sequence in which different sectors are closed. This is determined by the hierarchy of original data sources. Usually, the foreign sector is chosen as the first sector to be closed and this sector would be given priority over other sources in closing other sectors.

8.   Table 1 presents the flow of funds matrix for the current account and Table 2 for the capital account. As mentioned earlier, the rows represent the sources of revenue ("incomings") to a sector and the columns represent uses of revenue of that sector ("outgoings").

FOREIGN SECTOR:

Current Account

9.   Current revenues of the foreign sector are imports (IMt), interest payments from government (iF_g), private (iF_p) and monetary sector (iF_m); transfer payments from government (T_{gf}) and private sector (T_{pf}); profit remittances from private sector (PR_{pf}) (profit that overseas Chinese send back home), and other factor service payments ($OTHFSP_{gf}$). Similarly current expenditures of the foreign sector are equal to the exports (Xt), transfers from abroad to the government (T_{fg}) and the private sector (T_{fp}); workers remittances (WR) and profit remittances on Chinese investment from abroad (PR_{fp}), current official grants (COG), interest payments on foreign reserves ($iRES_m$) and finally foreign savings (S_f) (current account deficit). Foreign savings (S_f) is the residual in the current account of the foreign sector. It is a use for the foreign sector and a source for the national accounts (see Table 3).

$$IMt + iF_g + iF_p + iF_m + T_{gf} + T_{pf} + PR_{pf} + OTHFSP_{gf} =$$
$$Xt + T_{fg} + T_{fp} + WR + COG + PR_{fp} + iRES_m + S_f$$

Exports are introduced at the intersection of the production accounts with the foreign sector with a negative sign.

Capital Account

10.   The capital account of the foreign sector states that foreign savings (S_f) plus changes in foreign reserves ($dARES_m$) must equal the net financing flow of the foreign debt to the government (dAF_g), private (dAF_p) and monetary sectors (dAF_m); foreign direct investment (DFI), other long term flows (OTH LT), net flow from the IMF (NDFt), net short term flow (NDSTt), capital flows not elsewhere included (Capflow), official capital grants (KOG) and errors and omissions (E&O).

$$S_f + dARES_m = dAF_g + dAF_p + dAF_m + DFI + OTH\ LT + NDFt + NDSTt + Capflow + KOG + E\&O$$

Here net financing inflow to the private sector (dAF_p) is the residual.

GOVERNMENT:

Current Account

11.   The government's current revenues consist of direct (TD) and indirect tax revenue (TI) less subsidies (Sub), non tax revenue (NTR) current official grants (COG) and transfer payments from abroad (T_{fg}).   Revenues are used to finance interest payments on the foreign debt (iF_g), and domestic debt which includes the loans from PBC (iCR_g), and domestic bonds (iB_{gp}); transfer payments to the private sector (T_{gp}) and abroad (T_{gf}), other factor service payments ($OTHFSP_{gf}$), government consumption (C_g) and savings (S_g). Government savings (S_g) is the residual i.e. this is the balancing item between the excess resources over uses (see Table 4).

$$TD + TI - Sub + NTR + COG + T_{fg} =$$
$$iF_g + iCR_g + iB_{gp} + T_{gp} + T_{gf} + OTHFSP_{gf} + C_g + S_g$$

Capital Account

12.   The government savings (S_g) together with the increase in net foreign (dAF_g) and domestic indebtedness which includes loans from PBC (dCR_g) and sale of domestic bonds (dB_{gp}); and foreign capital grants (KOG) to finance the gross investment of the government (I_g) and its capital transfers to the private (dKT_{gp}) and monetary sectors (dKT_{gm}).

$$S_g + dB_{gp} + dCR_g + dAF_g + NDFt + KOG = I_g + dKT_{gp} + dKT_{gm}$$

Here dB_{gp} is the residual.

MONETARY SECTOR:

Capital Account

13.   For the monetary sector, we start with the capital account and determine its savings (change in net worth) and shift up to the current account. Assets and liabilities, denominated in local currency, are extracted from the balance sheets of Peoples Bank of China and Specialized Banks, and are used to derive the financing flows which are simply the changes in local currency stocks. In the case of foreign debt, to reconcile the stocks and flows three effects have to be considered - the timing effect, the revaluation effect and the cross-currency effect.

Timing Effect	=	$(E^{eop} - E^{avg}) * \$Flow$
Revaluation Effect	=	$(E^{eop} - E^{eop}_{-1}) * \$Stock_{-1}$
Cross-currency Effect	=	$(\$Stock - \$Stock_{-1} - \$Flow) * E^{eop}$

- 174 -

where E^{eop} = end-of-period exchange rate
E^{avg} = period average exchange rate
$\$Flow$ = US dollar flow of capital reported in the balance of payments
$\$Stock_{-1}$ = last periods debt stock

The revaluation and timing effects occur only when stock sources denominated in one currency are converted to flows in another. But these effects don't appear in flow accounts. In order to compensate for these effects in the foreign debt and reserve figures, an item in the liability side of the monetary flow account called "total revaluation effect" is created. This item is equal to the difference between the summation of the three effects for reserves and summation of the three effects for debt.

14.　　Liabilities (sources) include increases in demand (dDD_p) and time deposits (dTD_p), currency in circulation (dCU_p), capital grants from government (dKT_{gm}), foreign borrowing (dAF_m) and changes in net worth (dNW_m). Assets (uses) are increases in domestic credit to government (dCR_g) and the private sector (dCR_p) (including State-Owned enterprises), plus increase in reserves ($dARES_m$). The monetary sector's changes in net worth (dNW_m) closes the capital account. Details are given in Table 5.

$$dDD_p + dTD_p + dCU_p + dKT_{gm} + dAF_m + dNW_m = dCR_g + dCR_p + dARES_m$$

Current Account

15.　　Current revenue includes interest payments received from the government (iCR_g), private (iCR_p), and foreign sectors ($iRES_m$). It is used to pay interest on demand (iDD_p) and time deposits (iTD_p), interest on the foreign debt (iF_m), changes in net worth (dNW_m), and profits or loss ($P\&L_m$). Given that changes in net worth of the monetary sector was determined in the capital account, profit or loss ($P\&L_m$) becomes the adjusting residual in the current account. It is a use for the monetary sector and is transferred as current source to the private sector.

$$iCR_g + iCR_p + iRES_m = iDD_p + iTD_p + iF_m + dNW_m + P\&L_m$$

NATIONAL ACCOUNTS

Current Account

16.　　Consumption by the government (C_g) and private sector (C_p), savings by the government (S_g), private sector (S_p), and foreign sector (S_f), and changes in net worth of the monetary sector (dNW_m) should equal GDP at factor cost (GDPfc) plus indirect taxes (TI) less subsidies (Sub), plus the resource balance: imports (IMt) minus exports (Xt). This equation is the current price national income (see Table 6).

$$C_g + C_p + S_g + S_p + S_f + dNW_m = GDPfc + TI - Sub + (IMt - Xt)$$

Capital Account

17.　　Investment expenditure by the government (I_g) and private sector (I_p) is financed by the savings from the government (S_g), private (S_p) and foreign sectors (S_f) plus changes in net worth of monetary sector (dNW_m).

$$I_g + I_p = S_g + S_p + S_f + dNW_m$$

PRIVATE SECTOR

Current Account

18.   The private sector receives interest on government bonds (iB_{gp}), demand (iDD_p) and time deposits (iTD_p); transfer payments from government (T_{gp}) and abroad (T_{fp}), workers remittances from overseas Chinese (WR), profit remittances on overseas Chinese investments (PR_{fp}), output (GDP at factor cost: GDPfc) and profit or loss from monetary sector ($P\&L_m$).   It pays direct taxes (TD), depreciation funds and losses of state owned enterprises (NTR), interest on credit from monetary sector (iCR_p), interest on foreign loans (iF_p), and profit remittances on foreign investment in China (PR_{pf}), transfer payments (T_{pf}), consumption (C_p) and the rest is saved (S_p).

$$iB_{gp} + iDD_p + iTD_p + T_{gp} + T_{fp} + WR + PR_{fp} + GDPfc + P\&L_m =$$
$$TD + NTR + iCR_p + iF_p + PR_{pf} + T_{pf} + C_p + S_p$$

Private savings (S_p) is the residual.   It closes the current account of the private sector.   See Table 7 for details.

Capital account

19.   The private sector capital sources include foreign direct investment (DFI), net foreign loans (dAF_p), other long term loans (OTH LT), net short term loans (NDSTt), capital not elsewhere included (Capflow), errors and omissions (E&O), plus increase in capital grants from government (dKT_{gp}) and increase in credit from monetary sector (dCR_p) plus savings (S_p).   It is used to finance investment (I_p), purchase of government bonds (dB_{gp}), increase in demand (dDD_p) and time deposits (dTD_p), increase in currency holding (dCU_p).

$$DFI + dAF_p + OTH LT + NDSTt + Capflow + E\&O + dKT_{gp} + dCR_p + S_p =$$
$$I_p + dB_{gp} + dDD_p + dTD_p + dCU_p$$

B.2 Behavioral Structure

20.   The flow of funds framework developed above for China, is linked to the RMSM-X model that contains the behavioral and technical relationship among variables.   These rules describe how income, expenditures, and financial asset holdings of each economic sector in China will evolve over time.   The projection period for the model is 1991-2000 and the base year is 1990.   Detailed base case assumptions are given in Table 8, and it is these assumptions that are referred to below.   Assumptions for the two alternative scenarios in comparison with the base scenario can be found in Table 9.

The Real Economy

21.   Production in the Chinese domestic economy is broken down into three types of goods - agriculture, industry and services.

$$K\ GDP = K\ AGR + K\ IND + K\ SER$$

where the prefix K denotes real values. On the supply side GDP and agriculture are assumed to grow at a constant rate of 7.5% and 3.0% p.a respectively, while industry is assumed to grow at faster in the beginning of the decade (ranging from 13.0% to 9.0% p.a) and levels off at 7.5% at the end of the decade (starting from 1998). Given these assumptions the growth rate of services is determined residually/endogenously in the model.

22.   On the demand side there are four expenditure items - consumption, investment, exports and imports. The following behavioral rules are used -

a). <u>Exports</u>: Exports are disaggregated into four types - food, petroleum, manufacturing, and other. Food exports are assumed to grow at 5.0 percent p.a and petroleum exports are expected to decline at 2.0 percent p.a. Manufacturing exports start at 9.5 percent p.a during the beginning of the decade and rise to 10.0 percent by the end of the decade. Other exports and non factor service exports are assumed to grow at 9.0 and 8.5 percent respectively.

b). <u>Imports</u>: Imports are broken down into five categories - food, consumer goods, petroleum, intermediate goods, and capital goods. Imports are linked to GDP through import-GDP elasticities. Food and petroleum elasticities are assumed to be unity, which translates into a real growth rate of 7.5 percent (real GDP growth rate). Intermediate and manufactured goods elasticities are projected at 1.1. and 1.2 respectively. These five components are added to get the value of total imports on a cif basis, which therefore has an overall elasticity of about 1.1.

c). <u>Investment</u>: Investment is linked to GDP through assumption on the incremental capital output ratio (ICOR). GDP is already determined above and given the assumptions on the ICOR, total investment is determined endogenously. ICOR is assumed to decline from 5.2 in 1992 to 4.4 by 2000. Government investment is assumed at 3.5 percent of nominal GDP and thus private investment is the difference between the total investment and government investment.

d). <u>Consumption</u>: In the following income equation

$$K\ GDP = K\ Ct + K\ It + K\ Xt - K\ IMt$$

all other variables are defined before and thus total consumption is calculated as residual. We assumed government consumption to grow at 10.0 percent p.a, thus making private consumption the true residual.

23.   These are the behavioral rules for real variables. Nominal variables are just the product of the respective real variables and the corresponding deflator. This applies to nominal GDP, investment, imports and exports. The deflators for imports and exports are calculated using world market prices projected by the World Bank's commodities division. Consumption deflator is obtained as residual.

Fiscal Accounts:

All taxes are projected as a fixed percentage of nominal GDP. On the revenue side, direct taxes are calculated at 5.0 percent of nominal GDP, indirect taxes 13.0 percent, non tax revenue at 3.0. Government expenditures in addition to direct consumption and investment noted above, for example subsidies and transfers, are assumed to remain at 5.0 percent of nominal GDP.

Assets Market

24.   The RMSM-X model integrates both real and monetary blocks. This is the advantage over the earlier RMSM model which included only the real block. There are four assets in the model - money, credit from Peoples Bank of China, domestic bonds, and foreign debt.

25.   In the money market, money supply (M2) is projected as a ratio of GDP - the inverse of velocity of circulation - - and it is fixed exogenously at 1.30. This money supply is split into currency, demand deposits and time deposits using ratios that add up to unity (17.0, 41.5, and 42.5 percent respectively).

26.   In the domestic bond market, various types of bonds are issued by the government and they are bought by the private sector (both individuals and enterprises).

27.   In the domestic credit market, total credit of the Peoples Bank of China equals the credit to the government and to the private sector.

28.   In the foreign market, the net demand for foreign credit is calculated in the balance of payments current account, which should equal the total supply of foreign credit to the government, monetary and private sectors.

29.   We assume that China is not credit constrained in the foreign market. The amount of foreign financing required is transferred to the private commercial borrowing category in the debt model which in turn calculates the interest payments.

C. The Debt Module

30.   The World Bank's Debt Reporting System (DRS) contains detailed debt information by different types of creditors. The debt module for China consists of 12 types of creditors: 1). IDA, 2). Other Multilateral Concessional, 3). IBRD, 4). Other Multilateral Non-concessional, 5). Bilateral Concessional, 6). Bilateral Non-concessional, 7). Private Bonds, 8). Private Commercial Banks, 9). Other Private, 10). Private Non-Guaranteed, 11). IMF, and 12). Short-term.

31.   China has been a creditworthy country in the international capital market and has been in current status regarding its payments on international debt. A simple debt module is developed for China and debt restructuring and other complex options are not considered since they are not relevant for China.

32.   The debt module takes into account both the existing (pipeline) debt and new commitments by credit and projects debt stocks, amortization, and interest payments. This data is passed on to the RMSM-X model through import building block option. Then RMSM-X model calculates the required additional foreign borrowing needed, which is referred to as "Gapfil". Finally this Gapfil is transferred to the debt module again.

33.   The private commercial borrowing (category 8) is assumed to be the "marginal creditor" for China. This is the category to which the unidentified debt is assumed to be contracted with. The debt module then projects the debts stock, amortization, and interest payments on the unidentified debt or Gapfil.

D. Closing the Model

34.   There are two types of closing rules - normative, and positive. The purpose of the normative closure rule is to find the fiscal, monetary, and exchange rate policies that are consistent with a given set of macroeconomic policy objectives. This closure rule is relevant for our purpose. The other closure rule is applied to find the effect on the target variables of given fiscal, monetary, and exchange rate policies, and since China has not announced explicit future policies in this area, we have not formulated positive cases.

35.   In the goods market private consumption is determined endogenously. Given the money supply in the money market, credit to the private sector and the purchase of government bonds, balances the domestic market. The total inflow of foreign borrowing (after taking pipeline debt into account) is derived in the foreign sector and passed on to the private sector. Closure in this case, given a set of base assumptions and relationships, is ultimately a matter of judgement with respect to these residual variables in relation to past experience and trends in other variables, for example by examining marginal savings rates and debt service ratios.

Table 1

12 May 1992, 10:43 AM

C H I N A

MATRIX OF SOURCES AND USES OF FUNDS for 1990

(Billion Yuan)

CURRENT ACCOUNT:	Government Sector	Private Sector	Monetary Sector	Foreign Sector	Production Account	Total Sources
Government Sector	/////	TD 71.9 / NTR 47.0		COG 0.0 / Tfg 0.0	TI 227.6 / -Sub 95.8	250.7
Private Sector	Tgp 59.0 / iBgp 2.9	/////	P&Lm 56.9 / iDDp 37.6 / iTDp 33.3	WR 0.5 / Tfp 0.4 / PRfp 0.0	GDPfc 1642.2	1833.0
Monetary Sector	iCRg 0.0	iCRp 116.1	/////	iRESm 7.4		123.5
Foreign Sector	OTHFSPgf 0.4 / iFg 2.5 / Tgf 0.0	Tpf 0.0 / iFp 8.9 / PRpf 0.0	iFm 1.1	///// Sf	IMt 255.2 / -Xt 316.7	-48.7
Consumption & Savings Account	Cg 146.2 / Sg 39.6	Cp 876.5 / Sp 712.7	dNWm -5.4	Sf -57.1	/////	1712.5
Total Uses	250.7	1833.0	123.5	-48.7	1712.5	

- 179 -

C H I N A

Table 2

MATRIX OF SOURCES AND USES OF FUNDS for 1990

(Billion Yuan)

12 May 1992, 10:43 AM

CAPITAL ACCOUNT:	Government Sector	Private Sector	Monetary Sector	Foreign Sector	Savings Account	Total Sources
Government Sector		dBgp 10.2	dCRg 17.4	KOG 0.0 dAFg 11.6 NDFt -1.7	Sg 39.6	77.1
Private Sector	dKTgp 9.5		dCRp 261.3	DFI 12.7 dAFp 1.0 OTH LT -9.8 NDSTt -9.6 Capflow 0.0 E&O -11.1	Sp 712.7	967.0
Monetary Sector	dKTgm 0.0	dDDp 105.2 dTDp 199.5 dCUp 29.9		dAFm 3.1	dNWm -5.4	332.3
Foreign Sector			dARESm 53.6		Sf -57.1	-3.5
Investment Account	Ig 67.6	Ip 622.2		-3.8	689.8	689.8
Total Uses	77.1	967.0	332.3			

STATISTICAL APPENDIX

1.   National Accounts

2.   Balance of Payments

3.   Exports

4.   Imports

5.   Debt

6.   Money, Credit and Interest Rates

7.   Fiscal Accounts

8.   Agriculture

9.   Industry

10.   Wages

11.   Employment

12.   Prices

13.   Investment and Inventories

14.   Energy

15.   Transport

1. National Accounts:

1.1.	in Current Prices.
1.2.	in Constant 1980 Prices.
1.3	Implicit Price Deflators 1980=100
1.4	Percentage Shares to GNP in Current Prices.
1.5	Percentage Shares to GNP in Constant 1980 Prices.
1.6	Percentage Growth Rates in Current Prices
1.7.	Percentage Growth Rates in Constant 1980 Prices.
1.8.	Percentage Growth Rates of (1980 based) Implicit Price Deflators.
1.9.	Sources of Growth in Constant 1980 Prices.
1.2b.	in Constant 1987 Prices.
1.3b.	Implicit Price Deflators 1987=100.
1.7b.	Percentage Growth Rates in Constant 1987 Prices.
1.8b.	Percentage Growth Rates of (1987 based) Implicit Price Deflators.
1.9b.	Sources of Growth in Constant 1987 Prices.

2. Balance of Payments:

2.1.	in Billion US$.
2.2.	Percentage Growth Rates.
2.3.	Factor and Non-factor Services
2.4.	Foreign Transfers.
2.5.	International Reserves.

3. Exports:

3.1.	Merchandise Exports in Million US$).
3.2.	Percentage Shares of Merchandise Exports.
3.3.	Percentage Growth Rates of Merchandise Exports.
3.4.	Exports in Current and Constant 1980 Prices in Million US$.
3.5.	Exports in Current and Constant 1987 Prices in Million US$.
3.6.	Exports in Current and Constant 1980 Prices in Billion Yuan.
3.7.	Exports in Current and Constant 1987 Prices in Billion Yuan.
3.8.	Exports of Goods & Non Factor Services in Million US$ & Yuan
3.9.	Implicit Price Indices of Exports of Goods & NF Services.
3.10.	Total Exports and its Relative Share in the World Exports.

4. Imports:

4.1.	Imports in Million US$).
4.2.	Percentage Shares of Imports.
4.3.	Percentage Growth Rates of Imports.
4.4.	Imports in Current and Constant 1980 Prices in Million US$.
4.5.	Imports in Current and Constant 1987 Prices in Million US$.
4.6.	Imports in Current and Constant 1980 Prices in Billion Yuan.
4.7.	Imports in Current and Constant 1987 Prices in Billion Yuan.
4.8.	Imports of Goods & Non Factor Services in Million US$ & Yuan
4.9.	Implicit Price Indices of Exports of Goods & NF Services.

5. External and Domestic Debt:

5.1.	External Debt: Disbursements and Repayments.
5.2.	External Debt: Interest and Debt Outstanding.
5.3.	External Borrowing: Growth Rates, Ratios and Terms.
5.4.	Domestic Debt: Bonds Issued

6. Money, Credit and Interest Rates:

6.1.   Monetary Survey 1984-91.
6.2.   Operations of the People's Bank, 1985-91.
6.3.   Monetary and Velocity Developments, 1984-91 (% Growth Rate).
6.4.   Specialized and Universal Banks' Assets & Liabilities.
6.5.   Balance Sheets of Rural Credit Cooperatives 1986-91.
6.6.   Assets of the Specialized Banks.
6.7.   Liabilities of the Specialized Banks.
6.8.   Profit & Losses of the Specialized Banks.
6.9.   Banking System: Nominal Annual Interest Rates on Deposits.
6.10.   Banking System: Nominal Annual Interest Rates on Loans for Working
         Capital.
6.11.   Banking System: Nominal Annual Interest Rates on Loans for Fixed
         Capital.
6.12.   Banking System: Nominal Annual Interest Rates on Loans for Other
         Purposes.

7. Fiscal Accounts:

7.1.   Structure of Government Revenue in Billion Yuan.
7.2.   Structure of Government Revenue as a % of Total Revenue.
7.3.   Structure of Government Revenue as a % of GNP.
7.4.   Structure of Government Expenditure in Billion Yuan.
7.5.   Structure of Government Expenditure as a % of Total Revenue.
7.6.   Structure of Government Expenditure as a % of GNP.
7.7.   Budget and Its Financing 1978-91.

8. Agriculture:

8.1.   Production of Major Crops in Million Tons.
8.2.   Production of Major Crops in Percentage Growth Rates.
8.3.   Total Sown Area in Million Hectares.
8.4.   Total Sown Area in Percentage Growth Rates.
8.5.   Average Unit Area Yield of Major Crops in Kg/Hectare.
8.6.   Average Unit Area Yield of Major Crops in % Growth Rates.

9. Industry:

9.1.   Gross Output Value of Industry in Billion Yuan.
9.2.   Gross Output Value of Industry in Percentage Shares.
9.3.   Output of Major Industrial Products in Million Tons.
9.4.   Output of Major Industrial Products in % Growth Rates.
9.5.   Profits of State Owned Enterprises in Billion Yuan and Percentage
         Growth Rates.
9.6.   Losses of State Owned Enterprises in Billion Yuan and Percentage Growth
         Rates.
9.7.   Net Profits of State Owned Enterprises in Billion Yuan and Percentage
         Growth Rates.
9.8.   Taxes paid by the State Owned Enterprises in Billion Yuan and
         Percentage Growth Rates.

10. Wages:

10.1.   Total Wage Bill of Staff and Workers in Billion Yuan, Percentage Shares and Percentage Growth Rates.

10.2.   Average Annual Wage by Sector and Ownership of Staff and Workers, Staff and Workers in State Owned Enterprises and in Urban Collective Owned Enterprises in Billion Yuan.

10.3.   Average Annual Wage by Sector and Ownership of Staff and Workers, Staff and Workers in State Owned Enterprises and in Urban Collective Owned Enterprises in % Growth rates.

11. Employment:

11.1.   Social Labor force by Sector in Millions.

11.2.   Social Labor force by Sector in Percentage Shares and Growth Rates.

11.3.   Social Labor force by Ownership.

12. Prices:

12.1.   General Price Indices and Percentage Growth Rates.

12.2.   Percentage Growth Rates of Overall Retail Sales Price Index for the Whole Nation.

12.3.   Percentage Growth Rates of Overall Retail Price Index.

12.4.   Percentage Growth Rate of Cost of Living Index of Goods and Services of Staff and Workers .

12.5.   Monthly and Annual Rates of Inflation.

12.6.   Price Adjustments during 1990.

13. Investment and Inventories:

13.1.   Investment in Fixed Assets: Total and for State Owned Enterprises: in Billion Yuan and Percentage Shares.

13.2.   Investment in Capital Construction of State Owned Enterprises by Sector of National Economy in Billion Yuan and Percentage Shares.

13.3.   Investment in Capital Construction of State Owned Enterprises by Branch of Industry in Billion Yuan and Percentage Shares.

13.4.   Percentage Shares of Investment by Sector.

13.5.   Percentage Shares of Investment of State Owned Enterprises by Sector.

13.6.   Inventories of Commodities held by the Agencies Under the Ministry of Commerce: Inventories that have Increased.

13.7.   Inventories of Commodities held by the Agencies Under the Ministry of Commerce: Inventories that have Decreased.

13.8.   Inventories of Commodities held by the Agencies Under the Ministry of Commerce: Stocks at the end of Period in Billion Yuan and Percentage Shares.

13.9.   Inventories of Industrial Products by Branch of Industry in Billion Yuan and Percentage Shares.

14. Energy:

14.1.   Total Production and Consumption of Energy and Its Composition.

15. Transport:

15.1.	Freight Traffic: International Comparisons.
15.2.	Freight Traffic Composition of China.
15.3.	Passenger Traffic Composition of China.
15.4.	Transport Investment vs. Economic Output.
15.5.	Transport Investment by Five Year Plan Periods.
15.6.	Railway Asset Utilization: International Comparison.
15.7.	Cargo Throughput in Coastal Ports.
15.8.	Freight Traffic Volumes: International Comparisons.
15.9.	Passenger Traffic Volumes: International Comparisons.
15.10.	Railway Traffic Volumes: International Comparisons.
15.11.	Railway Network: International Comparisons.
15.12.	Road Network: International Comparisons.

- 185 -

Table 1.1 : CHINA: National Accounts
(in billions of yuan in Current prices)

	1978	1979	1980	1981	1982	1983	1984	1985	1986	1987	1988	1989	1990	1991
GDP at market prices	358.82	398.88	446.71	477.03	518.93	579.50	693.83	854.95	969.95	1133.04	1404.42	1598.58	1774.01	1976.03
GDP at factor cost														
Agriculture	101.91	126.05	135.80	154.56	175.92	195.87	228.96	253.92	276.44	321.78	383.41	425.22	503.82	531.55
Industry	160.75	177.10	199.68	204.65	215.88	237.02	278.23	344.54	396.71	460.01	578.62	650.62	700.73	822.03
Mining and quarrying	16.72	18.42	20.77	21.28	22.45	24.65	28.94	35.83	40.46	43.24	62.49	59.21	68.67	80.56
Manufacturing	144.03	158.68	178.91	183.36	193.42	212.37	249.29	308.71	356.24	416.77	516.13	591.41	632.06	741.47
Services, etc.	96.16	95.73	111.23	117.83	127.14	146.61	186.64	256.48	296.80	351.24	442.39	522.73	569.46	622.45
Imports of GNFS	18.33	24.38	29.89	37.52	36.49	42.26	63.59	124.08	148.14	160.85	205.74	222.67	255.18	339.59
Exports of GNFS	17.70	23.40	30.10	41.61	47.44	49.35	67.12	89.31	120.44	163.11	192.63	211.93	316.74	403.16
Resource balance	-0.63	-0.98	0.20	4.09	10.95	7.08	3.53	-34.78	-27.69	2.26	-13.11	-10.74	61.56	63.58
Total Expenditures	359.46	399.86	446.51	472.94	507.98	572.42	690.30	889.72	997.64	1130.78	1417.53	1609.32	1712.46	1912.46
Total consumption, etc	239.66	260.65	302.67	333.65	353.86	396.41	466.13	543.14	602.03	685.52	862.41	994.95	1063.38	1207.07
General government	27.32	33.88	36.93	38.70	42.46	47.17	61.06	71.15	84.28	94.60	112.11	131.33	152.06	172.61
Private, etc	212.34	226.77	265.74	294.94	311.40	349.23	405.07	471.99	517.75	590.92	750.30	863.62	911.31	1034.46
Statistical discrepancy														
Gross domestic investment	119.80	139.21	143.84	139.29	154.12	176.01	224.18	346.58	395.61	445.26	555.12	614.37	649.08	705.39
GDFI	96.28	100.69	107.39	96.10	123.04	143.01	183.29	254.32	301.96	364.09	449.65	413.77	445.10	527.85
Nonfinacial Pub. Sector	66.87	69.94	74.59	66.75	84.53	95.20	118.52	168.05	197.85	229.80	276.28	253.55	292.68	355.82
General Government														
Central Govt.														
State and Local Govt.														
Nonfinacial Pub. Enterp.														
Private Sector	29.40	30.75	32.80	29.35	38.51	47.81	64.77	86.27	104.11	134.29	173.38	160.23	152.42	172.04
Changes in stocks /a	23.52	38.52	36.45	43.19	31.08	33.01	40.89	92.26	93.65	81.17	105.47	200.60	203.98	177.54
Gross domestic saving	119.17	138.23	144.04	143.39	165.07	183.10	227.70	311.81	367.91	447.52	542.01	603.63	710.63	768.96
Net factor income	-0.01	-0.07	0.29	0.27	0.37	1.40	2.37	0.81	-0.32	-2.94	-2.60	-6.95	-5.40	-0.16
Net current transfers	1.01	1.02	0.96	0.79	1.00	0.86	0.71	0.50	0.88	0.93	1.55	0.90	0.93	1.73
Gross national saving	120.16	139.18	145.29	144.45	166.44	185.36	230.78	313.12	368.48	445.51	540.96	597.58	706.17	770.53
Net Indirect Taxes														
Indirect Taxes														
Subsidies														
Gross national product	358.81	398.81	447.00	477.30	519.30	580.90	696.20	855.76	969.63	1130.10	1401.82	1591.63	1768.61	1975.87
IFS conversion factor	1.6836	1.5550	1.4984	1.7045	1.8925	1.9757	2.3200	2.9367	3.4528	3.7221	3.7221	3.7651	4.7832	5.3234
IEC conversion factor	1.6836	1.5550	1.4984	1.7045	1.8925	1.9757	2.3200	2.9367	3.4528	3.7221	3.7221	3.7651	4.7832	5.3234
GDP at mp (curr. mill. US$)	213129	256514	298123	279865	274205	293315	299065	291125	280916	304409	377320	424577	370884	371198

REF: NABOP.WK1 06/23/92
Source: CHINA Statistical year book 1990 and 1988 pp.26, 44, 493, and 643 and IMF Recent Economic Developments 01/28/91.
Exports and Imports of goods and non-factor services are from customs statistics.
See Table 2.1 for explanation.
Note: /a Includes investment by enterprises not covered by the plan.

Table 1.2 : CHINA : National Accounts
(in billions of yuan in Constant 1980 prices)

	1978	1979	1980	1981	1982	1983	1984	1985	1986	1987	1988	1989	1990	1991
GDP at market prices	385.38	414.73	446.71	466.85	507.39	558.71	639.66	722.67	783.61	871.76	969.55	1013.73	1070.22	1144.93
Net Indirect Taxes	:	:	:	:	:	:	:	:	:	:	:	:	:	:
GDP at factor cost	:	:	:	:	:	:	:	:	:	:	:	:	:	:
Agriculture	129.81	137.73	135.80	145.31	162.02	175.46	198.27	201.84	208.50	218.30	223.76	230.70	248.00	255.93
Industry	163.14	177.33	199.68	203.07	214.85	235.69	270.81	320.10	351.15	397.50	458.32	481.69	509.15	567.19
Mining and quarrying	16.97	18.44	20.77	21.12	22.34	24.51	28.16	33.29	35.82	37.36	49.50	43.83	49.90	55.58
Manufacturing	146.17	158.89	178.91	181.95	192.51	211.18	242.65	286.81	315.33	360.13	408.82	437.86	459.25	511.60
Services, etc.	92.43	99.67	111.23	118.47	130.53	147.56	170.58	200.73	223.97	255.96	287.47	301.35	313.08	321.81
Imports of GNFS	19.69	25.35	29.89	32.85	29.16	30.07	36.25	53.76	54.44	55.73	69.67	78.09	67.94	77.08
Exports of GNFS	19.01	24.33	30.10	36.78	39.60	39.72	46.34	50.86	63.18	74.52	85.96	90.58	100.27	116.48
Resource balance	-0.68	-1.02	0.20	3.94	10.44	9.65	10.08	-2.90	8.73	18.79	16.29	12.48	32.33	39.40
Total Expenditures	386.06	415.75	446.51	462.92	496.95	549.06	629.58	725.57	774.88	852.97	953.25	1001.25	1037.89	1105.53
Total consumption, etc	254.93	271.01	302.67	326.59	346.25	379.36	422.91	435.51	458.40	510.37	570.01	611.62	646.32	696.83
General government	29.06	35.23	36.93	37.89	41.55	45.14	55.40	57.05	64.18	70.43	74.10	83.79	91.78	98.95
Private, etc	225.87	235.78	265.74	288.71	304.70	334.22	367.51	378.46	394.23	439.94	495.90	527.83	554.54	597.88
Statistical discrepancy	:	:	:	:	:	:	:	:	:	:	:	:	:	:
Gross domestic investment	131.13	144.74	143.84	136.32	150.70	169.70	206.67	290.06	316.48	342.60	383.25	389.63	391.57	408.71
GDFI	103.40	104.69	107.39	94.05	120.30	137.87	168.97	214.96	243.96	280.14	310.43	262.41	268.52	305.84
Nonfinancial Pub. Sector	71.82	72.71	74.59	65.33	82.65	91.78	109.26	142.05	159.84	176.82	190.74	160.80	176.57	206.16
General Government														
Central Govt.														
State and Local Govt.														
Nonfinacial Pub. Enterp.														
Private Sector	31.58	31.97	32.80	28.72	37.65	46.09	59.71	72.92	84.11	103.33	119.70	101.61	91.95	99.68
Changes in stocks	27.73	40.05	36.45	42.27	30.39	31.82	37.70	75.09	72.52	62.46	72.81	127.22	123.05	102.87
Net factor income	-0.01	-0.07	0.29	0.26	0.36	1.34	2.16	0.66	-0.25	-2.22	-1.75	-4.32	-3.27	-0.10
Net current transfers	1.08	1.06	0.96	0.77	0.98	0.83	0.65	0.41	0.68	0.70	1.04	0.56	0.57	1.00
Gross national product	385.37	414.66	447.00	467.11	507.75	560.05	641.82	723.33	783.37	869.54	967.80	1009.41	1066.95	1144.84
Gross domestic saving	130.45	143.72	144.04	139.90	159.45	174.74	208.68	274.99	306.30	343.38	378.81	385.87	407.96	423.14
Gross national saving	131.51	144.71	145.29	140.94	160.79	176.90	211.48	276.06	306.74	341.86	378.10	382.10	405.25	424.04
Capacity to import	19.01	24.33	30.10	36.43	37.91	35.11	38.26	38.69	44.27	56.51	65.23	74.33	84.33	91.51
Terms of trade adjustment	0.00	0.00	0.00	-0.35	-1.69	-4.61	-8.07	-12.17	-18.91	-18.01	-20.73	-16.25	-15.94	-24.96
Gross domestic income	385.38	414.73	446.71	466.50	505.70	554.10	631.59	710.50	764.70	853.75	948.81	997.48	1054.28	1119.97
Gross national income	385.37	414.66	447.00	466.76	506.06	555.44	633.75	711.16	764.46	851.53	947.06	993.16	1051.01	1119.87

REF: NABOP.WK1 06/23/92
Source: CHINA Statistical Year Book 1988, and Statistical Abstract 1989.

Table 1.3 : CHINA: National Accounts
(Implicit price deflators 1980=100)

	1978	1979	1980	1981	1982	1983	1984	1985	1986	1987	1988	1989	1990	1991
GDP at market prices	93.11	96.18	100.00	102.18	102.27	103.72	108.47	118.30	123.78	129.97	144.85	157.69	165.76	172.59
GDP at factor cost														
Agriculture	78.50	91.52	100.00	106.37	108.58	111.63	115.48	125.80	132.58	147.40	171.35	184.32	203.15	207.69
Industry	98.54	99.87	100.00	100.77	100.48	100.56	102.74	107.64	112.98	115.73	126.25	135.07	137.63	144.93
Mining and quarrying	98.54	99.87	100.00	100.77	100.48	100.56	102.74	107.64	112.98	115.73	126.25	135.07	137.63	144.93
Manufacturing	98.54	99.87	100.00	100.77	100.48	100.56	102.74	107.64	112.98	115.73	126.25	135.07	137.63	144.93
Services, etc.	104.04	96.05	100.00	99.45	97.40	99.36	109.42	127.78	132.52	137.23	153.89	173.47	181.89	193.42
Imports of GNFS	93.11	96.18	100.00	114.23	125.15	140.56	175.41	230.80	272.10	288.63	295.30	285.13	375.59	440.55
Exports of GNFS	93.11	96.18	100.00	113.13	119.79	124.24	144.85	175.58	190.65	218.89	224.08	233.98	315.88	346.13
Terms of Trade (Px/Pm)	100.00	100.00	100.00	99.04	95.72	88.39	82.58	76.07	70.07	75.84	75.88	82.06	84.10	78.57
Total Expenditures	93.11	96.18	100.00	102.17	102.22	104.25	109.65	122.62	128.75	132.57	148.70	160.73	164.99	172.99
Total consumption, etc	94.01	96.18	100.00	102.16	102.20	104.49	110.22	124.71	131.33	134.32	151.30	162.68	164.53	173.22
General government	94.01	96.18	100.00	102.16	102.20	104.49	110.22	124.71	131.33	134.32	151.30	156.74	165.69	174.44
Private, etc	94.01	96.18	100.00	102.16	102.20	104.49	110.22	124.71	131.33	134.32	151.30	163.62	164.34	173.02
Gross domestic investment	91.36	96.18	100.00	102.18	102.27	103.72	108.47	119.49	125.00	129.97	144.85	157.68	165.76	172.59
GDFI	93.11	96.18	100.00	102.18	102.27	103.72	108.47	118.31	123.78	129.97	144.85	157.68	165.76	172.59
Nonfinacial Pub. Sector	93.11	96.18	100.00	102.18	102.27	103.72	108.47	118.31	123.78	129.97	144.85	157.68	165.76	172.59
General Government	..	..	..	..	..	..	..	..	..	..	..	..	..	..
Central Govt.	..	..	..	..	..	..	..	..	..	..	..	..	..	..
State and Local Govt.	..	..	..	..	..	..	..	..	..	..	..	..	..	..
Nonfinacial Pub. Enterp.	..	..	..	..	..	..	..	..	..	..	..	..	..	..
Private Sector	93.11	96.18	100.00	102.18	102.27	103.72	108.47	118.31	123.78	129.97	144.85	157.68	165.76	172.59
Changes in stocks	84.84	96.18	100.00	102.18	102.27	103.72	108.47	122.87	129.12	129.97	144.85	157.68	165.76	172.59
Net factor income	93.11	96.18	100.00	102.17	102.22	104.25	109.65	122.62	128.75	132.57	148.70	160.73	164.99	172.99
Net current transfers	93.11	96.18	100.00	102.17	102.22	104.25	109.65	122.62	128.75	132.57	148.70	160.73	164.99	172.99
Gross national product	93.11	96.18	100.00	102.18	102.27	103.72	108.47	118.31	123.78	129.97	144.85	157.68	165.76	172.59
Gross domestic saving	91.35	96.18	100.00	102.49	103.53	104.78	109.12	113.39	120.11	130.33	143.08	156.43	174.19	181.73
Gross national saving	91.36	96.18	100.00	102.49	103.52	104.78	109.12	113.42	120.13	130.32	143.07	156.39	174.25	181.71

REF: NABOP.WK1 06/23/92
Source: Table 1.1 divided by Table 1.2.

Table 1.4 : CHINA : National Accounts
(Percentage SHARES to GNP in Current prices)

	1978	1979	1980	1981	1982	1983	1984	1985	1986	1987	1988	1989	1990	1991
GDP at market prices	100.0	100.0	99.9	99.9	99.9	99.8	99.7	99.9	100.0	100.3	100.2	100.4	100.3	100.0
GDP at factor cost														
Agriculture	28.4	31.6	30.4	32.4	33.9	33.7	32.9	29.7	28.5	28.5	27.4	26.7	28.5	26.9
Industry	44.8	44.4	44.7	42.9	41.6	40.8	40.0	40.3	40.9	40.7	41.3	40.9	39.6	41.6
Mining and quarrying														
Manufacturing														
Services, etc.	26.8	24.0	24.9	24.7	24.5	25.2	26.8	30.0	30.6	31.1	31.6	32.8	32.2	31.5
Imports of GNFS	5.1	6.1	6.7	7.9	7.0	7.3	9.1	14.5	15.3	14.2	14.7	14.0	14.4	17.2
Exports of GNFS	4.9	5.9	6.7	8.7	9.1	8.5	9.6	10.4	12.4	14.4	13.7	13.3	17.9	20.4
Resource balance	-0.2	-0.2	0.0	0.9	2.1	1.2	0.5	-4.1	-2.9	0.2	-0.9	-0.7	3.5	3.2
Total Expenditures	100.2	100.3	99.9	99.1	97.8	98.5	99.2	104.0	102.9	100.1	101.1	101.1	96.8	96.8
Total consumption, etc	66.8	65.4	67.7	69.9	68.1	68.2	67.0	63.5	62.5	60.7	61.5	62.5	60.1	61.1
General government	7.6	8.5	8.3	8.1	8.2	8.1	8.8	8.3	8.7	8.4	8.0	8.3	8.6	8.7
Private, etc	59.2	56.9	59.4	61.8	60.0	60.1	58.2	55.2	53.4	52.3	53.5	54.3	51.5	52.4
Statistical discrepancy														
Gross domestic investment	33.4	34.9	32.2	29.2	29.7	30.3	32.2	40.5	40.8	39.4	39.6	38.6	36.7	35.7
GDFI	26.8	25.2	24.0	20.1	23.7	24.6	26.3	29.7	31.1	32.2	32.1	26.0	25.2	26.7
Nonfinacial Pub. Sector	18.6	17.5	16.7	14.0	16.3	16.4	17.0	19.6	20.4	20.3	19.7	15.9	16.5	18.0
General Government														
Central Govt.														
State and Local Govt.														
Nonfinacial Pub. Enterp.														
Private Sector	8.2	7.7	7.3	6.1	7.4	8.2	9.3	10.1	10.7	11.9	12.4	10.1	8.6	8.7
Changes in stocks	6.6	9.7	8.2	9.0	6.0	5.7	5.9	10.8	9.7	7.2	7.5	12.6	11.5	9.0
Gross domestic saving	33.2	34.7	32.2	30.0	31.8	31.5	32.7	36.4	37.9	39.6	38.7	37.9	40.2	38.9
Net factor income	-0.3	-0.0	0.1	0.2	0.1	0.2	0.3	0.1	-0.0	-0.3	-0.2	-0.4	-0.3	-0.0
Net current transfers	-0.0	-0.3	0.2	0.2	0.2	0.1	0.1	0.1	0.1	0.1	0.1	0.1	0.1	0.1
Gross national saving	33.5	34.9	32.5	30.3	32.1	31.9	33.1	36.6	38.0	39.4	38.6	37.5	39.9	39.0
Net Indirect Taxes														
Indirect Taxes														
Subsidies														
Gross national product	100.0	100.0	100.0	100.0	100.0	100.0	100.0	100.0	100.0	100.0	100.0	100.0	100.0	100.0
IFS conversion factor														
IEC conversion factor														
GDP at mp (curr. mill. US$)														

REF: NABOP.WK1 06/23/92
Source: Table 1.1.

Table 1.5 : CHINA : National Accounts
(Percentage SHARES to GNP in Constant 1980 prices)

	1978	1979	1980	1981	1982	1983	1984	1985	1986	1987	1988	1989	1990	1991
GDP at market prices	100.0	100.0	99.9	99.9	99.9	99.8	99.7	99.9	100.0	100.3	100.2	100.4	100.3	100.0
Net Indirect Taxes	..	..	..											
GDP at factor cost	..	..												
Agriculture	33.7	33.2	30.4	31.1	31.9	31.3	30.9	27.9	26.6	25.1	23.1	22.9	23.2	22.4
Industry	42.3	42.8	44.7	43.5	42.3	42.1	42.2	44.3	44.8	45.7	47.4	47.7	47.7	49.5
Mining and quarrying	4.4	4.4	4.6	4.5	4.4	4.4	4.4	4.6	4.6	4.3	5.1	4.3	4.7	4.9
Manufacturing	37.9	38.3	40.0	39.0	37.9	37.7	37.8	39.7	40.3	41.4	42.2	43.4	43.0	44.7
Services, etc.	24.0	24.0	24.9	25.4	25.7	26.3	26.6	27.8	28.6	29.4	29.7	29.9	29.3	28.1
Imports of GNFS	5.1	6.1	6.7	7.0	5.7	5.4	5.6	7.4	6.9	6.4	7.2	7.7	6.4	6.7
Exports of GNFS	4.9	5.9	6.7	7.9	7.8	7.1	7.2	7.0	8.1	8.6	8.9	9.0	9.4	10.2
Resource balance	-0.2	-0.2	0.0	0.8	2.1	1.7	1.6	-0.4	1.1	2.2	1.7	1.2	3.0	3.4
Total Expenditures	100.2	100.3	99.9	99.1	97.9	98.0	98.1	100.3	98.9	98.1	98.5	99.2	97.3	96.6
Total consumption, etc	66.2	65.4	67.7	69.9	68.2	67.7	65.9	60.2	58.5	58.7	58.9	60.6	60.6	60.9
General government	7.5	8.5	8.3	8.1	8.2	8.1	8.6	7.9	8.2	8.1	7.7	8.3	8.6	8.6
Private, etc	58.6	56.9	59.4	61.8	60.0	59.7	57.3	52.3	50.3	50.6	51.2	52.3	52.0	52.2
Statistical discrepancy														
Gross domestic investment	34.0	34.9	32.2	29.2	29.7	30.3	32.2	40.1	40.4	39.4	39.6	38.6	36.7	35.7
GDFI	26.8	25.2	24.0	20.1	23.7	24.6	26.3	29.7	31.1	32.2	32.1	26.0	25.2	26.7
Nonfinacial Pub. Sector	18.6	17.5	16.7	14.0	16.3	16.4	17.0	19.6	20.4	20.3	19.7	15.9	16.5	18.0
General Government	..	..	..	..	..	..	..	..	..	..	..	..	..	0.0
Central Govt.	..	..	..	..	..	..	..	..	..	..	..	..	..	
State and Local Govt.	..	..	..	..	..	..	..	..	..	..	..	..	..	
Nonfinacial Pub. Enterp.	..	..	..	..	..	..	..	..	..	..	..	..	..	
Private Sector	8.2	7.7	7.3	6.1	7.4	8.2	9.3	10.1	10.7	11.9	12.4	10.1	8.6	8.7
Changes in stocks	7.2	9.7	8.2	9.0	6.0	5.7	5.9	10.4	9.3	7.2	7.5	12.6	11.5	9.0
Net factor income	-0.0	-0.0	0.1	0.1	0.1	0.2	0.3	0.1	-0.0	-0.3	-0.2	-0.4	-0.3	-0.0
Net current transfers	0.3	0.3	0.2	0.2	0.2	0.1	0.1	0.1	0.1	0.1	0.1	0.1	0.1	0.1
Gross national product	100.0	100.0	100.0	100.0	100.0	100.0	100.0	100.0	100.0	100.0	100.0	100.0	100.0	100.0
Gross domestic saving	33.9	34.7	32.2	30.0	31.4	31.2	32.5	38.0	39.1	39.5	39.1	38.2	38.2	37.0
Gross national saving	34.1	34.9	32.5	30.2	31.7	31.6	33.0	38.2	39.2	39.3	39.1	38.0	38.0	37.0
Capacity to import	4.9	5.9	6.7	7.8	7.5	6.3	6.0	5.3	5.7	6.5	6.7	7.4	7.9	8.0
Terms of trade adjustment	0.0	0.0	0.0	-0.1	-0.3	-0.8	-1.3	-1.7	-2.4	-2.1	-2.1	-1.6	-1.5	-2.2
Gross domestic income	100.0	100.0	99.9	99.9	99.6	98.9	98.4	98.2	97.6	98.2	98.0	98.8	98.8	97.8
Gross national income	100.0	100.0	100.0	99.9	99.7	99.2	98.7	98.3	97.6	97.9	97.9	98.4	98.5	97.8

REF: NABOP.WK1 06/23/92
Source: Table 1.2.

Table 1.6 : CHINA : National Accounts
(Percentage GROWTH RATES in Current prices)

	1978	1979	1980	1981	1982	1983	1984	1985	1986	1987	1988	1989	1990	1991
GDP at market prices	:	11.2	12.0	6.8	8.8	11.7	19.7	23.2	13.5	16.8	24.0	13.8	11.0	11.4
GDP at factor cost	:													
Agriculture	:	23.7	7.7	13.8	13.8	11.3	16.9	10.9	8.9	16.4	19.2	10.9	18.5	5.5
Industry	:	10.2	12.7	2.5	5.5	9.8	17.4	23.8	15.1	16.0	25.8	12.4	7.7	17.3
Mining and quarrying	:	10.2	12.7	2.5	5.5	9.8	17.4	23.8	12.9	6.9	44.5	-5.3	16.0	17.3
Manufacturing	:	10.2	12.7	2.5	5.5	9.8	17.4	23.8	15.4	17.0	23.8	14.6	6.9	17.3
Services, etc.	:	-0.5	16.2	5.9	7.9	15.3	27.3	37.4	15.7	16.3	26.0	18.2	8.9	9.3
Imports of GNFS	:	33.0	22.6	25.5	-2.8	15.8	50.5	95.1	19.4	8.6	27.9	8.2	14.6	33.1
Exports of GNFS	:	32.2	28.6	38.3	14.0	4.0	36.0	33.1	34.9	35.4	18.1	10.0	49.5	27.3
Resource balance	:													
Total Expenditures	:													
Total consumption, etc	:	11.2	11.7	5.9	7.4	12.7	20.6	28.9	12.1	13.3	25.4	13.5	6.4	11.7
General government	:	8.8	16.1	10.2	6.1	12.0	17.6	16.5	10.8	13.9	25.8	15.4	6.9	13.5
Private, etc	:	24.0	9.0	4.8	9.7	11.1	29.4	16.5	18.5	12.2	18.5	17.1	15.8	13.5
Statistical discrepancy	:	6.8	17.2	11.0	5.6	12.2	16.0	16.5	9.7	14.1	27.0	15.1	5.5	13.5
Gross domestic investment	:													
GDFI	:	16.2	3.3	-3.2	10.6	14.2	27.4	54.6	14.1	12.6	24.7	10.7	5.6	8.7
Nonfinacial Pub. Sector	:	4.6	6.7	-10.5	28.0	16.2	28.2	38.8	18.7	20.6	23.5	-8.0	7.6	18.6
General Government	:	4.6	6.7	-10.5	26.6	12.6	24.5	41.8	17.7	16.1	20.2	-8.2	15.4	21.6
Central Govt.	:													
State and Local Govt.	:													
Nonfinacial Pub. Enterp.	:													
Private Sector	:	4.6	6.7	-10.5	31.2	24.2	35.5	33.2	20.7	29.0	29.1	-7.6	-4.9	12.9
Changes in stocks	:	63.8	-5.4	18.5	-28.0	6.2	23.9	125.6	1.5	-13.3	29.9	90.2	1.7	-13.0
Gross domestic saving	:	16.0	4.2	-0.5	15.1	10.9	24.4	36.9	18.0	21.6	21.1	11.4	17.7	8.2
Net factor income	:													
Net current transfers	:													
Gross national saving	:	15.8	4.4	-0.6	15.2	11.4	24.5	35.7	17.7	20.9	21.4	10.5	18.2	9.1
Net Indirect Taxes	:													
Indirect Taxes	:													
Subsidies	:													
Gross national product	:	11.1	12.1	6.8	8.8	11.9	19.8	22.9	13.3	16.5	24.0	13.5	11.1	11.7
IFS conversion factor	:	-7.6	-3.6	13.8	11.0	4.4	17.4	26.6	17.6	7.8	0.0	1.2	27.0	11.3
IEC conversion factor	:	-7.6	-3.6	13.8	11.0	4.4	17.4	26.6	17.6	7.8	0.0	1.2	27.0	11.3
GDP at mp (curr. mill. US$)	:	20.4	16.2	-6.1	-2.0	7.0	2.0	-2.7	-3.5	8.4	24.0	12.5	-12.6	0.1

REF: NABOP.WK1 06/23/92
Source: Table 1.1.

Table 1.7 : CHINA: National Accounts
(Percentage GROWTH RATES in Constant 1980 prices)

	1978	1979	1980	1981	1982	1983	1984	1985	1986	1987	1988	1989	1990	1991
GDP at market prices	..	7.6	7.7	4.5	8.7	10.1	14.5	13.0	8.4	11.2	11.2	4.6	5.6	7.0
Net Indirect Taxes	..	..	..	..	..	..	..	..	..	..	..	..	..	..
GDP at factor cost	..	..	..	..	..	..	..	..	..	..	..	..	..	..
Agriculture	..	6.1	-1.4	7.0	11.5	8.3	13.0	1.8	3.3	4.7	2.5	3.1	7.5	3.2
Industry	..	8.7	12.6	1.7	5.8	9.7	14.9	18.2	9.7	13.2	15.3	5.1	5.7	11.4
Mining and quarrying	..	8.7	12.6	1.7	5.8	9.7	14.9	18.2	7.6	4.3	32.5	-11.4	13.8	11.4
Manufacturing	..	8.7	12.6	1.7	5.8	9.7	14.9	18.2	9.9	14.2	13.5	7.1	4.9	11.4
Services, etc.	..	7.8	11.6	6.5	10.2	13.0	15.6	17.7	11.6	14.3	12.3	4.8	3.9	2.8
Imports of GNFS	..	28.7	17.9	9.9	-11.2	3.1	20.6	48.3	1.3	2.4	25.0	12.1	-13.0	13.5
Exports of GNFS	..	28.0	23.7	22.2	7.7	0.3	16.7	9.8	24.2	18.0	15.4	5.4	10.7	16.2
Resource balance	..	..	..	..	..	..	..	..	..	..	..	..	..	..
Total Expenditures	..	7.7	7.4	3.7	7.4	10.5	14.7	15.2	6.8	10.1	11.8	5.0	3.7	6.5
Total consumption, etc	..	6.3	11.7	7.9	6.0	9.6	11.5	3.0	5.3	11.3	11.7	7.3	5.7	7.8
General government	..	21.2	4.8	2.6	9.7	8.6	22.7	3.0	12.5	9.7	5.2	13.1	9.5	7.8
Private, etc	..	4.4	12.7	8.6	5.5	9.7	10.0	3.0	4.2	11.6	12.7	6.4	5.1	7.8
Statistical discrepancy	..	..	..	..	..	..	..	..	..	..	..	..	..	..
Gross domestic investment	..	10.4	-0.6	-5.2	10.5	12.6	21.8	40.4	9.1	8.3	11.9	1.7	0.5	4.4
GDFI	..	1.2	2.6	-12.4	27.9	14.6	22.6	27.2	13.5	14.8	10.8	-15.5	2.3	13.9
Nonfinancial Pub. Sector	..	1.2	2.6	-12.4	26.5	11.0	19.0	30.0	12.5	10.6	7.9	-15.7	9.8	16.8
General Government	..	..	..	..	..	..	..	..	..	..	..	..	..	..
Central Govt.	..	..	..	..	..	..	..	..	..	..	..	..	..	..
State and Local Govt.	..	..	..	..	..	..	..	..	..	..	..	..	..	..
Nonfinancial Pub. Enterp.	..	..	..	..	..	..	..	..	..	..	..	..	..	..
Private Sector	..	1.2	2.6	-12.4	31.1	22.4	29.5	22.1	15.4	22.8	15.8	-15.1	-9.5	8.4
Changes in stocks	..	44.4	-9.0	16.0	-28.1	4.7	18.5	99.2	-3.4	-13.9	16.6	74.7	-3.3	-16.4
Net factor income	..	..	..	..	..	..	..	..	..	..	..	..	..	..
Net current transfers	..	..	..	..	..	..	..	..	..	..	..	..	..	..
Gross national product	..	7.6	7.8	4.5	8.7	10.3	14.6	12.7	8.3	11.0	11.3	4.3	5.7	7.3
Gross domestic saving	..	10.2	0.2	-2.9	14.0	9.6	19.4	31.8	11.4	12.1	11.9	1.9	5.7	3.7
Gross national saving	..	10.0	0.4	-3.0	14.1	10.0	19.5	30.5	11.1	11.5	10.6	1.1	6.1	4.6
Capacity to import	..	..	..	..	..	..	..	..	..	..	..	..	..	..
Terms of trade adjustment	..	..	..	..	..	..	..	..	..	..	..	..	..	..
Gross domestic income	..	7.6	7.7	4.4	8.4	9.6	14.0	12.5	7.6	11.6	11.1	5.1	5.7	6.2
Gross national income	..	7.6	7.8	4.4	8.4	9.8	14.1	12.2	7.5	11.4	11.2	4.9	5.8	6.6

REF: NABOP.WK1 06/23/92
Source: Table 1.2.

Table 1.8 : CHINA: National Accounts
(Percentage GROWTH RATES of 1980 based Implicit price deflators)

	1978	1979	1980	1981	1982	1983	1984	1985	1986	1987	1988	1989	1990	1991
GDP at market prices	..	3.3	4.0	2.2	0.1	1.4	4.6	9.1	4.6	5.0	11.4	8.9	5.1	4.1
GDP at factor cost	..	..	..	..	..	..	..	..	..	..	..	..	..	..
Agriculture	..	16.6	9.3	6.4	2.1	2.8	3.4	8.9	5.4	11.2	16.2	7.6	10.2	2.2
Industry	..	1.4	0.1	0.8	-0.3	0.1	2.2	4.8	5.0	2.4	9.1	7.0	1.9	5.3
Mining and quarrying	..	..	..	..	..	..	..	..	..	..	..	..	..	..
Manufacturing	..	..	..	..	..	..	..	..	..	..	..	..	..	..
Services, etc.	..	-7.7	4.1	-0.5	-2.1	2.0	10.1	16.8	3.7	3.6	12.1	12.7	4.9	6.3
Imports of GNFS	..	3.3	4.0	14.2	9.6	12.3	24.8	31.6	17.9	6.1	2.3	-3.4	31.7	17.3
Exports of GNFS	..	3.3	4.0	13.1	5.9	3.7	16.6	21.2	8.6	14.8	2.4	4.4	35.0	9.6
Terms of Trade (Px/Pm)	..	-0.0	0.0	-1.0	-3.4	-7.7	-6.6	-7.9	-7.9	8.2	0.1	8.1	2.5	-6.6
Total Expenditures	..	3.3	4.0	2.2	0.1	2.0	5.2	11.8	5.0	3.0	12.2	8.1	2.7	4.8
Total consumption, etc	..	2.3	4.0	2.2	0.0	2.2	5.5	13.2	5.3	2.3	12.6	7.5	1.1	5.3
General government	..	2.3	4.0	2.2	0.0	2.2	5.5	13.2	5.3	2.3	12.6	3.6	5.7	5.3
Private, etc	..	2.3	4.0	2.2	0.0	2.2	5.5	13.2	5.3	2.3	12.6	8.1	0.4	5.3
Gross domestic investment	..	5.3	4.0	2.2	0.1	1.4	4.6	10.2	4.6	4.0	11.5	8.9	5.1	4.1
GDFI	..	3.3	4.0	2.2	0.1	1.4	4.6	9.1	4.6	5.0	11.5	8.9	5.1	4.1
Nonfinacial Pub. Sector	..	3.3	4.0	2.2	0.1	1.4	4.6	9.1	4.6	5.0	11.5	8.9	5.1	4.1
General Government	..	..	..	..	..	..	..	..	..	..	..	..	..	..
Central Govt.	..	..	..	..	..	..	..	..	..	..	..	..	..	..
State and Local Govt.	..	..	..	..	..	..	..	..	..	..	..	..	..	..
Nonfinacial Pub. Enterp.	..	..	..	..	..	..	..	..	..	..	..	..	..	..
Private Sector	..	3.3	4.0	2.2	0.1	1.4	4.6	9.1	4.6	5.0	11.5	8.9	5.1	4.1
Changes in stocks	..	..	..	..	0.1	1.4	4.6	13.3	5.1	0.7	11.5	8.9	5.1	4.1
Net factor income	..	3.3	4.0	2.2	0.1	2.0	5.2	11.8	5.0	3.0	12.2	8.1	2.7	4.8
Net current transfers	..	..	..	2.2	0.1	2.0	5.2	11.8	5.0	3.0	12.2	8.1	2.7	4.8
Gross national product	..	3.3	4.0	2.2	0.1	1.4	4.6	9.1	4.6	5.0	11.5	8.9	5.1	4.1
Gross domestic saving	..	5.3	4.0	2.5	1.0	1.2	4.1	3.9	5.9	8.5	9.8	9.3	11.4	4.3
Gross national saving	..	5.3	4.0	2.5	1.0	1.2	4.1	3.9	5.9	8.5	9.8	9.3	11.4	4.3

REF: WABOP.WK1 06/23/92
Source: Table 1.3.

Table 1.9: CHINA: Sources of Growth (in Constant 1980 Prices)

	1978	1979	1980	1981	1982	1983	1984	1985	1986	1987	1988	1989	1990	1991
GDP growth rate (actual)	..	7.61	7.71	4.51	8.68	10.11	14.49	12.98	8.43	11.25	11.22	4.56	5.57	6.98
SUPPLY SIDE														
Agriculture growth rate	..	6.10	-1.40	7.00	11.50	8.30	13.00	1.80	3.30	4.70	2.50	3.10	7.50	3.20
Industry growth rate	..	8.70	12.60	1.70	5.80	9.70	14.90	18.20	9.70	13.20	15.30	5.10	5.70	11.40
Other growth rate	..	7.83	11.60	6.51	10.18	13.05	15.60	17.68	11.58	14.28	12.31	4.83	3.89	2.79
Agriculture Share into GDP	33.68	33.21	30.40	31.12	31.93	31.40	31.00	27.93	26.61	25.04	23.08	22.76	23.17	22.35
Industry Share into GDP	42.33	42.76	44.70	43.50	42.34	42.18	42.34	44.29	44.81	45.60	47.27	47.52	47.57	49.54
Other Share into GDP	23.98	24.03	24.90	25.38	25.73	26.41	26.67	27.78	28.58	29.36	29.65	29.73	29.25	28.11
Total Share	100.00	100.00	100.00	100.00	100.00	100.00	100.00	100.00	100.00	100.00	100.00	100.00	100.00	100.00
Agr. Share of last year * Weight	..	2.05	-0.46	2.13	3.58	2.65	4.08	0.56	0.92	1.25	0.63	0.72	1.71	0.74
Ind. Share of last year * Weight	..	3.68	5.39	0.76	2.52	4.11	6.29	7.71	4.30	5.92	6.98	2.41	2.71	5.42
Oth. Share of last year * Weight	..	1.88	2.79	1.62	2.58	3.36	4.12	4.71	3.22	4.08	3.62	1.43	1.16	0.82
Weighted Average Growth rate	..	7.61	7.71	4.51	8.68	10.11	14.49	12.98	8.43	11.25	11.22	4.56	5.57	6.98
DEMAND SIDE														
Total Consumption growth rate	..	6.31	11.68	7.91	6.02	9.56	11.48	2.98	5.26	11.34	11.69	7.30	5.67	7.81
Gross Domestic Investment gr. rate	..	10.38	-0.62	-5.23	10.55	12.61	21.79	40.35	9.11	8.25	11.86	1.67	0.50	4.38
Exports of goods & NFS growth rate	..	27.98	23.70	22.22	7.66	0.31	16.66	9.77	24.21	17.96	15.36	5.37	10.71	16.16
Imports of goods & NFS growth rate	..	28.74	17.92	9.88	-11.24	3.13	20.57	48.29	1.27	2.36	25.01	12.09	-13.00	13.45
Total Consumption Share into GDP	66.15	65.35	67.75	69.96	68.24	67.90	66.11	60.26	58.50	58.54	58.79	60.33	60.39	60.86
Gross Domestic Inv. Share into GDP	34.03	34.90	32.20	29.20	29.70	30.37	32.31	40.14	40.39	39.30	39.53	38.44	36.59	35.70
Exports of GNFS Share into GDP	4.93	5.87	6.74	7.88	7.80	7.11	7.24	7.04	8.06	8.55	8.87	8.93	9.37	10.17
Imports of GNFS Share into GDP	-5.11	-6.11	-6.69	-7.04	-5.75	-5.38	-5.67	-7.44	-6.95	-6.39	-7.19	-7.70	-6.35	-6.73
Total Share	100.00	100.00	100.00	100.00	100.00	100.00	100.00	100.00	100.00	100.00	100.00	100.00	100.00	100.00
Total Cons. Share(-1) * Weight	..	4.17	7.63	5.36	4.21	6.53	7.79	1.97	3.17	6.63	6.84	4.29	3.42	4.72
Gross Dom. Inv. Share(-1)* Weight	..	3.53	-0.22	-1.68	3.08	3.74	6.62	13.04	3.66	3.33	4.66	0.66	0.19	1.60
Exports of GNFS Share(-1) * Weight	..	1.38	1.39	1.50	0.60	0.02	1.18	0.71	1.70	1.45	1.31	0.48	0.96	1.51
Imports of GNFS Share(-1) * Weight	..	-1.47	-1.10	-0.66	0.79	-0.18	-1.11	-2.74	-0.09	-0.16	-1.60	-0.87	1.00	-0.85
Weighted Average Growth rate	..	7.61	7.71	4.51	8.68	10.11	14.49	12.98	8.43	11.25	11.22	4.56	5.57	6.98
Contribution to GDP growth in percent														
SUPPLY SIDE														
Agriculture	..	26.98	-6.03	47.19	41.22	26.20	28.18	4.30	10.93	11.12	5.58	15.70	30.63	10.62
Industry	..	48.36	69.87	16.85	29.05	40.61	43.38	59.38	50.95	52.59	62.19	52.90	48.61	77.69
Other	..	24.65	36.16	35.96	29.73	33.19	28.44	36.32	38.13	36.29	32.23	31.40	20.76	11.69
Total	..	100.00	100.00	100.00	100.00	100.00	100.00	100.00	100.00	100.00	100.00	100.00	100.00	100.00
DEMAND SIDE														
Total consumption	..	54.78	98.99	118.79	48.49	64.52	53.80	15.18	37.56	58.96	60.99	94.17	61.43	67.61
Gross domestic investment	..	46.38	-2.82	-37.33	35.44	37.02	45.67	100.46	43.36	29.63	41.57	14.45	3.43	22.94
Exports of goods & NFS	..	18.13	18.03	33.20	6.95	0.24	8.17	5.45	20.20	12.87	11.70	10.44	17.17	21.69
Imports of goods & NFS	..	-19.29	-14.20	-14.66	9.10	-1.78	-7.64	-21.09	-1.12	-1.46	-14.25	-19.06	17.97	-12.23
Total	..	100.00	100.00	100.00	100.00	100.00	100.00	100.00	100.00	100.00	100.00	100.00	100.00	100.00

REF: NABOP.WK1 06/23/92   NOTE: Other is calculated as residual.
Source: Table 1.2.

Table 1.2b: CHINA : National Accounts
(in billions of yuan in Constant 1987 prices)

	1978	1979	1980	1981	1982	1983	1984	1985	1986	1987	1988	1989	1990	1991
GDP at market prices	500.89	539.03	580.60	606.78	659.47	726.17	831.38	939.27	1018.48	1133.04	1260.14	1317.57	1390.99	1488.09
Net Indirect Taxes	..	..	..	..	..	..	..	..	..	..	..	..	..	..
GDP at factor cost	..	..	..	..	..	..	..	..	..	..	..	..	..	..
Agriculture	191.34	203.01	200.17	214.18	238.82	258.64	292.26	297.52	307.34	321.78	329.83	340.05	365.56	377.25
Industry	188.80	205.22	231.08	235.01	248.64	272.76	313.40	370.44	406.37	460.01	530.40	557.45	589.22	656.39
Mining and quarrying	19.64	21.34	24.03	24.44	25.86	28.37	32.59	38.53	41.45	43.24	57.28	50.73	57.74	64.33
Manufacturing	169.16	183.88	207.05	210.57	222.78	244.39	280.81	331.91	364.92	416.77	473.11	506.72	531.48	592.07
Services, etc.	120.75	130.79	149.34	157.58	172.01	194.77	225.72	271.31	304.77	351.24	399.91	420.07	436.21	454.44
Imports of GNFS	56.84	73.17	86.91	93.21	77.76	86.04	108.91	166.34	163.96	160.85	198.48	214.13	186.71	206.71
Exports of GNFS	41.61	53.25	68.01	85.20	91.66	93.68	107.68	112.11	138.00	163.11	187.19	201.94	227.25	258.92
Resource balance	-15.23	-19.92	-18.89	-8.01	13.90	7.64	-1.23	-54.23	-25.95	2.26	-11.29	-12.19	40.54	52.21
Total Expenditures	516.12	558.95	599.49	614.79	645.57	718.53	832.61	993.50	1044.43	1130.78	1271.43	1329.76	1350.45	1435.88
Total consumption, etc	345.69	370.84	412.55	437.62	449.72	497.98	564.02	616.52	633.12	685.52	773.34	823.37	841.54	904.71
General government	42.30	54.14	55.61	49.83	40.44	49.06	70.38	108.18	103.60	94.60	107.25	114.40	96.69	101.64
Private, etc	303.39	316.70	356.94	387.79	409.28	448.92	493.64	508.34	529.52	590.92	666.09	708.97	744.86	803.06
Statistical discrepancy	..	..	..	..	..	..	..	..	..	..	..	..	..	..
Gross domestic investment	170.42	188.11	186.94	177.17	195.85	220.55	268.59	376.97	411.32	445.26	498.09	506.39	508.91	531.18
GDFI	134.39	136.06	139.57	122.23	156.35	179.19	219.60	279.38	317.06	364.09	403.46	341.05	348.98	397.49
Nonfinacial Pub. Sector	93.34	94.50	96.94	84.90	107.42	119.28	142.00	184.61	207.74	229.80	247.89	208.98	229.48	267.94
General Government	..	..	..	..	..	..	..	..	..	..	..	..	..	..
Central Govt.	..	..	..	..	..	..	..	..	..	..	..	..	..	..
State and Local Govt.	..	..	..	..	..	..	..	..	..	..	..	..	..	..
Nonfinacial Pub. Enterp.	..	..	..	..	..	..	..	..	..	..	..	..	..	..
Private Sector	41.04	41.55	42.62	37.33	48.94	59.91	77.60	94.77	109.32	134.29	155.57	132.06	119.50	129.55
Changes in stocks	36.04	52.06	47.38	54.94	39.50	41.36	48.99	97.59	94.26	81.17	94.63	165.34	159.93	133.69
Net factor income	-0.02	-0.10	0.39	0.35	0.48	1.78	2.86	0.88	-0.33	-2.94	-2.32	-5.73	-4.34	-0.13
Net current transfers	1.43	1.41	1.27	1.03	1.30	1.10	0.86	0.54	0.91	0.93	1.38	0.74	0.75	1.33
Gross national product	500.87	538.94	580.98	607.13	659.95	727.95	834.24	940.15	1018.15	1130.10	1257.82	1311.84	1386.65	1487.96
Gross domestic saving	168.46	185.16	187.53	187.34	219.19	234.97	274.63	330.35	380.66	447.52	485.44	496.06	553.94	569.88
Gross national saving	169.87	186.47	189.19	188.71	220.97	237.84	278.35	331.77	381.24	445.51	484.50	491.07	550.35	571.08
Capacity to import	54.87	70.22	87.50	103.38	101.10	100.46	114.95	331.77	133.30	163.11	185.83	203.80	231.75	245.41
Terms of trade adjustment	13.26	16.97	19.48	18.18	9.43	6.78	7.27	7.61	-4.70	0.00	-1.36	1.86	4.50	-13.51
Gross domestic income	514.15	556.00	600.08	624.96	668.90	732.95	838.65	946.88	1013.78	1133.04	1258.78	1319.43	1395.48	1474.58
Gross national income	514.13	555.90	600.46	625.31	669.38	734.73	841.52	947.75	1013.45	1130.10	1256.46	1313.70	1391.15	1474.46
Population (in millions)	962.59	975.42	987.05	1000.72	1016.54	1030.08	1043.57	1058.51	1075.07	1093.00	1110.26	1127.04	1143.33	1158.23
Labor Force (in millions)	401.52	410.24	423.61	437.25	452.95	464.36	481.97	498.73	512.82	527.83	543.34	553.29	567.40	583.64

REF: NABOP.WK1 06/23/92
Source: Table 1.1 divided by Table 1.3b.

Table 1.3b : CHINA: National Accounts
(Implicit price deflators 1987=100)

	1978	1979	1980	1981	1982	1983	1984	1985	1986	1987	1988	1989	1990	1991
GDP at market prices	71.64	74.00	76.94	78.62	78.69	79.80	83.46	91.02	95.23	100.00	111.45	121.33	127.54	132.79
GDP at factor cost														
Agriculture	53.26	62.09	67.84	72.16	73.66	75.73	78.34	85.35	89.94	100.00	116.24	125.05	137.82	140.90
Industry	85.14	86.30	86.41	87.08	86.82	86.90	88.78	93.01	97.62	100.00	109.09	116.71	118.93	125.23
Mining and quarrying	85.14	86.30	86.41	87.08	86.82	86.90	88.78	93.01	97.62	100.00	109.09	116.71	118.93	125.23
Manufacturing	85.14	86.30	86.41	87.08	86.82	86.90	88.78	93.01	97.62	100.00	109.09	116.71	118.93	125.23
Services, etc.	79.64	73.19	74.48	74.77	73.91	75.27	82.69	94.54	97.39	100.00	110.62	124.44	130.55	136.97
Imports of GNFS	32.26	33.32	34.40	40.25	46.92	49.12	58.39	74.59	90.35	100.00	103.99	103.99	136.67	164.28
Exports of GNFS	42.54	43.94	44.25	48.84	51.75	52.67	62.33	79.65	87.28	100.00	102.91	104.94	139.38	155.71
Terms of Trade (Px/Pm)	131.86	131.86	128.64	121.34	110.29	107.24	106.75	106.79	96.59	100.00	99.27	100.92	101.98	94.78
Total Expenditures	70.23	72.55	75.43	77.06	77.11	78.64	82.71	92.50	97.12	100.00	112.17	121.24	124.46	130.49
Total consumption, etc	69.99	71.60	74.45	76.06	76.08	77.79	82.06	92.85	97.78	100.00	112.64	121.11	122.49	128.96
General government	69.99	71.60	74.45	76.06	76.08	77.79	82.06	92.85	97.78	100.00	112.64	116.69	123.35	129.87
Private, etc	69.99	71.60	74.45	76.06	76.08	77.78	82.06	92.85	97.78	100.00	112.64	121.81	122.35	128.81
Gross domestic investment	70.30	74.00	76.94	78.62	78.69	79.81	83.46	91.94	96.18	100.00	111.45	121.32	127.54	132.80
GDFI	71.64	74.00	76.94	78.62	78.69	79.81	83.46	91.03	95.24	100.00	111.45	121.32	127.54	132.80
Nonfinacial Pub. Sector	71.64	74.00	76.94	78.62	78.69	79.81	83.46	91.03	95.24	100.00	111.45	121.32	127.54	132.80
General Government	:	:	:	:	:	:	:	:	:	:	:	:	:	:
Central Govt.	:	:	:	:	:	:	:	:	:	:	:	:	:	:
State and Local Govt.	:	:	:	:	:	:	:	:	:	:	:	:	:	:
Nonfinacial Pub. Enterp.	:	:	:	:	:	:	:	:	:	:	:	:	:	:
Private Sector	71.64	74.00	76.94	78.62	78.69	79.81	83.46	91.03	95.24	100.00	111.45	121.32	127.54	132.80
Changes in stocks	65.28	74.00	76.94	78.62	78.69	79.81	83.46	94.54	99.35	100.00	111.45	121.32	127.54	132.80
Net factor income	70.23	72.55	75.43	77.06	77.11	78.64	82.71	92.50	97.12	100.00	112.17	121.24	124.46	130.49
Net current transfers	70.23	72.55	75.43	77.06	77.11	78.64	82.71	92.50	97.12	100.00	112.17	121.24	124.46	130.49
Gross national product	71.64	74.00	76.94	78.62	78.69	79.81	83.46	91.03	95.24	100.00	111.45	121.32	127.54	132.80
Gross domestic saving	70.09	73.80	76.73	78.64	79.44	80.40	83.73	87.00	92.16	100.00	109.79	120.03	133.66	139.44
Gross national saving	70.11	73.80	76.74	78.64	79.44	80.40	83.74	87.04	92.18	100.00	109.79	120.01	133.72	139.44

REF: NABOP.WK1 06/23/92
Source: Table 1.3 rebased to 1987.

Table 1.7b: CHINA: National Accounts
(Percentage GROWTH RATES in Constant 1987 prices)

	1978	1979	1980	1981	1982	1983	1984	1985	1986	1987	1988	1989	1990	1991
GDP at market prices	:	7.6	7.7	4.5	8.7	10.1	14.5	13.0	8.4	11.2	11.2	4.6	5.6	7.0
Net Indirect Taxes	:	:	:	:	:	:	:	:	:	:	:	:	:	:
GDP at factor cost	:	:	:	:	:	:	:	:	:	:	:	:	:	:
Agriculture	:	6.1	-1.4	7.0	11.5	8.3	13.0	1.8	3.3	4.7	2.5	3.1	7.5	3.2
Industry	:	8.7	12.6	1.7	5.8	9.7	14.9	18.2	9.7	13.2	15.3	5.1	5.7	11.4
Mining and quarrying	:	:	:	:	:	:	:	:	:	:	:	:	:	:
Manufacturing	:	:	:	:	:	:	:	:	:	:	:	:	:	:
Services, etc.	:	8.3	14.2	5.5	9.2	13.2	15.9	20.2	12.3	15.2	13.9	5.0	3.8	4.2
Imports of GNFS	:	28.7	18.8	7.2	-16.6	10.6	26.6	52.7	-1.4	-1.9	23.4	7.9	-12.8	10.7
Exports of GNFS	:	28.0	27.7	25.3	7.6	2.2	14.9	4.1	23.1	18.2	14.8	7.9	12.5	13.9
Resource balance	:	:	:	:	:	:	:	:	:	:	:	:	:	:
Total Expenditures	:	8.3	7.3	2.6	5.0	11.3	15.9	19.3	5.1	8.3	12.4	4.6	1.6	6.3
Total consumption, etc	:	7.3	11.2	6.1	2.8	10.7	13.3	9.3	2.7	8.3	12.8	6.5	2.2	7.5
General government	:	28.0	2.7	-10.4	-18.8	21.3	43.5	53.7	-4.2	-8.7	13.4	6.7	-15.5	5.1
Private, etc	:	4.4	12.7	8.6	5.5	9.7	10.0	3.0	4.2	11.6	12.7	6.4	5.1	7.8
Statistical discrepancy	:	:	:	:	:	:	:	:	:	:	:	:	:	:
Gross domestic investment	:	10.4	-0.6	-5.2	10.5	12.6	21.8	40.4	9.1	8.3	11.9	1.7	0.5	4.4
GDFI	:	1.2	2.6	-12.4	27.9	14.6	22.6	27.2	13.5	14.8	10.8	-15.5	2.3	13.9
Nonfinacial Pub. Sector	:	1.2	2.6	-12.4	26.5	11.0	19.0	30.0	12.5	10.6	7.9	-15.7	9.8	16.8
General Government	:	:	:	:	:	:	:	:	:	:	:	:	:	:
Central Govt.	:	:	:	:	:	:	:	:	:	:	:	:	:	:
State and Local Govt.	:	:	:	:	:	:	:	:	:	:	:	:	:	:
Nonfinacial Pub. Enterp.	:	:	:	:	:	:	:	:	:	:	:	:	:	:
Private Sector	:	1.2	2.6	-12.4	31.1	22.4	29.5	22.1	15.4	22.8	15.8	-15.1	-9.5	8.4
Changes in stocks	:	44.4	-9.0	16.0	-26.1	4.7	18.5	99.2	-3.4	-13.9	16.6	74.7	-3.3	-16.4
Net factor income	:	:	:	:	:	:	:	:	:	:	:	:	:	:
Net current transfers	:	:	:	:	:	:	:	:	:	:	:	:	:	:
Gross national product	:	7.6	7.8	4.5	8.7	10.3	14.6	12.7	8.3	11.0	11.3	4.3	5.7	7.3
Gross domestic saving	:	9.9	1.3	-0.1	17.0	7.2	16.9	20.3	15.2	17.6	8.5	2.2	11.7	2.9
Gross national saving	:	9.8	1.5	-0.3	17.1	7.6	17.0	19.2	14.9	16.9	8.8	1.4	12.1	3.8
Capacity to import	:	:	:	:	:	:	:	:	:	:	:	:	:	:
Terms of trade adjustment	:	:	:	:	:	:	:	:	:	:	:	:	:	:
Gross domestic income	:	8.1	7.9	4.1	7.0	9.6	14.4	12.9	7.1	11.8	11.1	4.8	5.8	5.7
Gross national income	:	8.1	8.0	4.1	7.0	9.8	14.5	12.6	6.9	11.5	11.2	4.6	5.9	6.0

REF: NABOP.WK1 06/23/92
Source: Table 1.2b

Table 1.8b : CHINA: National Accounts
(Percentage GROWTH RATES of 1987 based Implicit price deflators)

	1978	1979	1980	1981	1982	1983	1984	1985	1986	1987	1988	1989	1990	1991
GDP at market prices	:	3.3	4.0	2.2	0.1	1.4	4.6	9.1	4.6	5.0	11.4	8.9	5.1	4.1
GDP at factor cost	:													
Agriculture	:	16.6	9.3	6.4	2.1	2.8	3.4	8.9	5.4	11.2	16.2	7.6	10.2	2.2
Industry	:	1.4	0.1	0.8	-0.3	0.1	2.2	4.8	5.0	2.4	9.1	7.0	1.9	5.3
Mining and quarrying	:													
Manufacturing	:													
Services, etc.	:	-8.1	1.8	0.4	-1.2	1.8	9.8	14.3	3.0	2.7	10.6	12.5	4.9	4.9
Imports of GNFS	:	3.3	3.2	17.0	16.6	4.7	18.9	27.8	21.1	10.7	3.7	0.3	31.4	20.2
Exports of GNFS	:	3.3	0.7	10.4	6.0	1.8	18.3	27.8	9.6	14.6	2.9	2.0	32.8	11.7
Terms of Trade (Px/Pm)	:	-0.0	-2.4	-5.7	-9.1	-2.8	-0.5	0.0	-9.5	3.5	-0.7	1.7	1.0	-7.1
Total Expenditures	:	3.3	4.0	2.2	0.1	2.0	5.2	11.8	5.0	3.0	12.2	8.1	2.7	4.8
Total consumption, etc	:	2.3	4.0	2.2	0.0	2.2	5.5	13.2	5.3	2.3	12.6	7.5	1.1	5.3
General government	:	2.3	4.0	2.2	0.0	2.2	5.5	13.2	5.3	2.3	12.6	3.6	5.7	5.3
Private, etc	:	2.3	4.0	2.2	0.0	2.2	5.5	13.2	5.3	2.3	12.6	8.1	0.4	5.3
Gross domestic investment	:	5.3	4.0	2.2	0.1	1.4	4.6	10.2	4.6	4.0	11.5	8.9	5.1	4.1
GDFI	:	3.3	4.0	2.2	0.1	1.4	4.6	9.1	4.6	5.0	11.5	8.9	5.1	4.1
Nonfinacial Pub. Sector	:		4.0	2.2	0.1	1.4	4.6	9.1	4.6	5.0	11.5	8.9	5.1	4.1
General Government	:													
Central Govt.	:													
State and Local Govt.	:													
Nonfinacial Pub. Enterp.	:													
Private Sector	:	3.3	4.0	2.2	0.1	1.4	4.6	9.1	4.6	5.0	11.5	8.9	5.1	4.1
Changes in stocks	:	13.4	4.0	2.2	0.1	1.4	4.6	13.3	5.1	0.7	11.5	8.9	5.1	4.1
Net factor income	:	3.3	4.0	2.2	0.1	2.0	5.2	11.8	5.0	3.0	12.2	8.1	2.7	4.8
Net current transfers	:	3.3	4.0	2.2	0.1	2.0	5.2	11.8	5.0	3.0	12.2	8.1	2.7	4.8
Gross national product	:	3.3	4.0	2.2	0.1	1.4	4.6	9.1	4.6	5.0	11.5	8.9	5.1	4.1
Gross domestic saving	:	5.3	4.0	2.5	1.0	1.2	4.1	3.9	5.9	8.5	9.8	9.3	11.4	4.3
Gross national saving	:	5.3	4.0	2.5	1.0	1.2	4.1	3.9	5.9	8.5	9.8	9.3	11.4	4.3

REF: NABOP.WK1 06/23/92
Source: Table 1.3b.

Table 1.9b: CHINA: Sources of Growth (in Constant 1987 Prices)

	1978	1979	1980	1981	1982	1983	1984	1985	1986	1987	1988	1989	1990	1991
GDP growth rate (actual)	..	7.61	7.71	4.51	8.68	10.11	14.49	12.98	8.43	11.25	11.22	4.56	5.57	6.98
SUPPLY SIDE														
Agriculture growth rate	::	6.10	-1.40	7.00	11.50	8.30	13.00	1.80	3.30	4.70	2.50	3.10	7.50	3.20
Industry growth rate	::	8.70	12.60	1.70	5.80	9.70	14.90	18.20	9.70	13.20	15.30	5.10	5.70	11.40
Other growth rate	::	8.32	14.18	5.52	9.16	13.23	15.89	20.20	12.33	15.25	13.86	5.04	3.84	4.18
Agriculture Share into GDP	38.20	37.66	34.48	35.30	36.21	35.62	35.15	31.68	30.18	28.40	26.17	25.81	26.28	25.35
Industry Share into GDP	37.69	38.07	39.80	38.73	37.70	37.56	37.70	39.44	39.90	40.60	42.09	42.31	42.36	44.11
Other Share into GDP	24.11	24.26	25.72	25.97	26.08	26.82	27.15	28.88	29.92	31.00	31.74	31.88	31.36	30.54
Total Share	100.00	100.00	100.00	100.00	100.00	100.00	100.00	100.00	100.00	100.00	100.00	100.00	100.00	100.00
Agr. share of last year * Weight	::	2.33	-0.53	2.41	4.06	3.01	4.63	0.63	1.05	1.42	0.71	0.81	1.94	0.84
Ind. share of last year * Weight	::	3.28	4.80	0.68	2.25	3.66	5.60	6.86	3.83	5.27	6.21	2.15	2.41	4.83
Oth. share of last year * Weight	::	2.01	3.44	1.42	2.38	3.45	4.26	5.48	3.56	4.56	4.30	1.60	1.22	1.31
Weighted Average Growth rate	..	7.61	7.71	4.51	8.68	10.11	14.49	12.98	8.43	11.25	11.22	4.56	5.57	6.98
DEMAND SIDE														
Total Consumption growth rate	::	7.27	11.25	6.08	2.76	10.73	13.26	9.31	2.69	8.28	12.81	6.47	2.21	7.51
Gross Domestic Investment gr. rate	::	10.38	-0.62	-5.23	10.55	12.61	21.79	40.35	9.11	8.25	11.86	1.67	0.50	4.38
Exports of goods & NFS growth rate	::	27.98	27.72	25.26	7.59	2.20	14.94	4.12	23.09	18.20	14.76	7.88	12.53	13.94
Imports of goods & NFS growth rate	::	28.74	18.77	7.25	-16.57	10.64	26.58	52.74	-1.44	-1.89	23.39	7.89	-12.81	10.71
Total Consumption Share into GDP	69.02	68.80	71.06	72.12	68.19	68.58	67.84	65.64	62.16	60.50	61.37	62.49	60.50	60.80
Gross Domestic Inv. Share into GDP	34.02	34.90	32.20	29.20	29.70	30.37	32.31	40.13	40.39	39.30	39.53	38.43	36.59	35.70
Exports of GNFS Share into GDP	8.31	9.88	11.71	14.04	13.90	12.90	12.95	11.94	13.55	14.40	14.85	15.33	16.34	17.40
Imports of GNFS Share into GDP	-11.35	-13.57	-14.97	-15.36	-11.79	-11.85	-13.10	-17.71	-16.10	-14.20	-15.75	-16.25	-13.42	-13.89
Total Share	100.00	100.00	100.00	100.00	100.00	100.00	100.00	100.00	100.00	100.00	100.00	100.00	100.00	100.00
Total Cons. Share(-1) * Weight	::	5.02	7.74	4.32	1.99	7.32	9.09	6.32	1.77	5.15	7.75	3.97	1.38	4.54
Gross Dom. Inv. Share(-1)* Weight	::	3.53	-0.22	-1.68	3.08	3.74	6.62	13.04	3.66	3.33	4.66	0.66	0.19	1.60
Exports of GNFS Share(-1) * Weight	::	2.32	2.74	2.96	1.07	0.31	1.93	0.53	2.76	2.47	2.12	1.17	1.92	2.28
Imports of GNFS Share(-1) * Weight	::	-3.26	-2.55	-1.09	2.55	-1.26	-3.15	-6.91	0.25	0.30	-3.32	-1.24	2.08	-1.44
Weighted Average Growth rate	..	7.61	7.71	4.51	8.68	10.11	14.49	12.98	8.43	11.25	11.22	4.56	5.57	6.98

Contribution to GDP growth in percent

	1978	1979	1980	1981	1982	1983	1984	1985	1986	1987	1988	1989	1990	1991
SUPPLY SIDE														
Agriculture	::	30.60	-6.84	53.52	46.74	29.72	31.96	4.88	12.39	12.61	6.33	17.80	34.74	12.05
Industry	::	43.06	62.21	15.01	25.87	36.16	38.63	52.87	45.36	46.82	55.38	47.10	43.28	69.18
Other	::	26.33	44.62	31.48	27.39	34.12	29.41	42.25	42.24	40.57	38.29	35.10	21.98	18.78
Total	::	100.00	100.00	100.00	100.00	100.00	100.00	100.00	100.00	100.00	100.00	100.00	100.00	100.00
DEMAND SIDE														
Total consumption	::	65.92	100.35	95.77	22.95	72.36	62.77	48.67	20.95	45.74	69.09	87.12	24.75	65.05
Gross domestic investment	::	46.38	-2.82	-37.33	35.46	37.02	45.67	100.45	43.35	29.63	41.57	14.45	3.43	22.94
Exports of goods & NFS	::	30.53	35.51	65.63	12.28	3.03	13.30	4.11	32.68	21.92	18.94	25.69	34.47	32.61
Imports of goods & NFS	::	-42.83	-33.05	-24.07	29.31	-12.41	-21.74	-53.24	3.02	2.71	-29.60	-27.26	37.35	-20.60
Total	::	100.00	100.00	100.00	100.00	100.00	100.00	100.00	100.00	100.00	100.00	100.00	100.00	100.00

REF: NABOP.WK1 06/23/92
Source: Table 1.2b.   NOTE: Other is calculated as residual.

Table 2.1 : CHINA : Balance of Payments
(billions of US dollars)

	1978	1979	1980	1981	1982	1983	1984	1985	1986	1987	1988	1989	1990	1991
Exp. of GS (incl. Wrkrs Remitt.)	11.346	16.009	21.237	25.574	26.624	26.951	31.265	32.063	36.077	45.016	53.386	57.725	68.348	79.623
Exports of GNFS	10.513	15.048	20.085	24.413	25.066	24.977	28.930	30.410	34.883	43.823	51.753	56.287	66.219	75.734
Merchandise (FOB)	9.750	13.660	18.188	22.010	22.330	22.250	26.129	27.350	30.942	39.437	47.518	52.537	62.063	71.911
Non-factor services	0.763	1.388	1.897	2.403	2.736	2.747	2.801	3.060	3.941	4.386	4.235	3.750	4.156	3.823
Imports of GNFS	10.890	15.680	19.950	22.012	19.280	21.391	27.410	42.252	42.904	43.216	55.275	59.140	53.350	63.791
Merchandise (FOB)	9.986	14.379	18.294	20.185	17.680	19.616	25.135	38.745	39.343	39.629	50.687	54.231	48.922	58.496
Non-factor services	0.904	1.301	1.656	1.827	1.600	1.775	2.275	3.507	3.561	3.587	4.588	4.909	4.428	5.295
Resource balance	-0.377	-0.632	0.135	2.401	5.786	3.586	1.520	-11.842	-8.021	0.607	-3.522	-2.853	12.869	11.943
Net factor income	-0.008	-0.045	0.195	0.158	0.194	0.707	1.021	0.277	-0.092	-0.790	-0.699	-1.845	-1.129	-0.031
Factor receipts	0.236	0.305	0.512	0.697	1.017	1.528	2.018	1.473	0.986	1.027	1.504	1.362	2.021	3.710
Factor payments	0.244	0.350	0.317	0.539	0.823	0.821	0.997	1.196	1.078	1.817	2.203	3.207	3.150	3.741
Total interest DUE	..	0.350	0.317	0.539	0.823	0.821	0.997	1.182	1.063	1.815	2.195	3.203	3.146	3.741
Other factor payments and dis	..	..	..	..	..	..	..	..	..	..	..	..	..	..
Net current transfers	0.597	0.656	0.640	0.464	0.530	0.436	0.305	0.171	0.255	0.249	0.416	0.238	0.195	0.325
Current Receipts	0.597	0.656	0.640	0.464	0.543	0.446	0.317	0.180	0.266	0.260	0.428	0.247	0.200	0.331
Workers remittances	0.597	0.656	0.640	0.464	0.541	0.446	0.317	0.180	0.208	0.166	0.129	0.076	0.108	0.179
Other curr. transfers	0.000	0.000	0.000	0.000	0.002	0.000	0.000	0.000	0.058	0.094	0.299	0.171	0.092	0.152
Current Payments	0.000	0.000	0.000	0.000	0.013	0.010	0.012	0.009	0.011	0.011	0.012	0.009	0.005	0.006
Curr.A/C Bal before Off.Grants	0.212	-0.021	-0.970	3.023	6.510	4.729	2.846	-11.394	-7.858	0.066	-3.805	-4.460	11.935	12.237
Off. Capital Grants 1/	0.000	-0.030	-0.070	0.108	-0.044	0.075	0.137	0.072	0.124	-0.025	-0.003	-0.143	-0.065	0.134
Curr.A/C Bal after Off.Grants	0.212	-0.051	-0.900	3.131	6.466	4.804	2.983	-11.322	-7.734	0.041	-3.802	-4.317	12.000	12.371
LT Capital Inflows	-0.830	0.822	1.830	0.523	0.453	1.097	1.471	4.264	6.934	5.815	7.053	3.212	3.900	2.900
Direct investment	..	..	0.057	0.265	0.386	0.543	1.124	1.031	1.425	1.669	2.344	2.613	2.660	3.340
Net LT Borrowing	..	..	1.926	0.596	0.535	0.986	1.070	4.005	4.851	6.131	6.781	6.023	6.249	3.108
disbursements	..	..	2.539	1.204	1.857	2.375	2.357	5.302	6.725	8.047	9.130	8.424	9.620	7.425
repayments DUE	..	..	0.613	0.608	1.302	1.389	1.287	1.297	1.874	1.916	2.349	2.401	3.371	4.317
Other LT Inflows (net)	..	..	-0.153	-0.338	-0.468	-0.432	-0.723	-0.772	0.658	-1.985	-2.072	-5.424	-5.009	-3.548
Adj. to Scheduled Debt Service	0	0	0	0	0	0	0	0	0	0	0	0	0	0
1. Debt Service Not Paid	0	0	0	0	0	0	0	0	0	0	0	0	0	0
a). Interest Not Paid	0	0	0	0	0	0	0	0	0	0	0	0	0	0
b). Principal Not Paid	0	0	0	0	0	0	0	0	0	0	0	0	0	0
2. Arrears Red/Prepayments (-)	0	0	0	0	0	0	0	0	0	0	0	0	0	0
Total Other Items (Net)	-0.130	-0.168	-2.063	-1.447	-0.828	-2.334	-3.247	1.770	-1.345	-1.630	-1.588	-0.625	-4.330	-1.172
Net short-term capital	0.000	-0.000	0.000	0.000	-0.000	-0.000	0.000	0.819	-0.343	2.145	0.585	-1.899	-0.141	-3.000
Capital flows n.e.i.	-1.231	-0.622	-3.734	-2.209	-1.121	-1.980	-2.358	0.860	-1.582	-2.325	-1.079	1.229	-0.976	2.684
Errors and omissions	1.101	0.454	1.671	0.762	0.293	-0.354	-0.889	0.091	0.580	-1.450	-1.094	0.045	-3.213	-0.856
Changes in net reserves	0.748	-0.603	-0.667	-2.207	-6.091	-3.567	-1.207	5.288	2.145	-4.226	-1.663	1.730	-11.570	-14.099
Net credit from IMF	0.000	0.000	0.000	0.524	-0.027	-0.496	0.000	0.000	0.731	-0.081	-0.083	-0.079	-0.490	-0.409
Reserve changes n.e.i	0.748	-0.603	-0.667	-2.731	-6.064	-3.071	-1.207	5.288	1.414	-4.145	-1.580	1.809	-11.080	-13.690
Escrow Account														
Gross Reserves (excld. Gold)	1.557	2.154	2.545	5.058	11.349	14.987	17.366	12.728	11.453	16.305	18.541	17.960	29.586	43.674
Gross Reserves (incl. Gold) 1/	4.450	8.708	10.091	10.106	17.152	19.832	21.281	16.881	16.417	22.453	23.751	23.053	34.476	47.500
Mon. Off. (Ann. avg.)(rf)	1.6836	1.5550	1.4984	1.7045	1.8925	1.9757	2.3200	2.9367	3.4528	3.7221	3.7221	3.7651	4.7832	5.3234
Mon. Off. (Endofyear)(ae)	1.5771	1.4962	1.5303	1.7455	1.9227	1.9809	2.7957	3.2015	3.7221	3.7221	3.7221	4.7221	5.2221	5.4342
MUV-Manuf (% change)	..	..	..	..	..	..	..	..	..	..	..	..	..	..
Index Real Eff.(IMF)	..	..	..	..	..	..	..	..	..	..	..	..	..	..

Source: CHINA Statistical Yearbook 1990 and IMF. Merchandise exports (fob), and merchandise imports (cif) are from customs statistics. Exports of non factor services from IMF RED 01/28/91. Merchandise fob imports are calculated by multiplying cif imports by a constant factor 0.917 (from IFS) Imports of non-factor services are calculated as the difference between CIF and FOB imports. NOTE: 1/ Gold evaluated at London Price.

Table 2.2 : CHINA : Balance of Payments
(Percentage GROWTH RATES)

	1978	1979	1980	1981	1982	1983	1984	1985	1986	1987	1988	1989	1990	1991
Exports of GNFS	..	43.1	33.5	21.5	2.7	-0.4	15.8	5.1	14.7	25.6	18.1	8.8	17.6	14.4
Merchandise (FOB)	..	40.1	33.1	21.0	1.5	-0.4	17.5	4.7	13.1	27.5	20.5	10.6	18.1	15.9
Non-factor services	..	81.9	36.7	26.7	13.9	0.4	2.0	9.2	28.8	11.3	-3.4	-11.5	10.8	-8.0
Imports of GNFS	..	44.0	27.2	10.3	-12.4	10.9	28.1	54.1	1.5	0.7	27.9	7.0	-9.8	19.6
Merchandise (FOB)	..	44.0	27.2	10.3	-12.4	10.9	28.1	54.1	1.5	0.7	27.9	7.0	-9.8	19.6
Non-factor services	..	44.0	27.2	10.3	-12.4	10.9	28.1	54.1	1.5	0.7	27.9	7.0	-9.8	19.6
Resource balance	..	..	..	..	..	..	..	..	..	..	..	..	..	..
Net factor income	..	29.2	67.9	36.1	45.9	50.2	32.1	-27.0	-33.1	4.2	46.4	-9.4	48.4	83.6
Factor receipts	..	..	..	70.0	52.7	-0.2	21.4	20.0	-9.9	68.6	21.2	45.6	-1.8	18.8
Factor payments	..	..	..	70.0	52.7	-0.2	21.4	18.6	-10.1	70.7	20.9	45.9	-1.8	18.9
Total interest paid	..	..	..	..	..	..	..	..	..	..	..	..	..	..
Interest due but not paid	..	..	..	..	..	..	..	..	..	..	..	..	..	..
Other factor payments and dis	..	..	..	..	..	..	..	..	..	..	..	..	..	..
Net current transfers	..	..	..	..	..	..	..	..	..	..	..	..	..	..
Current Receipts	..	..	-2.4	-27.5	17.0	-17.9	-28.9	-43.2	47.8	-2.3	64.6	-42.3	-19.0	65.6
Workers remittances	..	..	-2.4	-27.5	16.6	-17.6	-28.9	-43.2	15.6	-20.2	-22.3	-41.1	42.1	65.6
Other curr. transfers	..	..	..	..	..	..	..	..	..	..	..	..	..	..
Current Payments	..	..	..	..	..	-23.1	20.0	-25.0	22.2	0.0	9.1	-25.0	-44.4	20.0
Curr.A/C Bal before Off.Grants	..	..	..	..	..	..	..	..	..	..	..	..	..	..
Off. Capital Grants 1/	..	..	..	..	..	..	..	..	..	..	..	..	..	..
Curr.A/C Bal after Off.Grants	..	..	..	..	..	..	..	..	..	..	..	..	..	..
LT Capital Inflows n.e.f	..	..	..	364.9	45.7	40.7	107.0	-8.3	38.2	17.1	40.4	11.5	1.8	25.6
Direct Investment	..	..	..	..	..	..	..	..	..	..	..	..	..	..
Net LT Borrowing (DRS)	..	..	..	..	..	..	..	..	..	..	..	..	..	..
disbursements	..	..	..	-29.1	2.1	29.3	-0.8	124.9	26.8	19.7	13.5	-7.7	14.2	-22.8
repayments	..	..	..	96.4	8.1	6.7	-7.3	0.8	44.5	2.2	22.6	2.2	40.4	28.1
Other LT Inflows (net)	..	..	..	..	..	..	..	..	..	..	..	..	..	..
Total Other Items (Net)	..	..	..	..	..	..	..	..	..	..	..	..	..	..
Net short-term capital	..	..	..	..	..	..	..	..	..	..	..	..	..	..
Interest Arrears	..	..	..	..	..	..	..	..	..	..	..	..	..	..
Other Net ST Capital	..	..	..	..	..	..	..	..	..	..	..	..	..	..
Capital flows n.e.i.	..	..	..	..	..	..	..	..	..	..	..	..	..	..
Errors and omissions	..	..	..	..	..	..	..	..	..	..	..	..	..	..
Changes in net reserves	..	..	..	..	..	..	..	..	..	..	..	..	..	..
Net credit from IMF	..	..	..	..	..	..	..	..	..	..	..	..	..	..
Reserve changes n.e.f	..	..	..	..	..	..	..	..	..	..	..	..	..	..
Escrow Account	..	..	..	..	..	..	..	..	..	..	..	..	..	..
Gross Reserves (excld. Gold)	..	38.3	18.2	98.7	124.4	32.1	15.9	-26.7	-10.0	42.4	13.7	-3.1	64.7	47.6
Gross Reserves (incl. Gold) 1/	..	95.7	15.9	0.2	69.7	15.6	7.3	-20.7	-2.7	36.8	5.8	-2.9	49.6	37.8
Exchange Rates:														
Nom. Off. (Ann. avg.)(rf)	..	-7.6	-3.6	13.8	11.0	4.4	17.4	26.6	17.6	7.8	0.0	1.2	27.0	11.3
Nom. Off. (Endofyear)(ae)	..	-5.1	2.3	14.1	10.2	3.0	41.1	14.5	16.3	0.0	0.0	26.9	10.6	4.1
MUV/PAC Estimate	..	..	..	..	..	..	..	..	..	..	..	..	..	..
Index Real Eff.(IMF)	..	..	..	..	..	..	..	..	..	..	..	..	..	..

REF: NABOP.WK1 06/23/92
Source: Table 2.1.

Table 2.3: CHINA : Services
(In millions of U.S. Dollars)

	1978	1979	1980	1981	1982	1983	1984	1985	1986	1987	1988	1989	1990	1991
A. Shipment of freight														
Credit	..	348	553	848	785	786	668	671	705	904	1308	1061	1937	1265
Debit	..	906	1187	1181	635	739	761	1224	850	1186	1387	2382	2139	1975
B. Insurance														
Credit	..	68	127	225	202	203	224	196	229	252	345	332	227	185
Debit	..	32	66	176	89	110	121	69	82	142	214	187	84	398
C. Other transportation														
Credit	..	33	106	113	140	174	209	271	304	152	169	153	480	101
Debit	..	0	0	0	0	0	0	0	0	0	0	0	0	0
D. Port expenses														
Credit	..	316	385	422	388	381	376	360	306	289	304	300	289	283
Debit	..	376	566	710	612	614	560	300	670	456	889	370	1106	320
E. Travel receipts														
Credit	..	413	511	672	703	767	922	979	1227	1693	2078	1707	1738	2557
Debit	..	..	..	69	66	53	150	314	308	387	633	429	470	368
F. Profits														
Credit	..	..	..	..	20	31	2	6	0	10	0	6	0	21
Debit	..	..	..	..	1	0	0	14	15	2	8	7	46	9
G. Interest														
Credit	..	..	..	..	5	707	925	484	216	177	427	247	667	2005
Debit	..	..	..	..	16	41	92	68	298	457	644	394	480	2351
H. Bank interest and charges														
Credit	..	305	512	697	992	715	995	897	685	789	1042	1641	2350	2854
Debit	..	624	612	821	624	254	296	464	611	732	978	1264	1536	1752
I. Posts														
Credit	..	..	..	..	0	0	0	0	15	12	24	118	159	180
Debit	..	..	..	..	0	0	0	0	15	14	11	16	13	18
J. Interofficial														
Credit	..	..	..	..	36	13	28	130	215	204	137	151	107	84
Debit	..	..	..	..	159	154	223	263	251	150	277	337	239	55
K. Labor income														
Credit	..	..	..	..	..	75	96	86	85	51	35	53	52	68
Debit	..	..	..	..	..	0	0	0	0	0	0	0	0	0
L. Other services														
Credit	..	210	215	123	407	402	384	448	940	880	458	727	866	705
Debit	..	316	272	376	463	324	563	354	100	150	193	189	291	154
M. Total services														
NET	..	-561	-294	-233	1088	1986	2053	1463	1727	1737	1094	922	2468	2787
Credit	..	1693	2409	3100	3753	4275	4819	4533	4927	5413	6327	6497	8872	10187
Debit	..	2254	2703	3333	2665	2289	2766	3070	3200	3676	5233	5575	6404	7400
N. Factor Services														
NET	..	-319	-100	-124	376	1233	1630	927	62	-164	-126	-303	1226	-402
Receipts (Credit)	..	305	512	697	1017	1528	2018	1473	986	1027	1504	1362	3288	3710
Payments (Debit)	..	624	612	821	641	295	388	546	924	1191	1630	1665	2062	4112
OTHER FACTOR RECEIPTS (ADJUSTMENT)										0	0	-585	219	-1238
O. Non-Factor Services														
NET														
Receipts (Credit) IMF definition	..	1388	1897	2403	2736	2747	2801	3060	3941	4386	4235	3750	4711	5057
Payments (Debit) IMF definition	..	1630	2091	2512	2024	1994	2378	2524	2276	2485	3603	3910	4342	3288
Payments (Debit) IFS definition	..	1301	1656	1827	1600	1775	2275	3507	3561	3587	4588	4909	4428	5295
(Imports cif customs basis * 0.083)														
OTHER NON-FACTOR RECEIPTS (ADJUSTMENT)									0	0	-588	-1385	-873	-1420

Source: IMF Recent Economic Developments 01/28/91 pp. 120, 01/17/90 pp.69 for 1984-89, 10/24/85 pp.115 for 1981-83, 11/03/83 pp.100 for 1979-80; and BESD data base file IMFBOPFC (which is identical to the data in IMF Recent Developments).

Table 2.4: CHINA : Transfers
(In millions of U.S. Dollars)

	1978	1979	1980	1981	1982	1983	1984	1985	1986	1987	1988	1989	1990	1991
Private unrequited transfers														
NET	...	656	640	464	530	436	305	171	255	249	416	238	195	325
Credit	...	656	640	464	543	446	317	180	266	260	428	247	200	331
Debit	..	0	0	0	13	10	12	9	11	11	12	9	5	6
Nonresident remittances														
NET	...	656	640	464	538	444	315	177	205	163	125	73	105	175
Credit	...	656	640	464	541	446	317	180	208	166	129	76	108	179
Debit	..	0	0	0	3	2	2	3	3	3	4	3	3	4
Migrants' transfers														
NET	...	...	...	...	-8	-8	-10	-6	50	86	291	165	90	150
Credit	...	...	...	...	2	0	0	0	58	94	299	171	92	152
Debit	..	..	..	..	10	8	10	6	8	8	8	6	2	2
Public unrequited transfers														
NET	...	-30	-70	108	-44	75	137	72	124	-25	3	143	65	134
Credit	...	0	21	156	129	174	279	259	250	129	140	230	123	204
Debit	..	30	91	48	173	99	142	187	126	154	137	87	58	70
International organizations														
NET	...	...	...	...	...	...	...	21	96	24	42	82	61	102
Credit	...	...	...	...	...	...	...	63	140	58	61	120	63	104
Debit	..	..	..	..	..	..	..	42	44	34	19	38	2	2
Grants and aid														
NET	...	...	...	...	...	...	...	52	28	-49	-39	61	5	33
Credit	...	...	...	...	...	...	...	197	110	71	79	110	60	99
Debit	..	..	..	..	..	..	..	145	82	120	118	49	55	66
TOTAL TRANSFERS														
NET	..	626	570	572	486	511	442	243	379	224	419	381	260	459
Credit	..	656	661	620	672	620	596	439	516	389	568	477	323	535
Debit	..	30	91	48	186	109	154	196	137	165	149	96	63	76

REF: NABOP.WK1 06/23/92
Source: IMF Recent Economic Developments 01/22/91 p. 121 for 1986-90; 01/17/90 pp.70 for 1985,01/30/89 pp.89 for 84, 10/24/85 pp.115 for 1981-3, 11/03/83 pp.100 for 1979-80.

Table 2.5: CHINA: INTERNATIONAL RESERVES
(US$ million)

	1978	1979	1980	1981	1982	1983	1984	1985	1986	1987	1988	1989	1990	1991
Total Reserves (minus Gold) (1l.d)	1557	2154	2545	5058	11349	14987	17366	12728	11453	16305	18541	17960	29586	43674
SDR's (1b.d)	0	0	92	275	214	335	406	483	569	640	586	540	562	577
Reserve Position with Fund(1c.d)	0	0	191	0	0	176	255	332	370	429	407	398	430	433
Foreign Exchange Reserves (1d.d)	1557	2154	2262	4783	11135	14476	16705	11913	10514	15236	17548	17022	28594	42664
GOLD														
Gold (mill. fine troy ounces)(1ad)	12.8	12.8	12.8	12.7	12.7	12.7	12.7	12.7	12.7	12.7	12.7	12.7	12.7	12.7
Gold (National valuation)1/ (1and)	584	590	571	516	491	464	435	486	541	629	594	587	623	634
London Gold Price(US$ per oz)(c)	226	512	590	398	457	382	308	327	391	484	410	401	385	354
Gold at London Price (Million US$)	2893	6554	7546	5048	5803	4845	3915	4153	4964	6148	5210	5093	4890	4491
Total Reserves incl. Gold (National	2141	2744	3116	5574	11840	15451	17801	13214	11994	16934	19135	18547	30209	44308
Total Reserves incl. Gold (London P	4450	8708	10091	10106	17152	19832	21281	16881	16417	22453	23751	23053	34476	48165

REF: NABOP.WK1 06/23/92
Source: IFS 3/1991, IMF RED 01/28/91 p.113.
Note: IFS line numbers in parenthesis.
1/ Gold valued at SDR 35 per fine ounce.

Table 3.1 : CHINA : Commodity Composition of Merchandise Exports (US $ million)

		1980	1981	1982	1983	1984	1985	1986	1987	1988	1989	1990	1991
PRIMARY GOODS	S0+S1+S2+S3+S4	9137	10251	10033	9623	11934	13828	11272	13231	14407	15077	15857	16213
FOOD	S0	2999	2925	2909	2854	3232	3803	4448	4781	5890	6145	6592	7226
of which													
Live animals chiefly for food	D00	..	..	..	..	326	304	338	348	386	395	430	439
Meat and meat products	D01	..	..	..	..	456	448	483	520	585	657	791	906
Fishes,shell-fish,molluscs etc.	D03	..	..	..	..	305	283	491	721	969	1039	1370	1181
Grain and grain products	D04	..	..	..	..	444	1065	898	579	681	719	614	1169
Vegetables and fruits	D05	..	..	..	..	829	825	1092	1290	1617	1623	1742	1946
Coffee, tea,cocoa etc.	D07	..	..	..	..	449	435	466	488	524	568	534	491
NON-FOOD	S2	1726	2098	1810	2102	2421	2653	2908	3650	4257	4212	3537	3486
of which													
Oil seeds & oil-containing fruits	D22	..	..	..	..	505	487	580	674	684	645	619	741
Textile fibers etc.	D26	..	..	..	..	929	1145	1160	1508	1672	1546	1095	1125
Animal and vegetable raw materials	D29	60	89	78	105	442	398	486	645	724	845	809	705
MINERAL FUELS	S3	4273	5228	5314	4667	6027	7132	3683	4544	3950	4321	5225	4821
of which													
Coal, coke and briquettes	D32	..	..	..	..	322	349	455	536	594	680	755	829
Petroleum,petroleum products etc.	D33	..	..	..	..	5701	6777	3224	4003	3350	3633	4460	3975
OTHER	S1+S4	139	0	0	0	254	240	233	256	310	400	503	679
MANUFACTURED GOODS	S5+S6+S7+S8+S9	9051	11759	12297	12607	14195	13522	19670	26206	33110	37460	46206	55698
CHEMICALS & RELATED PRODUCTS	S5	1125	1342	1196	1251	1364	1358	1733	2235	2897	3201	3730	3818
of which													
Organic	D51	..	..	..	..	294	309	411	500	575	690	838	911
Inorganic	D52	..	..	..	..	283	287	379	553	762	791	842	913
LIGHT INDUSTRY	S6	4019	4706	4302	4366	5054	4493	5886	8570	10489	10897	12576	14456
of which													
Yarn,fabrics,manuf. goods etc.	D65	..	..	..	..	3093	3243	4220	5790	6456	6994	6999	7734
Non-metallic minerals	D66	..	..	..	..	260	227	317	439	579	792	1316	1668
Metal products	D67	..	..	..	..	477	426	553	797	1006	1210	1283	1669
MACHINERY & TRANSPORT EQUIPMENT	S7	846	1087	1263	1220	1493	772	1094	1741	2769	3874	5588	7149
OTHER	S8	2850	3725	3702	3805	4687	3486	4948	6273	8268	10755	12687	16620
Clothing and garments	D84	..	..	..	..	2653	2050	2913	3749	4872	6130	6848	8998
PRODUCTS NOT CLASSIFIED ELSEWHERE	S9	210	899	1834	1965	1597	3413	6009	7387	8687	8733	11625	13655
TOTAL		18188	22010	22330	22230	26129	27350	30942	39437	47518	52537	62063	71910

REF: EXPORTS.WK1   06/23/92
Source: CHINA Customs Statistics 1992.1 for 1990, 1991.1 for 1990; Statistical Yearbook 1990 pp.603 for 1988-9, 1988 pp.644 for 1987, 1986;
1987 pp.520 for 1985; 1986 pp.482 for 1984; 1985 pp.494 for 1983; 1984 pp.381 for 1982;
1983 pp.405 for 1981; 1981 pp.73 for 1980.

Table 3.2 : CHINA : Commodity Composition of Merchandise Exports
(Percentage Shares)

		1980	1981	1982	1983	1984	1985	1986	1987	1988	1989	1990	1991
PRIMARY GOODS	S0+S1+S2+S3+S4	50.2	46.6	44.9	43.3	45.7	50.6	36.4	33.5	30.3	28.7	25.5	22.5
FOOD	S0	16.5	13.3	13.0	12.8	12.4	13.9	14.4	12.1	12.4	11.7	10.6	10.0
of which													
Live animals chiefly for food	D00	..	..	..	..	1.2	1.1	1.1	0.9	0.8	0.8	0.7	0.6
Meat and meat products	D01	..	..	..	..	1.7	1.6	1.6	1.3	1.2	1.2	1.3	1.3
Fishes,shell-fish,molluscs etc.	D03	..	..	..	..	1.7	1.0	1.6	1.8	2.0	2.0	2.2	1.6
Grain and grain products	D04	..	..	..	..	1.7	3.9	2.9	1.5	1.4	1.4	1.0	1.6
Vegetables and fruits	D05	..	..	..	..	3.2	3.0	3.5	3.3	3.4	3.1	2.8	2.7
Coffee, tea,cocoa etc.	D07	..	..	..	..	1.7	1.6	1.5	1.2	1.1	1.1	0.9	0.7
NON-FOOD	S2	9.5	9.5	8.1	9.5	9.3	9.7	9.4	9.3	9.0	8.0	5.7	4.8
of which													
Oil seeds & oil-containing fruits	D22	..	..	..	..	1.9	1.8	1.9	1.7	1.4	1.2	1.0	1.0
Textile fibers etc.	D26	..	..	..	..	3.6	4.2	3.7	3.8	3.5	2.9	1.8	1.6
Animal and vegetable raw materials	D29	0.3	0.4	0.3	0.5	1.7	1.5	1.6	1.6	1.5	1.6	1.3	1.0
MINERAL FUELS	S3	23.5	23.8	23.8	21.0	23.1	26.1	11.9	11.5	8.3	8.2	8.4	6.7
of which													
Coal, coke and briquettes	D32	..	..	..	..	1.2	1.3	1.5	1.4	1.2	1.3	1.2	1.2
Petroleum,petroleum products etc.	D33	..	..	..	..	21.8	24.8	10.4	10.2	7.0	6.9	7.2	5.5
OTHER	S1+S4	0.8	0.0	0.0	0.0	1.0	0.9	0.8	0.6	0.7	0.8	0.8	0.9
MANUFACTURED GOODS	S5+S6+S7+S8+S9	49.8	53.4	55.1	56.7	54.3	49.4	63.6	66.5	69.7	71.3	74.5	77.5
CHEMICALS & RELATED PRODUCTS	S5	6.2	6.1	5.4	5.6	5.2	5.0	5.6	5.7	6.1	6.1	6.0	5.3
of which													
Organic	D51	..	..	..	..	1.1	1.1	1.3	1.3	1.2	1.3	1.4	1.3
Inorganic	D52	..	..	..	..	1.1	1.0	1.2	1.4	1.6	1.5	1.4	1.3
LIGHT INDUSTRY	S6	22.1	21.4	19.3	19.6	19.3	16.4	19.0	21.7	22.1	20.7	20.3	20.1
of which													
Yarn,fabrics,manuf. goods etc.	D65	..	..	..	..	11.8	11.9	13.6	14.7	13.6	13.3	11.3	10.8
Non-ferrous metals	D68	..	..	..	..	1.0	0.8	1.0	1.1	1.2	1.5	2.1	2.3
Metal products	D67	..	..	..	..	1.8	1.6	1.8	2.0	2.1	2.3	2.1	2.3
MACHINERY & TRANSPORT EQUIPMENT	S7	4.7	4.9	5.7	5.5	5.7	2.8	3.5	4.4	5.8	7.4	9.0	9.9
OTHER	S8	15.7	16.9	16.6	17.1	17.9	12.7	16.0	15.9	17.4	20.5	20.4	23.1
Clothing and garments	D84	..	..	..	..	10.2	7.5	9.4	9.5	10.3	11.7	11.0	12.5
PRODUCTS NOT CLASSIFIED ELSEWHERE	S9	1.2	4.1	8.2	8.8	6.1	12.5	19.4	18.7	18.3	16.6	18.7	19.0
TOTAL		100.0	100.0	100.0	100.0	100.0	100.0	100.0	100.0	100.0	100.0	100.0	100.0

REF: EXPORTS.WK1   06/23/92
Source: Table 3.1.

Table 3.3 : CHINA : Commodity Composition of Merchandise Exports
(Percentage Growth Rates)

		1980	1981	1982	1983	1984	1985	1986	1987	1988	1989	1990	1991
PRIMARY GOODS	S0+S1+S2+S3+S4	..	12.2	-2.1	-4.1	24.0	15.9	-18.5	17.4	8.9	4.7	5.2	2.2
FOOD	S0	..	-2.5	-0.5	-1.9	13.2	17.7	17.0	7.5	23.2	4.3	7.3	9.6
of which													
Live animals chiefly for food	D00	..	..	..	..	..	-6.7	11.2	3.0	11.0	2.3	8.8	2.2
Meat and meat products	D01	..	..	..	..	..	-1.8	7.8	7.7	12.5	12.2	20.5	14.5
Fishes,shell-fish,molluscs etc.	D03	..	..	..	..	..	-7.2	73.5	46.8	34.3	7.3	31.8	-13.8
Grain and grain products	D04	..	..	..	..	..	139.9	-15.7	-35.5	17.6	5.6	-14.7	90.5
Vegetables and fruits	D05	..	..	..	..	..	-0.5	32.4	18.1	25.3	0.4	7.3	11.7
Coffee, tea,cocoa etc.	D07	..	..	..	..	..	-3.1	7.1	4.7	7.4	8.3	-6.0	-8.1
NON-FOOD	S2	..	21.5	-13.7	16.1	15.2	9.6	9.6	25.5	16.6	-1.1	-16.0	-1.5
of which													
Oil seeds & oil-containing fruits	D22	..	..	..	..	..	-3.6	19.1	16.2	1.4	-5.6	-4.1	19.8
Textile fibers etc.	D26	..	49.1	-12.4	34.6	321.0	23.3	1.3	30.0	10.9	-7.5	-29.1	2.7
Animal and vegetable raw materials	D29	..	..	..	..	..	-10.0	22.1	32.7	12.3	16.6	-4.2	-12.9
MINERAL FUELS	S3	..	22.4	1.6	-12.2	29.1	18.3	-48.4	23.4	-13.1	9.4	20.9	-7.7
of which													
Coal, coke and briquettes	D32	..	..	..	..	..	8.4	30.4	17.8	10.8	14.6	11.0	9.9
Petroleum,petroleum products etc.	D33	..	..	..	..	..	18.9	-52.4	24.2	-16.3	8.4	22.8	-10.9
OTHER	S1+S4	..	..	..	..	..	-5.5	-2.9	9.9	21.3	28.8	25.7	35.1
MANUFACTURED GOODS	S5+S6+S7+S8+S9	..	29.9	4.6	2.5	12.6	-4.7	45.5	33.2	26.3	13.1	23.3	20.5
CHEMICALS & RELATED PRODUCTS	S5	..	19.3	-10.9	4.6	9.0	-0.4	27.6	29.0	29.6	10.5	16.5	2.4
of which													
Organic	D51	..	..	..	..	..	5.1	33.0	21.7	15.1	19.9	21.5	8.7
Inorganic	D52	..	..	..	..	..	1.4	32.1	45.9	37.8	3.8	6.5	8.4
LIGHT INDUSTRY	S6	..	17.1	-8.6	1.5	15.8	-11.1	31.0	45.6	22.4	3.9	15.4	14.9
of which													
Yarn,fabrics,manuf. goods etc.	D65	..	..	..	..	..	4.8	30.1	37.2	11.5	8.3	0.1	10.5
Non-ferrous metals	D68	..	..	..	..	..	-12.7	39.6	38.5	31.9	36.7	66.2	26.8
Metal products	D67	..	..	..	..	..	-10.7	29.8	44.1	26.2	20.3	6.0	30.1
MACHINERY & TRANSPORT EQUIPMENT	S7	..	28.4	16.2	-3.4	22.4	-48.3	41.7	59.1	59.1	39.9	44.3	27.9
OTHER	S8	..	30.7	-0.6	2.8	23.2	-25.6	41.9	26.8	31.8	30.1	18.0	31.0
Clothing and garments	D84	..	..	..	..	..	-22.7	42.1	28.7	29.9	25.8	11.7	31.4
PRODUCTS NOT CLASSIFIED ELSEWHERE	S9	..	..	104.0	7.1	-18.7	113.7	76.1	22.9	17.6	0.5	33.1	17.5
TOTAL		..	21.0	1.5	-0.4	17.5	4.7	13.1	27.5	20.5	10.6	18.1	15.9

REF: EXPORTS.MK1   06/23/92
Source: Table 3.1.

Table 3.4: CHINA: Merchandise Exports in Current Prices and Constant (1980) Prices

Merchandise Exports in Current Prices (US$ million)

		1980	1981	1982	1983	1984	1985	1986	1987	1988	1989	1990	1991
Food	(S0+S1+S4)	3138	2925	2909	2854	3486	4043	4681	5037	6200	6544	7094	7906
Petroleum	(S3)	4273	5228	5314	4667	6027	7132	3683	4544	3950	4321	5225	4821
Manufacturing	(S5+S6+S7+S8+S9)	9051	11759	12297	12607	14195	13522	19670	26206	33110	37460	46206	55698
Other	(S2)	1726	2098	1810	2102	2421	2653	2908	3650	4257	4212	3537	3486
Total		18188	22010	22330	22230	26129	27350	30942	39437	47518	52537	62063	71910

Source: Table 3.1.

Price Indices (in US dollars) 1980=100

		1980	1981	1982	1983	1984	1985	1986	1987	1988	1989	1990	1991
Food	food	100.00	87.09	78.13	84.68	92.20	80.35	72.35	55.49	61.18	58.00	50.58	47.21
Petroleum	petroleum	100.00	112.01	102.81	95.40	95.40	91.84	39.40	45.68	33.68	40.62	50.19	39.87
Manufacturing	muv	100.00	100.41	98.87	96.62	94.56	95.32	112.39	123.45	132.44	131.47	139.28	141.73
Other	non-food	100.00	86.55	77.42	88.99	84.67	70.56	54.37	61.43	58.14	58.51	55.79	52.30

Source: World Bank Commodity Projections; IECCM 07/18/91

Growth Rate of Price Indices in US dollars (Percentage)

		1980	1981	1982	1983	1984	1985	1986	1987	1988	1989	1990	1991
Food	food	..	-12.91	-10.29	8.38	8.87	-12.85	-9.95	-23.30	10.24	-5.20	-12.79	-6.67
Petroleum	petroleum	..	12.01	-8.21	-7.21	0.00	-3.74	-57.10	15.95	-26.28	20.61	23.56	-20.56
Manufacturing	muv	..	0.41	-1.54	-2.28	-2.13	0.81	17.91	9.84	7.28	-0.73	5.94	1.76
Other	non-food	..	-13.45	-10.54	14.95	-4.86	-16.67	-22.93	12.98	-5.36	0.65	-4.66	-6.24

Merchandise Exports in 1980 Constant Prices (US$ million)

		1980	1981	1982	1983	1984	1985	1986	1987	1988	1989	1990	1991
Food	(S0+S1+S4)	3138	3359	3723	3370	3781	5032	6470	9077	10136	11284	14027	16747
Petroleum	(S3)	4273	4668	5169	4892	6317	7766	9348	9946	11729	10638	10411	12093
Manufacturing	(S5+S6+S7+S8+S9)	9051	11711	12438	13049	15012	14186	17501	21228	25001	28492	33175	39298
Other	(S2)	1726	2424	2338	2362	2859	3760	5348	5942	7322	7198	6340	6664
Total		18188	22161	23668	23673	27970	30744	38667	46193	54188	57612	63953	74802

REF: EXPORTS.WK1   06/23/92

Table 3.5: CHINA: Merchandise Exports in Current Prices and Constant (1987) Prices

Merchandise Exports in Current Prices (US$ million)

		1980	1981	1982	1983	1984	1985	1986	1987	1988	1989	1990	1991
Food	(S0+S1+S4)	3138	2925	2909	2854	3486	4043	4681	5037	6200	6544	7094	7906
Petroleum	(S3)	4273	5228	5314	4667	6027	7132	3683	4544	3950	4321	5225	4821
Manufacturing	(S5+S6+S7+S8+S9)	9051	11759	12297	12607	14195	13522	19670	26206	33110	37460	46206	55698
Other	(S2)	1726	2098	1810	2102	2421	2653	2908	3650	4257	4212	3537	3486
Total		18188	22010	22330	22230	26129	27350	30942	39437	47518	52537	62063	71910

Source: Table 3.4.

Price Indices (in US dollars) 1987=100

		1980	1981	1982	1983	1984	1985	1986	1987	1988	1989	1990	1991
Food	(S0+S1+S4)	180.21	156.94	140.80	152.60	166.15	144.79	130.38	100.00	110.24	104.51	91.15	85.07
Petroleum	(S3)	218.89	245.17	225.05	208.83	208.83	201.03	86.24	100.00	73.72	88.91	109.86	87.27
Manufacturing muv	(S5+S6+S7+S8+S9)	81.01	81.34	80.09	78.26	76.60	77.21	91.04	100.00	107.28	106.50	112.83	114.81
Other non-food	(S2)	162.79	140.89	126.03	144.87	137.83	114.85	88.51	100.00	94.64	95.25	90.81	85.15

Source: World Bank Commodity Projections; IECCM 10/26/90

Growth Rate of Price Indices in US dollars (Percentage)

		1980	1981	1982	1983	1984	1985	1986	1987	1988	1989	1990	1991
Food	(S0+S1+S4)	..	-12.91	-10.29	8.38	8.87	-12.85	-9.95	-23.30	10.24	-5.20	-12.79	-6.67
Petroleum	(S3)	..	12.01	-8.21	-7.21	0.00	-3.74	-57.10	15.95	-26.28	20.61	23.56	-20.56
Manufacturing muv	(S5+S6+S7+S8+S9)	..	0.41	-1.54	-2.28	-2.13	0.81	17.91	9.84	7.28	-0.73	5.94	1.76
Other non-food	(S2)	..	-13.45	-10.54	14.95	-4.86	-16.67	-22.93	12.98	-5.36	0.65	-4.66	-6.24

Merchandise Exports in 1987 Constant Prices (US$ million)

		1980	1981	1982	1983	1984	1985	1986	1987	1988	1989	1990	1991
Food	(S0+S1+S4)	1741	1864	2066	1870	2098	2792	3590	5037	5624	6262	7784	9293
Petroleum	(S3)	1952	2132	2361	2235	2886	3548	4271	4544	5358	4860	4756	5525
Manufacturing	(S5+S6+S7+S8+S9)	11173	14457	15355	16108	18532	17512	21605	26206	30863	35173	40954	48513
Other	(S2)	1061	1489	1436	1451	1757	2310	3285	3650	4498	4422	3895	4094
Total		15927	19942	21218	21664	25273	26162	32751	39437	46344	50717	57389	67425

REF: EXPORTS.WK1   06/23/92

Table 3.6: CHINA: Merchandise Exports in Current Prices and Constant (1980) Prices

Merchandise Exports in Current Prices
(Yuan million)

		1980	1981	1982	1983	1984	1985	1986	1987	1988	1989	1990	1991
Food	(S0+S1+S4)	4702	4986	5505	5639	8088	11873	16163	18748	23079	24641	33934	42085
Petroleum	(S3)	6403	8911	10057	9221	13983	20945	12717	16913	14702	16269	24993	25666
Manufacturing	(S5+S6+S7+S8+S9)	13562	20043	23272	24908	32932	39710	67917	97541	123240	141040	221014	296501
Other	(S2)	2587	3576	3425	4153	5617	7791	10041	13586	15845	15859	16918	18555
Total		27254	37516	42260	43920	60619	80319	106837	146788	176866	197808	296859	382807

Source: Table 3.4.

Price Indices (in Yuan)
1980=100

			1980	1981	1982	1983	1984	1985	1986	1987	1988	1989	1990	1991
Food	(S0+S1+S4)	food	100.00	99.07	98.68	111.66	142.75	157.47	166.72	137.84	151.96	145.73	161.46	167.71
Petroleum	(S3)	petroleum	100.00	127.41	129.86	125.79	147.71	179.99	90.79	113.48	83.66	102.07	160.21	141.64
Manufacturing	(S5+S6+S7+S8+S9)	muv	100.00	116.22	124.87	127.39	146.40	186.82	258.99	306.65	328.98	330.36	444.61	503.53
Other	(S2)	non-food	100.00	98.45	97.79	117.34	131.09	138.28	125.30	152.59	144.42	147.03	178.08	185.82

Source: World Bank Commodity Projections; IECCM 10/26/90

Merchandise Exports in 1980 Constant Prices
(Yuan million)

		1980	1981	1982	1983	1984	1985	1986	1987	1988	1989	1990	1991
Food	(S0+S1+S4)	4702	5032	5579	5050	5666	7540	9694	13601	15187	16908	21018	25094
Petroleum	(S3)	6403	6994	7745	7330	9466	11636	14007	14904	17575	15940	15600	18120
Manufacturing	(S5+S6+S7+S8+S9)	13562	17548	18637	19552	22494	21256	26224	31808	37461	42692	49709	58884
Other	(S2)	2587	3632	3503	3539	4285	5634	8014	8903	10972	10786	9500	9985
Total		27254	33206	35464	35471	41910	46067	57939	69216	81195	86327	95827	112084

	1980	1981	1982	1983	1984	1985	1986	1987	1988	1989	1990	1991
Exchange Rate	1.6984	1.7045	1.8925	1.9757	2.3200	2.9367	3.4528	3.7221	3.7221	3.7651	4.7832	5.3234

REF: EXPORTS.MK1   06/23/92

Table 3.7: CHINA: Merchandise Exports in Current Prices and Constant (1987) Prices

Merchandise Exports in Current Prices
(Yuan million)

	1980	1981	1982	1983	1984	1985	1986	1987	1988	1989	1990	1991
Food (S0+S1+S4)	4702	4986	5505	5639	8088	11873	16163	18748	23079	24641	33934	42085
Petroleum (S3)	6403	8911	10057	9221	13983	20945	12717	16913	14702	16269	24993	25666
Manufacturing (S5+S6+S7+S8+S9)	13562	20043	23272	24908	32952	39710	67917	97541	123240	141040	221014	296501
Other (S2)	2587	3576	3425	4153	5617	7791	10041	13586	15845	15859	16918	18555
Total	27254	37516	42260	43920	60619	80319	106837	146788	176866	197808	296659	382807

Source: Table 3.6.

Price Indices (in Yuan)
1987=100

		1980	1981	1982	1983	1984	1985	1986	1987	1988	1989	1990	1991
Food (S0+S1+S4)	food	72.55	71.87	71.59	81.00	103.56	114.24	120.95	100.00	110.24	105.72	117.13	121.67
Petroleum (S3)	petroleum	88.12	112.28	114.43	110.85	130.16	158.61	80.00	100.00	73.72	89.94	141.17	124.81
Manufacturing (S5+S6+S7+S8+S9)	muv	32.61	37.25	40.72	41.54	47.74	60.92	84.46	100.00	107.28	107.73	144.99	164.20
Other (S2)	non-food	65.53	64.52	64.08	76.90	85.91	90.62	82.11	100.00	94.64	96.35	116.70	121.78

Source: World Bank Commodity Projections; IECCM 10/26/90

Merchandise Exports in 1987 Constant Prices
(Yuan million)

	1980	1981	1982	1983	1984	1985	1986	1987	1988	1989	1990	1991
Food (S0+S1+S4)	6482	6937	7690	6961	7810	10393	13363	18748	20934	23307	28972	34590
Petroleum (S3)	7266	7937	8789	8318	10742	13205	15895	16913	19944	18089	17704	20563
Manufacturing (S5+S6+S7+S8+S9)	41588	53811	57152	59957	68979	65183	80416	97541	114876	130917	152635	180570
Other (S2)	3947	5543	5345	5401	6538	8598	12228	13586	16742	16459	14497	15257
Total	59283	74227	78976	80636	94069	97379	121903	146788	172497	188772	213607	250961

	1980	1981	1982	1983	1984	1985	1986	1987	1988	1989	1990	1991
Exchange Rate	1.4984	1.7045	1.8925	1.9757	2.3200	2.9367	3.4528	3.7221	3.7221	3.7651	4.7832	5.3234

REF: EXPORTS.WK1   06/23/92

Table 3.8: CHINA: Exports of Goods and Non Factor Services
(in million US$ and Yuan)

(US$ million)

	1980	1981	1982	1983	1984	1985	1986	1987	1988	1989	1990	1991
MERCHANDISE												
Current Prices	18188	22010	22330	22230	26129	27350	30942	39437	47518	52537	62063	71910
Constant 1980 Prices	18188	22161	23668	23673	27970	30744	38667	46193	54188	57612	63953	74802
Constant 1987 Prices	15927	19942	21218	21664	25273	26162	32751	39437	46344	50717	57389	67425
NON FACTOR SERVICES												
Current Prices	1897	2403	2736	2747	2801	3060	3941	4386	4235	3750	4157	4157
Constant 1980 Prices (use muv index)	1897	2393	2767	2843	2962	3210	3506	3553	3198	2852	2985	2933
Constant 1987 Prices (use muv index)	2342	2954	3416	3510	3657	3963	4329	4386	3948	3521	3684	3621
Total												
Current Prices	20085	24413	25066	24977	28930	30410	34883	43823	51753	56287	66220	76067
Constant 1980 Prices	20085	24554	26435	26516	30932	33954	42174	49746	57385	60465	66938	77735
Constant 1987 Prices	18269	22897	24634	25174	28930	30125	37080	43823	50291	54238	61073	71045
Exchange Rate	1.4984	1.7045	1.8925	1.9757	2.3200	2.9367	3.4528	3.7221	3.7221	3.7651	4.7832	5.3234

(Yuan million)

	1980	1981	1982	1983	1984	1985	1986	1987	1988	1989	1990	1991
GOODS												
In Curent Prices	27254	37516	42260	43920	60619	80319	106837	146788	176866	197808	296859	382807
Constant 1980 Prices	27254	33206	35464	35471	41910	46067	57939	69216	81195	86327	95827	112084
Constant 1987 Prices	59283	74227	78976	80636	94069	97379	121903	146788	172497	188772	213607	250961
NON FACTOR SERVICES												
In Curent Prices	2842	4096	5178	5427	6498	8986	13607	16325	15763	14119	19884	22129
Constant 1980 Prices	2842	3586	4147	4260	4439	4810	5254	5324	4791	4274	4472	4395
Constant 1987 Prices	8716	10996	12716	13064	13611	14751	16112	16325	14693	13106	13714	13477
Total												
Current Prices	30096	41612	47437	49347	67118	89305	120444	163114	192629	211927	316743	404936
Constant 1980 Prices	30096	36792	39610	39731	46349	50877	63193	74540	85986	90600	100300	116478
Constant 1987 Prices	68000	85224	91692	93701	107680	112129	138015	163114	187190	201878	227320	264438

REF: EXPORTS.WK1 06/23/92
Source: Tables 3.4 to 3.7

- 212 -

Table 3.9: CHINA: Implicit Price Indices of Exports of Goods and Services

in US dollars (1980=100)

	1980	1981	1982	1983	1984	1985	1986	1987	1988	1989	1990	1991
MERCHANDISE	100.00	99.32	94.35	93.91	93.42	88.96	80.02	85.37	87.69	91.19	97.04	96.13
NON FACTOR SERVICES	100.00	100.41	98.87	96.62	94.56	95.32	112.39	123.45	132.44	131.47	139.28	141.73
TOTAL	100.00	99.42	94.82	94.20	93.53	89.56	82.71	88.09	90.18	93.09	98.93	97.85

in Yuan (1980=100)

	1980	1981	1982	1983	1984	1985	1986	1987	1988	1989	1990	1991
MERCHANDISE	100.00	112.98	119.16	123.82	144.64	174.35	184.40	212.07	217.83	229.14	309.79	341.54
NON FACTOR SERVICES	100.00	114.22	124.87	127.39	146.40	186.82	258.99	306.65	328.98	330.36	444.61	503.53
TOTAL	100.00	113.10	119.76	124.20	144.81	175.53	190.60	218.83	224.02	233.91	315.80	347.65

in US dollars (1987=100)

	1980	1981	1982	1983	1984	1985	1986	1987	1988	1989	1990	1991
MERCHANDISE	114.20	110.37	105.24	102.61	103.39	104.54	94.48	100.00	102.53	103.59	108.14	106.65
NON FACTOR SERVICES	81.01	81.34	80.09	78.26	76.60	77.21	91.04	100.00	107.28	106.50	112.83	114.81
TOTAL	109.94	106.62	101.75	99.22	100.00	100.95	94.08	100.00	102.91	103.78	108.43	107.07

in Yuan (1987=100)

	1980	1981	1982	1983	1984	1985	1986	1987	1988	1989	1990	1991
MERCHANDISE	45.97	50.54	53.51	54.47	64.44	82.48	87.64	100.00	102.53	104.79	138.97	152.54
NON FACTOR SERVICES	32.61	37.25	40.72	41.54	47.74	60.92	84.46	100.00	107.28	107.73	144.99	164.20
TOTAL	44.26	48.83	51.74	52.66	62.33	79.64	87.27	100.00	102.91	104.98	139.34	153.13

REF: EXPORTS.WK1   06/23/92
Source: Table 3.8

Table 3.10: CHINA: Total Exports and its Relative Share in the World Exports

	1980	1981	1982	1983	1984	1985	1986	1987	1988	1989	1990	1991
(Billion US$ in Current Prices)												
China Exports	18.2	22.0	22.3	22.2	26.1	27.4	30.9	39.4	47.5	52.5	62.1	71.9
World Exports	1892.5	1861.4	1724.7	1674.6	1775.8	1800.1	1981.4	2333.2	2679.6	3090.0	3333.4	3441.7
(Growth Rate)												
China Exports	33.2	21.0	1.5	-0.4	17.5	4.7	13.1	27.5	20.5	10.6	18.1	15.9
World Exports	20.8	-1.6	-7.3	-2.9	6.0	1.4	10.1	17.8	14.8	15.3	7.9	3.2
(Percentage Share)												
China Exports into World Exports	1.0	1.2	1.3	1.3	1.5	1.5	1.6	1.7	1.8	1.7	1.9	2.1
China Exports into China GNP	6.1	7.9	8.1	7.6	8.7	9.4	11.0	13.0	12.6	12.4	16.8	19.4
Memo Items:												
China GNP in Current Prices (Billion Yuan)	447.00	477.30	519.30	580.90	696.20	855.76	969.63	1130.10	1401.82	1591.63	1768.61	1975.87
Exchange Rate (Yuan per US$)	1.498	1.705	1.893	1.976	2.320	2.937	3.453	3.722	3.722	3.765	4.783	5.323
China GNP in Current Prices (US$ Billion)	298.3	280.0	274.4	294.0	300.1	291.4	280.8	303.6	376.6	422.7	369.8	371.2

REF: EXPORTS.WK1   06/23/92
Source: CHINA Statistical Year Book 1990 pp.603 for 1978-87 and Statistical Abstract 1989 pp.82 for 1988.
International Financial Statistics for World Exports (June 1991 pp.72 for 1990) and Exchange rate.

Table 4.1: CHINA : Imports (CIF) Customs basis
(US $ million)

		1980	1981	1982	1983	1984	1985	1986	1987	1988	1989	1990	1991
FOOD	S0+S1+S4	3211	3932	4437	3238	2527	1881	2002	3055	4191	5269	4474	3718
Food	S0	2934	3620	4200	3122	2331	1553	1625	2443	3476	4192	3336	2799
Beverages	S1	36	213	130	46	116	206	172	263	346	202	157	200
Animal fat	S4	241	99	107	70	80	122	205	349	369	875	982	719
PETROLEUM (Mineral Fuels)	S3	203	83	183	111	139	172	504	539	787	1650	1272	2114
INTERMEDIATE S5+S2+D61+D63+D65 to D68		10639	10980	10091	12047	13856	19175	17552	16769	23391	23415	18327	23189
Chemicals and related products	S5	2899	2617	2936	3183	4237	4469	3771	5008	9139	7556	6650	9277
Crude materials (non-food)	S2	3574	4328	3250	2575	2542	3236	3143	3321	5090	4835	4107	5003
Leather+Cork=D61+D63=Light In.-D64 to D68		4165	4035	3905	6289	415	770	851	728	842	747	938	1267
Leather	D61	..	..	..	..	..	..	..	184	224	280	374	642
Cork	D63	..	..	..	..	..	..	..	544	618	467	564	625
Textile Yarn (yarn, fabrics etc.)	D65	..	..	..	..	953	1607	1632	1848	2388	2845	2748	3689
Non metallic minerals	D66	..	..	..	..	225	325	363	342	430	520	453	443
Iron and Steel	D67	..	..	..	..	4361	7120	6741	4787	4624	5797	2852	2694
Non-ferrous metals	D68	..	..	..	..	1123	1648	1051	735	878	1114	579	816
CONSUMER GOODS D64+D62 to D82 to D89		544	557	486	782	1423	2330	2431	1743	1757	1866	2051	2506
Paper (Paper and related products)	D64	544	557	486	782	241	428	554	727	610	634	745	969
D62+D82+D83+D84+D85		..	..	..	..	1182	1902	1877	108	150	165	186	205
Rubber	D62	..	..	..	..	..	..	..	45	51	50	50	76
Furniture	D82	..	..	..	..	..	..	..	42	61	68	72	49
Travel goods	D83	..	..	..	..	..	..	..	3	8	6	6	7
Clothing	D84	..	..	..	..	..	..	..	17	28	38	48	61
Footwear	D85	..	..	..	..	..	..	..	1	2	3	9	11
Photo supplies	D88	..	..	..	..	..	..	..	432	365	398	361	441
Miscellaneous	D89	..	..	..	..	..	..	..	476	632	669	759	892
MANUFACTURED (Residual)		5353	6461	4083	5213	9465	18694	20415	21110	25150	26940	27225	32264
Total		19950	22012	19280	21391	27410	42252	42904	43216	55275	59140	53350	63791

REF: IMPORTS.WK1 06/23/92
Source: CHINA Customs Statistics 1991.1 for 1990; Statistical Yearbook 1990 pp.604, 1988 pp.645 for 1987,1986;
1987 pp.521 for 1985; 1986 pp.483 for 1984; 1985 pp.495 for 1983; 1984 pp.382 for 1982;
1983 pp.406 for 1981; 1981 pp.73 for 1980 (in yuan).

- 214 -

Table 4.2: CHINA : Imports (CIF) Customs basis
(Percentage Shares)

		1980	1981	1982	1983	1984	1985	1986	1987	1988	1989	1990	1991
FOOD	S0+S1+S4	16.1	17.9	23.0	15.1	9.2	4.5	4.7	7.1	7.6	8.9	8.4	5.8
Food	S0	14.7	16.4	21.8	14.6	8.5	3.7	3.8	5.7	6.3	7.1	6.3	4.4
Beverages	S1	0.2	1.0	0.7	0.2	0.4	0.5	0.4	0.6	0.6	0.3	0.3	0.3
Animal fat	S4	1.2	0.4	0.6	0.3	0.3	0.3	0.5	0.8	0.7	1.5	1.8	1.1
PETROLEUM (Mineral Fuels)	S3	1.0	0.4	0.9	0.5	0.5	0.4	1.2	1.2	1.4	2.8	2.4	3.3
INTERMEDIATE S5+S2 +D61+D63+D65 to D68		53.3	49.9	52.3	56.3	50.6	45.4	40.9	38.8	42.3	39.6	34.4	36.4
Chemicals and related products	S5	14.5	11.9	15.2	14.9	15.5	10.6	8.8	11.6	16.5	12.8	12.5	14.5
Crude materials (non-food)	S2	17.9	19.7	16.9	12.0	9.3	7.7	7.3	7.7	9.2	8.2	7.7	7.8
Leather+Cork=D61+D63=Light In.-D64 to D68		20.9	18.3	20.3	29.4	1.5	1.8	2.0	1.7	1.5	1.3	1.8	2.0
Leather	D61	..	..	..	..	..	..	..	0.4	0.4	0.5	0.7	1.0
Cork	D63	..	..	..	..	..	..	..	1.3	1.1	0.8	1.1	1.0
Textile Yarn (yarn, fabrics etc.)	D65	..	..	..	..	3.5	3.8	3.8	4.3	4.3	4.8	5.2	5.8
Non metallic minerals	D66	..	..	..	..	0.8	0.8	0.8	0.8	0.8	0.9	0.8	0.7
Iron and Steel	D67	..	..	..	..	15.9	16.9	15.7	11.1	8.4	9.8	5.3	4.2
Non-ferrous metals	D68	..	..	..	..	4.1	3.9	2.4	1.7	1.6	1.9	1.1	1.3
CONSUMER GOODS D64+D62+D82 to D89		2.7	2.5	2.5	3.7	5.2	5.5	5.7	4.0	3.2	3.2	3.8	3.9
Paper (Paper and related products)	D64	2.7	2.5	2.5	3.7	0.9	1.0	1.3	1.7	1.1	1.1	1.4	1.5
D62+D82+D83+D84+D85		..	..	..	..	4.3	4.5	4.4	0.2	0.3	0.3	0.3	0.3
Rubber	D62	..	..	..	..	..	..	..	0.1	0.1	0.1	0.1	0.1
Furniture	D82	..	..	..	..	..	..	..	0.0	0.1	0.0	0.0	0.0
Travel goods	D83	..	..	..	..	..	..	..	0.0	0.0	0.1	0.1	0.1
Clothing	D84	..	..	..	..	..	..	..	0.0	0.1	0.0	0.0	0.0
Footwear	D85	..	..	..	..	..	..	..	0.0	0.0	0.0	0.0	0.0
Photo supplies	D88	..	..	..	..	..	..	..	1.0	0.7	0.7	0.7	0.7
Miscellaneous	D89	..	..	..	..	..	..	..	1.1	1.1	1.1	1.4	1.4
MANUFACTURED	(Residual)	26.8	29.3	21.2	24.4	34.5	44.2	47.6	48.8	45.5	45.6	51.0	50.6
Total		100.0	100.0	100.0	100.0	100.0	100.0	100.0	100.0	100.0	100.0	100.0	100.0

REF: IMPORTS.WK1 06/23/92
Source: Table 4.1.

Table 4.3: CHINA : Imports (CIF) Customs basis
(Percentage Growth Rates)

	Code	1980	1981	1982	1983	1984	1985	1986	1987	1988	1989	1990	1991
FOOD	S0+S1+S4	..	22.4	12.9	-27.0	-21.9	-25.6	6.4	52.6	37.2	25.7	-15.1	-16.9
Food	S0	..	23.4	16.0	-25.7	-25.3	-33.4	4.6	50.3	42.3	20.6	-20.4	-16.1
Beverages	S1	..	486.3	-38.8	-64.9	154.4	77.6	-16.5	52.9	31.6	-41.6	-22.3	27.8
Animal fat	S4	..	-58.9	8.1	-34.6	14.3	52.5	68.0	70.2	5.7	137.2	12.2	-26.8
PETROLEUM (Mineral Fuels)	S3	.	-59.0	120.5	-39.3	25.2	23.7	193.0	6.9	46.0	109.8	-22.9	66.2
INTERMEDIATE	S5+S2+D61+D63+D65 to D68	..	3.2	-8.1	19.4	15.0	38.4	-8.5	-4.5	39.5	0.1	-21.7	26.5
Chemicals and related products	S5	:	-9.7	12.2	8.4	33.1	5.5	-15.6	32.8	82.5	-17.3	-12.0	39.5
Crude materials (non-food)	S2	:	21.1	-24.9	-20.8	-1.3	27.3	-2.9	5.7	53.3	-5.0	-15.1	21.8
Leather+Cork=D61+D63=Light In.-D64 to D68		:	-3.1	-3.2	61.0	-93.4	85.5	10.5	-14.5	21.7	-11.3	25.5	35.1
Leather	D61		:	:	:	:	:	:	:	13.6	25.1	33.3	71.9
Cork	D63		:	:	:	:	:	:	:	:	-24.4	20.8	10.7
Textile Yarn (yarn, fabrics etc.)	D65		:	:	:	:	68.6	1.6	13.2	29.2	19.1	-3.4	34.2
Non metallic minerals	D66		:	:	:	:	44.4	11.7	-5.8	25.7	21.0	-12.9	-2.2
Iron and Steel	D67		:	:	:	:	63.3	-5.3	-29.0	-3.4	25.4	-50.8	-5.5
Non-ferrous metals	D68		:	:	:	:	46.7	-36.2	-30.1	19.4	26.9	-48.0	40.9
CONSUMER GOODS	D64+D62+D82 to D89	..	2.5	-12.7	60.9	82.0	63.7	4.3	-28.3	0.8	6.2	9.9	22.2
Paper (Paper and related products)	D64	:	2.5	-12.7	60.9	51.2	77.6	29.4	31.2	-16.1	4.0	17.4	30.0
D62+D82+D83+D84+D85		:	:	:	:	:	60.9	-1.3	-94.2	38.9	9.8	12.8	10.3
Rubber	D62	:	:	:	:	:	:	:	:	13.3	-2.9	0.9	52.7
Furniture	D82	:	:	:	:	:	:	:	:	45.2	10.8	7.1	-32.0
Travel goods	D83	:	:	:	:	:	:	:	:	166.7	-27.2	8.2	14.8
Clothing	D84	:	:	:	:	:	:	:	:	64.7	37.0	25.3	27.1
Footwear	D85	:	:	:	:	:	:	:	:	100.0	68.0	167.9	21.4
Photo supplies	D88	:	:	:	:	:	:	:	:	-15.5	9.1	-9.2	22.0
Miscellaneous	D89	:	:	:	:	:	:	:	:	32.8	5.8	13.5	17.5
MANUFACTURED	(Residual)	..	20.7	-36.8	27.7	81.6	97.5	9.2	3.4	19.1	7.1	1.1	18.5
Total		..	10.3	-12.4	10.9	28.1	54.1	1.5	0.7	27.9	7.0	-9.8	19.6

REF: IMPORTS.WK1   06/23/92
Source: Table 4.1.

- 217 -

Table 4.4: CHINA: Imports in Current Prices and Constant (1980) Prices

Imports (CIF) in Current Prices
(US $ million)

	1980	1981	1982	1983	1984	1985	1986	1987	1988	1989	1990	1991
FOOD S0+S1+S4	3211	3932	4437	3238	2527	1881	2002	3055	4191	5269	4474	3718
PETROLEUM (Mineral Fuels) S3	203	83	183	111	139	172	504	539	787	1650	1272	2114
INTERMEDIATE S5+S2 +D61+D63+D65 to D68	10639	10980	10091	12047	13856	19175	17552	16769	23391	23415	18327	23189
CONSUMER GOODS D64+D62+D82 to D89	544	557	486	782	1423	2330	2431	1743	1757	1866	2051	2506
MANUFACTURED (Residual)	5353	6461	4083	5213	9465	18694	20415	21110	25150	26940	27225	32264
Total	19950	22012	19280	21391	27410	42252	42904	43216	55275	59140	53350	63791

Source: Table 4.1.

Price Indices (in US dollars)
1980=100

	1980	1981	1982	1983	1984	1985	1986	1987	1988	1989	1990	1991
FOOD	100.00	87.09	78.13	84.68	92.20	80.35	72.35	55.49	61.18	58.00	50.58	47.21
PETROLEUM	100.00	112.01	102.81	95.40	95.40	91.84	39.40	45.68	33.68	40.62	50.19	39.87
INTERMEDIATE (Imports MUV)	100.00	103.80	107.74	111.84	116.09	120.50	125.08	129.83	134.77	133.96	140.12	151.47
CONSUMER GOODS (Imports MUV)	100.00	103.80	107.74	111.84	116.09	120.50	125.08	129.83	134.77	133.96	140.12	151.47
MANUFACTURED (Imports MUV)	100.00	103.80	107.74	111.84	116.09	120.50	125.08	129.83	134.77	133.96	140.12	151.47

Source: World Bank Commodity Projections; IECCM 02/08/90

Percentage Growth Rate of Price Indices in US dollars

	1980	1981	1982	1983	1984	1985	1986	1987	1988	1989	1990	1991
FOOD	..	-12.91	-10.29	8.38	8.87	-12.85	-9.95	-23.30	10.24	-5.20	-12.79	-6.67
PETROLEUM	..	12.01	-8.21	-7.21	0.00	-3.74	-57.10	15.95	-26.28	20.61	23.56	-20.56
INTERMEDIATE (Imports MUV)	..	3.80	3.80	3.80	3.80	3.80	3.80	3.80	3.80	-0.60	4.60	8.10
CONSUMER GOODS (Imports MUV)	..	3.80	3.80	3.80	3.80	3.80	3.80	3.80	3.80	-0.60	4.60	8.10
MANUFACTURED (Imports MUV)	..	3.80	3.80	3.80	3.80	3.80	3.80	3.80	3.80	-0.60	4.60	8.10

Imports (CIF) in 1980 Constant Prices
(US $ million)

	1980	1981	1982	1983	1984	1985	1986	1987	1988	1989	1990	1991
FOOD S0+S1+S4	3211	4514	5679	3823	2741	2341	2767	5505	6851	9086	8846	7876
PETROLEUM (Mineral Fuels) S3	203	74	178	116	146	187	1279	1180	2336	4063	2535	5302
INTERMEDIATE S5+S2 +D61+D63+D65 to D68	10639	10578	9366	10772	11936	15913	14033	12916	17357	17479	13080	15310
CONSUMER GOODS D64+D62+D82 to D89	544	537	451	699	1226	1934	1944	1343	1304	1393	1464	1655
MANUFACTURED (Residual)	5353	6224	3790	4662	8153	15514	16322	16259	18662	20111	19430	21301
Total	19950	21927	19463	20072	24201	35889	36344	37203	46509	52131	45355	51443

REF: IMPORTS.WK1 06/23/92

Table 4.5: CHINA: Imports in Current Prices and Constant (1987) Prices

Imports (CIF) in Current Prices
(US $ million)

	1980	1981	1982	1983	1984	1985	1986	1987	1988	1989	1990	1991
FOOD S0+S1+S4	3211	3932	4437	3238	2527	1881	2002	3055	4191	5269	4474	3718
PETROLEUM (Mineral Fuels) S3	203	83	183	111	139	172	504	539	787	1650	1272	2114
INTERMEDIATE S5+S2 +D61+D63+D65 to D68	10639	10980	10091	12047	13856	19175	17552	16769	23391	23415	18327	23189
CONSUMER GOODS D64+D62+D82 to D89	544	557	486	782	1423	2330	2431	1743	1757	1866	2051	2506
MANUFACTURED (Residual)	5353	6461	4083	5213	9465	18694	20415	21110	25150	26940	27225	32264
Total	19950	22012	19280	21391	27410	42252	42904	43216	55275	59140	53350	63791

Source: Table 4.4.

Price Indices (in US dollars)
1987=100

	1980	1981	1982	1983	1984	1985	1986	1987	1988	1989	1990	1991
FOOD	180.21	156.94	140.80	152.60	166.15	144.79	130.38	100.00	110.24	104.51	91.15	85.07
PETROLEUM	218.89	245.17	225.05	208.83	208.83	201.03	86.24	100.00	73.72	88.91	109.86	87.27
INTERMEDIATE (Imports MUV)	77.02	79.95	82.99	86.14	89.41	92.81	96.34	100.00	103.80	103.18	107.92	116.67
CONSUMER GOODS (Imports MUV)	77.02	79.95	82.99	86.14	89.41	92.81	96.34	100.00	103.80	103.18	107.92	116.67
MANUFACTURED (Imports MUV)	77.02	79.95	82.99	86.14	89.41	92.81	96.34	100.00	103.80	103.18	107.92	116.67

Source: World Bank Commodity Projections; IECCM 02/08/90

Percentage Growth Rate of Price Indices in US dollars

	1980	1981	1982	1983	1984	1985	1986	1987	1988	1989	1990	1991
FOOD	..	-12.91	-10.29	8.38	8.87	-12.85	-9.95	-23.30	10.24	-5.20	-12.79	-6.67
PETROLEUM	..	12.01	-8.21	-7.21	0.00	-3.74	-57.10	15.95	-26.28	20.61	23.56	-20.56
INTERMEDIATE (Imports MUV)	..	3.80	3.80	3.80	3.80	3.80	3.80	3.80	3.80	-0.60	4.60	8.10
CONSUMER GOODS (Imports MUV)	..	3.80	3.80	3.80	3.80	3.80	3.80	3.80	3.80	-0.60	4.60	8.10
MANUFACTURED (Imports MUV)	..	3.80	3.80	3.80	3.80	3.80	3.80	3.80	3.80	-0.60	4.60	8.10

Imports (CIF) in 1987 Constant Prices
(US $ million)

	1980	1981	1982	1983	1984	1985	1986	1987	1988	1989	1990	1991
FOOD S0+S1+S4	1782	2505	3151	2122	1521	1299	1535	3055	3802	5042	4909	4371
PETROLEUM (Mineral Fuels) S3	93	34	81	53	67	86	584	539	1067	1856	1158	2422
INTERMEDIATE S5+S2 +D61+D63+D65 to D68	13813	13734	12160	13985	15496	20660	18219	16769	22534	22694	16981	19877
CONSUMER GOODS D64+D62+D82 to D89	706	697	586	908	1591	2510	2523	1743	1692	1808	1900	2148
MANUFACTURED (Residual)	6950	8081	4920	6052	10586	20142	21191	21110	24229	26111	25226	27655
Total	23344	25050	20898	23120	29261	44697	44053	43216	53325	57510	50175	56473

REF: IMPORTS.WK1 06/23/92

Table 4.6: CHINA: Imports in Current Prices and Constant (1980) Prices

Imports (CIF) in Current Prices (Yuan million)

	1980	1981	1982	1983	1984	1985	1986	1987	1988	1989	1990	1991
FOOD S0+S1+S4	4812	6701	8397	6397	5863	5524	6913	11371	15599	19839	21402	19792
PETROLEUM (Mineral Fuels) S3	304	141	346	219	322	505	1740	2006	2928	6213	6085	11253
INTERMEDIATE S5+S2 +D61+D63+D65 to D68	15941	18715	19097	23801	32146	56311	60604	62416	87063	88159	87662	123445
CONSUMER GOODS D64+D62+D82 to D89	815	949	920	1545	3301	6843	8394	6488	6539	7024	9810	13343
MANUFACTURED (Residual)	8021	11012	7727	10300	21959	54899	70489	78574	93611	101432	130224	171754
Total	29893	37519	36487	42262	63591	124081	148139	160854	205739	222668	255182	339587

Source: Table 4.1.

Price Indices (in Yuan) 1980=100

	1980	1981	1982	1983	1984	1985	1986	1987	1988	1989	1990	1991
FOOD (Imports MUV)	100.00	99.07	98.68	111.66	142.75	157.47	166.72	137.84	151.96	145.73	161.46	167.71
PETROLEUM	100.00	127.41	129.86	125.79	147.71	179.99	90.79	113.48	83.66	102.07	160.21	141.64
INTERMEDIATE (Imports MUV)	100.00	118.08	136.08	147.46	179.74	236.17	288.22	322.51	334.76	336.60	447.29	538.13
CONSUMER GOODS (Imports MUV)	100.00	118.08	136.08	147.46	179.74	236.17	288.22	322.51	334.76	336.60	447.29	538.13
MANUFACTURED (Imports MUV)	100.00	118.08	136.08	147.46	179.74	236.17	288.22	322.51	334.76	336.60	447.29	538.13

Source: World Bank Commodity Projections; IECCM 02/08/90

Imports (CIF) in 1980 Constant Prices (Yuan million)

	1980	1981	1982	1983	1984	1985	1986	1987	1988	1989	1990	1991
FOOD S0+S1+S4	4812	6764	8509	5729	4107	3508	4146	8249	10265	13614	13256	11801
PETROLEUM (Mineral Fuels) S3	304	111	267	174	218	281	1917	1768	3500	6088	3798	7944
INTERMEDIATE S5+S2 +D61+D63+D65 to D68	15941	15850	14034	16140	17884	23844	21027	19353	26007	26191	19598	22940
CONSUMER GOODS D64+D62+D82 to D89	815	804	676	1048	1837	2897	2912	2012	1953	2087	2193	2480
MANUFACTURED (Residual)	8021	9326	5678	6985	12217	23246	24456	24363	27963	30134	29114	31917
Total	29893	32855	29164	30076	36263	53775	54458	55745	69689	78114	67960	77082

	1980	1981	1982	1983	1984	1985	1986	1987	1988	1989	1990	1991
Exchange Rate	1.6984	1.7045	1.8925	1.9757	2.3200	2.9367	3.4528	3.7221	3.7221	3.7651	4.7832	5.3234

REF: IMPORTS.WK1 06/23/92

Table 4.7: CHINA: Imports in Current Prices and Constant (1987) Prices

Imports (CIF) in Current Prices
(Yuan million)

	1980	1981	1982	1983	1984	1985	1986	1987	1988	1989	1990	1991
FOOD S0+S1+S4	4812	6701	8397	6397	5863	5524	6913	11371	15599	19839	21402	19792
PETROLEUM (Mineral Fuels) S3	304	141	346	219	322	505	1740	2006	2928	6213	6085	11253
INTERMEDIATE S5+S2 +D61+D63+D65 to D68	15941	18715	19097	23801	32146	56311	60604	62416	87063	88159	87662	123445
CONSUMER GOODS D64+D62+D82 to D89	815	949	920	1545	3301	6843	8394	6488	6539	7024	9810	13343
MANUFACTURED (Residual)	8021	11012	7727	10300	21959	54899	70489	78574	93611	101432	130224	171754
Total	29893	37519	36487	42262	63591	124081	148139	160854	205739	222668	255182	339587

Source: Table 4.6.

Price Indices (in Yuan)
1987=100

	1980	1981	1982	1983	1984	1985	1986	1987	1988	1989	1990	1991
FOOD	72.55	71.87	71.59	81.00	103.56	114.24	120.95	100.00	110.24	105.72	117.13	121.67
PETROLEUM (Imports MUV)	88.12	112.28	114.43	110.85	130.16	158.61	80.00	100.00	73.72	89.94	141.17	124.81
INTERMEDIATE (Imports MUV)	31.01	36.61	42.20	45.72	55.73	73.23	89.37	100.00	103.80	104.37	138.69	166.86
CONSUMER GOODS (Imports MUV)	31.01	36.61	42.20	45.72	55.73	73.23	89.37	100.00	103.80	104.37	138.69	166.86
MANUFACTURED (Imports MUV)	31.01	36.61	42.20	45.72	55.73	73.23	89.37	100.00	103.80	104.37	138.69	166.86

Source: World Bank Commodity Projections; IECCM 02/08/90

Imports (CIF) in 1987 Constant Prices
(Yuan million)

	1980	1981	1982	1983	1984	1985	1986	1987	1988	1989	1990	1991
FOOD S0+S1+S4	6633	9324	11729	7897	5661	4835	5715	11371	14150	18766	18272	16267
PETROLEUM (Mineral Fuels) S3	345	126	303	198	248	318	2175	2006	3972	6908	4310	9016
INTERMEDIATE S5+S2 +D61+D63+D65 to D68	51412	51118	45259	52054	57679	76899	67813	62416	83875	84468	63207	73983
CONSUMER GOODS D64+D62+D82 to D89	2627	2593	2180	3379	5924	9344	9392	6488	6299	6730	7073	7997
MANUFACTURED (Residual)	25870	30077	18313	22527	39400	74970	78874	78574	90184	97186	93895	102935
Total	86887	93238	77784	86055	108912	166366	163970	160854	198480	214059	186758	210198

	1980	1981	1982	1983	1984	1985	1986	1987	1988	1989	1990	1991
Exchange Rate	1.498	1.705	1.893	1.976	2.320	2.937	3.453	3.722	3.722	3.765	4.783	5.323

REF: IMPORTS.WK1 06/23/92

Table 4.8: CHINA: Total Imports of Goods and Services

(in million US$ and Yuan)

(US$ million)

	1980	1981	1982	1983	1984	1985	1986	1987	1988	1989	1990	1991
MERCHANDISE (91.7% of Total)												
Current Prices	18294	20185	17680	19616	25135	38745	39343	39629	50687	54231	48922	58497
Constant 1980 Prices	18294	20107	17848	18406	22193	32910	33328	34115	42649	47804	41590	47173
Constant 1987 Prices	21406	22971	19163	21201	26832	40987	40597	39629	48899	52737	46011	51786
SERVICES (8.3% of Total)												
Current Prices	1656	1827	1600	1775	2275	3507	3561	3587	4588	4909	4428	5295
Constant 1980 Prices	1656	1820	1615	1666	2009	2979	3017	3088	3860	4327	3764	4270
Constant 1987 Prices	1938	2079	1735	1919	2429	3710	3656	3587	4426	4773	4165	4687
TOTAL												
Current Prices	19950	22012	19280	21391	27410	42252	42904	43216	55275	59140	53350	63791
Constant 1980 Prices	19950	21927	19463	20072	24201	35889	36344	37203	46509	52131	45355	51443
Constant 1987 Prices	23344	25050	20898	23120	29261	44697	44053	43216	53325	57510	50175	56473
Exchange Rate	1.4984	1.7045	1.8925	1.9757	2.3200	2.9367	3.4528	3.7221	3.7221	3.7651	4.7832	5.3234

(Yuan million)

	1980	1981	1982	1983	1984	1985	1986	1987	1988	1989	1990	1991
MERCHANDISE (91.7% of Total)												
Current Prices	27412	34405	33459	38754	58313	113783	135843	147503	188663	204187	234002	311401
Constant 1980 Prices	27412	30128	26743	27580	33253	49312	49938	51118	63905	71630	62319	70684
Constant 1987 Prices	79675	85500	71328	78912	99872	152558	150360	147503	182006	196292	171257	192752
SERVICES (8.3% of Total)												
Current Prices	2481	3114	3028	3508	5278	10299	12296	13351	17076	18481	21180	28186
Constant 1980 Prices	2481	2727	2421	2496	3010	4463	4520	4627	5784	6483	5641	6398
Constant 1987 Prices	7212	7739	6456	7143	9040	13808	13609	13351	16474	17767	15501	17446
TOTAL												
Current Prices	29893	37519	36487	42262	63591	124081	148139	160854	205739	222668	255182	339587
Constant 1980 Prices	29893	32855	29164	30076	36263	53775	54458	55745	69689	78114	67960	77082
Constant 1987 Prices	86887	93238	77784	86055	108912	165666	163970	160854	198480	214059	186758	210198

REF: IMPORTS.WK1 06/23/92
Source: Tables 4.4 to 4.7.

Table 4.9: CHINA: Implicit Price Indices of Imports of Goods and Services

In US dollars (1980=100)

	1980	1981	1982	1983	1984	1985	1986	1987	1988	1989	1990	1991
MERCHANDISE	100.00	100.39	99.06	106.57	113.26	117.73	118.05	116.16	118.85	113.44	117.63	124.00
SERVICES	100.00	100.39	99.06	106.57	113.26	117.73	118.05	116.16	118.85	113.44	117.63	124.00
TOTAL	100.00	100.39	99.06	106.57	113.26	117.73	118.05	116.16	118.85	113.44	117.63	124.00

In Yuan (1980=100)

	1980	1981	1982	1983	1984	1985	1986	1987	1988	1989	1990	1991
MERCHANDISE	100.00	114.20	125.11	140.52	175.36	230.74	272.02	288.55	295.23	285.06	375.49	440.55
SERVICES	100.00	114.20	125.11	140.52	175.36	230.74	272.02	288.55	295.23	285.06	375.49	440.55
TOTAL	100.00	114.20	125.11	140.52	175.36	230.74	272.02	288.55	295.23	285.06	375.49	440.55

In US dollars (1987=100)

	1980	1981	1982	1983	1984	1985	1986	1987	1988	1989	1990	1991
MERCHANDISE	85.46	87.87	92.26	92.52	93.67	94.53	97.39	100.00	103.66	102.83	106.33	112.96
SERVICES	85.46	87.87	92.26	92.52	93.67	94.53	97.39	100.00	103.66	102.83	106.33	112.96
TOTAL	85.46	87.87	92.26	92.52	93.67	94.53	97.39	100.00	103.66	102.83	106.33	112.96

In Yuan (1987=100)

	1980	1981	1982	1983	1984	1985	1986	1987	1988	1989	1990	1991
MERCHANDISE	34.40	40.24	46.91	49.11	58.39	74.58	90.35	100.00	103.66	104.02	136.64	161.56
SERVICES	34.40	40.24	46.91	49.11	58.39	74.58	90.35	100.00	103.66	104.02	136.64	161.56
TOTAL	34.40	40.24	46.91	49.11	58.39	74.58	90.35	100.00	103.66	104.02	136.64	161.56

REF: IMPORTS.WK1 06/23/92
Source: Table 4.8

Table 5.1 : CHINA: External Debt: Disbursements and Repayments
(in US$ million)

	1978	1979	1980	1981	1982	1983	1984	1985	1986	1987	1988	1989	1990	1991
DISBURSEMENTS														
Public & Publicly Guar. LT	583	1779	2539	1800	1837	2375	2357	5302	6725	8047	9130	8424	9620	9590
1. Official Creditors	27	199	245	573	665	678	888	1166	1444	1126	1848	2741	2566	2624
a. Multilateral	0	0	0	0	1	78	208	599	620	720	1124	1149	1146	1320
of which IDA	0	0	0	0	1	67	124	212	282	399	557	486	557	611
of which IBRD	0	0	0	0	0	4	73	354	324	306	553	604	591	668
b. Bilateral	27	199	245	573	664	600	680	567	824	405	724	1592	1420	1305
2. Private Creditors	556	1580	2294	1227	1173	1697	1470	4137	5281	6921	7282	5684	7054	6966
a. Bonds	77	531	50	560	17	21	84	971	1333	1064	782	450	277	275
b. Commercial Banks	480	965	159	97	90	269	303	722	1776	4598	4484	2007	3217	3200
c. Other Private	0	83	2085	571	1083	1408	1084	2443	2172	1260	2016	3227	3560	3491
Private Non-Guaranteed LT	0	0	0	0	0	0	0	0	0	0	0	0	0	0
Total LT Disbursements	583	1779	2539	1800	1837	2375	2357	5302	6725	8047	9130	8424	9620	9590
IMF Purchases	0	0	0	896	0	0	0	0	701	0	0	0	0	0
Net Short-Term Capital	0	0	0	0	0	0	0	0	0	0	0	0	0	0
Total Disbursements	583	1779	2539	2696	1837	2375	2357	5302	7426	8047	9130	8424	9620	9590
REPAYMENTS														
Public & Publicly Guar. LT	0	0	613	1205	1302	1389	1287	1297	1874	1916	2349	2401	3371	4799
1. Official Creditors	0	0	50	78	77	56	57	49	279	395	493	486	861	790
a. Multilateral	0	0	0	0	0	0	0	0	2	99	41	63	220	146
of which IDA	0	0	0	0	0	0	0	0	0	0	0	0	0	1
of which IBRD	0	0	0	0	0	0	0	0	0	97	39	62	216	130
b. Bilateral	0	0	50	78	77	56	57	49	277	296	452	422	641	644
2. Private Creditors	0	0	563	1127	1226	1334	1230	1248	1595	1521	1856	1916	2510	4010
a. Bonds	0	0	0	475	17	17	0	0	0	24	37	38	329	334
b. Commercial Banks	0	0	161	333	313	168	126	77	331	469	754	870	831	2204
c. Other Private	0	0	401	318	896	1149	1104	1171	1265	1029	1065	1008	1349	1472
Private Non-Guaranteed LT	0	0	0	0	0	0	0	0	0	0	0	0	0	0
Adjust: Principal not paid														
Adjust: Arrears Red/Prepay (-)														
Total LT Repayments	0	0	613	1205	1302	1389	1287	1297	1874	1916	2349	2401	3371	4799
IMF Repurchases	0	0	0	0	0	481	0	0	36	81	83	79	490	451
Total LT Repay + IMF Repur.	0	0	613	1205	1302	1870	1287	1297	1910	1997	2432	2480	3860	5251
Net Flows:														
1. Official Creditors														
of which IDA														
of which IBRD														
COMMITMENTS														
IBRD commitments	0	0	0	100	165	299	616	660	672	692	856	1221	75	..
of which fast Disbursing	0	0	0	0	0	0	0	0	0	0	0	0	0	0
IDA commitments	0	0	0	96	165	139	343	432	448	613	576	539	878	..
of which fast Disbursing	0	0	0	0	0	0	0	0	0	0	0	0	0	0

REF: DEBT.WK1 06/23/92
Source: World Debt Tables 1991-2.

Table 5.2 : CHINA: External Debt : Interest and Debt Outstanding
(In US$ million)

	1978	1979	1980	1981	1982	1983	1984	1985	1986	1987	1988	1989	1990	1991
INTEREST														
Public & Publicly Guar. LT	0	61	318	518	541	523	610	586	644	1126	1610	2508	2534	3147
1. Official Creditors	0	5	17	55	78	104	131	172	262	402	434	456	531	696
a. Multilateral	0	0	0	0	0	3	9	30	76	126	143	179	226	315
of which IDA	0	0	0	0	0	1	3	4	8	12	15	14	18	23
of which IBRD	0	0	0	0	0	3	6	26	66	111	126	161	200	228
b. Bilateral	0	5	17	55	78	101	121	142	186	276	290	278	305	380
2. Private Creditors	0	56	301	463	463	418	479	414	382	723	1176	2051	2003	2451
a. Bonds	0	0	3	118	2	5	4	20	91	212	288	342	362	365
b. Commercial Banks	0	56	140	110	72	45	40	50	66	138	458	1063	963	1135
c. Other Private	0	0	158	235	388	368	436	343	225	373	431	647	677	951
Private Non-Guaranteed LT	0	0	0	0	0	0	0	0	0	0	0	0	0	0
Adjust: Interest not paid														
Adjust: Reduction in arrears														
Total LT Interest	0	61	318	518	541	523	610	586	644	1126	1610	2508	2534	3147
IMF Service Charges	0	0	0	21	34	21	2	2	2	50	51	67	65	24
Interest Paid on ST Debt	0	0	0	0	248	277	386	594	417	640	534	628	547	707
Total Interest Paid	0	61	318	539	823	821	998	1181	1063	1815	2195	3203	3146	3878
DEBT OUTSTANDING & DISB. (DOD)														
Public & Publicly Guar. LT	623	2183	4504	4913	5221	5301	6179	9963	16598	25927	32588	37032	45319	49097
1. Official Creditors	27	226	446	919	1453	2028	2812	4724	7028	9495	10533	12015	14466	15595
a. Multilateral	0	0	0	0	1	77	271	983	1810	2852	3753	4761	6076	6845
of which IDA	0	0	0	0	1	67	181	431	774	1330	1819	2274	2981	3670
of which IBRD	0	0	0	0		4	73	498	965	1427	1831	2330	2865	3494
b. Bilateral	27	226	446	919	1452	2104	2541	3741	5218	6642	6780	7254	8390	8750
2. Private Creditors	596	1957	4057	3994	3768	3121	3367	5239	9570	16432	22054	25017	30853	33602
a. Bonds	82	572	50	1041	17	65	140	1234	2811	4471	5129	5177	5366	5300
b. Commercial Banks	514	131	1514	632	369	406	546	802	1806	6111	10431	11454	14489	15329
c. Other Private	0	84	2492	2321	3383	2650	2681	3203	4953	5850	6495	8386	10998	12973
Private Non-Guaranteed LT	0	0	0	0	0	0	0	0	0	0	0	0	0	0
Total LT DOD	623	2183	4504	4913	5221	5301	6179	9963	16598	25927	32588	37032	45319	49097
Use of IMF Credit	0	0	0	884	838	324	303	340	1072	1155	1013	908	469	0
Short-Term Debt	0	0	0	0	2300	3984	5600	6419	6076	8221	8806	6907	6766	8000
Total External Debt	623	2183	4504	5798	8359	9609	12082	16722	23746	35303	42406	44847	52555	57097
Memorandum Item:														
% Debt on Concessional Terms	0	::	0.5	1.1	8.1	9.6	11.6	14.7	15.5	15	14.9	17.4	18.4	::
% Debt at Variable Int. Rates	::	::	::	::	::	::	::	::	::	::	::	::	::	::
Preferred Creditor DS	::	::	::	::	::	::	::	::	::	::	::	::	::	::
Share of IBRD Portfolio	::	::	::	::	::	::	::	::	::	::	::	::	::	::

REF: DEBT.WK1 06/23/92
Source: World Debt Tables 1991-2.

Table 5.3 : CHINA: External Borrowing: Growth rates, Ratios and Terms of Borrowing

	1978	1979	1980	1981	1982	1983	1984	1985	1986	1987	1988	1989	1990	1991
Percentage Shares														
Official Creditors	4.3	10.4	9.9	15.9	17.4	21.1	23.3	28.3	29.6	26.9	24.8	26.8	27.5	27.3
Private Creditors	95.7	89.6	90.1	68.9	45.1	32.5	27.9	31.3	40.3	46.5	52.0	55.8	58.7	58.9
Total LT DOD	100.0	100.0	100.0	84.8	62.5	55.2	51.1	59.6	69.9	73.4	76.8	82.6	86.2	86.0
of which Concessional	0.0	0.0	0.5	0.0	8.1	17.4	22.7	24.6	22.2	20.5	19.3	21.1	21.4	23.4
Short term	0.0	0.0	0.0	0.0	27.5	41.5	46.3	38.4	25.6	23.3	20.8	15.4	12.9	14.0
Total External Debt	100.0	100.0	100.0	100.0	100.0	100.0	100.0	100.0	100.0	100.0	100.0	100.0	100.0	100.0
of which Concessional	0.0	0.0	0.5	0.0	5.0	9.6	11.6	14.7	15.5	15.0	14.9	17.4	18.4	20.1
Percentage Growth Rates														
Official Creditors	..	743.3	97.3	106.1	58.0	39.6	38.6	68.0	48.8	35.1	10.9	14.1	20.4	7.8
Private Creditors	..	228.3	107.3	-1.6	-5.6	-17.2	7.9	55.6	82.7	71.7	34.2	13.4	23.3	8.9
Total LT DOD	..	250.4	106.3	9.1	6.3	1.5	16.6	61.2	66.6	56.2	25.7	13.6	22.4	8.3
of which Concessional	..	..	..	..	..	119.0	51.9	74.9	50.4	43.7	18.8	24.1	23.7	18.5
Short term	..	..	..	..	..	73.2	40.6	14.6	-5.3	35.3	7.1	-21.6	-2.0	18.2
Total External Debt	..	250.4	106.3	28.7	44.2	15.0	25.7	38.4	42.0	48.7	20.1	5.8	17.2	8.6
Average terms of new borrowing														
All Creditors														
Interest (%)	..	..	10.4	8.2	7.0	7.6	7.5	7.5	6.4	6.7	7.2	7.4	7.6	..
Maturity (years)	..	..	10.8	13.0	18.5	16.7	18.2	11.5	14.7	15.0	14.3	18.0	16.8	..
Grace period (years)	..	..	3.3	3.6	5.5	4.5	4.8	4.0	5.0	4.0	3.8	4.5	3.9	..
Grant element (%)	..	..	4.1	..	..	17.3	17.4	13.2	20.1	18.7	15.1	16.6	15.0	..
Official Creditors														
Interest (%)	..	..	4.9	5.2	4.3	5.6	5.9	5.8	5.5	4.9	5.0	5.9	3.8	..
Maturity (years)	..	..	18.8	22.8	28.1	25.9	28.2	26.6	26.6	29.4	24.1	24.9	27.7	..
Grace period (years)	..	..	7.7	7.0	8.5	6.9	7.1	6.8	6.5	6.7	7.0	6.8	7.9	..
Grant element (%)	..	..	35.3	..	..	33.7	32.6	32.3	34.5	40.3	37.3	30.3	49.0	..
Private Creditors														
Interest (%)	..	..	12.5	9.9	10.3	9.6	8.9	8.0	6.8	7.1	7.9	8.4	8.8	..
Maturity (years)	..	..	7.7	7.5	7.0	7.3	9.0	6.6	11.0	11.7	11.3	13.1	13.5	..
Grace period (years)	..	..	1.6	1.7	2.0	1.9	2.7	3.0	4.5	3.4	2.8	3.0	2.7	..
Grant element (%)	..	..	-8.0	..	..	0.4	3.8	7.0	15.5	13.8	8.4	7.0	4.7	..

REF: DEBT.WK1 06/23/92
Source: World Debt Tables 1990-1 and Table 5.1 & 5.2.

Table 5.4: CHINA: DOMESTIC DEBT: BONDS ISSUED

AMOUNT (Billion Yuan)

INSTRUMENT / BUYER	MINISTRY OF FINANCE										STATE KEY ENTERPRISES		STATE PLANNING COMMIS.		GRAND TOTAL
	1981	1982	1983	1984	1985	1986	1987	1988	1989	1990	1987	1989 /a	1988	1989	
T BONDS															
Enterprises/Institutions	4.86	2.41	2.07	2.05	2.18	2.29	2.26	3.49	5.61	9.30	..	..	..	..	36.52
Individuals	..	1.97	2.09	2.21	3.88	3.96	4.03	5.72	..	..	..	..	..	..	23.86
KEY CONSTRUCTION BONDS															
Local governments/Enterprises	..	..	..	..	..	..	4.90	..	..	..	3.00	3.50	0.50	..	11.90
Individuals	..	..	..	..	..	..	0.50	..	..	..	..	..	..	..	0.50
FISCAL BONDS															
Financial Institutions	..	..	..	..	..	..	..	6.61	..	7.10	..	..	..	..	13.71
STATE CONSTRUCTION BONDS															
Individuals	..	..	..	..	..	..	..	3.05	..	..	..	..	..	..	3.05
INDEX BONDS															
Individuals	..	..	..	..	..	..	..	..	12.50	..	..	..	..	..	12.50
SPECIAL STATE BONDS															
Enterprises	..	..	..	..	..	..	..	..	4.28	3.20	..	..	..	..	7.48
CAPITAL CONSTRUCTION BONDS															
Financial Institutions	..	..	..	..	..	..	..	..	..	..	..	..	8.00	1.00	8.00
Individuals	..	..	..	..	..	..	..	..	..	..	..	..	..	1.00	1.00
TOTAL OF ALL INSTRUMENTS BY YEAR	4.86	4.38	4.16	4.26	6.06	6.25	11.69	18.87	22.39	19.60	3.00	3.50	8.50	1.00	118.52
STOCK OF DOMESTIC DEBT	4.86	9.24	13.40	17.66	23.72	29.97	41.66	60.53	82.92	102.52	3.00	6.50	8.50	9.50	
STOCK OF DOMESTIC DEBT(w/SKE&SPC)	4.86	9.24	13.40	17.66	23.72	29.97	44.66	72.03	98.92	118.52					
BOND REPAYMENTS							1.80	2.10	3.50	12.10					19.50
OUTSTANDING DOMESTIC DEBT	4.86	9.24	13.40	17.66	23.72	29.97	42.86	68.13	91.52	99.02					99.02

INTEREST (%)

INSTRUMENT / BUYER	1981	1982	1983	1984	1985	1986	1987	1988	1989	1990	1987	1989	1988	1989
T BONDS														
Enterprises/Institutions	4.0	4.0	4.0	4.0	5.0	6.0	6.0	6.0	14.0	14.0	..	..		
Individuals	..	8.0	8.0	8.0	9.0	10.0	10.0	10.0	..	..				
KEY CONSTRUCTION BONDS														
Local governments/Enterprises	..	..	..	..	..	..	6.0	..	..	..	Nego.	7.2	6.0	..
Individuals	..	..	..	..	..	..	10.5	..	..	..				
FISCAL BONDS														
Financial Institutions	..	..	..	..	..	..	..	8.0	..	10.0				
STATE CONSTRUCTION BONDS														
Individuals	..	..	..	..	..	..	..	9.5	..	..				
INDEX BONDS														
Individuals	..	..	..	..	..	..	..	..	1.0 /b	..				
SPECIAL STATE BONDS														
Enterprises	..	..	..	..	..	..	..	..	15.0	15.0				
CAPITAL CONSTRUCTION BONDS														
Financial Institutions	..	..	..	..	..	..	..	..	..	..			7.5	..
Individuals	..	..	..	..	..	..	..	..	..	..			..	1.0 /b

MATURITY (Years)

INSTRUMENT	1981	1982	1983	1984	1985	1986	1987	1988	1989	1990	1987	1989	1988	1989
T BONDS	5-10	5-10	5-10	5-10	5	5	5	3	3	3	Nego.	5		3
KEY CONSTRUCTION BONDS	..	..	..	..	5	3	5	..	..				..	5
FISCAL BONDS	..	..	..	..	..	..	..	2	..	5				
STATE CONSTRUCTION BONDS	..	..	..	..	..	..	..	2	..	..				
INDEX BONDS	..	..	..	..	..	..	..	..	3	..				3
SPECIAL STATE BONDS	..	..	..	..	..	..	..	..	5	5				
CAPITAL CONSTRUCTION BONDS	..	..	..	..	..	..	..	..	..	..				5

REF: DEBT2.WK1   06/23/92   Source: Ministry of Finance & Peoples Bank of China.   SKE=State Key Enterprises; SPC=State Planning Commission
NOTE: /a:Key enterprises are those in the electrical, metallurgical, nonferrous, & petrochemical industries. Bonds sold to their customers.   /b + Inflation allowance

Table 6.1: CHINA : Monetary Survey, 1984-91

	1984	1985	1986	1987	1988	1989	1990				1991			
						Dec.	March	June	Sept.	Dec.	March	June	Sept.	Dec.
						(in billions of yuan; end of period)								
Net foreign assets	35.1	20.8	3.9	23.0	30.2	37.1	57.0	67.6	80.1	92.7	115.4	116.3	133.3	137.0
Peoples Bank of China	28.0	12.4	3.7	15.0	20.9	33.0	45.1	59.6	68.3	68.5	96.6	106.6	122.3	
Gold	1.2	1.2	1.2	1.2	1.2	1.2	1.2	1.2	1.2	1.2	1.2	1.2	1.2	
Foreign Exchange Claims	26.4	9.3	3.8	13.2	15.8	26.5	38.2	52.5	60.5	60.0	88.3	98.4	113.3	
Claims on Intl. Inst. (net)	0.4	1.9	-1.3	0.6	3.9	5.3	5.7	5.9	6.6	7.3	7.1	7.0	7.7	
Bank of China	7.1	8.4	0.2	8.0	9.4	4.2	11.9	8.0	11.8	24.2	18.7	9.7	11.1	
Foreign Exchange	17.3	29.7	31.4	45.8	52.8	54.2	61.6	63.9	68.4	91.4	87.6	68.6	104.8	
Foreign Liabilities	10.2	21.2	31.2	37.8	43.4	50.0	49.7	55.9	56.6	67.2	68.9	78.9	93.7	
Net domestic assets	408.9	499.3	668.3	812.0	979.7	1158.7	1191.9	1252.1	1343.8	1437.7	1508.6	1588.6	1690.9	1797.0
Loans to enterprises and individuals	509.9	628.9	814.5	980.3	1141.8	1346.9	1378.6	1436.2	1526.9	1653.6	1689.3	1750.5	1847.0	1981.0
Net Credit to Government 2/	9.5	-9.3	5.8	20.8	30.5	24.7	26.6	27.9	37.0	42.1	36.3	43.2	47.0	58.0
Other Items (net) 3/	-110.4	-120.4	-152.1	-189.1	-192.7	-212.9	-213.3	-211.9	-220.1	-258.3	-216.5	-205.3	-203.1	-242.0
Money plus quasi-money	444.0	520.0	672.2	835.0	1009.9	1195.9	1248.9	1319.7	1423.9	1530.4	1625.0	1704.7	1824.2	1935.0
Money	340.0	374.0	474.1	568.5	695.0	744.2	714.2	739.6	802.4	879.3	895.3	926.2	1009.0	1122.0
Currency	79.2	98.8	121.8	145.4	213.3	234.2	215.2	209.4	229.8	264.1	258.1	251.4	272.7	318.0
Household demand deposits	31.4	39.7	50.6	70.8	94.8	94.6	93.2	99.8	106.3	115.0	124.0	131.0	139.0	145.0
Enterprise deposits	197.0	203.0	262.1	307.3	347.7	367.0	356.8	378.4	411.5	438.6	454.7	483.0	530.0	584.0
Official institutions	32.4	32.6	39.6	44.9	39.3	48.4	49.1	52.1	54.9	61.0	58.0	61.0	67.0	75.0
Quasi-money	104.1	145.9	198.0	266.5	314.9	451.6	534.6	580.0	621.3	651.1	729.3	778.5	815.2	812.0
Capital construction deposits	14.0	23.5	25.1	30.9	31.2	42.0	53.0	60.2	65.3	65.1	75.4	87.5	92.7	52.0
Household term deposits	90.1	122.4	172.9	235.6	283.7	409.6	481.6	519.9	556.2	586.0	653.9	691.0	722.5	760.0
					(Percent change from same period of the preceding year)									
Net domestic assets	31.1	22.1	33.9	21.5	20.7	18.3	20.2	21.1	24.9	24.1	26.6	26.9	25.8	25.0
Of which: Loans to enterprises and individuals	33.5	22.3	29.5	20.3	16.5	18.0	19.7	21.7	24.8	22.8	22.5	21.9	21.0	19.8
Money and quasi-money	..	17.1	29.3	24.2	21.0	18.4	22.5	24.9	29.5	28.0	30.1	29.2	28.1	26.4
Of which: Currency	..	24.7	23.3	19.4	46.6	9.8	2.6	0.7	10.4	12.8	19.9	20.1	18.7	20.3
Memorandum Item:														
Ratio of currency to deposits (%)	21.9	19.0	18.1	17.4	21.1	19.6	17.2	15.9	16.1	17.3	15.9	14.7	14.9	16.4
(seasonally adjusted)	20.4	21.8	17.0	16.4	19.8	18.4	17.3	16.6	16.4	16.2	15.9	15.5	15.2	15.4

REF: MONEY.WK1 06/23/92
Source: IMF Recent Economic Developments 05/06/92.
1/ Covers the operations of the People's Bank, the four specialized banks, the two universal banks, and the rural credit cooperatives.
2/ Claims related to state budget operations less government deposits, which include extrabudgetary deposits of local governments.
3/ Includes financial bonds issued by banks.

Table 6.2: CHINA : Operations of the People's Bank, 1985-91

(in billions of yuan; end of period)

| | 1985 | 1986 | 1987 | 1988 | 1989 | 1990 | | | | 1991 | | | |
| | | | | | | | | | | | | | |
					Dec.	March	June	Sept.	Dec.	March	June	Sept.	Dec.
Net foreign assets	12.4	3.7	15.0	20.9	32.9	45.1	59.6	68.3	68.5	96.6	96.5	122.3	131.7
Claims on financial institutions	224.9	269.4	277.4	338.8	420.7	417.9	415.9	440.3	514.8	494.0	480.7	520.0	599.2
Other domestic assets	-8.7	9.6	29.9	45.8	48.1	57.6	58.9	65.8	74.0	85.2	105.8	70.0	94.2
Loans	8.6	13.0	22.7	30.6	34.5	35.0	36.1	37.5	40.7	40.8	41.6	42.5	44.9
Budgetary borrowing, net 1/	-9.3	5.8	20.8	30.5	24.7	26.6	27.9	37.0	42.1	36.3	43.2	47.0	58.2
Other items, net	-7.9	-9.3	-13.6	-15.3	-11.1	-4.0	-5.0	-8.8	-8.7	8.2	21.0	-19.5	-8.9
Reserve Money	228.6	282.7	322.3	405.5	501.7	520.5	534.4	574.3	657.2	675.9	683.0	712.2	825.2
Liabilities to banks	96.4	120.1	127.4	145.4	208.1	243.6	258.3	273.3	312.7	336.5	345.1	344.0	400.0
Required deposits	42.0	56.5	67.0	84.1	104.2	111.4	119.6	128.8	139.1	148.7	158.2	168.6	181.0
Other deposits	47.0	55.8	52.8	50.9	91.2	119.5	126.0	132.2	159.2	173.0	172.1	160.4	203.1
Cash in vault	7.3	7.8	7.6	10.4	12.8	12.7	12.7	12.3	14.4	14.8	14.8	15.0	15.9
Liabilities to nonbanks	132.2	162.6	194.8	260.1	293.6	276.9	276.1	301.0	344.6	339.4	337.9	368.3	425.2
Currency in circulation	98.8	121.8	145.4	213.3	234.2	215.2	209.4	229.8	264.1	258.1	251.4	272.7	317.4
Deposits	33.4	40.8	49.4	46.9	59.3	61.7	66.8	71.3	80.5	81.2	86.5	95.6	107.8
Total Liabilities	228.6	282.7	322.3	405.5	501.7	520.5	534.4	574.3	657.3	675.9	683.0	712.2	825.2
Memorandum Item:													
Money multiplier 2/	2.3	2.4	2.6	2.5	2.4	2.4	2.5	2.5	2.3	2.4	2.5	2.6	2.3
Ratio of excess reserves to deposits (%) 3	12.1	10.1	7.7	6.8	10.1	12.3	12.1	11.8	13.4	13.5	12.6	11.0	13.5
Currency deposit ratio				26.8	24.4	20.8	18.9	19.2	20.9	18.9	17.3	17.6	::
(seasonally adjusted)				24.8	22.6	21.0	20.2	19.7	19.3	19.0	18.5	::	::
Required Reserve Ratio				11.2	11.5	11.5	11.5	11.5	11.7	11.6	11.6	11.6	::

REF: MONEY.WK1 06/23/92
Source: IMF Recent Economic Developments 05/06/92.

1/ Claims related to state budget operations less government deposits, which include extrabudgetary deposits of local governments.
2/ The ratio of money and quasi-money to reserve money.
3/ Deposits exclude deposits with the PBC.

Table 6.3: CHINA : Monetary and Velocity Developments, 1984-1991

(Percentage fourth quarter to fourth quarter)

	1984	1985	1986	1987	1988	1989	1990	1991	
Money and quasi-money	42.4	17.1	29.3	24.2	20.9	18.4	28.0	26.4	
Currency	49.4	24.7	23.3	19.4	46.7	9.8	12.8	20.4	
Household deposits	32.6	33.4	37.9	37.1	23.5	33.2	39.0	29.1	
Demand	44.0	26.4	27.5	39.9	33.9	-0.2	21.6	26.1	
Time	29.1	35.8	41.3	36.3	20.4	44.4	43.1	29.7	
Enterprise deposits 1/	62.9	3.0	29.1	17.2	13.1	5.6	19.5	33.2	
Other deposits 2/	-14.3	0.6	21.5	13.4	-12.5	23.2	26.0	23.0	
Velocity (ratio) 3/	1.52	1.65	1.44	1.35	1.39	1.33	1.16	1.02	/4
(percent change)	-16.5	8.3	-12.4	-6.2	2.6	-4.1	-13.2	-11.6	
Memorandum item:									
Augmented money and quasi-money 5/	..	..	32.3	26.8	23.2	14.8	..	..	/6
GNP (Billion Yuan, Current Prices)	696.2	855.8	969.6	1130.1	1401.8	1591.6	1768.6	1975.9	

REF: MONEY.WK1 06/23/92
Source: IMF Recent Economic Developments 05/06/92.

1/ Includes deposits with the People's Construction Bank of China (PCBC).
2/ Deposits of official institutions.
3/ Ratio of GNP to the end-year money and quasi-money.
4/ Adjusted for seasonal factors.
5/ Includes deposits held at trust and investment companies and urban credit cooperatives.
6/ June 1989 over June 1988.

Table 6.4: CHINA : Specialized and Universal Banks'
Domestic Currency Assets and Liabilities, 1986-90

(billions of yuan; end of period)

	1986	1987	1988	1989	1990				1991			
				Dec.	March	June	Sept.	Dec.	March	June	Sept.	Dec.
Total deposits	463.5	573.9	668.6	798.3	860.7	921.4	991.6	1045.9	1130.4	1199.5	1282.9	1330.0
Enterprises	223.9	268.8	293.2	308.1	325.9	346.8	378.7	399.3	427.6	462.0	504.8	505.0
Sight	198.8	237.9	262.0	267.0	273.9	287.8	314.6	335.5	353.7	376.2	413.9	454.7
Term	25.1	30.9	31.2	41.1	52.0	59.0	64.0	63.7	73.9	85.8	90.9	50.3
Saving	146.4	202.8	258.9	363.0	407.7	440.7	473.4	500.9	554.0	586.9	616.7	647.1
Sight	28.0	41.0	59.7	61.4	60.5	65.6	70.2	76.4	82.5	88.2	93.9	101.7
Term	118.4	161.8	199.2	301.6	347.2	375.0	403.2	424.4	471.6	498.7	522.8	545.4
Township enterprises	4.6	5.6	6.2	1.7	5.8	1.6	6.1	7.1	6.6	7.6	8.3	9.2
Agricultural collectives	1.1	1.2	1.8	1.7	1.5	1.6	1.6	1.9	1.8	1.9	2.1	2.5
Rural credit cooperatives	50.2	56.3	58.8	63.9	68.2	69.3	70.6	75.9	77.6	75.7	80.0	91.8
Other deposits	37.3	39.2	49.7	55.6	52.2	57.2	61.3	60.9	62.8	65.4	70.9	74.5
Liabilities to the PBC	268.4	275.0	336.1	420.1	412.2	406.9	433.2	508.3	484.3	478.0	512.0	590.6
Self-owned funds of banks	74.1	81.5	91.4	91.4	102.3	102.3	102.3	111.5	102.3	102.3	102.3	102.3
Other liabilities, net	54.5	67.9	56.7	66.8	58.9	60.7	59.3	74.1	58.6	42.5	34.6	96.0
Total Liabilities	857.6	993.0	1152.7	1384.5	1434.1	1491.3	1586.4	1739.8	1775.6	1822.2	1931.7	2118.8
Loans	748.9	884.2	1023.9	1206.4	1222.0	1266.1	1346.4	1476.0	1488.8	1533.3	1621.0	1759.5
Industrial	189.4	221.2	260.4	330.5	348.6	364.4	394.8	421.0	432.0	449.0	470.6	493.0
Commercial	308.4	350.0	409.5	476.6	469.3	477.9	509.4	575.7	564.8	566.5	592.5	668.1
Construction	36.9	46.7	49.5	60.1	59.9	61.9	64.3	67.2	70.1	71.3	70.0	71.5
Urban collectives	41.5	53.6	63.6	69.3	71.1	74.1	77.8	81.5	83.6	87.4	90.5	93.3
Business loans to individuals	1.1	1.5	1.9	1.5	1.6	1.5	1.6	1.6	1.6	1.7	1.8	2.0
Agricultural loans	52.8	65.4	77.9	86.0	88.1	94.1	97.5	100.0	105.1	110.6	115.9	116.7
Loans to rural credit coops.	4.3	3.8	3.5	3.5	4.0	4.8	4.6	3.8	4.6	5.9	5.7	4.2
Fixed investment loans	88.6	111.9	138.7	157.0	157.1	162.9	172.2	198.2	200.6	211.1	243.4	274.4
Other loans	26.0	30.2	18.7	21.8	22.5	24.2	24.3	27.1	28.3	29.7	30.6	36.6
Cash in vault	7.8	7.6	10.4	12.8	12.7	12.7	12.3	14.4	14.8	14.8	15.0	15.9
Required deposits	56.3	65.8	80.9	100.8	107.7	115.6	124.3	133.7	142.8	151.9	161.7	173.5
Other deposits at the PBC	47.5	40.5	37.6	64.5	91.6	96.9	103.5	115.8	129.2	122.3	134.0	170.0
Total Assets	860.5	998.2	1152.7	1384.5	1434.1	1491.3	1586.4	1739.8	1775.6	1822.2	1931.7	2118.8

REF: MONEY.WK1 06/23/92
Source: IMF Recent Economic Developments 05/06/92.

Table 6.5: CHINA : Balance Sheets of Rural Credit Cooperatives, 1986-90

(in billions of yuan; end of period)

	1986	1987	1988	Dec.	1990				1991			
					March	June	Sept.	Dec.	March	June	Sept.	Dec.
Deposits	75.5	103.7	140.0	166.9	178.6	190.3	200.6	214.5	232.4	243.1	253.2	270.9
Rural collective enterprises	8.4	9.0	9.8	9.2	7.5	7.8	8.2	10.7	9.3	9.6	10.5	13.6
Township enterprises	9.2	10.5	12.8	12.6	10.6	11.6	12.5	15.0	13.5	14.9	16.3	19.2
Individual deposits	62.0	86.6	114.2	141.2	156.8	167.0	175.5	184.1	204.9	213.4	220.6	231.7
Sight	22.6	29.7	35.1	33.2	32.6	34.2	36.1	38.7	41.7	42.9	44.9	43.4
Term	54.0	70.8	79.2	108.0	124.1	132.8	139.4	145.4	163.2	170.6	175.7	188.3
Other deposits	2.1	2.5	3.1	3.9	3.7	3.9	4.4	4.7	4.7	5.1	5.8	6.5
Loans from banks	4.2	3.8	3.6	3.8	4.2	5.2	5.1	4.2	5.1	6.5	6.6	5.1
Other liabilities, net	5.8	10.0	5.2	4.6	9.6	10.8	10.9	-0.2	2.6	5.8	6.7	-3.6
Total liabilities	84.7	117.9	148.8	175.3	192.4	206.3	216.6	218.5	240.1	255.4	266.5	272.5
Domestic credit	49.0	75.5	90.9	109.5	125.6	138.8	147.7	141.1	164.4	181.6	189.2	180.9
Loans to collective enterprises	4.5	7.2	8.0	10.7	11.5	12.6	13.3	13.4	14.7	16.0	16.9	17.0
Loans to township enterprises	26.6	35.9	45.6	57.2	62.4	67.4	72.5	75.9	83.6	91.2	96.5	100.7
Loans to individuals	35.8	34.0	37.2	41.6	51.7	58.9	61.9	51.8	66.1	74.4	75.9	63.1
Redeposits at banks	49.3	59.1	58.0	65.8	66.9	67.4	68.9	77.4	75.8	73.8	77.2	91.6
Total assets	84.7	117.9	148.8	175.3	192.4	206.3	216.6	218.5	240.1	255.4	266.5	272.5

REF: MONEY.WK1 06/23/92
Source: IMF Recent Economic Developments 05/06/92.

Table 6.6: CHINA: ASSETS OF THE SPECIALIZED BANKS
(Million RMB)

ASSETS	PCBC 1987	1988	1989	1990	ABC 1987	1988	1989	1990	ICBC 1987	1988	1989	1990	BOC 1987	1988	1989	1990
LIQUID ASSETS 1/	13341	10147	16330	26383	4333	18152	30958	45371	12677	13775	22131	41013	728	1252	2009	2470
CASH	288	944	1436	1699	4333	4888	5958	6594	2854	4014	4710	5244	728	1252	2009	2470
DEPOSITS WITH PBC	23057	20871	29399	45235	n.e.	33497	50875	72792	46195	53953	69899	101912	..	..	..	..
(of which RRs)	10004	11668	14505	20551	..	20233	25875	34015	36372	44192	52478	66143	..	..	..	..
DUE FROM BANKS	5589	9026	13630	35977	..	..	10496	16810	..	..	..	4305	91337	118009	150157	210600
LOAN PORTFOLIO	99267	121297	149952	192805	232314	263155	305796	377434	444817	496976	575190	687190	167106	190730	259842	346053
Of which:																
FIXED ASSETS	54951	66260	76852	102072	4688	5846	6560	7643	57230	57530	63689	74998	..	..	..	..
WORKING CAPITAL	23069	31588	37010	46595	227626	257309	..	..	387587	439446	341174	608737	..	..	..	..
Industrial	..	..	..	..	13348	15443	18920	24954	216885	242298	159130	..	..	..	..	..
Commercial	..	..	..	..	138873	156939	187337	235928	116866	137622	..	..	..	..	..	..
TVEs	..	..	..	..	34969	40769	42061	46218	37112	47900	..	..	..	..	..	..
Urban Collectives & Ind.Enterprises	..	..	..	..	18320	21688	26022	31661	..	..	..	..	..	..	..	..
Rural Collectives & Rural SOEs	..	..	..	..	7926	8679	9060	9941	..	..	..	..	..	..	..	..
Loans to farmers	..	..	..	..	3646	3369	3398	3747	..	..	..	..	..	..	..	..
Loans to RCCs	..	..	..	..	..	10422	12438	17342	..	..	8991	3455	..	..	..	..
OTHER LOANS 2/	..	775	794	2303	..	..	..	..	..	..	..	10247	23899	29360	27453	43458
SECURITIES	142333	173419	193253	220958	..	..	..	..	..	..	2206	33600	..	..	..	..
TRUST PORTFOLIO	33196	54116	127968	139887	..	..	..	..	..	..	..	..	..	..	..	..
GOV. ENTRUSTED LOANS	109137	119303	65285	81071	..	..	..	..	..	..	..	59027	..	..	..	..
GOV. INVEST. LOANS	..	..	..	..	..	..	..	..	..	..	..	..	..	..	..	..
AGENCY BUSINESS	..	..	..	..	..	..	..	..	..	..	..	21750	95609	103004	132894	127202
LETTERS OF CREDIT 3/	..	..	..	..	..	..	..	..	..	..	..	..	17250	21690	39631	47051
RECEIVABLES & FORWARD CONTRACTS	..	..	..	..	..	..	..	..	..	..	..	..	43254	92584	56935	70208
COLLECTIONS & TRUSTS	7266	13114	19029	18861	..	..	..	6748	..	6709	7358	15093	2785	3072	8488	12060
OTHER ASSETS 4/	277800	339446	407493	517838	236647	301540	373125	480378	493866	561652	657157	938368	441968	559701	677410	859113
TOTAL ASSETS	135467	166027	214240	296880												
of which Own Assets																
TOTAL ASSETS Growth Rate%	..	22.2%	20.0%	27.1%	..	27.4%	23.7%	28.7%	..	13.7%	17.0%	42.8%	..	26.6%	21.0%	26.8%

REF: MONEY2.WK1 06/23/92
Source: Balance sheets of the banks.
1/ Cash plus Deposits at PBC (excluding RRs).
2/ Includes Special and Development Loans, Poverty Alleviation Subsidies and Other Loans.
3/ Includes International Businesses.
4/ Includes Net Value of Fixed Assets.

Table 6.7: CHINA: LIABILITIES OF THE SPECIALIZED BANKS
(Million Yuan)

LIABILITIES	PCBC				ABC				ICBC				BOC			
	1987	1988	1989	1990	1987	1988	1989	1990	1987	1988	1989	1990	1987	1988	1989	1990
TOTAL DEPOSITS	82351	96860	115157	158049	149795	171373	205546	264055	314459	356169	413109	517349	196070	214435	276347	390581
Enterprise	71434	76018	75817	93791	24717	28155	29466	34481	134631	144389	148007	223039	..	..	..	..
Industrial	..	..	..	..	..	2836	2843	3463	..	..	..	..	..	..	..	..
Commercial	..	..	..	..	..	25319	26623	31018	..	..	..	..	..	..	..	..
Individual	2327	11672	29627	51050	..	50	..	..	29694	37781	35917	n.a.	..	..	..	..
Other	8590	9170	9713	13208	5428	6215	5625	6633	..	..	..	..	..	..	..	..
TVEs	..	..	..	..	10699	10731	11096	13424	..	..	..	..	..	..	..	..
Agr.Collect. & SOEs	..	..	..	..	..	..	..	..	..	..	..	..	..	..	..	..
RCC DEPOSITS	..	..	..	..	55000	56491	61156	71943	..	..	..	..	..	..	..	..
SAVINGS DEPOSITS	..	..	..	..	42619	59371	84851	121210	125856	142956	194080	n.a.	..	..	..	..
TOTAL HOUSEHOLD DEPOSITS	..	..	..	..	..	..	..	..	155550	180737	229997	294310	..	..	..	..
OTHER DEPOSITS	..	..	..	..	11332	10360	13352	16364	24278	29529	34027	..	..	..	..	..
LIABILITIES WITH PBC	6019	10503	25273	43962	23437	99380	118287	143888	115769	140783	173654	202436	7925	9509	11704	13578
LIABILITIES WITH GOV.	105504	114309	128159	140002	..	..	..	..	..	..	..	..	13029	20961	24074	23416
INTERNATIONAL BUSINESS	..	..	..	..	..	..	..	..	..	..	..	21203	95609	103004	132694	127202
FINANCIAL BONDS	1062	1982	1933	2761	..	..	..	..	2779	3085	2464	3239	51333	72358	102176	140276
OTHER LIABILITIES	17803	23310	25895	34593	61115	4775	6384	16890	42424	29461	32588	43617	17791	22212	37002	51050
GUARANTEES 1/ & LCs	..	..	..	..	..	..	..	..	..	..	..	62129	43254	92583	56935	70208
DUE TO OTHER BANKS 2/	4076	9161	13703	22303	..	..	15981	27588	..	..	..	3785	5000	10000	15000	15000
PAYABLES & FORW.CONTRACTS	..	..	..	..	..	..	..	..	..	..	..	..	..	..	..	..
TRUSTS & INVESTMENTS	34744	55416	67535	83777	..	..	..	..	..	1514	1078	29290	..	..	..	..
CAPITAL 3/	24583	26314	27900	30229	..	26012	26927	27957	18435	32154	35342	55320	11956	14638	21276	27771
SURPLUS & RESERVES	1578	1591	1735	1923	..	..	..	..	..	..	..	..	..	..	..	..
PROVISION FOR BAD DEBTS	..	161	203	239	..	..	..	..	..	..	..	..	..	..	..	..
TOTAL LIABILITIES & NW	277800	339446	407493	517838	236647	301540	373125	480378	493866	561652	657157	938368	441968	559701	677410	859113
TOTAL LIABILITIES Growth%	..	22.2%	20.0%	27.1%	..	27.4%	23.7%	28.7%	..	13.7%	17.0%	42.8%	..	26.6%	21.0%	26.8%

REF: MONEY2.WK1 06/23/92
Source: Balance sheets of the banks.
1/ Includes Agency Businesses.
2/ Interbank Borrowing.
3/ Credit Fund plus Self-Owned Funds and Retained Earnings.

Table 6.8: CHINA: PROFIT & LOSSES OF THE SPECIALIZED BANKS

(Million Yuan)

	PCBC 1987	PCBC 1988	PCBC 1989	PCBC 1990	ABC 1987	ABC 1988	ABC 1989	ABC 1990	ICBC 1987	ICBC 1988	ICBC 1989	ICBC 1990	BOC 1987	BOC 1988	BOC 1989	BOC 1990
GROSS INTEREST																
Income	6967	9889	15528	17739	..	..	28911	27342	29667	37457	60270	..	15024	20866	37784	44611
Expenses	1937	4081	8902	9995	..	..	9009	9726	15147	21400	31899	..	11675	17065	32318	37843
NET INTEREST INCOME	5030	5808	6626	7744	..	..	19902	17616	14520	16057	28371	..	3350	3801	5466	6768
COMMISSION & OTHER																
Income	35	67	133	181	..	..	47434	47592	297	366	1689	..	3291	3715	3888	4942
Expenses 1/	..	161	46	45	..	..	57179	58168	3312	5095	14784	..	2254	2576	3282	4102
OPERATING & OTH. EXPENSES (Expenses)	886	1500	1591	2193	..	..	6733	5885	604	759	62	..	511	715	1011	1447
OPERATING PROFIT (Before Taxes)	4179	4214	5122	5687	..	..	3424	1155	10901	10569	15214	..	3875	4224	5060	6161
INCOME & ADJ. TAX	2601	2623	3387	3764	..	..	2198	n.a.	n.a.	n.a.	n.a.	n.a.	n.a.	n.a.	n.a.	n.a.
NET PROFIT 2/ (After Taxes)	1578	1591	1735	1923	n.a.	n.a.	1226	1155	n.a.	n.a.	n.a.	n.a.	n.a.	n.a.	n.a.	n.a.

REF: MONEY2.WK1 06/23/92
Source: Balance sheets of the banks.
1/ Includes Provisions for Bad Debts.
2/ ICBC and BOC do not indicate taxes paid, however they report "Net Profits". It is possible that such payments are classified as "Other Expenses", in which case the table's "Operating Profits" would correspond to the banks' reported "Net Profits".

Table 6.9: CHINA: BANKING SYSTEM: Nominal Annual Interest Rates on Deposits

	1971	1979	1980	1982	1983	1985	1985	1986	1986	1987	1987	1988	1989	1990	1990	1991
	10/01	04/01	04/01	04/01	12/21	04/01	08/01	03/01	08/01	06/21	08/14	09/01	02/01	04/15	08/21	04/21
HOUSEHOLD DEPOSITS																
Sight	2.16	2.16	2.88	2.88	2.88	2.88	2.88	2.88	2.88	2.88	2.88	2.88	2.88	2.88	2.16	1.80
Time																
Fixed IN, Fixed OUT																
1/2 Year		3.60	4.32	4.32	4.32	5.40	6.12	6.12	6.12	6.12	6.12	6.48	9.00	7.74	6.48	5.40
1 Year	3.24	3.96	5.40	5.76	5.76	6.84	7.20	7.20	7.20	7.20	7.20	8.64	11.34	10.08	8.64	7.56
2 Years		4.80	6.12	6.84	6.84	7.92	8.28	8.28	8.28	8.28	8.28	9.18	12.24	10.98	9.36	7.90
3 Years		5.04	6.84	7.92	7.92	8.28	9.36	9.36	9.36	9.36	9.36	9.72	13.14	11.88	10.08	8.28
5 Years		5.04	6.84	9.00	9.00	9.00	10.44	10.44	10.44	10.44	10.44	10.80	14.94	13.68	11.52	9.00
8 Years												12.42	17.64	16.20	13.68	10.08
Flexible IN, Fixed OUT & Flexible OUT																
1 Year		3.60	4.32	4.68	4.68	5.40	6.12	6.12	6.12	6.12	6.12	7.20	9.54	8.28	7.20	6.12
3 Years		3.96	5.40	6.12	6.12	6.84	7.20	7.20	7.20	7.20	7.20	8.64	11.34	10.08	8.64	6.84
5 Years		4.50	6.12	7.20	7.20	7.56	7.92	7.92	7.92	7.92	7.92	9.72	13.14	11.88	10.08	7.56
Fixed Principal																
1 Year		3.60	4.32	4.32	4.32	5.40	6.12	6.12	6.12	6.12	6.12	7.20				
3 Years		3.96	5.40	5.76	5.76	6.84	7.20	7.20	7.20	7.20	7.20	8.64				
5 Years		4.50	6.12	6.84	6.84	7.56	7.92	7.92	7.92	7.92	7.92	9.72				
Convertible Deposit																
1/2 Year or less							2.88	2.88	2.88	2.88	2.88	5.83				
1/2 - 1 Year							5.51	5.51	5.51	5.51	5.51	6.80				
1 Year or more							6.48	6.48	6.48	6.48	6.48	8.02				
DEPOSITS FROM OVERSEAS CHINESE																
1 Year	3.96	4.68	5.76	6.48	6.48	7.20	8.28	8.28	8.28	8.28	8.28	9.72	13.14	11.88	10.08	8.28
3 Years		5.04	5.40	7.20	7.20	8.28	9.36	9.36	9.36	9.36	9.36	10.80	14.94	13.68	11.52	9.00
5 Years		6.48	7.20	8.28	8.28	9.00	10.44	10.44	10.44	10.44	10.44	11.88	16.74	15.48	13.68	9.90
ENTERPRISE DEPOSITS																
Sight	1.80	1.80	1.80	1.80	1.80	1.80	1.80	1.80	1.80	1.80	1.80	2.88	2.88	2.88	2.16	1.80
Time																
1/2 Year				3.60	3.60	4.32	4.32	4.32	4.32	4.32	4.32	6.48	9.00	7.74	6.48	5.40
1 Year				4.32	4.32	5.04	5.04	5.04	5.04	5.04	5.04	8.64	11.34	10.08	8.64	7.56
2 Years				5.04	5.04	5.76	5.76	5.76	5.76	5.76	5.76	9.18	12.24	10.98	9.36	7.90
3 Years										6.48	6.48	9.72	13.14	11.88	10.08	8.28
5 Years												10.80	14.94	13.68	11.52	9.00
8 Years												12.42	17.64	16.20	13.68	10.08
INSURANCE COMPANY DEPOSITS																
Sight			1.80	1.80	1.80	1.80	1.80	1.80	1.80	1.80	1.80	2.88	2.88	2.16	2.16	1.80
Reserves of different kind 1/ 2/				4.20	4.20	4.20	4.20	5.04	5.04	5.76	5.76	9.18	8.64	7.92	6.84	6.12
INDIVIDUAL ENTERPRISE DEPOSITS 3/		1.80	1.80	1.80	1.80	2.88	2.88	2.88	2.88	2.88	2.88	2.88	2.88	2.88	2.88	2.88

REF: MONEY3.WK1 06/23/92
Source: Peoples Bank of China
1/ Same rates paid by PBC to the SBs.
2/ Reserves include Contingent reserves, Reserves against property claims, and Life insurance reserves.
3/ Same rates paid on enterprise deposits.
Note 1: This Table does not include PBC's interest rates on SBs' deposits.
Note 2: Before September 21, 1988, interest rates on deposits in Trust & Investment Companies could float within a 20% range from quoted rates.
Note 3: Since September 10, 1988, interest rates on time deposits with maturities of 3 years or more were indexed to the rate of inflation (CPI).

Table 6.10 : CHINA: BANKING SYSTEM: Nominal Annual Interest Rates on Loans for Working Capital

	1971	1979	1980	1980	1981	1982	1983	1984	1985	1985	1986	1987	1988	1989	1990	1990	1991
	01/01	01/01	01/01	04/01	01/01	01/01	01/01	01/01	04/01	08/01	09/21	01/01	09/01	02/01	04/15	08/21	04/21
Industry	5.04	5.04	5.04	5.04	5.04	7.20	7.20	7.20	7.92	7.92	7.92	7.92	9.00	11.34	11.34	11.34	11.34
Commerce	5.04	5.04	5.04	5.04	5.04	7.20	7.20	7.20	7.92	7.92	7.92	7.92	9.00	11.34	11.34	11.34	11.34
Agriculture	4.32	4.32	4.32	4.32	4.32	7.20	7.20	7.20	7.92	7.92	7.92	7.92	9.00	11.34	11.34	11.34	11.34
Construction	5.04	5.04	5.04	5.04	5.04	3.60	3.60	3.60	4.32	4.32	4.32	4.32	9.00	11.34	11.34	11.34	11.34
Foreign trade	5.04	5.04	5.04	5.04	5.04	7.20	7.20	7.20	7.20	7.20	7.20	7.20	9.00	11.34	11.34	11.34	11.34
Town & Village Enterprises (TVE)	4.32	4.32	4.32	4.32	5.04	7.20	7.20	7.20	8.64	8.64	8.64	8.64	9.00	11.34	11.34	11.34	11.34
Individual Enterprises				5.04	5.04	7.20	7.20	8.64	11.52	11.52	11.52	11.52	9.00	11.34	11.34	11.34	11.34
Farmers	4.32	4.32	4.32	4.32	5.04	7.20	7.20	7.20	7.92	7.92	7.92	7.92	9.00	11.34	11.34	11.34	11.34
Preferential Rates																	
Listed Price Food & Oil		2.52	2.52	2.52	2.52	3.60	3.60	3.60	3.60	3.60	3.96	3.96	9.00	9.00	9.00	9.00	9.00
Food Purchases		4.32	4.32	4.32	4.32	5.76	5.76	5.76	5.76	5.76	3.96	3.96	9.00	9.00	9.00	9.00	9.00
Rice Seed Companies		2.52	2.52	2.52	2.52	3.60	3.60	3.60	3.60	3.60	4.32	7.92	9.00	7.92	7.92	7.92	7.92
Youth Run TAVE's		4.32	4.32	4.32	4.32	4.32	4.32	4.32	4.32	4.32	3.96	5.04	7.92	8.46	8.46	8.46	8.46
Minorities: Production & Trade					3.96	3.96	3.96	3.96	3.96	3.96	3.96	5.04	6.12	8.46	8.46	8.46	8.46
Minorities: Handicrafts					3.96	3.96	3.96	5.76	5.76	5.76	5.76	7.92	6.12	7.92	7.92	7.92	7.92
Chinese Medicine: not in Beijing...						5.76	5.76	5.76	5.76	5.76	5.76	7.92	7.92	7.92	7.92	7.92	7.92
Chinese Medicine: in Beijing...							5.76	5.76	5.76	5.76	5.76	7.92	7.92	7.50	7.50	7.50	7.50
Household Items						5.76	5.76	5.76	6.34	6.34	6.34	6.34	7.50	7.50	7.50	7.50	7.50
Non-Profit Government Entities																	
State-run Commercial Entities (SCE)																	
Working Capital							6.84	6.84	6.84	6.84	6.84	6.84	6.84	6.84	6.84	6.84	6.84
Short-term Loans							7.20	7.20	7.20	7.20	7.20	7.20	9.00	9.00	9.00	9.00	9.00
Other Loans							7.56	7.56	7.56	7.56	7.56	7.56	9.00	9.00	9.00	9.00	9.00
Cotton									7.20	7.20	7.20	7.20	9.00	9.00	9.00	9.00	9.00
SCE: Commerce & Medicine					3.93	3.96	3.96	3.96	3.96	3.96	3.96	5.04	6.12	6.12	6.12	6.12	6.12
Settlement Loans		5.04	5.04	5.04	5.04	7.20	3.60	3.60	3.60	3.60	3.60	7.92	9.00	9.00	9.00	9.00	9.00
Discounting of Bills					< +3% higher than working capital loans >												

REF: MONEY3.WK1   06/23/92
Source: Peoples Bank of China

Table 6.11 : CHINA: BANKING SYSTEM: Nominal Annual Interest Rates on Loans for Fixed Capital

	1971	1979	1980	1980	1981	1982	1983	1984	1985	1985	1986	1987	1988	1989	1990	1990	1991
	01/01	01/01	01/01	04/01	01/01	01/01	01/01	01/01	04/01	08/01	09/21	01/01	09/01	02/01	04/15	08/21	04/21
Agricultural Development Loans																	
1 year or less						5.04	5.04	5.04	5.04	7.92	7.92	7.92	9.00	11.34	10.08	9.36	8.64
1 - 3 years						5.76	5.76	5.76	5.76	8.64	8.64	8.64	9.90	12.78	10.80	9.36	8.64
3 - 5 years						6.48	6.48	6.48	6.48	9.36	9.36	9.36	10.80	14.40	11.52	10.08	9.54
5 - 10 years						6.48	6.48	6.48	6.48	10.08	10.08	10.08	13.32	19.26	11.88	10.08	9.54
More than 10 years						6.48	6.48	6.48	6.48	10.80	10.80	10.80	16.20				
14 Coastal Cities & SEZ's (Up to Y 2 billion)																	
5 years or less												5.88	5.88				
More than 5 years												7.32	7.32				
1983 S&M-Term Equipment Loans							2.52										
Ships: Sixth Five Year Plan Period (SFYP)					4.03	4.03	4.03	4.03	4.03	4.03	4.03	4.03	4.03	4.03	4.03	4.03	4.03
Motorcycles & Cars: SFYP					5.04	5.04	5.04	5.04	5.04	5.04	5.04	5.04	5.04	5.04	5.04	5.04	5.04
Gold Production																	
1 year		2.16	2.16	2.16	2.16	4.32	4.32	4.32	5.04	5.04	5.04	5.04	6.12	8.46	7.92	7.20	7.20
3 years		2.16	2.16	2.16	2.16	4.32	4.32	4.32	5.76	5.76	5.76	5.76	6.84	9.18	7.92	5.76	5.76
5 years		2.16	2.16	2.16	2.16	4.32	4.32	4.32	6.48	6.48	6.48	6.48	7.56	9.9	7.92	5.76	5.76
Rural Enterprises (TVE's)	4.32	4.32	4.32	4.32	5.04	7.20	7.20	7.92	9.36	9.36	9.36	9.36	13.32	11.34	10.08	9.36	8.64

REF: MONEY3.WK1   06/23/92
Source: Peoples Bank of China

Table 6.12 : CHINA: BANKING SYSTEM: Nominal Annual Interest Rates on Loans for Other Purposes

	1971 01/01	1979 01/01	1980 01/01	1980 04/01	1981 01/01	1982 01/01	1983 01/01	1984 01/01	1985 04/01	1985 08/01	1986 09/21	1987 01/01	1988 09/01	1989 02/01	1990 04/15	1990 08/21	1991 04/21
GRANTS INTO LOANS (Since 01/01/85)																	
Electronics, textiles, light industries, petrochemical, oil processing					3.60	3.60	3.60	3.60	4.20	4.20	4.20	4.20	4.20	4.20	4.20	4.20	4.20
Steel, machinery, chemical, automotive, power, oil exploration					3.00	3.00	3.00	3.00	3.60	3.60	3.60	3.60	3.60	3.60	3.60	3.60	3.60
Agriculture, forestry, energy conservation, farming, water conservation, animal husbandry, acquatic production, meterology, defense, coal, building material, telecommunications, food grain					2.40	2.40	2.40	2.40	2.40	2.40	2.40	2.40	2.40	2.40	2.40	2.40	2.40
Surplus products & energy intensive projects								12.00	12.00	12.00	12.00	12.00	12.00	12.00	12.00	12.00	12.00
Other					3.00	3.00	3.00	3.00	3.00	3.00	3.00	3.00	3.00	3.00	3.00	3.00	3.00
SPECIAL LOANS								12%-14%	12%-14%	12%-14%	10.8%-14.4%		10.8%-14.4%	10.8%-14.4%		10.8%-14.4%	
INTERBANK LOANS		(Negotiate)															
INTEREST PENALTIES																	
Overdue loans				+20%	+20%	+20%	+20%	+20%	+20%	+20%	+20%	+20%	+20%	+20%	+20%	+20%	+20%
Loans above working capital limits				+30%	+30%	+30%	+30%	+30%	+30%	+30%	+30%	+30%	+30%	+30%	+30%	+30%	+30%
Surplus & problem products				+30%	+30%	+30%	+30%	+30%	+30%	+30%	+30%	+30%	+30%	+30%	+30%	+30%	+30%
Loans used for unauthorized purposes				+50%	+50%	+50%	+50%	+50%	+50%	+50%	+50%	+50%	+50%	+50%	+50%	+50%	+50%

238

REF: MONEY3.WK1 06/23/92
Source: Peoples Bank of China

Table 7.1: CHINA: Structure of Consolidated Government Revenue, 1978-91 /a
(Billion Yuan)

	1978	1979	1980	1981	1982	1983	1984	1985	1986	1987	1988	1989	1990	1991
Tax Revenue /b /c	120.6	122.7	128.1	135.4	136.8	153.5	175.5	218.8	224.8	232.1	257.6	301.7	313.9	336.8
Taxes on income and profits /d	74.0	73.7	75.6	77.1	72.1	75.1	80.6	69.7	68.9	66.5	69.6	68.8	73.5	68.6
Enterprises income tax	74.0	73.4	75.4	76.7	71.6	72.6	78.0	69.7	68.9	66.5	69.6	68.8	73.5	68.6
Collectives /e	5.4	4.5	4.5	4.4	4.8	6.0	6.2	10.1	9.3	10.2	10.5	10.5	13.1	11.3
State enterprises /f	68.6	68.9	70.9	72.3	66.8	66.6	71.8	59.6	59.6	56.3	59.1	58.3	60.4	57.3
Other	0.0	0.3	0.2	0.4	0.5	2.5	2.6	..	..	..	..	..	..	..
Taxes on goods and services	43.7	46.4	49.1	52.8	58.6	60.2	71.4	100.5	111.2	117.1	136.0	155.3	160.5	176.3
General sales taxes /g	39.5	42.5	45.4	49.1	54.7	55.9	66.9	95.3	104.0	109.5	126.3	144.8	149.7	169.1
Product tax	..	..	..	..	..	..	..	59.4	54.7	53.9	48.1	53.0	58.1	61.7
VAT	..	..	..	..	..	..	..	14.8	23.2	25.4	38.4	43.1	40.0	43.7
Business tax	..	..	..	..	..	..	..	21.1	26.1	30.2	39.8	48.7	51.6	63.7
Special Tax on Oil	..	..	..	..	..	..	..	..	1.6	0.2	1.4	1.2	1.1	0.0
Salt Tax	1.1	1.0	0.9	0.9	1.0	1.0	1.0	1.0	1.1	0.9	0.9	1.0	0.9	0.9
Agricultural tax	3.1	2.9	2.8	2.8	2.9	3.3	3.5	4.2	4.5	5.2	7.4	8.3	8.8	6.3
Taxes on international trade /h	2.9	2.6	3.4	5.4	4.7	5.4	10.3	20.5	15.2	14.2	15.5	17.9	15.9	18.0
Other taxes	0.0	0.0	0.0	0.1	1.4	12.8	13.2	28.1	29.5	34.3	36.5	59.7	64.0	73.9
of which:														
Tax on extrabudgetary receipts	0.0	0.0	0.0	0.0	0.0	9.3	12.2	14.7	15.7	18.0	18.6	20.2	18.5	20.5
Tax on extrabudgetary construction	0.0	0.0	0.0	0.0	0.0	0.2	1.0	2.3	2.4	3.0	2.6	2.8	3.8	3.9
Nontax revenue	2.7	3.6	3.5	3.2	4.4	5.9	8.0	9.5	19.8	25.5	22.8	24.7	37.9	28.0
Gross profit remittances from SOE /j	0.0	0.0	0.0	0.0	0.0	0.0	0.0	4.4	4.2	4.3	5.1	6.4	7.8	7.6
Depreciation funds	2.4	2.5	2.7	2.6	2.6	2.7	2.7	..	..	..	..	..	..	..
Other	0.3	1.1	0.8	0.6	1.8	3.2	5.3	5.1	15.6	21.2	17.7	18.3	30.1	20.4
Total revenue /i	123.3	126.3	131.6	138.6	141.2	159.4	183.5	228.3	244.6	257.6	280.4	326.4	351.8	364.8
Memorandum item:														
Gross profit remittances from SOE	68.6	68.9	70.9	72.3	66.8	66.6	68.7	4.4	4.2	4.3	5.1	6.4	7.8	

REF: FISCAL.WK1 06/23/92
Source: Ministry of Finance and The World Bank/IMF.

/a This includes all government revenue, with the exception of extrabudgetary receipts of the various levels of government.
/b Proceeds of the profit tax on state enterprises introduced in 1983 are classified under profit remittances, as the breakdown of enterprise payments in 1983-4 between profit tax and profit transfers is not available. Beginning with 1985, profit taxes on state enterprises are included under tax revenue.
/c Chinese definition of tax revenues plus energy and communications tax.
/d for 1987: Residual: 231.0 less all identifiable items below.
/e Until 1985, the industrial and commercial income tax levied on collective enterprises. Beginning in 1986, official data no longer separately identify income tax on collectives.
/f The profit tax and adjustment tax on state enterprises, gross profit remittances from state enterprises until 1984.
/g The consolidated industrial and commercial tax.
/h for 1982: Includes 2.9 billion yuan from the tax on crude oil consumption introduced in 1982.
/i According to the definition contained in IMF, Manual on Government Finance Statistics (GFS), 1986.
/j Until 1984, included in income tax on state enterprises, as of 1988, only banks and financial institutions are subject to remittance.

Table 7.2: CHINA: Structure of Consolidated Government Revenue, 1978-91
(as a % of Total Revenue)

	1978	1979	1980	1981	1982	1983	1984	1985	1986	1987	1988	1989	1990	1991
Tax Revenue	42.2	42.6	43.5	45.5	49.6	54.5	58.2	95.8	91.9	90.1	91.9	92.4	89.2	94.4
Taxes on income and profits	6.9	6.1	5.7	5.5	5.8	7.4	8.4	32.4	30.0	27.8	27.5	23.6	23.4	22.6
Profit tax	4.4	3.6	3.4	3.2	3.4	3.8	5.1	30.5	28.2	25.8	24.8	21.1	20.9	20.9
Agricultural tax	2.5	2.3	2.1	2.0	2.1	2.1	1.9	1.8	1.8	2.0	2.6	2.5	2.5	1.7
Other	0.0	0.2	0.2	0.3	0.4	1.6	1.4	0.0	0.0	0.0	0.0	0.0	0.0	0.0
Taxes on goods and services	32.9	34.4	35.2	36.1	39.4	35.7	37.0	42.2	43.6	43.4	45.9	45.0	43.1	46.6
Product tax	0.0	0.0	0.0	0.0	0.0	0.0	0.0	26.0	22.4	20.9	17.2	16.2	16.5	16.9
VAT	0.0	0.0	0.0	0.0	0.0	0.0	0.0	6.5	9.5	9.9	13.7	13.2	11.4	12.0
Business tax	0.0	0.0	0.0	0.0	0.0	0.0	0.0	9.2	10.7	11.7	14.2	14.9	14.7	17.5
Taxes on international trade	2.4	2.1	2.6	3.9	3.3	3.4	5.6	9.0	6.2	5.5	5.5	5.5	4.5	4.9
Other taxes	0.0	0.0	0.0	0.1	1.0	8.0	7.2	12.3	12.1	13.3	13.0	18.3	18.2	20.3
Nontax revenue	57.8	57.4	56.5	54.5	50.4	45.5	41.8	4.2	8.1	9.9	8.1	7.6	10.8	5.6
of which: Profit remittances	55.6	54.6	53.9	52.2	47.3	41.8	37.4	1.9	1.7	1.7	1.8	2.0	2.2	0.0
Memorandum items:														
Revenue from enterprises	60.0	58.1	57.3	55.3	50.7	45.5	42.5	32.5	29.9	27.5	26.6	23.0	23.1	20.9
Profit tax	4.4	3.6	3.4	3.2	3.4	3.8	5.1	30.5	28.2	25.8	24.8	21.1	20.9	20.9
Profit remittances	55.6	54.6	53.9	52.2	47.3	41.8	37.4	1.9	1.7	1.7	1.8	2.0	2.2	0.0
Extrabudgetary receipts	0.0	0.0	0.0	0.0	0.0	1.0	1.0	0.9	0.8	0.7	0.5	0.4	0.4	0.3
Total Revenue	100.0	100.0	100.0	100.0	100.0	100.0	100.0	100.0	100.0	100.0	100.0	100.0	100.0	100.0

REF: FISCAL.WK1 06/23/92
Source: Ministry of Finance and The World Bank/IMF.

Table 7.3: CHINA: Developments in Government Revenue 1978-91
(as a % of GNP)

	1978	1979	1980	1981	1982	1983	1984	1985	1986	1987	1988	1989	1990	1991
Total Revenue	34.4	31.6	29.4	29.0	27.2	27.4	26.4	26.7	25.2	22.8	20.0	20.5	19.9	18.6
Taxes on income and profits	2.4	1.9	1.7	1.6	1.6	2.0	2.2	8.6	7.6	6.3	5.5	4.8	4.7	4.2
Profit tax	1.5	1.1	1.0	0.9	0.9	1.0	1.3	8.1	7.1	5.9	5.0	4.3	4.2	3.9
Agricultural tax	0.9	0.7	0.6	0.6	0.6	0.6	0.5	0.5	0.5	0.5	0.5	0.5	0.5	0.3
Other	0.0	0.1	0.0	0.1	0.1	0.4	0.4	0.0	0.0	0.0	0.0	0.0	0.0	0.0
Taxes on goods and services	11.3	10.9	10.4	10.5	10.7	9.8	9.8	11.3	11.0	9.9	9.2	9.2	8.6	8.7
Product tax	0.0	0.0	0.0	0.0	0.0	0.0	0.0	6.9	5.6	4.8	3.4	3.3	3.3	3.2
VAT	0.0	0.0	0.0	0.0	0.0	0.0	0.0	1.7	2.4	2.2	2.7	2.7	2.3	2.2
Business tax	0.0	0.0	0.0	0.0	0.0	0.0	0.0	2.5	2.7	2.7	2.8	3.1	2.9	3.3
Taxes on international trade	0.8	0.7	0.8	1.1	0.9	0.9	1.5	2.4	1.6	1.3	1.1	1.1	0.9	0.9
Other taxes	0.0	0.0	0.0	0.0	0.3	2.2	1.9	3.3	3.0	3.0	2.6	3.8	3.6	3.8
Nontax revenue	19.9	18.1	16.6	15.8	13.7	12.5	11.0	1.1	2.0	2.3	1.6	1.6	2.1	1.0
of which: Profit remittances	19.1	17.2	15.9	15.1	12.9	11.5	9.9	0.5	0.4	0.4	0.4	0.4	0.4	0.0
Memorandum items:														
Revenue from enterprises	20.6	18.4	16.9	16.1	13.8	12.5	11.2	8.7	7.5	6.3	5.3	4.7	4.6	3.9
Profit tax	1.5	1.1	1.0	0.9	0.9	1.0	1.3	8.1	7.1	5.9	5.0	4.3	4.2	3.9
Profit remittances	19.1	17.2	15.9	15.1	12.9	11.5	9.9	0.5	0.4	0.4	0.4	0.4	0.4	0.0
Extrabudgetary receipts	0.0	0.0	0.0	0.0	0.0	0.3	0.3	0.2	0.2	0.2	0.1	0.1	0.1	0.1

REF: FISCAL.WK1 06/23/92
Source: Ministry of Finance and The World Bank/IMF.

Table 7.4: CHINA: Structure of Government Expenditure, 1978-91
(Billion Yuan)

	1978	1979	1980	1981	1982	1983	1984	1985	1986	1987	1988	1989	1990	1991
Total Expenditure and net lending /a	122.5	146.9	146.4	144.4	148.3	169.0	193.9	232.4	263.2	282.4	313.7	364.3	388.5	413.3
Current expenditure	69.2	86.2	99.1	107.1	113.2	126.4	138.1	168.1	188.0	206.8	237.6	288.7	306.9	330.2
Administration	4.9	5.7	6.7	7.1	8.2	10.1	13.7	14.4	18.2	19.5	23.9	28.5	33.3	34.8
Defense	16.8	22.3	19.5	16.8	17.6	17.7	18.1	19.2	20.1	21.0	21.8	25.1	29.0	33.0
Culture, education, public health science, and broadcasting	11.3	13.2	15.7	17.0	19.7	22.3	26.3	31.7	38.0	40.3	48.6	55.1	61.7	69.9
of which: Education	..	..	..	..	..	..	14.8	18.4	21.4	22.7	27.9	31.6	35.3	40.6
Economic services	17.9	18.7	19.2	16.8	17.6	18.8	20.4	22.4	25.2	26.0	28.9	34.6	37.9	42.0
Geological survey	..	..	..	..	..	..	2.6	3.0	3.1	3.0	3.3	3.3	3.6	4.0
Agriculture	..	..	..	..	..	..	9.6	10.1	12.4	13.4	15.4	19.7	22.2	24.3
Operating expenditure for industry, communication and commerce	..	..	..	..	..	..	3.0	3.5	3.7	3.3	3.9	4.5	4.7	4.9
Development of new products	..	..	..	..	..	..	4.2	4.4	5.0	5.1	5.3	5.9	6.3	7.9
Working capital for SOE	..	..	..	..	..	..	1.0	1.4	1.0	1.2	1.0	1.2	1.1	1.0
Social welfare relief	..	..	..	..	..	..	..	..	3.6	3.9	4.1	5.0	5.5	6.0
Subsidies	11.4	19.5	27.4	36.8	37.2	42.6	41.0	50.7	58.2	67.0	76.3	97.3	96.0	87.7
Daily living necessities /b	7.8	16.0	24.0	30.5	30.0	30.9	31.5	31.4	25.7	29.5	31.7	37.4	38.1	37.1
Agricultural inputs	0.0	0.0	0.0	2.2	2.1	1.4	1.0	1.3	..	..	..	..	..	..
Operating losses of SOE	3.6	3.5	3.4	4.2	5.2	10.3	8.5	18.0	32.5	37.5	44.6	59.9	57.9	50.6
Interest payments	..	..	..	..	..	..	..	..	1.9	2.8	3.0	3.3	4.4	8.0
Other	6.9	6.8	10.7	12.6	12.8	15.0	18.6	29.7	22.8	26.3	31.0	39.6	39.1	48.8
Capital expenditure	53.3	60.7	47.3	37.3	35.1	42.6	55.8	64.3	75.2	75.6	76.1	75.6	81.6	83.1
Capital construction	..	..	..	..	..	..	48.9	58.4	67.2	68.2	66.4	66.9	72.6	72.6
Development of the productive capacity of existing enterprises	..	..	..	..	..	..	6.9	5.9	8.0	7.4	9.7	8.7	9.0	10.5
Memorandum Items:														
(as percent of GNP)														
Current expenditure	19.3	21.6	22.2	22.4	21.8	21.8	19.8	19.6	19.4	18.3	16.9	18.1	17.4	16.9
Subsidies	3.2	4.9	6.1	7.7	7.2	7.3	5.9	5.9	6.0	5.9	5.4	6.1	5.4	4.5
Daily living necessities	2.2	4.0	5.4	6.4	5.8	5.3	4.5	3.7	2.7	2.6	2.3	2.3	2.2	1.9
Operating losses of SOE	1.0	0.9	0.8	0.9	1.0	1.8	1.2	2.1	3.4	3.3	3.2	3.8	3.3	2.6
Capital expenditure	14.9	15.2	10.6	7.8	6.8	7.3	8.0	7.5	7.8	6.7	5.4	4.7	4.6	4.2
(as percentage of total expenditure)														
Subsidies	9.3	13.3	18.7	25.5	25.1	25.2	21.1	21.8	22.1	23.7	24.3	26.7	24.7	21.2
Capital expenditure	43.5	41.3	32.3	25.8	23.7	25.2	28.8	27.7	28.6	26.8	24.3	20.8	21.0	20.1

REF: FISCAL.WK1 06/23/92
Source: Ministry of Finance and The World Bank/IMF.

Table 7.5: CHINA: Structure of Government Expenditure, 1978-91
(as a % of Total Expenditure)

	1978	1979	1980	1981	1982	1983	1984	1985	1986	1987	1988	1989	1990	1991
Total Expenditure and net lending	100.0	100.0	100.0	100.0	100.0	100.0	100.0	100.0	98.6	98.6	98.7	98.6	98.6	98.5
Current expenditure	56.5	58.7	67.7	74.2	76.3	74.8	71.2	72.3	70.1	71.8	74.4	77.9	77.6	78.4
Administrative	4.0	3.9	4.6	4.9	5.5	6.0	7.1	6.2	6.9	6.9	7.6	7.8	8.6	8.4
Defense	13.7	15.2	13.3	11.6	11.9	10.5	9.3	8.3	7.6	7.4	6.9	6.9	7.5	8.0
Culture, education , public health	9.2	9.0	10.7	11.8	13.3	13.2	13.6	13.6	14.4	14.3	15.5	15.2	15.9	16.9
Economic services	14.6	12.7	13.1	11.6	11.9	11.1	10.5	9.6	9.6	9.2	9.2	9.5	9.8	10.2
Subsidies	9.3	13.3	18.7	25.5	25.1	25.2	21.1	21.8	22.1	23.7	24.3	26.7	24.7	21.2
Daily necessities	6.4	10.9	16.4	21.1	20.2	18.3	16.2	13.5	9.8	10.4	10.1	10.3	9.8	9.0
Agricultural inputs	0.0	0.0	0.0	1.5	1.4	0.8	0.5	0.6	0.0	0.0	0.0	0.0	0.0	0.0
Enterprise losses	2.9	2.4	2.3	2.9	3.5	6.1	4.4	7.7	12.3	13.3	14.2	16.4	14.9	12.2
Other	5.6	4.6	7.3	8.7	8.6	8.9	9.6	12.8	9.4	10.3	10.8	11.8	11.2	13.7
Developmental expenditure	43.5	41.3	32.3	25.8	23.7	25.2	28.8	27.7	28.6	26.8	24.3	20.8	21.0	20.1

REF: FISCAL.WK1 06/23/92
Source: Ministry of Finance and The World Bank/IMF.

Table 7.6: CHINA: Developments in Government Expenditure, 1978-91
(as a % of GNP)

	1978	1979	1980	1981	1982	1983	1984	1985	1986	1987	1988	1989	1990	1991
Total Expenditure and net lending	34.1	36.7	32.8	30.2	28.6	29.1	27.9	27.2	27.1	25.0	22.4	22.9	22.0	21.1
Current expenditure	19.3	21.6	22.2	22.4	21.8	21.8	19.8	19.6	19.4	18.3	16.9	18.1	17.4	16.9
Administrative	1.4	1.4	1.5	1.5	1.6	1.7	2.0	1.7	1.9	1.7	1.7	1.8	1.9	1.8
Defense	4.7	5.6	4.4	3.5	3.4	3.1	2.6	2.2	2.1	1.9	1.6	1.6	1.6	1.7
Culture, education, public health	3.1	3.3	3.5	3.6	3.8	3.8	3.8	3.7	3.9	3.6	3.5	3.5	3.5	3.6
Economic services	5.0	4.7	4.3	3.5	3.4	3.2	2.9	2.6	2.6	2.3	2.1	2.2	2.1	2.1
Subsidies	3.2	4.9	6.1	7.7	7.2	7.3	5.9	5.9	6.0	5.9	5.4	6.1	5.4	4.5
Daily necessities	2.2	4.0	5.4	6.4	5.8	5.3	4.5	3.7	2.7	2.6	2.3	2.3	2.2	1.9
Agricultural inputs	0.0	0.0	0.0	0.5	0.4	0.2	0.1	0.2	0.0	0.0	0.0	0.0	0.0	0.0
Enterprise losses	1.0	0.9	0.8	0.9	1.0	1.8	1.2	2.1	3.4	3.3	3.2	3.8	3.3	2.6
Other	1.9	1.7	2.4	2.6	2.5	2.6	2.7	3.5	2.5	2.6	2.4	2.7	2.5	2.9
Developmental expenditure	14.9	15.2	10.6	7.8	6.8	7.3	8.0	7.5	7.8	6.7	5.4	4.7	4.6	4.2

REF: FISCAL.WK1 06/23/92
Source: Ministry of Finance and The World Bank/IMF.

Table 7.7: CHINA: Budget and Its Financing 1978-91

	1978	1979	1980	1981	1982	1983	1984	1985	1986	1987	1988	1989	1990	1991
(Billion Yuan)														
Revenue	123.3	126.3	131.6	138.6	141.2	159.4	183.5	228.3	244.6	257.6	280.4	326.4	351.8	364.8
Expenditure	122.4	146.9	146.4	144.3	148.3	169.2	193.9	232.3	263.2	282.4	313.7	364.3	388.5	413.3
Deficit	0.9	-20.6	-14.8	-5.7	-7.1	-9.8	-10.4	-4.1	-18.6	-24.8	-33.3	-37.9	-36.7	-48.5
Financing	-0.9	20.6	14.8	5.7	7.1	9.8	10.4	4.1	18.1	24.6	33.5	37.4	36.8	31.0
Domestic	-1.2	17.0	12.6	2.5	7.3	8.7	8.6	4.0	12.8	17.8	22.0	26.1	23.7	20.3
PBC	-1.2	17.0	12.6	-2.2	2.9	4.4	4.5	-2.1	12.7	8.4	11.5	-7.5	17.4	12.3
Nonbank	0.0	0.0	0.0	4.8	4.4	4.3	4.2	6.1	0.1	9.4	10.5	33.6	6.3	8.0
Foreign	0.2	3.6	2.2	3.1	-0.2	1.1	1.8	0.1	5.3	6.8	11.5	11.3	13.1	10.7
Gross foreign borrowing	..	..	..	..	..	..	..	..	7.6	10.6	13.9	14.4	17.8	16.2
Amortization	..	..	..	..	..	..	..	..	-2.3	-3.8	-2.4	-3.1	-4.7	-5.5
(as a % of GNP)														
Revenue	34.4	31.6	29.4	29.0	27.2	27.4	26.4	26.7	25.2	22.8	20.0	20.5	19.9	18.6
Expenditure	34.1	36.7	32.8	30.2	28.6	29.1	27.9	27.2	27.1	25.0	22.4	22.9	22.0	21.1
Deficit	0.3	-5.2	-3.3	-1.2	-1.4	-1.7	-1.5	-0.5	-1.9	-2.2	-2.4	-2.4	-2.1	-2.5
Financing	-0.3	5.2	3.3	1.2	1.4	1.7	1.5	0.5	1.9	2.2	2.4	2.3	2.1	1.6
Domestic	-0.3	4.3	2.8	0.5	1.4	1.5	1.2	0.5	1.3	1.6	1.6	1.6	1.3	1.0
PBC	-0.3	4.3	2.8	-0.5	0.6	0.8	0.6	-0.2	1.3	0.7	0.8	-0.5	1.0	0.6
Nonbank	0.0	0.0	0.0	1.0	0.8	0.7	0.6	-0.7	0.0	0.8	0.7	2.1	0.4	0.4
Foreign	0.1	0.9	0.5	0.7	-0.0	0.2	0.3	0.0	0.5	0.6	0.8	0.7	0.7	0.5
Gross foreign borrowing	..	..	..	..	..	..	..	..	0.8	0.9	1.0	0.9	1.0	0.8
Amortization	..	..	..	..	..	..	..	..	-0.2	-0.3	-0.2	-0.2	-0.3	-0.3
(as a % of Total Deficit)														
Financing	100.0	100.0	100.0	100.0	100.0	100.0	100.0	100.0	97.3	99.2	100.6	98.7	100.3	63.9
Domestic	125.0	82.5	84.9	44.8	102.8	88.6	82.9	97.6	68.8	71.8	66.1	68.9	64.6	41.9
PBC	125.0	82.5	84.9	-39.7	40.8	44.8	42.9	-51.2	68.5	33.9	34.5	-19.8	47.4	25.4
Nonbank	0.0	0.0	0.0	84.5	62.0	43.8	40.0	148.8	0.5	37.9	31.5	88.7	17.2	16.5
Foreign	-25.0	17.5	15.1	55.2	-2.8	11.4	17.1	2.4	28.5	27.4	34.5	29.8	35.7	22.1
Gross foreign borrowing	..	..	..	..	..	..	..	..	40.9	42.7	41.7	38.0	48.5	33.4
Amortization	..	..	..	..	..	..	..	..	-12.4	-15.3	-7.2	-8.2	-12.8	-11.3

REF: FISCAL.WK1 06/23/92
Source: Ministry of Finance and The World Bank/IMF.

Table 8.1 : CHINA : Production of Major Crops
(Million Tons)

	1978	1979	1980	1981	1982	1983	1984	1985	1986	1987	1988	1989	1990	1991
Total Food Grains	304.8	332.1	320.6	325.0	354.5	387.3	407.3	379.1	391.5	403.0	394.1	407.5	446.2	435.3
Rice	136.9	143.8	139.9	144.0	161.6	168.9	178.3	168.6	172.2	174.3	169.1	180.1	189.3	183.8
Wheat	53.8	62.7	55.2	69.6	68.5	81.4	87.8	85.8	90.0	85.9	85.4	90.8	98.2	96.0
Corn	56.0	60.0	62.6	59.2	60.6	68.2	73.4	63.9	70.9	79.2	77.4	78.9	96.8	98.8
Soybeans	7.6	7.5	7.9	9.3	9.0	9.8	9.7	10.5	11.6	12.5	11.7	10.2	11.0	9.7
Tuber	31.7	28.5	28.7	26.0	27.1	29.3	28.5	26.0	25.3	28.2	27.0	27.3	27.4	27.2
Total Oil Seeds	5.2	6.4	7.7	10.2	11.8	10.6	11.9	15.8	14.7	15.3	13.2	12.9	16.1	16.4
Peanuts	2.4	2.8	3.6	3.8	3.9	4.0	4.8	6.7	5.9	6.2	5.7	5.4	6.4	6.3
Rapeseed	1.9	2.4	2.4	4.1	5.7	4.3	4.2	5.6	5.9	6.6	5.0	5.4	7.0	7.4
Cotton	2.2	2.2	2.7	3.0	3.6	4.6	6.3	4.1	3.5	4.2	4.1	3.8	4.5	5.7
Sugarcane	21.1	21.5	22.8	29.7	36.9	31.1	39.5	51.5	50.2	47.4	49.1	48.6	57.6	67.9
Beetroots	2.7	3.1	6.3	6.4	6.7	9.2	8.3	8.9	8.3	8.1	12.8	9.4	14.5	16.3
Cured Tobacco	1.1	0.8	0.7	1.3	1.8	1.2	1.5	2.1	1.4	1.6	2.3	2.4	2.3	2.7
Fruits	6.6	7.0	6.8	7.8	7.7	9.5	9.8	11.6	13.5	16.7	16.7	18.4	18.7	21.8
Apples	2.3	2.9	2.4	3.0	2.4	3.5	2.9	3.6	3.3	4.3	4.3	4.5	4.3	4.5
Citrus	0.4	0.6	0.7	0.8	0.9	1.3	1.5	1.8	2.5	3.2	2.6	4.6	4.9	6.3
Pears	1.5	1.4	1.5	1.6	1.8	1.8	2.1	2.1	2.3	2.5	2.7	2.6	2.4	2.5
Bananas	0.1	0.1	0.1	0.1	0.2	0.2	0.3	0.6	1.3	2.0	1.8	1.4	1.5	2.0

REF: AGR.WK1 06/23/92
Source: Statistical Abstract 1992 (in Chinese) pp.58-60 for 1991; Yearbook 1991 pp.315-7.

- 247 -

Table 8.2 : CHINA : Production of Major Crops
(Percentage GROWTH RATES)

	1978	1979	1980	1981	1982	1983	1984	1985	1986	1987	1988	1989	1990	1991
Total Food Grains	..	9.0	-3.5	1.4	9.1	9.2	5.2	-6.9	3.3	2.9	-2.2	3.4	9.5	-2.5
Rice	..	5.0	-2.7	2.9	12.3	4.5	5.6	-5.4	2.2	1.2	-3.0	6.5	5.1	-2.9
Wheat	..	16.5	-12.0	26.1	-1.7	18.9	7.9	-2.3	4.9	-4.6	-0.5	6.3	8.2	-2.3
Corn	..	7.3	4.3	-5.4	2.3	12.6	7.6	-13.0	10.9	11.8	-2.4	2.0	22.7	2.0
Soybeans	..	-1.5	6.4	17.5	-3.2	8.1	-0.6	8.2	10.6	7.4	-6.6	-12.2	7.5	-11.7
Tuber	..	-10.3	0.9	-9.6	4.2	8.1	-2.6	-8.6	-2.7	11.3	-4.4	1.2	0.5	-1.0
Total Oil Seeds	..	23.3	19.5	32.7	15.8	-10.7	12.9	32.5	-6.6	3.7	-13.6	-2.2	25.0	1.6
Peanuts	..	18.7	27.6	6.3	2.4	0.9	21.9	38.4	-11.7	4.9	-7.7	-5.8	18.7	-1.0
Rapeseed	..	28.6	-0.7	70.5	39.1	-24.2	-1.9	33.3	4.9	12.3	-23.6	7.9	27.9	6.9
Cotton	..	1.8	22.7	9.6	21.2	28.9	35.0	-33.7	-14.6	19.9	-2.3	-8.7	18.9	25.9
Sugarcane	..	1.9	6.0	30.1	24.3	-15.6	26.9	30.4	-2.6	-5.7	3.6	-1.0	18.6	17.8
Beetroots	..	15.0	103.0	0.9	5.5	36.8	-9.8	7.7	-6.9	-2.0	57.4	-26.9	55.2	12.1
Cured Tobacco	..	-23.4	-11.0	78.4	44.5	-37.7	34.1	34.5	-33.8	19.1	42.8	3.1	-6.3	18.2
Fruits	..	6.8	-3.2	14.8	-1.1	23.0	3.8	18.2	15.8	23.8	-0.1	10.3	2.0	16.1
Apples	..	26.1	-17.6	27.2	-19.2	45.7	-16.9	22.9	-7.7	27.8	1.9	3.6	-4.0	5.1
Citrus	..	44.9	28.5	11.9	17.7	38.0	15.7	20.6	40.9	26.5	-20.6	78.2	6.4	30.4
Pears	..	-5.2	1.9	8.7	10.2	2.3	17.0	1.8	9.9	6.0	9.3	-5.7	-8.3	6.2
Bananas	..	-12.9	-17.6	106.6	59.5	3.0	44.9	110.3	98.3	62.2	-9.8	-23.3	3.7	36.1

REF: AGR.WK1 06/23/92
Source: Table 8.1.

Table 8.3 : CHINA : Total Sown Area
(Million Hectares)

	1978	1979	1980	1981	1982	1983	1984	1985	1986	1987	1988	1989	1990	1991
Total Food Grains	121	119	117	115	114	114	113	109	111	111	110	112	114	112
Rice	34	34	34	33	33	33	33	32	32	32	32	33	33	33
Wheat	29	29	29	28	28	29	30	29	30	29	29	30	31	31
Corn	20	20	20	19	19	19	19	18	19	20	20	20	21	22
Soybeans	7	7	7	8	8	8	7	8	8	8	8	8	8	7
Tuber	12	11	10	10	9	9	9	9	9	9	9	9	9	9
Peanuts	2	2	2	2	2	2	2	3	3	3	3	3	3	3
Rapeseed	3	3	3	4	4	4	3	4	5	5	5	5	6	6
Cotton	5	5	5	5	6	6	7	5	4	5	6	5	6	7
Sugarcane	1	1	0	1	0	1	1	1	1	1	1	1	1	1
Beetroots	0	0	0	0	0	1	1	1	1	0	1	1	1	1
Cured Tobacco	1	1	0	1	0	1	1	1	1	1	1	2	1	2
Fruits	..	..	..	..	..	..	..	3	4	5	5	5	..	..
Apples	..	..	..	..	..	..	..	1	1	1	2	2	..	..
Citrus	..	..	..	..	..	..	..	1	5	5	1	1	..	..
Pears	..	..	..	..	..	..	..	0	0	0	0	0	..	..
Bananas	..	..	..	..	..	..	..	0	0	0	0	0	..	..
Total Sown Area	150	149	146	145	145	144	144	144	144	145	145	147	148	150
Total Irrigated Area	..	45	45	45	44	45	44	44	44	44	44	45	47	48

Percentage to Total Sown Area

	1978	1979	1980	1981	1982	1983	1984	1985	1986	1987	1988	1989	1990	1991
Grain Crops	80.3	80.3	80.1	79.2	78.4	79.2	79.3	75.8	76.9	76.8	76.0	76.6	76.5	75.1
Total Industrial Crops	9.6	10.0	10.9	12.1	13.0	12.3	13.4	15.6	14.1	14.3	14.8	14.3	14.4	15.7

REF: AGR.WK1 06/23/92
Source: Statistical Abstract 1992 (in Chinese) pp.57-9, 65 for 1991; Yearbook 1990 pp.342-3, 348, 333; 1988 pp.197, 206, 211.
(converted into hectares with 1 mu=0.0667 ha).

Table 8.4 : CHINA : Total Sown Area
(Percentage GROWTH RATES)

	1978	1979	1980	1981	1982	1983	1984	1985	1986	1987	1988	1989	1990	1991
Total Food Grains	..	-1.1	-1.7	-1.9	-1.3	0.5	-1.0	-3.6	1.9	0.3	-1.0	1.9	1.1	-1.0
Rice	..	-1.6	0.0	-1.7	-0.7	0.2	0.1	-3.3	0.6	-0.2	-0.6	2.2	1.1	-1.4
Wheat	..	0.6	-0.4	-3.2	-1.2	3.9	1.8	-1.2	1.4	-2.8	-0.0	3.7	3.1	0.6
Corn	..	0.9	1.1	-4.6	-4.5	1.5	-1.5	-4.5	8.1	5.7	-2.6	3.4	5.1	0.8
Soybeans	..	1.4	-0.3	11.0	4.9	-10.1	-3.7	5.9	7.5	1.8	-3.8	-0.8	-6.2	-6.9
Tuber	..	-7.2	-7.3	-5.2	-2.6	0.3	-4.4	-4.6	1.3	2.1	2.1	0.5	0.3	-0.5
Peanuts	..	17.3	12.8	5.7	-2.3	-8.9	10.0	37.1	-2.0	-7.1	-1.5	-1.0	-1.3	-0.9
Rapeseed	..	7.0	3.0	33.6	8.5	-11.0	-7.0	31.7	9.4	7.1	-6.3	1.1	10.2	11.4
Cotton	..	-7.3	9.0	5.4	12.4	4.3	13.9	-25.7	-16.2	12.5	14.3	-6.0	7.4	17.0
Sugarcane	..	-6.7	-6.4	15.0	18.5	0.1	11.3	32.5	-1.5	-9.6	7.6	3.8	5.1	15.4
Beetroots	..	-1.6	36.1	-1.5	6.0	17.7	-7.7	11.7	-7.1	-4.4	49.5	-23.5	17.7	16.9
Cured Tobacco	..	-17.0	-22.0	47.9	51.5	-35.6	25.1	50.6	-17.0	2.1	42.8	15.3	-10.7	16.4
Fruits	..	..	..	..	..	..	..	..	34.2	22.8	12.4	6.0	..	..
Apples	..	..	..	..	..	..	..	..	35.6	22.8	15.2	1.8	..	..
Citrus	..	..	..	..	..	..	..	..	32.6	28.5	10.6	7.4	..	..
Pears	..	..	..	..	..	..	..	..	16.7	11.9	10.4	-1.1	..	..
Bananas	..	..	..	..	..	..	..	..	51.3	113.2	-7.1	-21.9	..	..
Total Sown Area	..	-1.1	-1.4	-0.8	-0.3	-0.5	0.2	-0.4	0.4	0.5	-0.1	1.2	1.2	0.8
Total Irrigated Area	..	..	-0.3	-0.7	-0.9	1.1	-0.4	-0.9	0.4	0.4	-0.1	1.2	5.5	0.9

GROWTH RATE OF Percentage to Total Sown Area

	1978	1979	1980	1981	1982	1983	1984	1985	1986	1987	1988	1989	1990	1991
Grain Crops	..	0.0	-0.2	-1.1	-1.0	1.0	0.1	-4.4	1.5	-0.1	-1.0	0.8	-0.1	-1.8
Total Industrial Crops	..	4.2	9.0	11.0	7.4	-5.4	8.9	16.4	-9.6	1.4	3.5	-3.4	0.7	9.0

REF: AGR.WK1 06/23/92
Source: Table 8.3.

Table 8.5 : CHINA : Average Unit Area Yield of Major Crops
(At sown area   kg/hectare)

	1978	1979	1980	1981	1982	1983	1984	1985	1986	1987	1988	1989	1990	1991
Total Food Grains	2535	2835	2745	2835	3135	3405	3615	3480	3525	3615	3585	3630	3930	..
Rice	3975	4245	4140	4320	4890	5100	5370	5250	5340	5415	5280	5505	5730	..
Wheat	1845	2145	1890	2115	2445	2805	2970	2940	3045	2985	2970	3045	3195	..
Corn	2805	2985	3075	3045	3270	3630	3960	3600	3705	3915	3930	3885	4530	..
Soybeans	1065	1035	1095	1170	1080	1290	1335	1365	1395	1470	1440	1275	1455	..
Tuber	2700	2595	2835	2700	2895	3120	3165	3030	2910	3180	2985	3000	3015	..
Peanuts	1350	1365	1545	1545	1620	1800	1800	2010	1815	2040	1905	1815	2190	..
Rapeseed	720	870	840	1080	1380	1170	1230	1245	1200	1260	1020	1095	1260	..
Cotton	450	495	555	570	615	765	915	810	825	870	750	735	810	..
Sugarcane	38505	42030	47565	53820	56460	47610	54285	53430	52860	55140	53115	50850	57120	..
Beetroots	8175	9555	14250	14595	14520	16890	16500	15915	15960	16350	17190	16245	21660	..
Cured Tobacco	1725	1590	1815	2190	2085	2010	2160	1920	1530	1785	1800	1605	1680	..

REF: AGR.WK1   06/23/92
Source: CHINA Statistical Yearbook 1991 pp.321.

Table 8.6 : CHINA : Average Unit Area Yield of Major Crops
(Percentage GROWTH RATES)

	1978	1979	1980	1981	1982	1983	1984	1985	1986	1987	1988	1989	1990	1991
Total Food Grains	..	11.8	-3.2	3.3	10.6	8.6	6.2	-3.7	1.3	2.6	-0.8	1.3	8.3	..
Rice	..	6.8	-2.5	4.3	13.2	4.3	5.3	-2.2	1.7	1.4	-2.5	4.3	4.1	..
Wheat	..	16.3	-11.9	11.9	15.6	14.7	5.9	-1.0	3.6	-2.0	-0.5	2.5	4.9	..
Corn	..	6.4	3.0	-1.0	7.4	11.0	9.1	-9.1	2.9	5.7	0.4	-1.1	16.6	..
Soybeans	..	-2.8	5.8	6.8	-7.7	19.4	3.5	2.2	2.2	5.4	-2.0	-11.5	14.1	..
Tuber	..	-3.9	9.2	-4.8	7.2	7.8	1.4	-4.3	-4.0	9.3	-6.1	0.5	0.5	..
Peanuts	..	1.1	13.2	0.0	4.9	11.1	0.0	11.7	-9.7	12.4	-6.6	-4.7	20.7	..
Rapeseed	..	20.8	-3.4	28.6	27.8	-15.2	5.1	1.2	-3.6	5.0	-19.0	7.4	15.1	..
Cotton	..	10.0	12.1	2.7	7.9	24.4	19.6	-11.5	1.9	5.5	-13.8	-2.0	10.2	..
Sugarcane	..	9.2	13.2	13.2	4.9	-15.7	14.0	-1.6	-1.1	4.3	-3.7	-4.3	12.3	..
Beetroots	..	16.9	49.1	2.4	-0.5	16.3	-2.3	-3.5	0.3	2.4	5.1	-5.5	33.3	..
Cured Tobacco	..	-7.8	14.2	20.7	-4.8	-3.6	7.5	-11.1	-20.3	16.7	0.8	-10.8	4.7	..

REF: AGR.WK1 06/23/92
Source: Table 8.5.

Table 9.1: CHINA: Gross Output Value of Industry
(Billion yuan)

	1985	1986	1987	1988	1989	1990	1991
Total	971.6	1119.4	1381.3	1822.5	2201.7	2392.4	2822.5
BY TYPE OF OWNERSHIP							
State-owned	630.2	697.1	825.0	1035.1	1234.3	1306.4	1491.5
Collective-owned	311.7	375.2	478.2	658.7	785.8	852.3	1008.8
Township	76.1	98.1	128.4	184.7	219.4	244.1	291.3
Village	66.3	83.8	116.5	170.4	211.8	239.4	291.9
Joint Urban-Rural	15.7	24.8	31.6	43.9	49.6	53.9	...
Joint City-Town	0.0	2.1	3.0	3.9	5.0	5.5	...
Joint Rural	15.2	22.7	28.6	40.0	44.6	48.4	...
Individual-Owned	18.0	30.9	50.2	79.0	105.8	129.0	161.0
Urban	3.3	2.9	5.0	6.8	9.0	10.7	...
Rural	14.6	27.9	45.2	72.2	96.8	118.3	...
Other	11.7	16.3	27.9	49.5	75.8	104.8	161.2
BY TYPE OF INDUSTRY							
Light	457.5	533.0	665.6	897.9	1076.1	1181.3	1379.6
Heavy	514.1	586.4	715.7	924.5	1125.6	1211.3	1442.9

Source: CHINA Statistical Abstract 1992 pp.70-1; CHINA Statistical Yearbook 1991 pp.353 for 1985-90.

Table 9.2: CHINA: Gross Output Value of Industry
(Percentage Shares)

	1985	1986	1987	1988	1989	1990	1991
Total	100.0	100.0	100.0	100.0	100.0	100.0	100.0
BY TYPE OF OWNERSHIP							
State-owned	64.9	62.3	59.7	56.8	56.1	54.6	52.8
Collective-owned	32.1	33.5	34.6	36.1	35.7	35.6	35.7
Township	7.8	8.8	9.3	10.1	10.0	10.2	10.3
Village	6.8	7.5	8.4	9.3	9.6	10.0	10.3
Joint Urban-Rural	1.6	2.2	2.3	2.4	2.3	2.3	0.0
Joint City-Town	0.0	0.2	0.2	0.2	0.2	0.2	...
Joint Rural	1.6	2.0	2.1	2.2	2.0	2.0	...
Individual-Owned	1.8	2.8	3.6	4.3	4.8	5.4	5.7
Urban	0.3	0.3	0.4	0.4	0.4	0.4	...
Rural	1.5	2.5	3.3	4.0	4.4	4.9	...
Other	1.2	1.5	2.0	2.7	3.4	4.4	5.7
BY TYPE OF INDUSTRY							
Light	47.1	47.6	48.2	49.3	48.9	49.4	48.9
Heavy	52.9	52.4	51.8	50.7	51.1	50.6	51.1

REF: INDUSTRY.WK1 06/23/92
Source: Table 9.1

Table 9.3: CHINA: Output of Major Industrial Products

Product	Unit	1979	1980	1981	1982	1983	1984	1985	1986	1987	1988	1989	1990	1991
Coal	million tons	635.0	620.0	622.0	666.0	715.0	789.0	872.0	894.0	928.0	980.0	1054.0	1080.0	1062.0
Crude Oil	million tons	106.2	106.0	101.2	102.1	106.1	114.6	124.9	130.7	134.1	136.9	137.0	138.3	139.6
Natural Gas	billion cu m	14.5	14.3	12.7	11.9	12.2	12.4	12.9	13.4	13.9	14.3	15.1	15.3	15.3
Electricity	billion kWh	282.0	300.6	309.3	327.7	351.4	377.0	410.7	449.5	497.3	545.2	584.8	621.2	671.2
Hydro power	billion kWh	50.1	58.2	65.5	74.4	86.4	86.8	92.4	94.7	100.0	109.2	118.2	126.7	123.1
Steel	million tons	34.5	37.1	35.6	37.2	40.0	43.5	46.8	52.2	56.3	59.2	61.2	66.4	70.6
Rolled Steel	million tons	25.0	27.2	36.7	29.0	30.7	33.7	36.9	40.6	43.9	47.0	48.7	51.5	55.5
Cement	million tons	73.9	79.9	82.9	95.2	108.3	123.0	146.0	166.1	186.3	210.1	210.3	209.7	243.6
Timber	million cu m	54.4	53.6	49.4	50.4	52.3	63.9	63.2	65.0	64.1	62.1	58.0	55.7	58.0
Railway Freight Cars	1000 units	16.0	10.6	8.8	10.6	15.8	18.1	19.3	20.6	21.6	23.3	24.7	18.6	22.3

REF: INDUSTRY.WK1 06/23/92
Source: CHINA Statistical Abstract 1992 (in Chinese) pp.75-7 for 1991;CHINA Statistical Yearbook 1991 pp.383-9.

Table 9.4: CHINA: Percentage Growth Rates of Output of Major Industrial Products

Product	1980	1981	1982	1983	1984	1985	1986	1987	1988	1989	1990	1980-5	1986-90	1980-90
Coal	-2.4	0.3	7.1	7.4	10.3	10.5	2.5	3.8	5.6	7.6	2.5	5.5	4.4	5.0
Crude Oil	-0.2	-4.5	0.9	3.9	8.1	9.0	4.6	2.6	2.0	0.1	1.0	2.9	2.1	2.5
Natural Gas	-1.7	-10.7	-6.4	2.3	1.8	4.0	3.5	3.8	2.9	5.6	1.3	-1.8	2.0	-0.0
Electricity	6.6	2.9	5.9	7.2	7.3	8.9	9.4	10.6	9.6	7.3	6.2	6.5	8.6	7.5
Hydro power	16.2	12.5	13.6	16.1	0.5	6.5	2.5	5.6	9.2	8.2	7.2	10.9	6.5	8.9
Steel	7.7	-4.1	4.4	7.7	8.6	7.8	11.6	8.1	5.2	3.6	8.3	5.3	7.3	6.2
Rolled Steel	8.8	35.1	-20.9	5.9	9.8	9.5	9.9	8.1	7.1	3.6	5.9	8.0	6.9	7.5
Cement	8.1	3.8	14.8	13.7	13.6	18.6	13.8	12.2	12.8	0.1	-0.3	12.1	7.7	10.1
Timber	-1.5	-7.8	2.0	3.8	22.0	-1.0	2.8	-1.4	-3.0	-6.6	-4.0	2.9	-2.5	0.5
Railway Freight Cars	-33.8	-17.0	20.5	49.1	14.6	6.6	6.7	4.9	7.9	6.0	-24.7	6.7	0.2	3.7

REF: INDUSTRY.WK1 06/23/92
Source: Table 9.3.

Table 9.5: CHINA: Profits of State Owned Enterprises

	1978	1979	1980	1981	1982	1983	1984	1985	1986	1987	1988	1989	1990	1991
(Billion Yuan)														
TOTAL	59.9	65.4	69.2	63.9	62.8	75.3	83.8	94.4	87.8	100.5	119.0	100.0		
Refine Industry	4.8	5.9	7.1	6.3	6.4	8.6	9.8	11.0	11.4	12.3	15.1	15.7		
Electricity	5.1	5.6	5.8	5.5	5.0	6.3	5.8	5.2	5.4	6.4	6.7	6.7		
Coal and Coke	0.4	0.9	0.7	0.0	-0.0	0.2	0.3	0.1	-0.8	-1.2	-1.2	-2.7		
Petroleum	9.6	9.6	9.6	9.1	8.5	8.6	9.8	8.1	7.7	8.4	6.1	6.1		
Chemical	7.4	7.9	8.4	7.7	8.6	10.6	11.1	9.7	9.0	12.2	16.3	14.9		
Machinery	16.1	16.7	14.8	11.4	13.0	18.7	23.2	30.8	25.4	27.2	33.6	29.2		
Building materials	1.9	2.3	2.6	2.3	3.0	3.6	3.8	5.1	5.5	5.1	6.3	5.2		
Forestry	0.8	0.9	1.1	1.2	1.3	1.4	1.4	1.6	1.4	2.3	2.6	1.8		
Food	2.2	2.6	3.2	3.5	3.6	3.7	4.6	5.5	5.4	6.3	8.5	6.3		
Textile yarn	6.8	7.8	10.1	11.4	8.2	7.5	7.3	9.0	9.1	12.2	14.7	12.6		
Clothing	0.5	0.6	1.0	1.1	0.9	1.0	1.1	1.3	1.0	1.2	1.5	1.5		
Leather	0.3	0.4	0.5	0.5	0.3	0.3	0.4	0.6	0.7	0.7	0.7	0.4		
Paper	0.7	1.0	0.9	0.7	0.6	0.8	0.9	1.3	1.3	1.6	2.2	1.8		
Art & Education	1.2	1.3	1.5	1.6	1.9	1.8	1.8	2.4	2.3	2.7	3.0	2.9		
Other	2.1	1.9	1.7	1.7	1.9	2.2	2.3	2.8	2.9	3.1	3.9	3.1		
(Percentage growth rates)														
TOTAL	..	9.2	5.8	-7.7	-1.7	19.9	11.2	12.7	-7.0	14.5	18.4	-15.9		
Refine Industry	:	23.7	19.2	-10.2	0.3	35.5	14.0	11.9	3.6	8.5	22.7	3.4		
Electricity	:	10.6	3.5	-4.7	-9.8	25.1	-6.6	-11.2	4.7	17.9	-11.7	18.6		
Coal and Coke	:	159.1	-21.5	-98.6	-340.0	-1054.2	40.2	-80.4	-1444.4	41.8	-1.0	122.9		
Petroleum	:	-0.4	0.4	-5.6	-6.2	0.9	14.1	-17.6	-4.8	9.7	-27.3	-1.3		
Chemical	:	6.8	6.5	-8.4	12.1	23.2	4.7	-12.5	-6.9	35.3	33.3	-8.6		
Machinery	:	3.5	-11.4	-23.2	14.3	44.0	24.2	32.5	-17.7	7.2	23.5	-12.9		
Building materials	:	22.9	15.0	-14.5	31.9	20.9	5.4	33.3	9.8	-8.5	25.0	-17.8		
Forestry	:	13.4	25.1	6.5	4.8	12.6	0.7	9.3	-10.2	64.5	10.1	-31.1		
Food	:	17.8	23.3	10.1	1.6	3.0	24.2	19.8	-2.2	16.7	34.2	-25.7		
Textile yarn	:	14.0	29.8	12.5	-28.2	-8.2	-2.8	23.0	1.4	33.6	20.9	-14.5		
Clothing	:	17.0	57.3	5.9	-18.4	13.6	12.9	20.5	-22.9	16.8	29.0	0.1		
Leather	:	18.5	55.5	-6.9	-38.4	10.5	8.3	68.2	6.0	3.6	0.1	-42.8		
Paper	:	39.1	-7.2	-26.6	-7.7	27.8	15.1	40.8	0.2	20.2	42.4	-20.9		
Art & Education	:	9.0	18.4	3.8	17.2	-4.0	-0.2	30.6	-1.9	15.6	11.6	-3.8		
Other	:	-9.1	-10.9	-2.3	12.9	13.9	7.6	23.0	3.0	5.9	25.2	-19.2		

REF: INDUSTRY.WK1 06/23/92
Source: CHINA Industrial Statistical Yearbook (in Chinese) "Zhongguo Gongye Jingji Tongji Nianjian", 1990 pp.74.

Table 9.6: CHINA: Losses of State Owned Enterprises

(Billion Yuan)

	1978	1979	1980	1981	1982	1983	1984	1985	1986	1987	1988	1989	1990	1991
TOTAL	4.5	4.0	3.9	5.4	5.6	3.8	3.4	4.1	7.2	8.5	10.7	23.4		
Refine Industry	1.2	1.0	0.5	0.5	0.4	0.2	0.1	0.1	0.2	0.3	0.3	0.6		
Electricity	0.2	0.1	0.1	0.0	0.1	0.1	0.1	0.1	0.2	0.3	0.7	1.4		
Coal and Coke	0.8	0.8	1.0	1.3	1.4	1.4	1.4	1.6	2.3	2.7	3.3	5.5		
Petroleum	0.0	0.0	0.0	0.0	0.0	0.0	0.0	0.0	0.0	0.2	1.1	4.4		
Chemical	1.1	0.9	0.6	0.6	0.5	0.2	0.2	0.6	1.0	0.5	0.5	1.3		
Machinery	0.7	0.6	1.0	1.7	1.7	0.7	0.4	0.5	1.4	1.7	1.6	2.9		
Building materials	0.2	0.2	0.1	0.2	0.2	0.2	0.2	0.2	0.4	0.6	0.6	1.2		
Forestry	0.0	0.0	0.0	0.1	0.1	0.1	0.1	0.1	0.1	0.1	0.1	0.3		
Food	0.2	0.2	0.2	0.3	0.5	0.5	0.5	0.4	0.6	0.9	1.0	2.7		
Textile yarn	0.1	0.1	0.0	0.1	0.2	0.2	0.3	0.2	0.4	0.5	0.5	1.3		
Clothing	0.0	0.0	0.0	0.0	0.1	0.0	0.0	0.0	0.1	0.1	0.1	0.2		
Leather	0.0	0.0	0.0	0.0	0.1	0.1	0.0	0.0	0.0	0.1	0.1	0.3		
Paper	0.0	0.0	0.1	0.1	0.1	0.1	0.0	0.0	0.1	0.1	0.1	0.3		
Art & Education	0.0	0.0	0.0	0.0	0.0	0.0	0.0	0.0	0.1	0.1	0.1	0.2		
Other	0.1	0.1	0.1	0.2	0.2	0.1	0.1	0.1	0.3	0.4	0.4	0.9		

(Percentage growth rates)

	1978	1979	1980	1981	1982	1983	1984	1985	1986	1987	1988	1989	1990	1991
TOTAL	..	-11.0	-3.4	38.0	4.3	-32.6	-8.9	18.3	78.7	16.9	25.9	119.6		
Refine Industry	..	-16.4	-47.4	-4.2	-13.8	-55.6	-42.4	-11.8	133.0	35.4	8.2	74.0		
Electricity	..	-21.5	-14.5	-9.4	193.7	-51.1	-15.9	112.1	73.2	26.8	162.6	96.6		
Coal and Coke	..	-2.3	32.4	34.3	6.3	-5.1	1.0	19.0	41.1	19.4	19.1	68.3		
Petroleum	..	66.7	40.0	342.9	-45.2	-23.5	-92.3	100.0	1250.0	640.7	472.0	280.2		
Chemical	..	-13.5	-35.8	4.5	-20.0	-56.3	-20.0	246.0	60.8	-49.8	9.6	147.2		
Machinery	..	-11.4	60.4	69.7	-2.4	-57.8	-37.2	5.2	209.4	17.1	-5.7	83.3		
Building materials	..	-24.2	-14.0	60.1	-22.4	-14.7	13.4	11.8	79.9	57.5	-1.8	115.2		
Forestry	..	-4.0	25.0	140.0	26.4	-14.3	-29.5	-5.5	101.7	-2.6	22.8	137.1		
Food	..	-8.1	20.6	38.2	33.5	0.9	5.9	-15.5	54.4	38.2	16.8	161.1		
Textile yarn	..	14.8	-25.8	84.8	147.1	-11.4	34.4	-23.6	118.8	19.1	2.4	163.3		
Clothing	..	-64.7	16.7	171.4	205.3	-43.1	6.1	17.1	217.1	5.4	2.9	68.1		
Leather	..	-40.0	50.0	100.0	255.6	-15.6	-24.1	-48.8	109.5	61.4	54.9	131.8		
Paper	..	-25.0	116.7	111.5	20.9	-45.9	-41.7	-35.7	81.5	63.3	10.0	209.1		
Art & Education	..	137.5	-31.6	138.5	16.1	-27.8	50.0	-5.1	40.5	48.1	40.3	81.5		
Other	..	38.4	16.0	29.7	-7.8	-12.1	0.7	1.4	77.7	35.7	15.1	112.4		

REF: INDUSTRY.WK1 06/23/92
Source: Table 9.5

Table 9.7: CHINA: Net Profits/Losses of State Owned Enterprises

(Billion Yuan)

	1978	1979	1980	1981	1982	1983	1984	1985	1986	1987	1988	1989	1990	1991
TOTAL	55.4	61.4	65.4	58.6	57.2	71.6	80.4	90.4	80.5	92.0	108.3	76.6		
Refine Industry	3.6	4.9	6.5	5.8	5.9	8.4	9.7	10.9	11.1	12.0	14.8	15.1		
Electricity	5.0	5.6	5.8	5.5	4.9	6.2	5.8	5.1	5.2	6.1	4.9	5.3		
Coal and Coke	-0.4	0.2	-0.3	-1.3	-1.4	-1.1	-1.0	-1.6	-3.1	-3.9	-4.4	-8.1		
Petroleum	9.6	9.6	9.6	9.0	8.5	8.6	9.8	8.1	7.7	8.2	5.0	1.7		
Chemical	6.3	6.9	7.8	7.0	8.1	10.4	10.9	9.1	8.0	11.7	15.7	13.5		
Machinery	15.4	16.1	13.8	9.6	11.3	18.0	22.8	30.3	23.9	25.5	32.0	26.3		
Building materials	1.6	2.1	2.5	2.0	2.8	3.4	3.6	4.9	5.2	4.5	5.8	4.0		
Forestry	0.8	0.9	1.1	1.1	1.2	1.4	1.4	1.5	1.3	2.2	2.4	1.4		
Food	2.0	2.4	3.0	3.2	3.2	3.3	4.1	5.1	4.8	5.4	7.4	3.6		
Textile yarn	6.8	7.7	10.1	11.3	8.0	7.3	7.1	8.8	8.7	11.7	14.2	11.2		
Clothing	0.5	0.6	1.0	1.0	0.8	0.9	1.1	1.3	0.9	1.1	1.4	1.3		
Leather	0.3	0.3	0.5	0.5	0.3	0.3	0.3	0.6	0.6	0.6	0.6	0.1		
Paper	0.7	1.0	0.9	0.6	0.5	0.7	0.9	1.3	1.3	1.5	2.1	1.5		
Art & Education	1.2	1.3	1.5	1.6	1.8	1.8	1.8	2.3	2.3	2.6	2.9	2.7		
Other	2.0	1.8	1.6	1.5	1.7	2.0	2.2	2.7	2.7	2.7	3.5	2.3		

(Percentage growth rates)

	1978	1979	1980	1981	1982	1983	1984	1985	1986	1987	1988	1989	1990	1991
TOTAL	..	10.8	6.4	-10.4	-2.3	25.0	12.3	12.4	-10.9	14.3	17.7	-29.3		
Refine Industry	..	36.9	32.5	-10.7	1.5	42.1	15.2	12.2	2.4	7.9	23.1	1.8		
Electricity	..	11.1	3.7	-4.6	-11.5	27.4	-6.4	-12.4	3.0	17.5	-19.4	7.4		
Coal and Coke	..	-141.5	-257.6	390.4	8.9	-22.5	-7.0	49.6	101.1	25.5	13.0	82.9		
Petroleum	..	-0.4	0.4	-5.8	-6.0	1.0	14.3	-17.6	-5.1	7.5	-39.5	-65.8		
Chemical	..	10.3	12.2	-9.4	14.9	28.1	5.3	-16.7	-11.4	45.6	34.3	-13.9		
Machinery	..	4.2	-14.3	-30.0	17.3	59.1	26.6	33.0	-21.2	6.6	25.4	-17.7		
Building materials	..	29.5	17.3	-18.9	38.2	23.3	5.0	34.3	6.9	-13.1	28.3	-30.5		
Forestry	..	14.0	25.1	2.9	3.4	14.6	2.4	9.5	-14.5	70.5	9.4	-40.8		
Food	..	20.7	23.5	7.7	-1.8	3.3	26.8	23.9	-6.7	13.9	37.0	-51.4		
Textile yarn	..	14.0	30.3	12.2	-29.5	-8.1	-3.7	24.6	-1.1	34.3	21.7	-20.9		
Clothing	..	19.7	57.7	4.8	-22.5	17.7	13.1	20.6	-30.5	18.5	32.4	-6.7		
Leather	..	20.5	55.6	-8.7	-49.1	17.1	14.3	82.4	2.4	-0.5	-6.1	-75.5		
Paper	..	42.1	-10.3	-34.9	-13.2	47.7	20.7	44.5	-1.6	18.6	44.1	-30.3		
Art & Education	..	8.2	19.1	2.7	17.2	-3.6	-0.9	31.4	-2.5	14.9	10.7	-7.0		
Other	..	-11.1	-12.7	-5.1	15.4	16.4	8.1	24.5	-1.1	3.0	26.5	-34.8		

REF: INDUSTRY.WK1 06/23/92
Source: Table 9.5 minus 9.6.

Table 9.8: CHINA: Taxes Paid by the State Owned Enterprises

(Billion Yuan)

	1978	1979	1980	1981	1982	1983	1984	1985	1986	1987	1988	1989	1990	1991
TOTAL	31.7	34.0	36.8	44.2	48.6	45.6	52.5	72.0	78.8	88.8	109.9	127.5		
Refine Industry	2.2	2.3	2.5	3.0	4.0	3.3	4.1	6.5	7.7	8.9	10.9	13.4		
Electricity	2.0	2.1	2.3	2.9	3.8	2.9	3.5	5.6	6.3	7.2	7.4	8.9		
Coal and Coke	0.9	1.0	1.0	1.4	1.3	1.2	1.1	0.8	0.9	1.0	1.2	1.7		
Petroleum	2.5	2.7	2.7	2.8	3.2	3.5	4.3	7.1	7.4	7.7	8.9	4.3		
Chemical	3.8	4.1	4.3	5.0	5.6	5.5	6.3	7.9	9.2	10.8	13.9	15.5		
Machinery	4.8	5.2	5.3	6.1	7.0	6.7	8.3	12.3	11.9	14.0	18.0	19.4		
Building materials	1.2	1.2	1.4	1.5	1.6	1.6	0.9	2.6	3.0	3.6	4.7	5.3		
Forestry	0.5	0.5	0.6	0.7	0.8	0.8	0.9	1.0	1.1	1.5	1.7	1.7		
Food	6.8	7.3	7.7	9.6	10.5	10.6	11.9	14.7	17.7	21.5	27.5	33.4		
Textile yarn	5.0	5.3	6.4	8.0	7.6	6.3	6.7	8.7	8.3	6.8	8.5	10.7		
Clothing	0.3	0.3	0.4	0.5	0.5	0.5	0.6	0.8	0.8	0.8	1.0	1.2		
Leather	0.1	0.2	0.2	0.3	0.3	0.3	0.3	0.4	0.5	0.5	0.5	0.5		
Paper	0.5	0.6	0.6	0.7	0.7	0.7	0.8	1.1	1.2	1.5	1.9	2.0		
Art & Education	0.4	0.5	0.5	0.6	0.4	0.6	0.7	1.0	1.2	1.4	1.6	1.7		
Other	0.9	0.9	0.9	1.0	1.1	1.1	1.2	1.4	1.6	1.8	2.2	2.4		

(Percentage growth rates)

	1978	1979	1980	1981	1982	1983	1984	1985	1986	1987	1988	1989	1990	1991
TOTAL	..	7.3	8.4	19.9	9.9	-6.1	15.2	37.0	9.4	12.8	23.7	16.0		
Refine Industry	..	5.6	6.8	23.8	30.9	-16.9	23.3	58.9	18.4	16.6	22.0	22.7		
Electricity	..	5.0	8.0	29.8	29.4	-25.1	22.8	59.7	12.9	14.1	3.2	19.8		
Coal and Coke	..	13.7	7.5	34.7	-10.4	-8.5	-4.8	-25.2	7.2	12.2	26.4	35.5		
Petroleum	..	7.9	1.9	4.4	12.0	8.5	25.4	64.0	4.4	3.8	15.5	-51.3		
Chemical	..	6.0	5.8	16.9	10.8	-0.6	14.6	25.1	16.3	16.6	29.2	11.4		
Machinery	..	8.2	2.0	15.7	15.7	-4.2	23.1	48.5	-3.4	17.7	28.6	7.4		
Building materials	..	4.5	10.2	13.3	2.5	-2.7	17.1	37.4	16.9	17.2	30.5	13.8		
Forestry	..	10.8	16.1	14.8	16.1	0.7	8.6	12.6	9.1	38.4	16.8	0.8		
Food	..	8.3	5.8	23.7	9.6	0.7	12.1	24.4	20.1	21.4	28.0	21.3		
Textile yarn	..	5.8	21.4	24.0	-5.0	-16.4	5.3	30.4	-4.9	-18.2	25.2	26.2		
Clothing	..	5.4	49.5	18.9	-4.3	2.8	14.3	33.0	3.6	3.6	22.5	18.4		
Leather	..	27.5	23.7	14.9	-2.2	1.5	12.3	39.9	8.3	9.4	5.4	-0.0		
Paper	..	21.0	4.6	11.9	11.9	-3.0	14.5	31.5	14.5	20.6	25.8	8.8		
Art & Education	..	15.0	8.5	16.7	-25.3	38.9	13.3	49.8	13.4	17.2	14.1	9.4		
Other	..	-0.2	7.0	13.0	11.0	-1.0	8.1	15.9	12.2	10.1	22.5	11.8		

REF: INDUSTRY.WK1 06/23/92
Source: CHINA Industrial Statistical Yearbook (in Chinese) "Zhongguo Gongye Jingji Tongji Nianjian", 1990 pp.74.

Table 10.1: CHINA: Total Wage Bill of Staff and Workers

	1978	1979	1980	1981	1982	1983	1984	1985	1986	1987	1988	1989	1990	1991
(Billion Yuan)														
Total Wage Bill	56.9	64.7	77.2	82.0	88.2	93.5	113.3	138.3	166.0	188.1	231.6	261.9	295.1	332.4
State-owned	46.9	52.9	62.8	66.0	70.9	74.8	87.6	106.5	128.9	145.9	180.7	205.0	232.4	259.5
Collectives	10.0	11.7	14.5	16.0	17.3	18.7	25.4	31.2	36.3	40.9	48.8	53.4	58.1	65.9
(Percentage share)														
Total Wage Bill	100.0	100.0	100.0	100.0	100.0	100.0	100.0	100.0	100.0	100.0	100.0	100.0	100.0	100.0
State-owned	82.4	81.9	81.3	80.5	80.4	80.0	77.3	77.0	77.6	77.6	78.0	78.3	78.8	78.1
Collectives	17.6	18.1	18.7	19.5	19.6	20.0	22.4	22.6	21.9	21.7	21.1	20.4	19.7	19.8
(Growth rate)														
Total Wage Bill	..	13.7	19.5	6.2	7.6	6.0	21.3	22.0	20.0	13.3	23.1	13.1	12.7	12.6
State-owned	..	13.0	18.6	5.2	7.3	5.5	17.1	21.6	21.0	13.3	23.8	13.5	13.4	11.7
Collectives	..	17.0	23.3	10.4	8.5	7.7	36.2	23.0	16.2	12.8	19.2	9.6	8.7	13.4
GDP (Current prices, Billion Yuan)	358.8	398.9	446.7	477.0	518.9	579.5	693.8	855.0	970.0	1133.0	1404.4	1598.6	1774.0	1976.0
% Share of Wage bill into GDP	15.9	16.2	17.3	17.2	17.0	16.1	16.3	16.2	17.1	16.6	16.5	16.4	16.6	16.8

REF: WAGES.WK1 06/23/92
Source: CHINA Statistical Abstract 1992 (in Chinese) pp.44 for 1991; Statistical Year Book 1991 pp.101.
Note: Total Wage bill includes various joint units for 1984-88.

Table 10.2: CHINA: Average Annual Wage by Sector and Ownership

(Yuan in Current Prices)

Staff and Workers

Sector	1978	1979	1980	1981	1982	1983	1984	1985	1986	1987	1988	1989	1990	1991
Total	615	668	762	772	798	826	974	1148	1329	1459	1747	1935	2140	2340
Farming & forestry, etc.	486	540	626	645	668	701	786	901	1075	1162	1311	1417	1577	1703
Industry	631	691	784	789	802	819	989	1158	1336	1479	1782	2001	2203	2424
Geological Survey	809	885	1029	1058	1088	1116	1357	1590	1800	1980	2298	2558	2902	3129
Construction	713	771	857	873	914	961	1160	1370	1543	1692	1967	2171	2391	2653
Transport & Communications	689	758	842	847	884	908	1095	1292	1504	1663	2008	2288	2520	2796
Commerce & Services etc.	569	616	694	704	714	728	868	1008	1166	1287	1564	1674	1833	1966
Real Estate & Services etc.	576	633	712	714	743	792	918	1128	1320	1458	1726	1933	2173	2418
Health care, Sports & Welfare	573	598	718	750	833	867	948	1124	1343	1446	1752	1959	2209	2370
Education, Culture & Arts etc.	545	584	700	716	811	836	920	1166	1330	1409	1747	1883	2117	2243
Scientific research	669	717	851	850	857	990	1072	1272	1492	1620	1931	2118	2403	2573
Banking & Insurance	610	652	720	750	768	779	973	1154	1353	1458	1739	1867	2097	2255
Government agencies	655	684	800	815	821	923	989	1127	1356	1468	1707	1874	2113	2275

Staff and Workers in State-Owned Enterprises

Sector	1978	1979	1980	1981	1982	1983	1984	1985	1986	1987	1988	1989	1990	1991
Total	644	705	803	812	836	865	1034	1213	1414	1546	1853	2055	2284	:
Farming & forestry, etc.	492	548	635	653	676	712	796	913	1085	1171	1318	1428	1591	:
Industry	681	755	852	851	863	877	1070	1259	1448	1601	1931	2177	2409	:
Geological Survey	811	887	1031	1061	1091	1119	1340	1600	1804	1982	2300	2563	2904	:
Construction	756	819	920	940	978	1023	1276	1532	1730	1882	2193	2413	2659	:
Transport & Communications	734	808	907	910	935	959	1178	1390	1627	1800	2182	2490	2763	:
Commerce & Services etc.	588	640	721	735	746	761	957	1095	1280	1407	1733	1858	2039	:
Real Estate & Services etc.	626	688	777	782	806	856	1005	1187	1400	1539	1820	2021	2271	:
Health care, Sports & Welfare	605	625	751	781	861	895	981	1164	1376	1481	1793	1999	2263	:
Education, Culture & Arts etc.	566	606	722	738	827	851	934	1184	1344	1422	1764	1899	2134	:
Scientific research	670	719	853	852	860	992	1074	1268	1494	1624	1935	2123	2411	:
Banking & Insurance	650	689	754	788	806	813	1038	1234	1427	1540	1842	1960	2200	:
Government agencies	661	691	807	820	826	928	993	1133	1361	1472	1708	1875	2115	:

Staff and Workers in Urban Collective-Owned Enterprises

Sector	1978	1979	1980	1981	1982	1983	1984	1985	1986	1987	1988	1989	1990	1991
Total	506	542	623	642	671	698	811	967	1092	1207	1426	1557	1681	:
Farming & forestry, etc.	378	407	478	520	547	559	642	745	903	1008	1170	1199	1282	:
Industry	499	531	622	644	659	684	804	969	1079	1195	1419	1556	1670	:
Geological Survey	600	640	709	720	776	837	936	1018	1189	1241	1457	1187	1928	:
Construction	594	652	716	737	794	847	959	1101	1232	1380	1597	1763	1935	:
Transport & Communications	597	561	697	702	763	783	881	1030	1165	1272	1480	1656	1723	:
Commerce & Services etc.	467	497	570	580	592	606	763	907	1033	1141	1354	1439	1566	:
Real Estate & Services etc.	467	528	593	596	635	685	768	952	1085	1198	1378	1563	1715	:
Health care, Sports & Welfare	484	522	618	647	735	768	831	975	1212	1296	1570	1774	1956	:
Education, Culture & Arts etc.	317	339	433	433	523	535	634	779	945	1033	1202	1352	1533	:
Scientific research	500	500	571	667	600	750	900	1052	1286	1319	1636	1710	1995	:
Banking & Insurance	526	571	640	654	667	690	800	945	1150	1235	1450	1597	1806	:
Government agencies	455	467	538	615	615	714	885	1046	1227	1368	1648	1860	2042	:

REF: WAGES.WK1 06/23/92
Source: CHINA Statistical Abstract 1992 (in Chinese) pp.45 for1991; Statistical Yearbook 1991 pp.113-7.

Table 10.3: CHINA: Average Annual Wage GROWTH RATES by Sector and Ownership

(Percentage Growth Rates)

Staff and Workers

Sector	1978	1979	1980	1981	1982	1983	1984	1985	1986	1987	1988	1989	1990	1991
Total	..	8.6	14.1	1.3	3.4	3.5	17.9	17.9	15.8	9.8	19.7	10.8	10.6	9.3
Farming & forestry, etc.	:	11.1	15.9	3.0	3.6	4.9	12.1	14.6	19.3	8.1	12.8	8.1	11.3	8.0
Industry	:	9.5	13.5	0.6	1.6	2.1	20.8	17.1	15.4	10.7	20.5	12.3	10.1	10.0
Geological Survey	:	9.4	16.3	2.8	2.8	2.6	19.8	18.9	13.2	10.0	16.1	11.3	13.4	7.8
Construction	:	8.1	11.2	1.9	4.7	5.1	20.7	18.1	12.6	9.7	16.3	10.4	10.1	11.0
Transport & Communications	:	10.0	11.1	1.4	4.4	2.7	20.6	18.0	16.4	10.6	20.7	13.9	10.1	11.0
Commerce & Services etc.	:	8.3	12.7	0.3	1.4	2.0	19.2	16.1	15.7	10.4	21.5	7.0	9.5	8.3
Real Estate & Services etc.	:	9.9	12.5	4.5	4.1	6.6	15.9	22.9	17.0	10.5	18.4	12.0	12.4	11.3
Health care, Sports & Welfare	:	4.4	20.1	2.3	11.1	4.1	9.3	18.6	19.5	7.7	21.2	11.8	12.8	7.3
Education, Culture & Arts etc.	:	7.2	19.9	-0.1	13.3	4.1	10.0	26.7	14.1	5.9	24.0	7.8	12.4	6.0
Scientific research	:	7.2	18.7	4.2	0.8	15.5	8.3	18.7	17.3	8.6	19.2	9.7	13.5	7.1
Banking & Insurance	:	6.9	10.4	4.2	2.4	1.4	24.9	18.6	17.2	7.8	19.3	7.4	12.3	7.5
Government agencies	:	4.4	17.0	1.9	0.7	12.4	7.2	14.0	20.3	8.3	16.3	9.8	12.8	7.7

Staff and Workers in State-Owned Enterprises

Sector	1978	1979	1980	1981	1982	1983	1984	1985	1986	1987	1988	1989	1990	1991
Total	..	9.5	13.9	1.1	3.0	3.5	19.5	17.3	16.6	9.3	19.9	10.9	11.1	:
Farming & forestry, etc.	:	11.4	15.9	2.8	3.5	5.3	11.8	14.7	18.8	7.9	12.6	8.3	11.4	:
Industry	:	10.9	12.8	-0.1	1.4	1.6	22.0	15.8	16.9	10.6	20.6	12.7	10.7	:
Geological Survey	:	9.4	16.2	2.9	2.8	2.6	19.7	19.4	12.8	9.9	16.0	11.4	13.3	:
Construction	:	8.3	12.3	2.2	4.0	4.6	24.7	20.1	12.9	8.8	16.5	10.0	10.2	:
Transport & Communications	:	10.1	12.3	0.3	2.7	2.6	22.8	18.0	17.1	10.6	21.2	14.1	11.0	:
Commerce & Services etc.	:	8.8	12.7	1.9	1.5	2.0	25.8	14.4	16.9	9.9	23.2	7.2	9.7	:
Real Estate & Services etc.	:	9.9	12.9	0.6	3.1	6.2	17.4	18.1	17.9	9.9	18.3	11.0	12.4	:
Health care, Sports & Welfare	:	3.3	20.2	4.0	10.2	3.9	9.6	18.7	18.2	7.6	21.1	11.5	13.2	:
Education, Culture & Arts etc.	:	7.1	19.1	2.2	12.1	2.9	8.3	26.8	13.5	5.8	24.1	7.7	12.4	:
Scientific research	:	7.3	18.6	-0.1	0.9	15.3	8.3	18.1	17.8	8.7	19.2	9.7	13.6	:
Banking & Insurance	:	6.0	9.4	4.5	2.3	0.9	27.7	18.9	15.6	7.9	19.6	6.4	12.2	:
Government agencies	:	4.5	16.8	1.6	0.7	12.3	7.0	14.1	20.1	8.2	16.0	9.8	12.8	:

Staff and Workers in Urban Collective-Owned Enterprises

Sector	1978	1979	1980	1981	1982	1983	1984	1985	1986	1987	1988	1989	1990	1991
Total	..	7.1	14.9	3.0	4.5	4.0	16.2	19.2	12.9	10.5	18.1	9.2	8.0	:
Farming & forestry, etc.	:	7.7	17.4	8.8	5.2	2.2	14.8	16.0	21.2	11.6	16.1	2.5	6.9	:
Industry	:	6.4	17.1	3.5	2.3	3.8	17.5	20.5	11.4	10.8	18.7	9.7	7.3	:
Geological Survey	:	6.7	10.8	1.6	7.8	7.9	11.8	4.8	16.8	4.4	17.4	-18.5	62.4	:
Construction	:	9.8	9.8	2.9	7.7	6.7	13.2	14.8	11.9	12.0	15.7	10.4	9.8	:
Transport & Communications	:	-6.0	24.2	0.7	8.7	2.6	12.5	16.9	13.1	9.2	16.4	11.9	4.0	:
Commerce & Services etc.	:	6.4	14.7	1.8	2.1	2.4	25.9	18.9	13.9	10.5	18.7	6.3	8.8	:
Real Estate & Services etc.	:	13.1	12.3	0.5	6.5	7.9	12.1	24.0	14.0	10.4	15.0	13.4	9.7	:
Health care, Sports & Welfare	:	7.9	18.4	4.7	13.6	4.5	8.2	17.3	24.3	6.9	21.1	13.0	10.3	:
Education, Culture & Arts etc.	:	6.9	27.7	0.0	20.8	2.3	18.5	22.9	21.3	9.3	16.4	12.5	13.4	:
Scientific research	:	0.0	14.2	16.8	-10.0	25.0	20.0	16.9	22.2	2.6	24.0	4.5	16.7	:
Banking & Insurance	:	8.6	12.1	2.2	2.0	3.4	15.9	18.1	21.7	7.4	17.4	10.1	13.1	:
Government agencies	:	2.6	15.2	14.3	0.0	16.1	23.9	18.2	17.3	11.5	20.5	12.9	9.8	:

REF: WAGES.WK1 06/23/92
Source: Table 10.2.

Table 11.1: CHINA: Social Labor force by Sector

(Million)

	1978	1979	1980	1981	1982	1983	1984	1985	1986	1987	1988	1989	1990	1991
Farming forestry, animal husbandry, fishery & water conservancy	283.73	286.92	291.81	298.36	309.17	312.09	309.27	311.87	313.11	317.20	323.08	332.84	341.77	350.17
Industry	60.91	62.98	67.14	69.75	72.04	73.97	79.30	83.49	89.80	93.43	96.61	95.68	96.97	99.49
Geological survey & exploration	0.97	0.99	1.00	0.99	1.02	1.03	1.06	1.06	1.05	1.07	1.07	1.04	1.00	0.99
Construction	8.79	9.43	10.22	10.58	11.73	13.14	16.92	20.69	22.71	24.19	25.27	24.48	24.61	25.22
Transportation, posts & telecommunications	7.35	7.65	7.87	8.24	8.50	9.07	10.81	12.22	13.05	13.73	14.34	14.32	14.69	15.15
Commerce, catering trade, supply & marketing of materials and warehouses	11.55	12.48	13.81	15.11	16.04	17.62	20.36	23.63	24.85	26.55	28.29	28.60	29.37	31.00
Real estate administration, public utilities, residential & consultancy services	2.10	2.44	3.13	3.43	3.60	4.03	4.74	4.37	5.04	5.40	5.77	5.92	6.37	6.52
Public health, sports and social welfare	3.63	3.86	3.89	3.75	3.99	4.15	4.35	4.67	4.82	4.96	5.08	5.18	5.36	5.53
Education, culture, art, radio and television broadcasting	10.93	11.31	11.47	10.95	11.28	11.51	12.04	12.73	13.24	13.75	14.03	14.26	14.58	14.97
Scientific research, technical service	0.92	1.00	1.13	1.27	1.32	1.33	1.37	1.44	1.52	1.58	1.61	1.65	1.73	1.79
Banking and insurance	0.76	0.86	0.99	1.07	1.13	1.17	1.27	1.38	1.52	1.70	1.93	2.05	2.18	2.34
Governments, parties and organizations	4.67	5.05	5.27	5.56	6.11	6.46	7.43	7.99	8.73	9.25	9.71	10.22	10.79	11.37
Others	5.21	5.27	5.88	8.19	7.02	8.79	13.05	13.19	13.38	15.02	16.55	17.09	17.98	19.10
TOTAL	401.52	410.24	423.61	437.25	452.95	464.36	481.97	498.73	512.82	527.83	543.34	553.29	567.40	583.64

REF: LABOR.WK1 06/23/92
Source: CHINA Abstract (in Chinese) 1991 pp.16; Statistical Year book 1990 pp.77.

Table 11.2: CHINA: Social Labor force by Sector

(Percentage Shares)

	1978	1979	1980	1981	1982	1983	1984	1985	1986	1987	1988	1989	1990	1991
Farming forestry, animal husbandry, fishery & water conservancy	70.7	69.9	68.9	68.2	68.3	67.2	64.2	62.5	61.1	60.1	59.5	60.2	60.2	60.0
Industry	15.2	15.4	15.8	16.0	15.9	15.9	16.5	16.7	17.5	17.7	17.8	17.3	17.1	17.0
Geological survey & exploration	0.2	0.2	0.2	0.2	0.2	0.2	0.2	0.2	0.2	0.2	0.2	0.2	0.2	0.2
Construction	2.2	2.3	2.4	2.4	2.6	2.8	3.5	4.1	4.4	4.6	4.7	4.4	4.3	4.3
Transportation, posts & telecommunications	1.8	1.9	1.9	1.9	1.9	2.0	2.2	2.5	2.5	2.6	2.6	2.6	2.6	2.6
Commerce, catering trade supply & marketing of materials and warehouses	2.9	3.0	3.3	3.5	3.5	3.8	4.2	4.7	4.8	5.0	5.2	5.2	5.2	5.3
Real estate administration, public utilities, residential & consultancy services	0.5	0.6	0.7	0.8	0.8	0.9	1.0	0.9	1.0	1.0	1.1	1.1	1.1	1.1
Public health, sports and social welfare	0.9	0.9	0.9	0.9	0.9	0.9	0.9	0.9	0.9	0.9	0.9	0.9	0.9	0.9
Education, culture, art, radio and television broadcasting	2.7	2.8	2.7	2.5	2.5	2.5	2.5	2.6	2.6	2.6	2.6	2.6	2.6	2.6
Scientific research, technical service	0.2	0.2	0.3	0.3	0.3	0.3	0.3	0.3	0.3	0.3	0.4	0.4	0.3	0.3
Banking and insurance	0.2	0.2	0.2	0.2	0.2	0.3	0.3	0.3	0.3	0.3	0.4	0.4	0.4	0.4
Governments, parties and organizations	1.2	1.2	1.2	1.3	1.3	1.4	1.5	1.6	1.7	1.8	1.8	1.8	1.9	1.9
Others	1.3	1.3	1.4	1.9	1.5	1.9	2.7	2.6	2.6	2.8	3.0	3.1	3.2	3.3
TOTAL	100.0	100.0	100.0	100.0	100.0	100.0	100.0	100.0	100.0	100.0	100.0	100.0	100.0	100.0

(Growth Rates)

	1978	1979	1980	1981	1982	1983	1984	1985	1986	1987	1988	1989	1990	1991
Farming forestry, animal husbandry, fishery & water conservancy	..	1.1	1.7	2.2	3.6	0.9	-0.9	0.8	0.4	1.3	1.9	3.0	2.7	2.5
Industry	..	3.4	6.6	3.9	3.3	2.7	7.2	5.3	7.6	4.0	3.4	-1.0	1.3	2.6
Geological survey & exploration	..	2.1	1.0	-1.0	3.0	1.0	2.9	0.0	-0.9	1.9	0.0	-2.8	-3.8	-1.0
Construction	..	7.3	8.4	3.5	10.9	12.0	28.8	22.3	9.8	6.5	4.5	-3.1	0.5	2.5
Transportation, posts & telecommunications	..	4.1	2.9	4.7	3.2	6.7	19.2	13.0	6.8	5.2	4.4	-0.1	2.6	3.1
Commerce, catering trade, supply & marketing of materials and warehouses	..	8.1	10.7	9.4	6.2	9.9	15.6	16.1	5.2	6.8	6.6	1.1	2.7	5.5
Real estate administration, public utilities, residential & consultancy services	..	16.2	28.3	9.6	5.0	11.9	17.6	-7.8	15.3	7.1	6.9	2.6	7.6	2.4
Public health, sports and social welfare	..	6.3	0.8	-3.6	6.4	4.0	4.8	7.4	3.2	2.9	2.4	2.0	3.5	3.2
Education, culture, art, radio and television broadcasting	..	3.5	1.4	-4.5	3.0	2.0	4.6	5.7	4.0	3.9	2.0	1.6	2.2	2.7
Scientific research, technical service	..	8.7	13.0	12.4	3.9	0.8	3.0	5.1	5.6	3.9	1.9	2.5	4.8	3.5
Banking and insurance	..	13.2	15.1	8.1	5.6	3.5	8.5	8.7	10.1	11.8	13.5	6.2	6.3	7.3
Governments, parties and organizations	..	8.1	4.4	5.5	9.9	5.7	15.0	7.5	9.3	6.0	5.0	5.3	5.6	5.4
Others	..	1.2	11.6	39.3	-14.3	25.2	48.5	1.1	1.4	12.3	10.2	3.3	5.2	6.2
TOTAL	..	2.2	3.3	3.2	3.6	2.5	3.8	3.5	2.8	2.9	2.9	1.8	2.6	2.9

REF: LABOR.WK1 06/23/92
Source: Table 11.1.

Table 11.3: CHINA: Social Labor force by Ownership

	1978	1979	1980	1981	1982	1983	1984	1985	1986	1987	1988	1989	1990	1991
						(Million)								
Total	401.52	410.24	423.61	437.25	452.95	464.36	481.97	498.73	512.82	527.83	543.34	553.29	567.40	583.64
Staff and Workers	94.99	99.67	104.44	109.40	112.81	115.15	118.90	123.58	128.09	132.14	136.08	137.42	140.59	145.08
State-owned	74.51	76.93	80.19	83.72	86.30	87.71	86.37	89.90	93.33	96.54	99.84	101.08	103.46	106.64
Urban Collective-owned	20.48	22.74	24.25	25.68	26.51	27.44	32.16	33.24	34.21	34.88	35.27	35.02	35.49	36.28
Other Ownership	0.00	0.00	0.00	0.00	0.00	0.00	0.37	0.44	0.55	0.72	0.97	1.32	1.64	2.16
Urban Individual Laborers	0.15	0.32	0.81	1.13	1.47	2.31	3.39	4.50	4.83	5.69	6.59	6.48	6.71	7.63
Rural Laborers	306.38	310.25	318.36	326.72	338.67	346.90	359.68	370.65	379.90	390.00	400.67	409.39	420.10	430.93
						(Percentage Shares)								
Total	100.0	100.0	100.0	100.0	100.0	100.0	100.0	100.0	100.0	100.0	100.0	100.0	100.0	100.0
Staff and Workers	23.7	24.3	24.7	25.0	24.9	24.8	24.7	24.8	25.0	25.0	25.0	24.8	24.8	24.9
State-owned	18.6	18.8	18.9	19.1	19.1	18.9	17.9	18.0	18.2	18.3	18.4	18.3	18.2	18.3
Urban Collective-owned	5.1	5.5	5.7	5.9	5.9	5.9	6.7	6.7	6.7	6.6	6.5	6.3	6.3	6.2
Other Ownership	0.0	0.0	0.0	0.0	0.0	0.0	0.1	0.1	0.1	0.1	0.2	0.2	0.3	0.4
Urban Individual Laborers	0.0	0.1	0.2	0.3	0.3	0.5	0.7	0.9	0.9	1.1	1.2	1.2	1.2	1.3
Rural Laborers	76.3	75.6	75.2	74.7	74.8	74.7	74.6	74.3	74.1	73.9	73.7	74.0	74.0	73.8
						(Growth Rates)								
Total	..	2.2	3.3	3.2	3.6	2.5	3.8	3.5	2.8	2.9	2.9	1.8	2.6	2.9
Staff and Workers	..	4.9	4.8	4.7	3.1	2.1	3.3	3.9	3.6	3.2	3.0	1.0	2.3	3.2
State-owned	..	3.2	4.2	4.4	3.1	1.6	-1.5	4.1	3.8	3.4	3.4	1.2	2.4	3.1
Urban Collective-owned	..	11.0	6.6	5.9	3.2	3.5	17.2	3.4	2.9	2.0	1.1	-0.7	1.3	2.2
Other Ownership	..	..	..	..	..	..	..	18.9	25.0	30.9	34.7	36.1	24.2	31.7
Urban Individual Laborers	..	113.3	153.1	39.5	30.1	57.1	46.8	32.7	7.3	17.8	15.8	-1.7	3.5	13.7
Rural Laborers	..	1.3	2.6	2.6	3.7	2.4	3.7	3.0	2.5	2.7	2.7	2.2	2.6	2.6

REF: LABOR.WK1 06/23/92
Source: CHINA Statistical Abstract 1992 (in Chinese) pp.16-8 for 1991; Statistical Yearbook 1991 pp.76.

Table 12.1 : CHINA : General Price Indices /1
(1980=100)

	1978	1979	1980	1981	1982	1983	1984	1985	1986	1987	1988	1989	1990	1991
Retail Prices	92.5	94.3	100.0	102.4	104.4	105.9	108.9	118.5	125.6	134.8	159.7	188.2	192.1	197.7
Cost of Living of Staff & Workers	91.3	93.0	100.0	102.5	104.6	106.7	109.6	122.6	131.2	142.8	172.3	200.4	203.0	213.3
Purchasing Price of Farm & Sideline Products	76.4	93.4	100.0	105.9	108.2	113.0	117.5	127.6	135.8	152.0	187.0	215.1	209.5	205.3
Retail Prices of Industrial Products in Rural Areas	99.1	99.2	100.0	101.0	102.6	103.6	106.9	110.3	113.8	119.3	137.5	163.2	170.7	175.6
Price Parity between Industrial & Agricultural Products	129.5	106.2	100.0	95.4	94.6	91.5	90.8	86.4	83.8	78.5	73.3	75.9	81.3	..
Market Price of Consumer goods	102.7	98.0	100.0	105.8	109.3	113.9	113.4	132.9	143.7	167.1	217.7	241.2	..	..

Percentage GROWTH RATES over last year

	1978	1979	1980	1981	1982	1983	1984	1985	1986	1987	1988	1989	1990	1991
Retail Prices	..	2.0	6.0	2.4	1.9	1.5	2.8	8.8	6.0	7.3	18.5	17.8	2.1	2.9
Cost of Living of Staff & Workers	..	1.9	7.5	2.5	2.0	2.0	2.7	11.9	7.0	8.8	20.7	16.3	1.3	5.1
Purchasing Price of Farm & Sideline Products	..	22.1	7.1	5.9	2.2	4.4	4.0	8.6	6.4	12.0	23.0	15.0	-2.6	-2.0
Retail Prices of Industrial Products in Rural Areas	..	0.1	0.8	1.0	1.6	1.0	3.1	3.2	3.2	4.8	15.2	18.7	4.6	2.9
Price Parity between Industrial & Agricultural Products	..	-18.0	-5.8	-4.6	-0.8	-3.3	-0.8	-4.8	-3.0	-6.4	-6.5	3.5	7.1	..
Market Price of Consumer goods	..	-4.5	2.0	5.8	3.3	4.2	-0.4	17.2	8.1	16.3	30.3	10.8	..	..

REF: PRICE.WK1 06/23/92
Source: CHINA Statistical Abstract 1992 (in Chinese) pp.39; Statistical Yearbook 1991 pp.199.
Note: 1/ Average for the year.

Table 12.2: CHINA: Growth Rate of Overall Retail Sales Price Index for the Whole Nation
(Growth rate over same month last year)

	Food	Grain	Non Staple Food	Fresh Vegeta-bles	Dried Vegeta-bles	Meat Poultry & Eggs	Aquatic Products	Fresh Fruit	Dried Fruit	Garments	Daily Use Articles	Overall
1988												
January												
February	15.3	6.2	23.9	48.3	13.6	27.6	25.5	7.7	17.6	5.6	3.3	11.2
March	15.8	5.7	24.3	30.2	12.7	30.3	26.3	13.7	16.6	6.8	4.8	11.6
April	16.1	7.4	24.7	16.0	14.7	35.4	27.1	7.5	16.2	8.6	6.5	12.6
May	17.7	8.9	26.9	17.8	15.6	37.7	26.5	6.0	17.4	10.1	8.4	14.7
June	20.2	13.5	29.5	13.2	15.0	40.3	33.0	8.7	17.6	11.0	10.7	16.5
July	23.6	12.3	32.3	30.3	16.6	41.0	31.6	29.0	16.5	12.5	12.8	19.3
August	28.9	18.6	37.4	47.8	19.1	42.6	37.1	18.2	17.6	15.2	15.6	23.2
September												
October	30.4	12.3	39.0	42.0	23.9	43.8	38.7	32.2	28.8	18.7	19.3	26.1
November	31.9	26.0	35.6	30.5	23.5	38.8	36.5	45.0	30.8	19.8	21.4	26.0
December	30.5	29.2	31.2	16.8	25.6	33.8	32.9	44.0	32.1	21.2	21.8	26.7
1989												
January	29.2	29.8	29.5	16.5	27.4	30.4	34.3	45.0	36.1	20.8	22.2	27.0
February	29.3	29.8	30.1	14.7	29.5	31.7	33.7	37.8	35.8	22.8	23.0	27.9
March	27.2	33.6	26.2	-3.7	27.5	30.7	28.9	24.9	37.9	23.4	22.6	26.2
April	26.6	33.6	25.0	6.2	26.5	26.5	27.4	22.4	38.3	22.7	21.4	25.8
May	24.4	32.8	21.1	15.4	25.3	19.7	25.2	28.8	36.8	22.4	20.4	24.4
June												
July	17.8	26.8	13.8	8.1	21.7	12.3	18.7	21.1	35.8	20.0	16.8	19.0
August	12.3	19.6	9.6	0.3	19.8	9.1	18.9	11.7	35.5	17.9	14.0	15.2
September	8.0	15.8	5.1	-6.3	15.0	4.3	7.2	2.9	29.5	15.1	13.4	11.4
October	4.6	9.9	2.2	-4.6	11.2	0.2	4.7	-2.1	17.7	13.5	0.3	8.7
November	3.1	5.9	1.9	-10.1	9.2	2.3	-0.4	-10.1	11.2	12.4	6.8	7.1
December												
1990												
January	1.0	-1.4	2.5	-8.3	4.0	1.6	-2.2	-16.4	-0.4	9.8	4.2	4.1
February	1.8	-1.7	3.1	-2.5	4.4	1.0	-1.0	-16.6	-0.9	9.6	3.4	4.1
March	1.3	-1.5	3.0	6.5	2.6	0.0	-6.0	-10.7	-3.2	8.5	2.3	3.3
April												
May	1.5	-6.3	1.6	-7.0	1.0	-0.4	3.1	30.6	-2.9	7.0	0.7	2.6
June												
July												
August	-1.7	-8.1	-1.0	-8.5	-1.6	-3.8	-1.3	-0.6	-5.4	5.8	1.2	0.4
September	-0.7	-7.7	0.7	5.5	-0.9	-4.1	-1.3	-0.2	-6.5	5.8	1.8	0.8
October	-0.2	-6.3	0.8	3.3	0.2	-4.1	-0.2	4.1	-5.6	5.7	2.0	1.1
November	0.2	-6.9	1.5	5.1	-0.2	-4.5	-1.6	7.8	-5.7	6.1	2.0	1.6
December	1.3	-5.7	2.4	13.9	1.3	-3.7	3.8	13.4	-4.1	6.2	2.2	2.2
1991												
January												
February												
March												
Average 1988												
Average 1989												
Average 1990												

REF: PRICE.WK1 06/23/92
Source: China Statistics Monthly, University of Illinois, Chicago.

Table 12.3: CHINA: Growth Rate of Overall Retail Price Index

(Same month last year = 100)

	Beijing	Tianjin	Shenyang	Shanghai	Nanjing	Wuhan	Guangzhou	Chengdu	Xian	Urban
1988										
January	10.2	6.5	7.9	15.4	16.0	13.7	15.5	14.4	13.0	11.7
February	10.0	9.9	15.5	15.6	16.9	16.1	20.9	14.5	14.2	13.4
March	10.1	10.7	12.4	15.9	18.2	15.2	20.7	22.0	16.7	14.2
April	12.2	10.2	8.8	13.4	20.8	17.7	20.0	17.7	14.8	14.2
May	12.5	11.5	10.9	19.4	22.7	17.8	23.8	17.6	13.9	16.0
June	22.2	14.8	17.2	23.7	21.9	16.4	20.8	18.4	15.6	18.1
July	25.9	22.6	20.4	24.2	25.3	21.6	27.5	21.6	18.5	22.0
August	30.7	25.1	26.7	24.3	32.2	28.2	35.9	31.7	26.7	27.4
September	29.9	24.0	32.2	25.4	32.0	32.9	44.3	37.8	28.3	29.8
October	33.3	24.9	31.0	28.8	29.4	31.9	41.7	41.1	31.0	30.2
November	29.1	25.1	29.9	27.4	27.5	29.4	43.4	38.4	34.0	30.4
December	30.5	24.9	32.1	25.4	29.2	28.1	38.6	35.0	32.8	28.9
1989										
January	28.9	24.4	34.1	26.4	27.5	24.5	44.0	32.9	37.9	27.8
February	28.5	22.0	31.3	29.7	30.5	25.3	45.0	32.7	34.9	27.8
March	28.4	20.2	28.9	26.9	25.8	23.9	41.5	23.7	31.0	26.0
April	25.6	19.9	27.4	26.5	21.1	20.0	39.5	26.2	32.8	25.6
May										
June	14.8	14.6	19.6	21.3	18.4	19.2	40.1	19.8	25.9	21.0
July	16.4	10.3	15.4	16.9	15.9	16.3	21.4	16.7	21.9	17.2
August	12.1	8.4	12.5	14.4	12.7	9.8	12.6	10.5	19.2	12.6
September	10.6	7.6	9.7	12.4	11.8	6.4	10.9	5.7	14.0	8.6
October	10.1	7.5	9.0	9.2	8.6	6.4	9.0	3.8	7.8	6.0
November										
December	7.6	6.4	2.0	5.7	4.9	6.0	2.1	2.7	0.3	3.2
1990										
January	1.2	1.7	0.8	7.8	6.3	5.0	-2.0	3.3	0.2	3.4
February	3.2	8.6	4.7	8.5	8.7	6.3	-2.6	0.9	3.6	4.6
March										
April	6.0	4.5	7.0	7.4	7.1	5.5	-2.3	4.7	3.8	4.6
May										
June										
July										
August	4.5	1.0	4.8	6.8	4.8	4.3	-4.0	2.1	0.0	2.7
September	5.1	2.3	0.2	5.2	3.9	1.3	-4.8	2.2	-1.4	2.2
October	4.8	1.7	0.8	6.0	3.4	1.2	-3.6	1.7	1.6	2.6
November	5.2	2.9	1.2	8.0	4.6	2.6	-0.8	3.3	3.7	4.1
December	8.8	4.9	5.2	7.3	6.0	3.3	0.6	2.6	7.1	5.4
1991										
January										
February										
March										
Average 1988	21.4	17.5	20.4	21.6	24.3	22.4	29.4	25.8	21.6	21.4
Average 1989										
Average 1990										

REF: PRICE.WK1 06/23/92
Source: China Statistics Monthly, University of Illinois, Chicago.

Table 12.4: CHINA: Growth Rate of Cost of Living Index of Staff & Workers (Goods & Services)

(Growth rate over same month last year)

	Beijing	Tianjin	Shenyang	Shanghai	Nanjing	Wuhan	Guangzhou	Chengdu	Xian	Urban
1988										
January	9.6	6.1	7.4	13.9	14.7	12.6	13.8	13.4	12.8	11.2
February	9.6	9.3	10.7	14.6	15.6	14.8	19.1	13.5	14.1	12.8
March	9.6	10.2	11.6	15.0	16.7	14.1	19.2	20.2	16.6	13.6
April	11.5	9.7	8.2	13.4	19.2	16.4	18.2	16.5	14.9	13.7
May	12.0	11.0	10.3	18.8	21.0	16.5	17.9	16.5	14.1	15.4
June	20.7	14.0	16.1	22.7	20.4	15.3	19.3	17.7	15.6	17.5
July	24.1	21.4	19.0	23.2	23.6	20.1	25.5	20.5	18.4	21.2
August	28.6	23.8	24.8	23.2	30.1	26.6	33.3	30.1	25.8	26.6
September	27.9	22.9	29.7	24.4	27.3	31.1	42.1	36.6	27.8	29.7
October	31.0	23.8	29.4	26.8	27.3	30.3	39.9	39.9	30.2	29.8
November	27.1	24.0	28.4	25.4	25.8	28.1	41.6	37.5	33.0	29.8
December	28.3	23.8	30.5	23.6	27.3	26.9	37.4	34.4	31.9	28.6
1989										
January	26.6	23.2	32.6	25.4	26.3	23.5	42.5	32.6	36.1	27.3
February	26.2	21.0	29.1	28.2	29.9	24.3	43.4	32.3	33.3	27.4
March	26.2	19.4	26.9	25.7	25.5	23.0	40.2	24.4	30.3	25.7
April	23.6	19.0	25.5	24.5	21.1	19.3	38.7	26.7	31.7	25.3
May										
June	13.8	16.0	18.3	19.7	18.6	18.4	39.1	20.3	25.9	21.0
July	15.3	9.9	14.4	15.7	16.3	15.7	22.1	17.6	22.2	17.5
August	11.4	8.2	11.9	13.5	13.2	9.3	14.2	11.3	20.0	13.0
September	10.2	7.6	9.4	12.4	13.1	6.4	10.5	5.8	15.2	9.2
October	9.8	7.5		10.0	6.5	3.9	9.7	3.9	9.4	6.8
November										
December	7.5	6.7	3.2	6.4	6.9	6.1	3.3	3.2	2.6	4.3
1990										
January	1.6	2.0	2.8	10.0	8.8	5.2	3.6	-0.3	2.0	4.6
February	3.0	8.7	2.5	6.0	7.6	6.3	-3.8	0.2	2.0	3.5
March										
April	6.0	4.6	6.0	4.9	5.8	5.4	-3.2	4.2	2.3	3.6
May										
June										
July										
August	3.4	0.5	1.5	3.8	3.1	3.0	-5.1	1.3	-2.1	1.1
September	8.0	2.5	1.1	5.7	4.5	2.3	-3.7	2.8	0.9	3.3
October	7.7	2.1	1.6	6.4	4.1	2.2	-2.5	2.6	3.7	3.6
November	8.1	3.5	3.8	8.9	4.8	3.5	0.2	4.1	5.7	5.3
December	11.3	5.4	9.7	8.3	6.4	4.1	1.3	3.7	9.3	6.6
1991										
January										
February										
March										
Average 1988	20.0	16.7	18.8	20.4	22.7	21.1	27.3	24.7	21.3	20.8
Average 1989										
Average 1990										

REF: PRICE.MK1 06/23/92
Source: China Statistics Monthly, University of Illinois, Chicago.

Table 12.5: CHINA: Monthly and Annual Rates of Inflation

	Overall Retail Price Index					Consumer Price Index (Whole Nation)					Free market Price Index of Consumer Goods				
	1987	1988	1989	1990	1991	1987	1988	1989	1990	1991	1987	1988	1989	1990	1991
January	5.0	9.5	27.0	4.1	1.4	5.0	9.7	27.4	3.5	1.5	22.0	20.0	27.5	-5.1	-2.3
February	5.1	11.2	27.9	4.1	1.0	5.3	10.7	28.4	3.5	1.0	7.9	27.9	26.9	-6.6	-0.8
March	5.5	11.6	26.3	3.3	0.9	5.6	11.6	27.0	2.7	0.8	7.4	28.8	19.2	-5.1	-5.2
April	6.5	12.6	25.8	3.1	0.6	6.6	12.6	26.5	2.5	0.4	14.2	23.1	21.0	-2.0	-6.9
May	7.6	14.7	24.3	2.6	3.1	7.7	14.5	24.7	2.0	3.0	15.6	21.5	20.1	-5.7	-5.5
June	7.8	16.5	21.5	3.0	3.8	7.9	16.7	22.5	2.4	3.8	20.1	22.4	15.0	-5.3	0.3
July	8.0	19.3	19.0	0.7	4.2	8.0	19.8	18.9	0.2	4.3	16.9	27.7	14.9	-7.3	1.8
August	8.4	23.2	15.2	0.4	4.0	8.4	24.1	14.8	-0.1	4.1	20.0	33.2	9.1	-7.5	0.6
September	7.9	25.4	11.4	0.8	4.3	7.8	26.4	10.8	0.5	4.4	16.5	37.3	3.3	-4.4	-0.2
October	7.6	26.1	8.7	1.1	4.0	7.6	27.0	7.7	0.9	4.0	19.9	36.5	0.9	-4.3	1.7
November	8.5	26.0	7.1	1.6	4.4	8.5	26.8	6.4	1.4	4.6	22.6	34.8	-6.4	-3.8	1.0
December	9.1	26.7	6.4	2.2	4.0	9.2	27.7	5.5	2.1	4.0	20.8	30.6	-6.6	-0.5	0.8
AVERAGE	7.3	18.6	18.4	2.3	3.0	7.3	19.0	18.4	1.8	3.0	17.0	28.7	12.1	-4.8	-1.2

REF: PRICE.WK1 06/23/92
Source: State Statistical Bureau Monthly Statistics pp.28 for 1991;
CHINA Statistics Monthly of University of Illinois, Chicago, Jan-Feb-March 1992 for 1991; 3/1991 pp.26 for 1990; March 1990 pp.23 for 1989; March 1989

Table 12.6 : CHINA : Price Adjustments during 1990   a/

Commodity	Notes	Unit	Increased in Month	OLD Price	NEW Price	Percent Increase	Absolute Increase
AGRICULTURAL COMMODITIES	Procurement Price						47
Cooking oil		50 kg	April	165	215	30%	
Soybean oil		50 kg	April	125	140	12%	
Sugar cane		Ton	April	140	155	11%	
Sugar beet		50 kg	April	109	121	10%	
Tobacco		50 kg	April	236	300	27%	
Cotton		50 kg	April	145	215	48%	
Timber		Meter	November				
INDUSTRIAL COMMODITIES	Producer Price						60
Crude oil		Ton	March	137	167	22%	
Residual oil		Ton	March	0.020	0.025	25%	
Railway freight		Ton-km	March	0.01051	0.01353	29%	
Water freight		Ton-km	March			29%	
Mineral ore (42%)		Ton	July	188	242	23%	
Iron ore (68%)		Ton	July	94	115	23%	
Postal rates		1 Letter	July	0.08	0.20	150%	
Oxidating aluminium		Ton	August	600	1000	67%	10
Coal		Ton	September	5700	7560	33%	
Copper ore (25%)		Ton	September	7500	9700	29%	
Electric copper (99.95%)		Ton	September	2700	3550	31%	
Tin ore (60%)		Ton					
COMMODITIES FOR DAILY USE	Retail Price						0.4
Detergent		500g	July	..	2.8	..	
White cloth		Meter	October	..	1.9	..	
Sugar		500g	November	..	..	..	

REF: PRICE.WK1 06/23/92
Source: Price Bureau, June 1990.

Note: a/ Price Adjustment during the first three months of 1991.

Agricultural products in the state-rationed shops for urban residents: Grain; including wheat flour, rice and maize, increased by an average of 0.2 yuan/kg; cooking oil including peanut oil, sesame oil, rape oil, cotton-seed oil, tea-seed oil and soybean oil increased an at average of 2.7 yuan/kg.

Industrial products: Coal, Plastic film, fertilizer, ferrous metal (ore), nonferrous metal (ore), petroleum products, and electricity have also increased. (percentage increase not known).

Daily use commodities: Bus ticket (percentage increase not known).

Table 13.1: CHINA: Total Investment in Fixed Assets

	1978	1979	1980	1981	1982	1983	1984	1985	1986	1987	1988	1989	1990	1991
						(Billion Yuan)								
Total Investment	66.9	69.9	74.6	96.1	123.0	143.0	183.3	254.3	302.0	364.1	449.7	413.8	444.9	527.9
State-Owned				66.8	84.5	95.2	118.5	168.1	197.9	229.8	276.3	253.5	291.9	355.8
Collective-Owned				11.5	17.4	15.6	23.9	32.7	39.2	54.7	71.2	57.0	52.9	62.9
Individual-Owned				17.8	21.1	32.2	40.9	53.5	64.9	79.6	102.2	103.2	100.2	109.2
						(Percentage Shares)								
Total Investment				100.0	100.0	100.0	100.0	100.0	100.0	100.0	100.0	100.0	100.0	100.0
State-Owned				69.5	68.7	66.6	64.7	66.1	65.5	63.1	61.4	61.3	65.6	67.4
Collective-Owned				12.0	14.2	10.9	13.0	12.9	13.0	15.0	15.8	13.8	11.9	11.9
Individual-Owned				18.5	17.1	22.5	22.3	21.0	21.5	21.9	22.7	24.9	22.5	20.7
GNP (Billion Yuan,Current Prices)				477.3	519.3	580.9	696.2	855.7	969.6	1130.1	1401.8	1591.6	1768.6	1975.9
Total Investment into GNP (%)				20.1	23.7	24.6	26.3	29.7	31.1	32.2	32.1	26.0	25.2	26.7
STATE-OWNED ENTERPRISES						(Billion Yuan)								
Total	66.9	69.9	74.6	66.8	84.5	95.2	118.5	168.1	197.9	229.8	276.3	253.5	291.9	355.8
Capital Construction	50.1	52.3	55.9	44.3	55.6	59.4	74.3	107.4	117.6	134.3	157.4	155.2	170.4	207.5
Technical Updating	16.8	17.6	18.7	19.5	25.0	29.1	30.9	44.9	61.9	75.9	98.0	78.0	83.0	99.7
Other	0.0	0.0	0.0	2.9	3.9	6.7	13.3	15.7	18.3	19.6	20.8	19.2	38.5	48.7
						(Percentage Shares)								
Total				100.0	100.0	100.0	100.0	100.0	100.0	100.0	99.9	99.5	100.0	100.0
Capital Construction				66.4	65.7	62.4	62.7	63.9	59.4	58.4	57.0	61.2	58.4	58.3
Technical Updating				29.3	29.6	30.6	26.1	26.7	31.3	33.0	35.5	30.8	28.4	28.0
Other				4.4	4.7	7.0	11.2	9.3	9.3	8.5	7.5	7.6	13.2	13.7

REF: INVEST.WK1 06/23/92
Source: CHINA Statistical Abstract 1992 (in Chinese) pp.20-1;Yearbook 1992 pp.119-121; Statistical Year Book of China 1990 pp.146; 1988 pp.493 for 1981-87 and
        Statistical Year Book of China (in Chinese) 1989 pp.477 for 1988.

Table 13.2: CHINA: Investment in Capital Constuction of State-Owned Enterprises by Sector of National Economy

(Billion Yuan)

	1978	1979	1980	1981	1982	1983	1984	1985	1986	1987	1988	1989	1990	1991
All Sectors	50.1	52.3	55.9	44.3	55.6	59.4	74.3	107.4	117.6	134.3	157.4	155.2	170.4	207.5
Agriculture			5.1	2.9	3.4	3.5	3.7	3.6	3.5	4.2	4.7	5.1	6.7	8.5
Industry			27.6	21.6	26.1	28.2	34.2	44.6	53.2	68.3	81.3	82.2	95.3	112.7
Geology				0.3	0.3	0.3	0.4	0.7	0.7	0.7	0.5	0.5	0.5	0.5
Construction				0.9	1.1	1.0	1.1	2.2	1.9	1.5	1.5	1.4	1.0	1.8
Transport			6.2	4.0	5.7	7.8	10.8	17.1	18.1	19.0	21.2	16.7	20.7	31.1
Commerce			2.9	2.8	3.6	2.9	3.5	4.7	4.2	4.7	5.4	4.5	4.3	7.8
Real Estate & Public Utilities			3.4	1.3	2.0	1.9	2.4	11.8	11.0	9.3	13.4	11.2	8.2	11.0
Educaiton, Health, & Culture etc.			3.5	3.4	4.1	4.9	6.6	10.1	11.6	12.6	13.2	12.9	13.8	13.9
Research			0.9	1.0	1.1	1.1	1.4	2.1	2.5	2.6	2.9	2.2	2.1	2.4
Banking & Insurance			0.3	0.3	0.6	0.3	0.3	0.7	0.8	1.3	1.9	1.6	1.5	2.0
Government Agencies & Other			4.5	5.8	7.8	7.3	10.0	9.8	10.1	10.0	12.0	17.0	16.3	15.7

(Percentage Shares)

	1978	1979	1980	1981	1982	1983	1984	1985	1986	1987	1988	1989	1990	1991
All Sectors			97.5	100.0	100.0	100.0	100.0	100.0	100.0	100.0	100.0	100.0	100.0	100.0
Agriculture			9.2	6.5	6.1	5.9	4.9	3.3	3.0	3.1	3.0	3.3	3.9	4.1
Industry			49.3	48.8	46.9	47.5	46.0	41.6	45.2	50.8	51.6	53.0	55.9	54.3
Geology			0.0	0.6	0.5	0.6	0.5	0.7	0.6	0.5	0.3	0.3	0.3	0.2
Construction			0.0	2.1	1.9	1.7	1.5	2.0	1.6	1.1	1.0	0.9	0.6	0.9
Transport			11.2	9.1	10.3	13.1	14.6	15.9	15.4	14.1	13.5	10.7	12.2	15.0
Commerce			5.1	6.3	6.5	4.9	4.7	4.4	3.6	3.5	3.4	2.9	2.5	3.8
Real Estate & Public Utilities			6.0	3.0	3.6	3.3	3.2	11.0	9.4	6.9	8.5	7.2	4.8	5.3
Educaiton, Health, & Culture etc.			6.3	7.7	7.4	8.2	8.8	9.4	9.9	9.3	8.4	8.3	8.1	6.7
Research			1.7	2.2	1.9	1.9	1.9	1.9	2.2	2.0	1.5	1.4	1.2	1.2
Banking & Insurance			0.5	0.7	1.1	0.6	0.4	0.7	0.7	1.0	1.2	1.0	0.9	1.0
Government Agencies & Other			8.1	13.0	14.0	12.4	13.4	9.1	8.6	7.5	7.6	10.9	9.6	7.5

REF: INVEST.WK1 06/23/92
Source: CHINA Statistical Abstract 1992 (in Chinese) pp.24.

Table 13.3: CHINA: Investment in Capital Constuction of State-Owned Enterprises by Branch of Industry

(Billion Yuan)

	1978	1979	1980	1981	1982	1983	1984	1985	1986	1987	1988	1989	1990	1991
Total Industry				21.6	26.1	28.2	34.2	44.6	53.2	68.3	81.3	82.2	95.3	
Metallurgical				2.7	4.3	4.2	4.7	5.2	5.4	7.9	9.5	9.0		
Power				4.0	4.6	5.7	7.7	10.8	16.0	20.9	24.4	26.5		
Coal				2.3	3.0	4.0	5.5	5.5	5.8	6.0	6.4	7.1		
Petroleum				2.8	2.5	2.9	3.1	3.3	3.9	5.9	8.6	9.4		
Chemical				1.9	2.6	3.0	3.6	5.4	5.9	8.4	10.1	8.7		
Machine Building				2.4	2.7	2.7	3.0	4.7	4.2	5.0	5.7	6.3		
Forest				0.7	0.8	0.6	0.7	0.6	0.7	1.0	0.9	0.9		
Building materials				0.9	1.2	1.4	1.8	2.7	3.2	3.4	3.2	2.8		
Textiles				2.0	2.1	1.7	1.8	2.1	2.7	3.1	3.6	4.3		
Food				0.9	1.4	1.1	1.2	1.7	2.2	3.1	2.9	2.8		
Paper making				0.2	0.2	0.2	0.2	0.3	0.4	0.5	0.7	0.6		

(Percentage Shares)

	1978	1979	1980	1981	1982	1983	1984	1985	1986	1987	1988	1989	1990	1991
Total Industry				100.0	100.0	100.0	100.0	100.0	100.0	100.0	100.0	100.0	100.0	
Metallurgical				12.7	16.5	15.0	13.7	11.7	10.2	11.6	11.7	10.9		
Power				18.6	17.7	20.4	22.5	24.2	30.0	30.6	30.1	32.2		
Coal				10.7	11.5	14.2	16.1	12.3	10.9	8.7	7.8	8.6		
Petroleum				12.9	9.7	10.3	9.0	7.4	7.3	8.6	10.6	11.4		
Chemical				8.8	9.9	10.7	10.5	12.0	11.1	12.3	12.5	10.6		
Machine Building				11.3	10.4	9.5	8.9	10.6	7.9	7.3	7.0	10.6		
Forest				3.1	3.0	2.3	2.1	1.5	1.4	1.4	1.1	1.1		
Building materials				4.1	4.5	5.0	4.9	6.1	6.0	5.0	4.0	3.4		
Textiles				9.2	8.1	6.1	5.3	4.6	5.1	4.5	4.4	5.2		
Food				4.3	5.4	4.0	3.5	3.9	4.2	4.5	3.6	3.5		
Paper making				0.9	0.6	0.6	0.6	0.8	0.8	0.8	0.8	0.7		
SUBTOTAL				96.5	97.4	97.9	97.0	95.2	94.7	95.3	93.7	95.2		

REF: INVEST.WK1 06/23/92
Source: CHINA: Statistical Yearbook 1990 pp.157.

Table 13.4: CHINA   : Sectoral Breakdown of Investment
(Percentage Shares)

	1978	1979	1980	1981	1982	1983	1984	1985	1986	1987	1988	1989	1990	1991
Capital Construction of which				100.0	100.0	100.0	100.0	100.0	100.0	100.0	100.0	100.0	100.0	100.0
Agriculture				6.6	6.1	6.0	5.0	3.3	3.0	3.1	3.0	3.3	3.9	4.1
Industry				48.8	46.9	47.5	46.0	41.6	45.2	50.9	51.6	53.0	55.9	54.3
Energy				21.4	18.4	21.5	22.3	19.0	22.7	25.3	26.1	28.8	32.8	30.4
Communications				9.1	10.3	13.1	14.6	15.9	15.4	14.1	13.5	10.7	12.2	15.2
Technical Updating of which				100.0	100.0	100.0	100.0	100.0	100.0	100.0	100.0			
Agriculture				2.6	2.2	2.1	1.7	1.4	1.2	1.3	..			
Industry				73.2	70.0	71.3	72.9	78.2	77.4	77.1	..			
Energy				13.0	12.6	13.0	13.1	10.4	10.3	9.8	..			
Communications				11.2	10.9	11.2	11.3	9.0	8.9	8.5	..			
Collectives of which				100.0	100.0	100.0	100.0	100.0	100.0	100.0	100.0			
Agriculture				22.5	20.2	18.5	13.3	9.3	8.4	8.1	..			
Industry				72.0	70.2	69.0	67.5	62.1	63.2	63.4	..			
Energy				1.0	1.0	1.0	1.0	1.0	1.0	0.9	..			
Communications				2.4	2.5	2.3	2.0	1.3	5.2	5.4				

REF: INVEST.WK1 06/23/92
Source: CHINA Statistical Abstract 1992 (in Chinese) pp.26 for 1991; Year book (in Chinese) 1991 pp.156 ;1988 pp. 258,277,493,503f,543,545f,571,573,579;
State Statistical Bureau, Statistics for 1988 Socioeconomic Development;
Beijing Review, March 6-12, 1989, and World Bank estimates.

Note: Technical updating investment in energy has been calculated by assuming the
       .: of energy to transport investment in 1987 throughout. Sectoral investment ratios
       for collectives assume that the ratio of sectoral investment to sectoral GVIO is
       the same as in 1987 for all years.

- 274 -

Table 13.5: CHINA : Capital Construction Investment of State Owned Enterprises
(Percentage Shares by Sector)

	1980	1981	1982	1983	1984	1985	1986	1987	1988	1989	1990	1991
Agriculture	9.3	6.6	6.1	6.0	5.0	3.3	3.0	3.1	3.0	3.3	4.1	
Light Industry	9.1	9.8	8.4	6.5	5.7	5.9	7.0	7.4	7.4	7.9	7.2	
Heavy Industry	40.2	39.0	38.5	41.0	40.3	35.7	38.2	43.5	44.8	45.1	47.2	

	1953-87	1958-62	1963-65	1966-70	1971-75	1976-80	1981-85	1986-90
Agriculture	7.1	11.3	17.7	10.7	9.8	10.5	5.1	3.3
Light Industry	6.4	6.4	3.9	4.4	5.8	6.7	6.9	7.5
Heavy Industry	36.2	54.0	45.9	51.1	49.6	45.9	38.5	43.9

REF: INVEST.WK1 06/23/92
Source: CHINA Statistical Abstract 1991 pp.25 for 1990; Yearbook 1990 pp.155 for 1953-89.
Note: Data are based on new classification since 1985; agriculture excludes metereology which is included in poly-technical services.

Table 13.6 : CHINA: Inventories of Commodities held by the Agencies Under the Ministry of Commerce

Inventories that have Increased in April 1991

(Stocks at the end of the period)

Serial	COMMODITY	UNIT	1989 Dec.	1990 Dec.	1989 April	1990 April	1991 April	GROWTH RATES		
								Between December 1989 & 90	Between April 1989 & 90	Between April 1990 & 91
1	Oranges	10,000 tons	6.3	11.3	2.2	2.1	6.3	79.4	-2.9	200.0
2	Pencils	100 mil	39.1	43.7	9.8	7.2	11.2	11.8	-26.5	55.6
3	Yellow & red yarn	10,000 tons		12.1	43.7	21.4	33.0		-51.0	54.2
4	Eggs	10,000 tons	5.7	7.2		4.8	7.3	26.3		52.1
5	Apples	10,000 tons		30.3		5.2	7.8			50.0
6	Poultry	10,000		3241.4		1563.1	2279.5			45.8
7	Video recorders	10,000		15.6		12.2	17.6			44.3
8	Soaps	10,000 boxes	943.6	948.1	843.1	964.3	1337.7	0.5	14.4	38.7
9	Honey	tons		42119.0		37894.0	48373.0			27.7
10	Bulbs	10,000	41198.0	51437.1	37977.0	39550.1	48596.6	24.9	4.1	22.9
11	Rubber shoes	10,000	32399.7	39233.7	33033.0	32602.1	39158.0	21.1	-1.3	20.1
12	TVs	10,000	423.1	524.1	248.5	374.3	438.5	23.9	50.6	17.2
13	Cotton underwear	10,000	25555.9	26360.2	23015.9	22228.3	25233.0	3.1	-3.4	13.5
14	Tea	10,000 tons	22.3	18.3	10.9	14.9	16.8	-17.9	36.7	12.8
15	Wool yarn	10,000 tons	9.0	11.7	5.0	8.8	9.8	30.0	76.0	11.4
16	Radios	10,000	420.0	480.0	416.2	418.5	459.6	14.3	0.6	9.8
17	Fans	10,000	629.1	957.8	895.9	1331.1	1461.8	52.2	48.6	9.8
18	Enamel basins	10,000		4282.4		3745.4	4102.0			9.5
19	Tape recorders	10,000	318.7	356.2	334.2	322.6	352.8	11.8	-3.5	9.4
20	Watches	10,000	1718.8	1936.3	1708.3	1762.3	1926.8	12.7	3.2	9.3
21	Old iron stuff	10,000 tons		181.6		176.0	192.2			9.2
22	Soda	10,000 tons	9.4	12.0	8.0	11.1	12.0	27.7	38.7	8.1
23	Match boxes	10,000 boxes	440.4	515.5	371.1	452.1	488.3	17.1	21.8	8.0
24	Liquor	10,000 tons	80.0	89.8	86.8	78.5	84.7	12.2	-9.6	7.9
25	Washing machines	10,000	154.5	167.0	127.9	147.2	155.6	8.1	15.1	5.7
26	Big clocks	10,000		1288.4		1144.5	1209.2			5.7
27	Washing powder	10,000 tons	18.8	21.7	12.7	20.0	21.1	15.4	57.5	5.5
28	Iron bowls	10,000 tons	3086.0	3614.0	2937.0	3099.0	3243.0	17.1	5.5	4.6
29	Cotton thread	10,000 tons		24.7		22.7	23.7			4.4
30	Garments	10,000	17833.3	18539.6	18709.9	18291.5	18771.9	4.0	-2.2	2.6
31	Thermos flasks	10,000	5484.1	5578.8	5851.6	5000.4	5112.7	1.7	-14.5	2.2
32	Sleeveless dress	10,000	42794.2	47069.1	47042.0	48538.6	49502.1	10.0	3.2	2.0
33	Wool yarn	kgs	4483.6	3714.9	3049.1	3134.2	3192.0	-17.1	2.8	1.8
34	Bedsheets	10,000		4874.8		4054.7	4114.8			1.5
35	Plastic shoes	10,000		15183.2		18006.8	18224.3			1.2
36	Nails	10,000 tons	10.9	12.4	9.9	11.4	11.5	13.8	15.2	0.9
37	Iron wire	10,000 tons	13.0	16.9	11.7	15.0	15.1	30.0	28.2	0.7

REF: INVENTOR.WK1 06/23/92
Source: CHINA: Ministry of Commerce

Table 13.7 : CHINA: Inventories of Commodities held by the Agencies Under the Ministry of Commerce

Inventories that have Decreased in April 1991

(Stocks at the end of the period)

Serial COMMODITY	UNIT	1989 Dec.	1990 Dec.	1989 April	1990 April	1991 April	GROWTH RATES		
							Between December 1989 & 90	Between April 1989 & 90	Between April 1990 & 91
1 Bamboo	10,000	686.7	488.8	969.5	636.7	416.1	-28.8	-34.3	-34.6
2 Sheep & goat	10,000	..	579.0	..	465.9	311.9	..	..	-33.1
3 Pigs	10,000	1903.9	1563.9	1891.5	1919.4	1337.3	-17.9	1.5	-30.3
4 Sewing machines	10,000	240.6	208.2	190.3	236.2	187.8	-13.5	24.1	-20.5
5 Enamil bouls	10,000	84243.0	76983.0	67275.0	77005.0	61407.0	-8.6	14.5	-20.3
6 Bicycles	10,000	748.8	689.1	779.5	757.8	606.6	-8.0	-2.8	-20.0
7 Timber	10,000	..	51.3	..	54.0	43.8	..	..	-18.9
8 Beef	10,000	..	133.9	..	90.1	75.3	..	..	-16.4
9 Kerosene	10,000 tons	..	6.2	..	5.9	5.3	..	..	-10.2
10 Cardboard paper	10,000 tons	..	4.9	..	4.1	3.7	..	..	-9.8
11 Thin paper	10,000 tons	17.8	17.0	19.0	16.6	15.1	-4.5	-12.6	-9.0
12 Aluminium pots	10,000	..	3395.6	..	2737.6	2522.5	..	..	-7.9
13 Underwear	10,000	4430.6	3917.7	5010.0	3907.2	3692.6	-11.6	-22.0	-5.5
14 Diesel	10,000 tons	..	23.7	..	23.8	22.5	..	..	-5.5
15 Motorcycles	10,000	..	11.3	..	10.3	9.8	..	..	-4.9
16 Refrigirators	10,000	83.0	89.6	85.9	94.1	89.9	8.0	9.5	-4.5
17 Towels	10,000	..	41527.1	..	41635.3	40026.8	..	..	-3.9
18 Cigarettes	10,000 boxes	94.7	98.1	89.1	86.2	83.9	3.6	-3.3	-2.7
19 Fresh Vegetables	10,000 tons	..	21.5	..	4.0	3.9	..	..	-2.5
20 Cameras	10,000	..	49.7	..	54.8	54.7	..	..	-0.2

REF: INVENTOR.WK1 06/23/92
Source: CHINA: Ministry of Commerce

Table 13.8 : CHINA: Inventories of Commodities held by the Agencies Under the Ministry of Commerce

(Stocks at the end of the period)

	(Billion Yuan)					GROWTH RATES		
	1989 Dec.	1990 Dec.	1989 April	1990 April	1991 April	Between December 1989 & 90	Between April 1989 & 90	Between April 1990 & 91
National Total	36.7	39.3	29.0	33.2	35.4	6.9	14.3	6.8
for Domestic Trade	23.1	25.8	19.1	21.3	22.0	11.6	11.4	3.5
for External Trade (residual)	13.6	13.5	9.9	11.9	13.4	-1.2	20.1	12.8
	(Percentage Shares)							
National Total	100.0%	100.0%	100.0%	100.0%	100.0%			
for Domestic Trade	62.9%	65.7%	65.9%	64.1%	62.2%			
for External Trade (residual)	37.1%	34.3%	34.1%	35.9%	37.8%			

REF: INVENTOR.WK1 06/23/92
Source: CHINA: Ministry of Commerce

Table 13.9 : CHINA: Inventories of Industrial Products by Branch of Industry

(Stocks at the end of the period)

(Billion Yuan)	1989 August	1989 Dec.	1990 August	1991 Feb.	August 90 Over August 89	February 91 Over January 91
Total Industry	130.5	152.3	184.1	199.0	41.1	6.2
Light	68.7	82.4	95.2	105.4	38.5	4.9
Heavy	61.8	69.9	88.9	93.6	44.0	7.8

(Percentage Shares)	1989 August	1989 Dec.	1990 August	1991 Feb.
Total Industry	100.0%	100.0%	100.0%	100.0%
Light	52.7%	54.1%	51.7%	53.0%
Heavy	47.3%	45.9%	48.3%	47.0%

(Billion Yuan)	1989 August	1989 Dec.	1990 August	1991 Feb.	August 90 Over August 89	February 91 Over January 91
Total Industry	130.5	152.3	184.1	199.0		
Extraction	7.6	7.9	9.6	9.8	25.9	7.1
Coal mining and dressing	2.0	1.8	2.8	3.1	42.2	3.6
Mining & dressing of buildingg materials	0.5	0.7	0.8	0.9	55.0	2.9
Manufacturing	122.9	144.4	174.5	189.3	42.0	6.2
Food, Beverages and Tobacco	15.5	17.4	17.6	22.1	13.6	6.3
Textiles	17.0	22.1	26.0	31.7	53.4	8.2
Machine building, electrical, & electronics	42.2	46.8	57.2	57.2	35.3	2.9

(Percentage Shares)	1989 August	1989 Dec.	1990 August	1991 Feb.
Total Industry	100.0%	100.0%	100.0%	100.0%
Extraction	5.8%	5.2%	5.2%	4.9%
Coal mining and dressing	1.5%	1.2%	1.5%	1.6%
Mining & dressing of buildingg materials	0.4%	0.5%	0.5%	0.5%
Manufacturing	94.2%	94.8%	94.8%	95.1%
Food, Beverages and Tobacco	11.9%	11.4%	9.6%	11.1%
Textiles	13.0%	14.5%	14.1%	15.9%
Machine building, electrical, & electronics	32.4%	30.7%	31.1%	28.7%

REF: INVENTOR.WK1 06/23/92
Source: CHINA: State Statistical Bureau.

Table 14.1: CHINA: Total Production and Consumption of Energy and its Composition

	1978	1979	1980	1981	1982	1983	1984	1985	1986	1987	1988	1989	1990	1991
PRODUCTION (millions of tons of coal equivalent)	628	646	637	632	668	713	779	855	881	913	958	1016	1039	1047
Proportion (%)														
Coal	70.3	70.2	69.4	70.2	71.3	71.6	72.4	72.8	72.4	72.6	73.1	74.1	74.2	74.4
Crude Oil	23.7	23.5	23.8	22.9	21.8	21.3	21.0	20.9	21.2	21.0	20.4	19.3	19.0	19.0
Natural Gas	2.9	3.0	3.0	2.7	2.4	2.3	2.1	2.0	2.1	2.0	2.0	2.0	2.0	2.0
Hydro Power	3.1	3.3	3.8	4.2	4.5	4.8	4.5	4.3	4.3	4.4	4.5	4.6	4.8	4.6
CONSUMPTION (millions of tons of coal equivalent)	571	586	603	594	621	660	709	767	809	866	930	969	987	1023
Proportion (%)														
Coal	70.7	71.3	72.2	72.7	73.7	74.2	75.3	75.8	75.8	76.2	76.2	76.0	76.2	76.0
Crude Oil	22.7	21.8	20.7	20.0	18.9	18.1	17.4	17.1	17.2	17.0	17.0	17.2	16.6	17.0
Natural Gas	3.2	3.3	3.1	2.8	2.5	2.4	2.4	2.2	2.3	2.1	2.1	2.0	2.1	2.0
Hydro Power	3.4	3.6	4.0	4.5	4.9	5.3	4.9	4.9	4.7	4.7	4.7	4.9	5.1	5.0
GDP (Billion Yuan) (Constant 1980 Prices)	385.4	416.7	446.7	466.9	507.4	558.7	639.7	722.7	783.6	871.8	969.6	1013.7	1070.2	1144.9
Energy Consumption (million ton per billion yuan)	1.5	1.4	1.3	1.3	1.2	1.2	1.1	1.1	1.0	1.0	1.0	1.0	0.9	0.9

REF: ENERGY.WK1 06/23/92
Source: CHINA Statistical Abstract 1992 (in Chinese) pp.83 for 1991; Yearbook 1990 pp.459-60 for 1978-89.

NOTES:

Excluding bio-energy, solar, geothermal and nuclear energy.
All fuels are converted into standard fuel with thermal
equivalent of 7000 kilocalorie per kilogram. The conversion is
1 kg of coal (5000 kcal)   = 0.714 kg of standard fuel.
1 kg of crude oil (10000 kcal) = 1.43 kg of standard fuel.
1 cubic metre of natural gas (9310 kcal) = 1.33 kg of standard fuel.
The conversion of hydropower into standard fuel is calculated on
the basis of the consumption quota of standard coal for thermal
power generation of the year.

Table 15.1: CHINA: Freight Traffic: International Comparisons

	CHINA	USSR	USA	INDIA	BRAZIL	JAPAN
FREIGHT TRAFFIC INTENSITIES						
Country Area (Million Square km)	9.6	22.4	9.4	3.3	8.5	0.4
Freight Traffic (Billion Ton-km)	1817	8773	5818	335	453	508
Average Distance (Ton-km)	199.7	624.0	704.0	608.0	419.0	82.6
Estimated GNP (Billion US$)	359.2	1,065.0	4,886.6	277.3	311.9	2,577.1
Ton-km / GNP ($)	5.1	8.2	1.2	1.2	1.5	0.2
Ton-km / Area	189.2	391.7	620.7	101.9	53.2	1344.0
RAILWAY AND ROAD NETWORK DENSITIES						
Population (Million)	1088	307	246	816	144	123
Rail Length (1000 km)	53.4	146.7	205.0	62.2	31.2	43.0
Rail Density						
km/Population	0.05	0.48	0.83	0.08	0.22	0.35
km/Area	5.56	6.55	21.87	18.93	3.66	113.71
Road Length (1000 km)	1028.3	1174.8	6230.0	1800.0	1675.0	1110.0
Road Density						
km/Population	0.94	3.83	25.29	2.21	11.60	9.05
km/Area	107.11	52.45	664.68	547.61	196.78	2936.46

REF: TRANSPORT.WK1 06/23/92

SOURCE:

CHINA: A Statistical Survey of China (Zhongguo Tongji Zhaiyao) 1991, pp. 84-85. Figures: 1990.

USSR: A Study of the Soviet Economy, Volume 3, (International Monetary Fund, The World Bank, Organization for Economic Co-operation and
         Development, and European Bank for Reconstruction and Development), February 1991, p.106-8. Data for 1988.

USA: National Transportation Statistics Annual Report, U.S. Department of Transportation, Reserarch and Special Programs Administration,
         July 1990,pp.103. Transportation in America, 1989, P. 8. World Transport Data, International Road Transport Union, p.180.Data for 1988.

INDIA: World Bank estimates based on Government of India, Economic Survey, 1988/89 and Perspective Planning for Transport Development, 1988.
         Data for 1987-88.
         Rail: Transport Sector Strategy Note -- Statistical Appendix, The World Bank, 1991. Rail Data for 1989.
         Roads: Estimate based on World Transport Data, Op. cit. and World Bank information. Road data for 1987-88.

BRAZIL: World Road Statistics 1985-1989, International Road Federation, 1990, Section 5.
         World Transport Data, International Road Transport Union, p. 130. World Bank
         Appraisal Report, Highways Management and Rehabilitation Report, 1989.
         Rail Figures: 1988; Road Figures: 1987.

JAPAN: World Road Statistics 1985-1989, International Road Federation, 1990, Section 5.
         World Transport Data, International Road Transport Union, p. 214-216. Road, rail
         and water figures: 1988. Air figures: 1986-87.

Population Area & GNP: The World Bank Development Report, pp. 178-179.

Table 15.2: CHINA: Freight Traffic Composition of China

FREIGHT TRAFFIC (Billion Ton-km)

	1952	1977	1978	1979	1980	1981	1982	1983	1984	1985	1986	1987	1988	1989	1990	Avg.80-90
Rail	60.2	456.8	534.5	559.8	571.7	571.2	612.0	664.6	724.7	812.6	876.5	947.1	987.8	1039.4	1056.3	805.8
Road	1.4	25.1	27.4	74.5	76.4	78.0	94.9	108.4	153.6	169.3	211.3	266.0	322.0	337.5	344.1	196.5
Domestic Waterways	11.8	102.1	129.2	139.0	152.3	150.7	170.8	181.1	196.1	237.1	270.0	288.9	310.4	349.8	361.2	242.6
Pipelines	0.0	38.7	43.0	47.6	49.1	49.9	50.1	52.4	57.2	60.3	61.2	62.5	65.0	62.9	63.0	57.6
Civil Aviation	0.0	0.1	0.1	0.1	0.1	0.2	0.2	0.2	0.3	0.4	0.5	0.7	0.7	0.7	0.8	0.4
OVERALL	73.4	622.8	734.2	821.0	849.6	850.0	928.0	1006.7	1131.9	1279.7	1419.5	1565.2	1685.9	1790.3	1825.4	1302.9
Ocean Shipping	2.8	174.1	248.7	317.4	353.2	364.3	376.9	397.7	437.4	532.9	594.8	657.6	696.6	768.9	632.1	528.4

FREIGHT TRAFFIC Composition (Percentage Share) (MODAL SPLIT)

	1952	1980	1990
Rail	82.0%	67.3%	57.9%
Road	1.9%	9.0%	18.9%
Domestic Waterways	16.1%	17.9%	19.8%
Pipelines	0.0%	5.8%	3.5%
Civil Aviation	0.0%	0.0%	0.0%
OVERALL	100.0%	100.0%	100.0%

FREIGHT TRAFFIC Growth Rates (Percentage)

	/a	1980	1981	1982	1983	1984	1985	1986	1987	1988	1989	1990	Avg.80-90
Rail	8.4%	2.1%	-0.1%	7.1%	8.6%	9.0%	12.1%	7.9%	8.1%	4.3%	5.2%	1.6%	6.0%
Road	12.2%	2.6%	2.1%	21.7%	14.2%	41.7%	10.2%	24.8%	25.9%	21.1%	4.8%	2.0%	15.5%
Domestic Waterways	9.0%	9.6%	-1.1%	13.3%	6.0%	8.3%	20.9%	13.9%	7.0%	7.4%	12.7%	3.2%	9.2%
Pipelines	..	3.2%	1.6%	0.4%	4.6%	9.2%	5.4%	1.5%	2.1%	4.0%	-3.2%	0.2%	2.6%
Civil Aviation	15.7%	14.6%	20.6%	16.5%	15.7%	35.8%	33.4%	15.9%	35.1%	12.3%	-5.5%	15.9%	19.1%
OVERALL	8.9%	3.5%	0.0%	9.2%	8.5%	12.4%	13.1%	10.9%	10.3%	7.7%	6.2%	2.0%	7.6%
Ocean Shipping	18.0%	11.3%	3.1%	3.5%	5.5%	10.0%	21.8%	11.6%	10.6%	5.9%	10.4%	-17.8%	6.9%

REF: TRANSPORT.WK1 06/23/92
Source: Statistical Yearbook of China, 1991, p. 85.
NOTE:
- Data for Rail in 1990 is an estimate.
- There was a drop in the freight traffic of Domestic Waterways from 1988 to 1989 and 1990 can be partially explained by a tariff increase of 24% for all modes except highways and inland waterways.
/a Average annual growth rate between 1952 and 1977.

Table 15.3: CHINA: Passenger Traffic Composition of China

	1952	1977	1978	1979	1980	1981	1982	1983	1984	1985	1986	1987	1988	1989	1990	Avg.80-90
PASSENGER TRAFFIC (Billion Passenger-km)																
Rail	20.1	102.3	109.3	121.6	138.3	147.3	157.5	177.7	204.6	241.6	258.7	284.3	326.0	303.7	261.6	227.4
Road	2.3	44.8	52.1	60.3	73.0	83.9	96.4	110.6	133.7	172.5	198.2	219.0	252.8	266.2	260.0	169.7
Domestic Waterways	2.5	9.7	10.1	11.4	12.9	13.8	14.5	15.4	15.4	17.9	18.2	19.6	20.4	18.8	17.8	16.8
Civil Aviation	0.0	1.8	2.8	3.4	3.9	5.0	5.9	5.8	8.3	11.6	14.6	18.7	21.4	18.6	21.8	12.3
OVERALL	24.9	158.6	174.3	196.7	228.1	250.0	274.3	309.5	362.0	443.6	489.7	541.6	620.6	607.3	561.2	426.2
PASSENGER TRAFFIC Composition (Percentage Share) (MODAL SPLIT)																
Rail	80.7%				60.6%										46.6%	
Road	9.2%				32.0%										46.3%	
Domestic Waterways	10.0%				5.7%										3.2%	
Civil Aviation	0.0%				1.7%										3.9%	
OVERALL	100.0%				100.0%										100.0%	
PASSENGER TRAFFIC Growth Rates (Percentage)																
Rail	..	6.7% /b			13.7%	6.5%	6.9%	12.8%	15.1%	18.1%	7.1%	9.9%	14.7%	-6.8%	-13.9%	7.7%
Road	..	12.6%			21.1%	14.9%	14.9%	14.7%	20.9%	29.0%	14.9%	10.5%	15.4%	5.3%	-2.3%	14.5%
Domestic Waterways	..	5.6%			13.2%	7.0%	5.1%	6.2%	0.0%	16.2%	1.7%	7.7%	4.1%	-7.8%	-5.3%	4.4%
Civil Aviation	..	..			14.7%	28.2%	18.0%	-1.7%	43.1%	39.8%	25.9%	28.1%	14.4%	-13.1%	17.2%	19.5%
OVERALL	..	7.7%			16.0%	9.6%	9.7%	12.8%	17.0%	22.5%	10.4%	10.6%	14.6%	-2.1%	-7.6%	10.3%

REF: TRANSPORT.WK1 06/23/92
Source: Statistical Yearbook of China, 1991, p. 85.
NOTE: The drop in passenger traffic of rail from 1988 to 1990 can be partially explained by a tariff increase of 112% in 1989.
/a: Average annual growth rate between 1952 and 1977.

Table 15.4: CHINA: Transport Investment vs. Economic Output

By Five Year Plan Periods

Billion Yuan

| | in Current Prices | | | 6th FYP | | | | | | | 7th FYP | | | | | | |
	3rd FYP 1966-70	4th FYP 1971-75	5th FYP 1976-80	1981	1982	1983	1984	1985	Current Prices Total	1987 Prices Total	1986	1987	1988	1989	1990	Current Prices Total	1987 Prices Total
Transport Investment																	
Current Prices	16.0	31.8	30.2	3.6	5.2	7.2	10.0	15.9	41.9		16.7	17.4	19.0	18.0	24.1	95.2	
Constant 1987 prices				4.6	6.6	9.0	12.0	17.4		49.6	17.5	17.4	17.0	14.8	18.9		85.7
GNP																	
Current Prices	935	1323	1758	477	519	581	696	856	3130		970	1130	1402	1592	1740	6833	
Constant 1987 prices				607	660	728	834	939		3768	1018	1130	1256	1419	1363		6187
Transport Investment as % of GNP																	
Current Prices	1.7%	2.4%	1.7%	0.8%	1.0%	1.2%	1.4%	1.9%	1.3%		1.7%	1.5%	1.4%	1.1%	1.4%	1.4%	

REF: TRANSPORT.WK1 08/15/91
Source: CHINA Statistical Yearbook 1991 pp.5, 23; 1990 pp.33, 171.

*: Estimate
Note: Investment of the 3rd, 4th, and 5th FYPS includes Post and Telecommunications (approximately 4 percent).

Table 15.5: CHINA: Investment in the Transport Sector (including Posts and Telecommunications)

By Five Year Plan Periods

(Billion Yuan)

	in Current Prices			6th FYP					Current Prices Total	1987 Prices Total	7th FYP					Current Prices Total	1987 Prices Total
	3rd FYP 1966-70	4th FYP 1971-75	5th FYP 1976-80	1981	1982	1983	1984	1985	Total	Total	1986	1987	1988	1989	1990	Total	Total
Transport:																	
Railway	11.3	17.3		1.4	2.6	4.2	5.9	7.7	21.9	25.9	8.5	8.7	10.2	9.0	12.1	48.5	43.6
Highway				0.8	0.9	0.7	1.2	2.3	5.9	7.0	2.7	3.3	4.2	4.3	5.5	20.0	17.8
Waterway				1.3	1.5	1.9	2.6	3.7	11.1	13.2	3.7	3.9	3.2	3.6	4.8	19.2	17.4
Aviation				0.1	0.1	0.3	0.3	2.1	2.9	3.3	1.3	1.4	1.3	1.0	1.5	6.5	6.0
Pipeline				0.0	0.0	0.0	0.0	0.1	0.2	0.2	0.5	0.1	0.1	0.1	0.1	0.9	0.9
Subtotal				3.6	5.2	7.2	10.0	15.9	41.9	49.6	16.7	17.4	19.0	18.0	24.1	95.2	85.7
Post & Telecom.				0.4	0.5	0.6	0.9	1.2	3.6	4.3	1.3	1.6	1.8	2.3	3.0	10.0	8.8
Total	16.0	31.8	30.2	4.0	5.7	7.8	10.8	17.1	45.5	54.0	18.0	19.0	20.8	20.3	27.1	105.2	94.5
Investment	97.6	176.4	234.2	44.3	55.6	59.4	74.3	107.4	341.0	408.3	117.6	134.3	152.6	155.2	170.3	730.0	655.6
Transport as % of Total Investment	16.4%	18.0%	12.9%	8.2%	9.4%	12.1%	13.4%	14.8%	12.3%	12.2%	14.2%	13.0%	12.5%	11.6%	14.2%	13.0%	13.1%

REF: TRANSPORT.WK1 08/15/91
Source: CHINA Statistical Yearbook 1991, pp.23, 1990 pp.157, 167, 171.

/_1: Investment of FYPs, before 1980, includes Post and Telecommunications (about 4% of total).
*:Estimates

Table 15.6: CHINA: Railway Asset Utilization: International Comparison

	Unit	CHINA	USSR	USA /a	INDIA /c	BRAZIL
Freight Ton-km/Route-km	Million	18.7	26.2	6.5	3.6	8.0
Passenger-km/Route-km	Million	6.2	2.8	0.1	4.4	0.05
Freight Ton-km/freight car owned	Million	2.9	2.2	0.8 (b)	0.6	1.7
Freight tonnage/car loaded	Ton/Car	54.1	53.6	66.6	20.1	55.0
Freight cars per train	1 Car	40-50 /e	50-75 /e	71	n.a.	35
Freight car turnaround time	Days	3.9	6.6	18.8	11.6	12.0
Freight car turnaround distance	km	952	1,610	2,125	1,274	750
Freight hauling distance	km	702	945	1,106	776	460
Freight tons-km/locomotive owned	Million	74.9	68.5	70.6	24.3	25.0
Freight train-km/route-km/day	km/day	36.1 /e	42.9	6.1	10.6	6.4
Freight train speed (inc. stops)	km/hour	28.3	31.8	n.a.	22.7	30.0
Freight train gross trailing weight	Tons	2,365	3,085	4,300	2,050	2,200
Freight tonnage per train	Train	1300-150/e	1,800 /e	2,390	1,053	1,200

REF: TRANSPORT.WK1 06/23/92
SOURCE:

CHINA: Ministry of Railways and mission estimates.

USSR: Narodnoe khozyalstvo SSR v 1987g. (The USSR National Economy in 1987), pp.21, 307-308, 312, 315. Various estimates from Hunter and Kaple, 1983; Hunter and Kontorovich, 1986; Kaple, 1984, and Szyrmyr and Dunn, 1985.

INDIA: Economic Survey, 1988-89, pp. 27, 35-36, s-30; India Railways Yearbook 1987-8, pp.viii, 40, 70, 78-9 and 80-1.

USA: Railroad Facts, 1988, pp. 9, 31,32,35,36,43,46. The World Bank, Railroad Database, June 1989.

BRAZIL: Official Government Sources.

NOTE:
/a Class 1 Railroads only.
/b Includes cars owned by car companies and shippers.
/c 90.58% of all freight ton-kilometers are carried on broad-gauge rails, so Estimates above estimates are for braod gauge only. See Indian Railways Yearbook, 1987-8, pp.23.
/e Estimate:most above estimates are for broad gauge only.

- 285 -

Table 15.7: CHINA: Cargo Throughput in Coastal Ports
(Million)

PORT	1952	1957	1965	1978	1980	1985	1988	1989
Dalian	1.5	5.9	10.6	28.6	32.6	43.8	48.5	50.9
Qinhuangdao	1.8	2.8	4.8	22.2	26.4	44.2	58.1	65.7
Tianjin	0.7	2.8	5.5	11.3	11.9	18.6	21.1	24.4
Qingdao	1.8	2.2	4.5	20.0	17.1	26.1	31.1	31.1
Shanghai	6.6	16.5	31.9	79.6	84.8	112.9	133.2	146.0
Ningbo	..	..	..	..	3.3	10.4	20.0	22.1
Guangzhou	0.5	1.9	4.7	10.5	12.1	17.7	47.4	47.0
Other main ports	1.6	5.2	9.8	26.1	29.1	37.8	96.5	103.0
Other medium size ports	..	..	..	..	..	..	43.2	48.1
TOTAL	14.4	37.3	71.8	198.3	217.3	311.5	455.9	490.3

Source:
China Statistical Yearbook, 1990, p. 555.

Table 15.8: CHINA: Freight Traffic Volumes: International Comparison

(countries with over 15,000 km of track)

		USSR	Canada	USA	Poland	France	Germany	Italy	Argentin	Brazil	Japan	U.K.	Mexico	China	India
FREIGHT VOLUME															
RAIL	Billion Ton-km	3835	212	1454	111	52	57	18	8	110	23	16	41	947	231
ROAD	Billion Ton-km	489	52	1028	38	144	151	157	103	260	246	101	98	241	211
TOTAL	Billion Ton-km	4323	265	2482	150	195	208	176	111	370	270	117	139	1188	442
Population	Million	291	26	246	38	56	61	57	32	144	123	57	84	1088	816
FREIGHT VOLUME PER PERSON															
RAIL	Ton-km/Person	13182	8164	5903	2932	923	931	318	262	758	192	275	485	870	283
ROAD	Ton-km/Person	1679	2012	4173	1014	2572	2470	2741	3271	1803	2008	1771	1174	221	259
TOTAL	Ton-km/Person	14861	10176	10076	3947	3496	3401	3060	3533	2562	2199	2046	1659	1091	542

REF: TRANSPORT.WK1 06/23/92
Sources:

ARGENTINA: World Transport Data, 1988. Roads: PCR Fourth Highway Project, World Bank, 1988. Freight traffic volume figures are estimates.

BRAZIL: World Road Statistics 1985-1989, International Road Federation (I.R.F.), 1990.

CANADA: Rail: World Bank Railway Data, 1990. Roads: Transport Review: Trends and Selected Issues, 1985, pp. 39-42.

CHINA: World Transport Data, 1988.

FRANCE: World Road Statistics 1985-1989, International Road Federation (I.R.F.), 1990.

GERMANY: World Transport Data, 1988.

INDIA: Roads: Policy Issues in Road Transport, World Bank, (Green cover), 1989, Annex 3.1

ITALY: World Road Statistics 1985-1989, International Road Federation (I.R.F.), 1990.

JAPAN: World Road Statistics 1985-1989, International Road Federation (I.R.F.), 1990.

MEXICO: Manual Estadistico del Sector Transporte, Institute Mexicano del Transporte, Qro. 1989, p. 63 (1986 figures)

POLAND: World Road Statistics 1985-1989, International Road Federation (I.R.F.), 1990.

USA: World Transport Data, 1988.

USSR: World Transport Data, 1988.

U.K.: World Transport Data, 1988.

Table 15.9: CHINA: Passenger Traffic Volumes: International Comparison

(countries with over 15,000 km of track)

		USA	France	Germany	Italy	U.K.	Canada	Japan	Brazil	USSR	Mexico	Poland	Argentin	India	China
PASSENGER VOLUME															
RAIL	Billion Passenger-km	20	74	39	44	34	2	362	15	402	6	48	13	269	284
ROAD	Billion Passenger-km	4472	614	617	506	512	221	608	519	515	220	38	56	893	220
TOTAL	Billion Passenger-km	4492	688	656	550	546	223	970	534	917	226	87	69	1162	504
Population	Million	246	56	61	57	57	26	123	144	291	84	38	32	816	1088
PASSENGER VOLUME PER PERSON															
RAIL	Passenger-km/Person	80	1324	639	764	602	81	2951	102	1383	70	1274	421	330	261
ROAD	Passenger-km/Person	18157	10984	10067	8823	8967	8500	4961	3595	1770	2631	1014	1762	1095	202
TOTAL	Passenger-km/Person	18236	12308	10706	9587	9569	8581	7912	3698	3152	2702	2288	2183	1425	463

REF: TRANSPORT.WK1 06/23/92
Sources:

ARGENTINA: World Transport Data, 1988. Staff Appraisal Report: Highway Sector Project, Argentina, May 4, 1983. Roads: PCR Fourth Highway Project, World Bank, 1988. Freight Traffic volume figures are estimates.

BRAZIL: World Road Statistics 1985-1989, International Road Federation (I.R.F.), 1990.

CANADA: Rail: World Bank Railway Data, 1990. Roads: Transport Review: Trends and Selected Issues, 1985, pp. 10.

CHINA: World Transport Data, 1988.

FRANCE: World Road Statistics 1985-1989, International Road Federation (I.R.F.), 1990.

GERMANY: World Transport Data, 1988.

INDIA: Roads: Policy Issues in Road Transport, World Bank, (Green cover), 1989, Annex 3.1

ITALY: World Road Statistics 1985-1989, International Road Federation (I.R.F.), 1990.

JAPAN: World Road Statistics 1985-1989, International Road Federation (I.R.F.), 1990.

MEXICO: Manual Estadistico del Sector Transporte, Instituto Mexicano del Transporte, Qro. 1989, p. 127 (1986 figures)

POLAND: World Road Statistics 1985-1989, International Road Federation (I.R.F.), 1990.

USA: World Transport Data, 1988.

USSR: World Transport Data, 1988.

U.K.: World Transport Data, 1988.

Table 15.10: CHINA: Railway Traffic Volume: International Comparison

(countries with over 15,000 km of track)

Country		USSR	China	Japan	India	Poland	USA	Brazil	Italy	France	Germany	U.K.	Mexico	Canada	Argentina
RAIL TRAFFIC VOLUME															
Freight	Billion Ton-km	3,835	947	23	231	111	1,454	110	18	52	57	16	41	212	8
Passenger	Billion Passenger-km	402	284	362	269	48	20	15	44	74	39	34	6	2	13
Total	Billion (Ton-km + Passenger-km)	4,237	1,231	385	501	159	1,474	124	62	126	96	50	46	214	22
Track Length	Thousand Km	146	53	21	62	27	252	27	16	35	27	17	16	103	34
Rail Traffic Units Per Unit of Track Length	Million (Ton-km + Passenger-km)/Km	29.0	23.4	18.2	8.1	6.0	5.8	4.6	3.9	3.6	3.5	3.0	2.9	2.1	0.6

Sources: See Tables 15.8, 15.9, and 15.11.

Table 15.11: CHINA: Railway Network: International Comparison

		Canada	Germany	Poland	France	U.K.	Japan	Italy	USA	Argentin	USSR	India	Mexico	Brazil	China
Track Length	1000 km	103	27	27	35	17	21	16	252	34	146	62	16	22	53
Population	Millions	26	61	38	56	57	123	57	246	32	291	816	84	144	1088
Track Length per person	km/Person	3949	447	703	620	291	173	278	1023	1084	502	76	189	153	48
Population Density Scaled	Canada=1.0	1.00	0.11	0.18	0.16	0.07	0.04	0.07	0.26	0.27	0.13	0.02	0.05	0.04	0.01
Total Area	1000 Sq km	9976	249	313	552	245	378	301	9373	2767	22402	3288	1958	8512	9561
Arable Land	1000 Sq km	5160	198	284	462	213	306	245	7172	2406	15622	2796	1477	2532	5563
Track Length per Sq. km of Arable land	km/Sq.km	20	139	94	75	78	69	65	35	14	9	22	11	9	9
Arable Area Density Scaled	Germany=1.0	0.14	1.00	0.68	0.54	0.56	0.50	0.47	0.25	0.10	0.07	0.16	0.08	0.06	0.07
Total Area Density Scaled (Population Density + +Arable area Density)		1.14	1.11	0.86	0.70	0.64	0.54	0.54	0.51	0.38	0.19	0.18	0.12	0.10	0.08

REF: TRANSPORT.WK1 06/23/92

Sources:

The World Bank Development Report, 1990, pp. 178-179.

FAO Yearbook: Production, Vol. 43, FAO Statistics Series No. 94, 1989, Table 1, pp. 47-58.

The World Bank Railway Database.

Table 15.12: CHINA: Road Network: International Comparison

		Japan	Canada	USA	Germany	France	U.K.	Poland	Brazil	Italy	Argentin	India	USSR	Mexico	China
Road Length	1000 km	1110	844	6229	497	805	354	361	1664	302	211	1621	1610	226	963
Population	Millions	123	26	246	61	56	57	38	144	57	32	816	291	84	1088
Road Length per person	km/Person	9054	32476	25289	8102	14409	6205	9521	11523	5259	6710	1987	5534	2696	885
Population Density Scaled	Canada=1.0	0.28	1.00	0.78	0.25	0.44	0.19	0.29	0.35	0.16	0.21	0.06	0.17	0.08	0.03
Total Area	1000 Sq km	378	9976	9373	249	552	245	313	8512	301	2767	3288	22402	1958	9561
Arable Land	1000 Sq km	306	5160	7172	198	462	213	284	2532	245	2406	2796	15622	1477	5563
Road Length per Sq. km of Arable land	km/Sq.km	3627	164	868	2508	1743	1663	1271	657	1232	88	580	103	153	173
Arable Area Density Scaled	Japan=1.0	1.00	0.05	0.24	0.69	0.48	0.46	0.35	0.18	0.34	0.02	0.16	0.03	0.04	0.05
Total Area Density Scaled (Population Density + Arable area Density)		1.28	1.05	1.02	0.94	0.92	0.65	0.64	0.54	0.50	0.23	0.22	0.20	0.13	0.07

REF: TRANSPORT.WK1 06/23/92
Sources:

The World Bank Development Report, 1990, pp. 178-179.

FAO Yearbook: Production, Vol. 43, FAO Statistics Series No. 94, 1989, Table 1, pp. 47-58.

World Road Statistics 1965-1989, International Road Federation, 1990. Section 1.

World Transport Data, International Road Transport Union, 1989.

Distributors of World Bank Publications

ARGENTINA
Carlos Hirsch, SRL
Galeria Guemes
Florida 165, 4th Floor-Ofc. 453/465
1333 Buenos Aires

**AUSTRALIA, PAPUA NEW GUINEA,
FIJI, SOLOMON ISLANDS,
VANUATU, AND WESTERN SAMOA**
D.A. Books & Journals
648 Whitehorse Road
Mitcham 3132
Victoria

AUSTRIA
Gerold and Co.
Graben 31
A-1011 Wien

BANGLADESH
Micro Industries Development
 Assistance Society (MIDAS)
House 5, Road 16
Dhanmondi R/Area
Dhaka 1209

Branch offices:
156, Nur Ahmed Sarak
Chittagong 4000

76, K.D.A. Avenue
Kulna 9100

BELGIUM
Jean De Lannoy
Av. du Roi 202
1060 Brussels

CANADA
Le Diffuseur
C.P. 85, 1501B rue Ampère
Boucherville, Québec
J4B 5E6

CHINA
China Financial & Economic
 Publishing House
8, Da Fo Si Dong Jie
Beijing

COLOMBIA
Infoenlace Ltda.
Apartado Aereo 34270
Bogota D.E.

COTE D'IVOIRE
Centre d'Edition et de Diffusion
 Africaines (CEDA)
04 B.P. 541
Abidjan 04 Plateau

CYPRUS
Cyprus College Bookstore
6, Diogenes Street, Engomi
P.O. Box 2006
Nicosia

DENMARK
SamfundsLitteratur
Rosenoerns Allé 11
DK-1970 Frederiksberg C

DOMINICAN REPUBLIC
Editora Taller, C. por A.
Restauración e Isabel la Católica 309
Apartado de Correos 2190 Z-1
Santo Domingo

EGYPT, ARAB REPUBLIC OF
Al Ahram
Al Galaa Street
Cairo

The Middle East Observer
41, Sherif Street
Cairo

EL SALVADOR
Fusades
Alam Dr. Manuel Enrique Araujo #3530
Edificio SISA, ler. Piso
San Salvador 011

FINLAND
Akateeminen Kirjakauppa
P.O. Box 128
SF-00101 Helsinki 10

FRANCE
World Bank Publications
66, avenue d'Iéna
75116 Paris

GERMANY
UNO-Verlag
Poppelsdorfer Allee 55
D-5300 Bonn 1

GUATEMALA
Librerias Piedra Santa
5a. Calle 7-55
Zona 1
Guatemala City

HONG KONG, MACAO
Asia 2000 Ltd.
46-48 Wyndham Street
Winning Centre
2nd Floor
Central Hong Kong

INDIA
Allied Publishers Private Ltd.
751 Mount Road
Madras - 600 002

Branch offices:
15 J.N. Heredia Marg
Ballard Estate
Bombay - 400 038

13/14 Asaf Ali Road
New Delhi - 110 002

17 Chittaranjan Avenue
Calcutta - 700 072

Jayadeva Hostel Building
5th Main Road Gandhinagar
Bangalore - 560 009

3-5-1129 Kachiguda Cross Road
Hyderabad - 500 027

Prarthana Flats, 2nd Floor
Near Thakore Baug, Navrangpura
Ahmedabad - 380 009

Patiala House
16-A Ashok Marg
Lucknow - 226 001

Central Bazaar Road
60 Bajaj Nagar
Nagpur 440010

INDONESIA
Pt. Indira Limited
Jl. Sam Ratulangi 37
P.O. Box 181
Jakarta Pusat

ISRAEL
Yozmot Literature Ltd.
P.O. Box 56055
Tel Aviv 61560
Israel

ITALY
Licosa Commissionaria Sansoni SPA
Via Duca Di Calabria, 1/1
Casella Postale 552
50125 Firenze

JAPAN
Eastern Book Service
Hongo 3-Chome, Bunkyo-ku 113
Tokyo

KENYA
Africa Book Service (E.A.) Ltd.
Quaran House, Mfangano Street
P.O. Box 45245
Nairobi

KOREA, REPUBLIC OF
Pan Korea Book Corporation
P.O. Box 101, Kwangwhamun
Seoul

MALAYSIA
University of Malaya Cooperative
 Bookshop, Limited
P.O. Box 1127, Jalan Pantai Baru
59700 Kuala Lumpur

MEXICO
INFOTEC
Apartado Postal 22-860
14060 Tlalpan, Mexico D.F.

NETHERLANDS
De Lindeboom/InOr-Publikaties
P.O. Box 202
7480 AE Haaksbergen

NEW ZEALAND
EBSCO NZ Ltd.
Private Mail Bag 99914
New Market
Auckland

NIGERIA
University Press Limited
Three Crowns Building Jericho
Private Mail Bag 5095
Ibadan

NORWAY
Narvesen Information Center
Book Department
P.O. Box 6125 Etterstad
N-0602 Oslo 6

PAKISTAN
Mirza Book Agency
65, Shahrah-e-Quaid-e-Azam
P.O. Box No. 729
Lahore 54000

PERU
Editorial Desarrollo SA
Apartado 3824
Lima 1

PHILIPPINES
International Book Center
Fifth Floor, Filipinas Life Building
Ayala Avenue, Makati
Metro Manila

POLAND
ORPAN
Palac Kultury i Nauki
00-901 Warzawa

PORTUGAL
Livraria Portugal
Rua Do Carmo 70-74
1200 Lisbon

SAUDI ARABIA, QATAR
Jarir Book Store
P.O. Box 3196
Riyadh 11471

**SINGAPORE, TAIWAN,
MYANMAR,BRUNEI**
Information Publications
 Private, Ltd.
02-06 1st Fl., Pei-Fu Industrial
 Bldg.
24 New Industrial Road
Singapore 1953

SOUTH AFRICA, BOTSWANA
For single titles:
Oxford University Press
 Southern Africa
P.O. Box 1141
Cape Town 8000

For subscription orders:
International Subscription Service
P.O. Box 41095
Craighall
Johannesburg 2024

SPAIN
Mundi-Prensa Libros, S.A.
Castello 37
28001 Madrid

Librería Internacional AEDOS
Consell de Cent, 391
08009 Barcelona

SRI LANKA AND THE MALDIVES
Lake House Bookshop
P.O. Box 244
100, Sir Chittampalam A.
 Gardiner Mawatha
Colombo 2

SWEDEN
For single titles:
Fritzes Fackboksforetaget
Regeringsgatan 12, Box 16356
S-103 27 Stockholm

For subscription orders:
Wennergren-Williams AB
Box 30004
S-104 25 Stockholm

SWITZERLAND
For single titles:
Librairie Payot
1, rue de Bourg
CH 1002 Lausanne

For subscription orders:
Librairie Payot
Service des Abonnements
Case postale 3312
CH 1002 Lausanne

TANZANIA
Oxford University Press
P.O. Box 5299
Maktaba Road
Dar es Salaam

THAILAND
Central Department Store
306 Silom Road
Bangkok

**TRINIDAD & TOBAGO, ANTIGUA
BARBUDA, BARBADOS,
DOMINICA, GRENADA, GUYANA,
JAMAICA, MONTSERRAT, ST.
KITTS & NEVIS, ST. LUCIA,
ST. VINCENT & GRENADINES**
Systematics Studies Unit
#9 Watts Street
Curepe
Trinidad, West Indies

UNITED KINGDOM
Microinfo Ltd.
P.O. Box 3
Alton, Hampshire GU34 2PG
England

VENEZUELA
Libreria del Este
Aptdo. 60.337
Caracas 1060-A